GENESIS

BERIT OLAM
Studies in Hebrew Narrative & Poetry

Genesis

David W. Cotter, O.S.B.

David W. Cotter, O.S.B.
Editor

Jerome T. Walsh
Chris Franke
Associate Editors

A Michael Glazier Book

THE LITURGICAL PRESS
Collegeville, Minnesota

www.litpress.org

A Michael Glazier Book published by The Liturgical Press.

Cover design by Ann Blattner.

1   2   3   4   5   6   7   8   9

Library of Congress Cataloging-in-Publication Data

Cotter, David W.
   Genesis / David W. Cotter.
      p.   cm. — (Berit olam)
   "A Michael Glazier book."
   Includes bibliographical references and index.
   ISBN 0-8146-5040-6 (alk. paper)
   1. Bible. O.T. Genesis—Criticism, interpretation, etc.   I. Title.   II. Series.

   BS1235.52 .C68 2003
   222'.11066—dc21   2002029846

*This book is dedicated to
the people of
Our Lady of Lourdes Parish
Bishopton in Renfrewshire
Scotland
with affection and gratitude.*

CONTENTS

PREFACE

Whenever I speak to groups of people interested in reading and studying the Bible in a more serious fashion I am inevitably asked which translation one should use or which translation is the best. I always respond that, ideally, one would have a variety of translations at hand because each has strengths and weaknesses, does some things well and others perhaps less well. The same is true of commentaries. Some focus on questions of source analysis and attempt to discover the origins and development of the text to its final canonical form. Others are oriented toward linguistic analysis and concentrate on trying to find the best and most accurate way to understand the meaning of sometimes very obscure and difficult ancient languages. Still others, such as this one, are more interested in the final form of the text, although the questions they pose to that final form differ widely. In particular, I am interested in the way Genesis functions as a narrative, what its plot is, how its characters develop and change.

All of this is a roundabout way of saying that, ideally, one would have access to a number of commentaries. While this one, I hope, will make some modest contribution to the ongoing discussion of the way biblical narrative works and the ways in which traditional biblical commentary (such as patristic or medieval Jewish and Christian) may be used today, it will not answer many other questions that will perplex a reader of the Bible. It is not a book that should be read in isolation. I would suggest that one also avail oneself of at least one of the great historical-critical commentaries. There is also an increasing number of fine studies that treat particular texts or particular themes. Many of these I will mention in the course of the commentary, but in particular I would mention Professor Gary Anderson's recent book *The Genesis of Perfection: Adam and Eve in Jewish and Christian Imagination*,[1] which

---

[1] Louisville: Westminster John Knox Press, 2001.

I received just as I was finishing this study. Although it came to me too late to utilize in writing this book, it shows the way forward for all of us interested in reconnecting contemporary biblical scholarship with traditional readings. There are many others, far too numerous to mention here, since the bibliography on Genesis is vast beyond the capacity of any individual either to read or simply to list.

I hope that in reading this book you find some modest profit. I have been working at it for some ten years and could have continued for many more; doubtless the result would have been better. At some point, however, the time comes to put a final period. Before I do so I would like to thank some of those people who have been of especial assistance. Jerry Walsh and Chris Franke, my associate editors in this series, have always been most eager to do whatever I asked of them, from editing manuscripts, keeping up with current authors and sharing ideas about the series and its development, to finding and photocopying articles that were not easily available to me. In addition editor extraordinaire Annette Kmitch has helped me in all sorts of ways, with generous friendship and skillful expertise. Similarly, my confreres Fr. Michael Patella, Fr. Bill Schipper, and Fr. Joseph Feders have done whatever I asked of them and asked only friendship in return. To all of these and to many others I have neglected to mention I extend my most hearty thanks.

In a special way I would like to thank Fr. Michael McMahon, Parish Priest of Our Lady of Lourdes Parish in the village of Bishopton in Renfrewshire; Fr. Mark Cassidy, RN, chaplain to the Royal Navy currently serving H.M.S. Raleigh at Torpoint in Cornwall; and P. Thomas Wagner of Benediktinerabtei Weltenburg in Bavaria for their longstanding and generous friendship and their gracious hospitality while I was writing this book. I cannot finish any list of those to whom I owe thanks without mentioning the many people of Our Lady of Lourdes Parish who have made me feel welcome and at home while in their midst. To all of these, and many more, I can only say that I thank you for all that you have done for me and, more importantly, for who you are.

A final note to the reader. In this book the name of God is represented as YHWH—and on a few occasions as LORD—and in referring to God the male personal pronoun is used. The former represents the ineffable name revealed in Exodus 3, and the latter is simply to avoid stylistic awkwardness and implies nothing about the nature of God.

There are many things we do not know about the history of Genesis. Among them are when it was given the final form in which we have it today, who put it into that form, and what role that person had in its composition. For some time it was more or less taken for granted that the person who put it into its final form was simply an editor of previously existing documentary sources. I suspect, although no one can know, that whoever this inspired person was, the task was much more like modern authorship than we would suspect. While no one would deny that the composer of the final form of the book used previously existing sources, whether documentary or oral, those sources were refined and reworked in such a way that the composer was a real contributor to the final effort. As a result, but ultimately for convenience only, I have chosen to call this person the author (cf. *Dei verbum* § 11) and, again simply to avoid stylistic awkwardness, have from time to time referred to the author with the masculine pronoun. This implies nothing about the gender of the person, or persons, to whom God revealed the book of Genesis.

This is a commentary on the traditional Hebrew text of the book of Genesis, the so-called Masoretic Text [MT]. Since many of those reading it will not have access to the original language I have had an eye on a translation as well, in particular the New Revised Standard Version of the Bible [NRSV], and from time to time I comment on the ways that translation, a fine and widely used one, departs from the original. Of course, one could equally well turn to the Jerusalem Bible, the New American Bible, or the Jewish Publication Society Tanakh or any other of the widely used biblical translations.

One final word on a similar topic. I hope that those who read this book have their appetites whetted for reading more of the traditional commentaries, both Christian and Jewish, which they will have sampled here. Many of these readers will be nonspecialists, so I have consciously cited fairly popular compendia of this material, more readily available in the bookshops and public libraries to which most people have access, rather than the specialist editions found in university libraries.

> The tectonic layers of our lives rest so tightly one on top of the other we
> always come up against earlier events in the later ones, not as a matter
> that has been fully formed and pushed aside, but absolutely present and
> alive. I understand this. Nevertheless, I sometimes find it hard to bear.
> Maybe I did write our story to be free of it, even if I never can be.
> —Bernhard Schlink[1]

Introduction

MICHELANGELO, PORCELAIN MINIATURES, AND METHOD

A discussion of the method I will follow in this commentary on Genesis must begin with two stories,[2] one set in Florence and the other in Rome. For it was viewing two very different sorts of works of art in those two cities that provided me with a metaphor for my own exegesis and so gave me the impetus I needed to write as an exegete about the texts to which I and so many other people of faith turn in order to find life and meaning.

In an art museum in Florence, the Galleria dell'Accademia, one finds Michelangelo's statue of David. It stands alone in a rotunda which is so large that the statue, although eighteen feet in height, does not seem unduly encumbered by having been brought indoors in the nineteenth century. One sees it first from the far end of a long gallery. The gallery is itself the site of some of the artist's greatest, albeit unfinished, pieces, the Four Prisoners for the tomb of Pope Julius II. But as beautiful as they are, the visitor hardly notices them. Instead, one is drawn toward the colossal representation of the young king of Israel that commands the entire space. One can walk around the statue, viewing it from all angles, seeing it from a variety of perspectives. All of the resulting views are true, although some of them

---

[1] *The Reader* (New York: Pantheon Books, 1997) 217–8.

[2] The words "story" and "narrative" will be used interchangeably in this commentary since that is the way they are used in normal English. Literary theorists ordinarily distinguish between them, using the one to refer to a series of events and the other to refer to an ordering of that series.

may not be very interesting or really worth coming back to for a second glance. If one wished, one could lie on the floor and contemplate the statue's feet. A close inspection could equally well be made of its pedestal. In fact, one could move inch by inch around the statue viewing it from a near infinity of postures and perspectives. All of the resulting views would be true, at least for that viewer, given the viewer's interests and skills.

Or, motivated by different interests, one could view the form as an engineer, interested in its structural integrity. One could ask whether the statue represented the likely physiognomy of an early adult Israelite male of the period in which the historical David lived. One might well be interested in the place of this statue in the development of Michelangelo's career as sculptor. Or in its place in the history of Renaissance sculpture. Or, indeed, by any number of other concerns.

Exegesis is very much like viewing the statue of David. True, it is only a metaphor and doubtless an imperfect one, but it has helped me to understand my task. And that task is this: I have to tell you what I see from where I stand. You may find my report of interest to you and worthy of your own consideration. You may go and find where I stood to compare our impressions. You may think me hopelessly naive and blind to what is truly important about the piece. I cannot control your reaction, nor do I wish to. But, in order to undertake the task of exegesis so understood, I must provide a preface to my reflections. I have to tell you who I am, where I am standing, and what I am seeing. Only in that way will I have given you what you need to know in order to weigh the value of my reading, to test my experience against your own.

Some readers may find this approach, with its apparently autobiographical focus on the *I*, to be needlessly solipsistic, idiosyncratic, and lacking in the scientific objectivity toward which we are all supposed to aspire as scholars. All of which brings me to the second story, about porcelain miniatures in a museum on the Campidoglio in Rome.

Roman museums tend to be very crowded places. One day while visiting a museum that seemed especially crowded, I was attracted to a particular gallery simply because, as far as I could tell, it was empty. As I walked down its length, I discovered that it was devoted entirely to a collection of very small 18th-century porcelain figurines, mostly figures of the elegant rich relaxing, talking, being involved with lovers. I was tempted at first simply to return to the large and dramatic works of art I had been viewing, but it was cool and quiet, so I stayed. I found that these works of art were able to yield great delight if one learned to look at them properly. But in order to do that, one had to pay extraordinary attention to very small details: the lift of a tiny eye, the shape of a miniature hand, the turning away of a head. If one paid attention to these tiny details, a world began to come to life.

This led me to my second insight about the nature of exegesis, one that removes it from the realm of the purely personal: the Bible presents us with literary miniatures, which must be read differently from the other texts with which we come into contact. We are used to huge piles of words,[3] an approach foreign to the Bible where a character appears, develops, and disappears in a few paragraphs or a few chapters. In order to see them at all, one must look carefully at the details of the language with which they are presented.

I wrote my dissertation on the first speech of Eliphaz (Job 4–5), the first of Job's so-called friends to speak. Eliphaz neither sounded nor acted like a friend to me, and I decided that in the narrative that is the book of Job the three supposed friends were not friends, none of them. But how could I know this? Where did I get this idea? I could get it only from the words with which Eliphaz and the others were described and the words they spoke. I could get it only from the way in which those words of speech and description, even their very sounds, came into contact with what I knew and had discovered about the nature of friendship. The literary critic George Steiner, from whose work I have profited greatly, makes the point better than I when he writes:

> We must learn to parse sentences and to analyze the grammar of our text for . . . there is no access to the grammar of poetry, to the nerve and sinew of the poem, if one is blind to the poetry of grammar.[4]

The text's meaning, at least the meaning that I found in it, was a result of the intersection of the text, with all of the complexities of literary artifice and linguistic subtlety with which its author endowed it, and one perhaps not overly skilled reader.[5]

So, here are two metaphors that inform my work as an exegete. I have to tell you who I am, where I am standing and what I am seeing. And I have to respect the form our biblical writers imposed upon their raw materials and look very carefully at the details of their craft.

---

[3] In 1994 Vikram Seth published his novel *A Suitable Boy* (San Francisco: Harper-Collins). A wonderful book, it is said, at 1376 pages, to be the longest novel ever published.

[4] George Steiner, "The Uncommon Reader," in *No Passion Spent* (New Haven: Yale University Press, 1996) 18.

[5] The reader of this book is free to judge how well I accomplished the task by dipping into my *A Study of Job 4-5 in the Light of Contemporary Literary Theory* (Atlanta: Scholars Press, 1992).

Who Am I?

Some exegetes maintain a certain professional distance from the texts on which they work, approaching them much as I suppose a classicist would approach the texts of Greece or Rome or an archeologist would approach a shard of some long-broken vase. They are bits of evidence with which the scholar can build up a picture of a world that is no more and come to a better understanding of how those people lived, what they felt, what they believed.

However, as useful as such an approach is, it accords only with difficulty with the desire to be transformed that draws most people to the Bible. And I cannot deny that I am among those desirous of transformation and certain that it may be found here. Is there a God who cares about me? Does my life have meaning? I answer "Yes" to both questions. And I must, for as much as I bring my skills, linguistic, historical, hermeneutical, to my study of these texts, I also bring the fact that I am a Roman Catholic priest and have long been a Benedictine monk.[6] These too inform my reading. But how?

The fundamental text that should inform the work of any Catholic exegete of our day is the Dogmatic Constitution on Divine Revelation *(Dei verbum)* of the Second Vatican Council, promulgated in 1965. On the task of the interpreter of Scripture, the Council taught:

> 12. However, since God speaks in Sacred Scripture through men in human fashion, the interpreter of Sacred Scripture, in order to see clearly what God wanted to communicate to us, should carefully investigate what meaning the sacred writers really intended, and what God wanted to manifest by means of their words.
>
> To search out the intention of the sacred writers, attention should be given, among other things, to "literary forms." For truth is set forth and expressed differently in texts which are variously historical, prophetic, poetic, or of other forms of discourse. The interpreter must investigate what meaning the sacred writer intended to express and actually expressed in particular circumstances by using contemporary literary forms in accordance with the situation of his own time and culture. For the correct understanding of what the sacred author wanted to assert, due at-

---

[6] This catalogue could be extended almost endlessly, so I choose to include those characteristics that seem to me most salient. Others might well wonder why I do not refer to my maleness, my race, my class, my ethnicity, the fact that I am an American. One could as well catalogue one's education, listing, for example, languages in which one has proficiency. And there are doubtless other items as well that affect the way I read. At some point, though—and I readily admit that the point is not objectively testable—this seems to cease being exegesis and to become confession.

tention must be paid to the customary and characteristic styles of feeling, speaking and narrating which prevailed at the time of the sacred
writer, and to the patterns men normally employed at that period in their
everyday dealings with one another.

But, since Holy Scripture must be read and interpreted in the sacred
spirit in which it was written, no less serious attention must be given to
the content and unity of the whole of Scripture if the meaning of the sacred texts is to be correctly worked out. The living tradition of the whole
Church must be taken into account along with the harmony which exists
between elements of the faith. It is the task of exegetes to work according
to these rules toward a better understanding and explanation of the meaning of Sacred Scripture, so that through preparatory study the judgment
of the Church may mature. For all of what has been said about the way
of interpreting Scripture is subject finally to the judgment of the Church,
which carries out the divine commission and ministry of guarding and
interpreting the word of God.[7]

Even the most casual reading of this text shows what a daunting
task the scholar has. One must become intimately aware of and con-
versant with the ways in which people, at the time the text in question
was written, thought, felt, and wrote. Moreover the text at hand is not
a secular text, but the Word from God to humanity. The texts have been
a part of a living tradition of commentary, interpretation, and liturgy
for thousands of years. So, working *now*, the scholar must be immersed
in *then* and, at the same time, be aware of all that has linked these two
times. And it is a sacred task.

The explicit religiosity of the approach taken here will cause some
to feel ill at ease. The result will be dismissed as devotional reading,
mere spirituality. That there is an anti-religious tendency in some seg-
ments of academe today, even if only among a minority, is clear and
needs to be acknowledged. A very powerful article entitled "Is Nothing Sacred? Casting out the Gods from Religious Studies" appeared in
Lingua Franca's November 1996 issue. The author, Charlotte Allen, described several members of an academic society for the study of religion whose attitudes toward their former faiths are said to range from
"ambivalent to downright hostile." While other members are quoted
to the effect that the imputation to them of anti-religious sentiments is
"nonsense," one of them defines religion as a "social way of thinking
about social identity and social relationships" and so conceives of a

---

[7] Vatican II, Dogmatic Constitution on Divine Revelation *(Dei verbum)*, *Vatican
Council II: The Conciliar and Post Conciliar Documents*, rev. ed., ed. Austin Flannery
(Collegeville: The Liturgical Press, 1992) III, 12; 757–8.

realm of concern very far removed from those of us engaged as persons of faith in biblical scholarship.[8]

Central to the way I read the Bible is the fact of my Benedictine monastic life, for which the Bible, encountered daily by means of the practice known as *lectio divina*, is the very foundation. Of this practice, a recent writer says:

> *Lectio* is sometimes presented as a method or technique of prayer, but it is really a kind of anti-technique, a disposition more than a method. Therefore it is hard to describe or teach because it varies so much from person to person, shaped by temperament, individual needs and ways of thinking. Some people read slowly but steadily. Others ponder a word or phrase for the whole time. Others sweep the pages, trawling for morsels of nourishment. . . . *Lectio* is meant to be a conversation with God about one's life. To foster that conversation, some people employ structured exercises of reflection on their reading or take notes. Others find *lectio* time valuable precisely because it is not structured. They find their *lectio* of the Bible flowing naturally into *lectio* of life or of natural beauty.[9]

As a monk one reads the Bible daily, using it as the language with which one converses with God, connecting it to all other parts of one's life. The resulting conversation, in my experience, spans centuries daily. The author of Genesis speaks to Reynolds Price, Annie Dillard, Anne Lamott, Eddie Vedder, Rashi, and whatever other films, novels, or poems I have just seen or read. And the conversation all flows through the person of Christ, who is for me the reason why the conversation happens at all.

Where Am I Standing?

For a very long time, the historical critical method has held sway among exegetes. In recent decades some have come to view it with suspicion. However, of its use the Pontifical Biblical Commission, in its 1994 document entitled *The Interpretation of the Bible in the Church,* said,

> The historical-critical method is the indispensable method for the scientific study of the meaning of ancient texts. Holy Scripture, inasmuch as it

---

[8] Charlotte Allen, "Is Nothing Sacred? Casting out the Gods from Religious Studies," *Lingua Franca* (1996) 30–40.

[9] Columba Stewart, *Prayer and Community: The Benedictine Tradition,* Traditions of Christian Spirituality (Maryknoll: Orbis, 1998) 39–41.

is the "word of God in human language," has been composed by human authors in all its various parts and in all the sources that lie behind them. Because of this, its proper understanding not only admits the use of this method but actually requires it.[10]

The document is well worth reading in its entirety, giving, as it does, a concise summary of this and other methods of biblical study. It is not possible to repeat all of its points here, but the document makes a concerted effort to respond to the idea that exegesis informed by the historical critical method is dry, merely scientific, and fails to find application and contemporary meaning for the scriptures. The Commission writes, describing the final stage of the method:

> At this point the text is explained as it stands, on the basis of the mutual relationships between its diverse elements, and with an eye to its character as a message communicated by the author to his contemporaries. At this point one is in a position to consider the demands of the text from the point of view of action and life.[11]

Essential to this method, despite what some of its skeptical critics think, is the application of the text to the contemporary situation. Not all are convinced. Consider the following evaluation by Schuyler Brown.

> For all that we have learned from historical criticism, we must acknowledge its principal shortcoming: by isolating a text in its own age and situation of origin, it prevents it from saying something to the present, and that is precisely what scripture is expected to do. By distancing the reader from the text, historical criticism runs the risk of frustrating the immediacy which is characteristic of religious literature. Instead of being summoned to question and deepen the way in which we view ourselves and the world, we are allowed, and even encouraged, to take a detached "objective" point of view: we analyze what the author intended to communicate to the original readers; we ourselves do not stand within the hermeneutical circle.[12]

According to Brown, one of the shortcomings of the dominant historical critical method is that it leaves the text in the past and so is unable

---

[10] Pontifical Biblical Commission, *The Interpretation of the Bible in the Church* (Rome: 1994) I. A.

[11] Ibid., I. A. 3.

[12] Schuyler Brown, *Text and Psyche: Experiencing Scripture Today* (New York: Continuum, 1998) 19. There is a large and growing body of literature on this question. I mention only one item here: Peter Williamson, "Actualization: A New Emphasis in Catholic Scripture Study," *America* (May 20, 1995) 17–9.

to effect the transformation that a contemporary reader of religious literature seeks. He does not advert to another issue that has come to perplex postmodern literary theorists in our day, i.e., whether it is possible to determine what a text means at all.

In 1985 George Steiner delivered the Leslie Stephen Memorial Lecture to Cambridge University. Entitled "Real Presences," it has recently been published in his collection *No Passion Spent*[13] and is a very accessible evaluation, much to be recommended for reading and pondering, of current literary theory. Steiner also has a suggestion for interpretation and criticism in the aftermath of the post-modernist challenge.

> The post-structuralist, the deconstructionist, remind us (justly) that there is no difference in substance between primary text and commentary, between the poem and the explication or critique. . . . The notion that we can grasp an author's intentionality, that we should attend to what he would tell us of his own purpose in or understanding of his text, is utterly naive. What does he know of the meanings hidden by or projected from the interplay of semantic potentialities which he has momentarily circumscribed and formalized? . . . The adage had it: "do not trust the teller but the tale." Deconstruction asks: why trust either?[14]

At the same time, the Catholic exegete reads in *Dei verbum* that

> The interpreter must investigate what meaning the sacred writer intended to express and actually expressed in particular circumstances by using contemporary literary forms in accordance with the situation of his time and culture.[15]

It might seem that these two stand in opposition, that *Dei verbum* directs the Catholic exegete to do something that cannot be done. Steiner offers a way out.

> We must read *as if*.
> We must read as if the text before us had meaning. This will not be a single meaning if the text is a serious one, if it makes us answerable to its force of life. . . . Above all, the meaning striven towards will never be one which exegesis, commentary, translation, paraphrase, psychoanalytic or sociological decoding can ever exhaust, can ever define as total. Only weak poems can be exhaustively interpreted or understood. Only in trivial or opportunistic texts is the sum of significance that of the parts.

[13] Steiner, "Real Presences," in *No Passion Spent*, 20–39.

[14] Steiner, "Presences," 28–9.

[15] Vatican II, Dogmatic Constitution on Divine Revelation *(Dei verbum)*, III, 11; 756–7.

We must read as if the temporal and executive setting of a text does matter. The historical surroundings, the cultural and formal circumstances, the biological stratum, what we can construe or conjecture of an author's intentions, constitute vulnerable aids. We know that they ought to be stringently ironized and examined for what is in them of subjective hazard. They matter nonetheless. They enrich the levels of awareness and enjoyment; they generate constraints on the complacencies and licence of interpretative anarchy.[16]

What does this look like, this exegesis that is, in my case, both Christian and also engaged with the philosophical realities of our day? I suggest that it looks like the books in this series, Berit Olam: Studies in Hebrew Narrative and Poetry. In particular, one might peruse David Jobling's commentary on 1 Samuel. The first part is called "The Reader and the Book."[17] He offers a fine, brief statement of the connection a believing Christian makes with our own day, how it is that we dare to read "as if."

Jobling's method, the model with which he approaches scripture by viewing it successively through the prisms of race, class, and gender, the so-called postmodern triad, is not mine. I am much more in tune with the approach described by Avivah Gottlieb Zornberg in the introduction to her book *Genesis: The Beginning of Desire.*[18] Zornberg is an Israeli, an Orthodox Jewish woman who is both a biblical scholar and a student of English literature. She says of her method:

> My mode of inquiry was closer to the "rhetorical" than the "methodical," in terms of Gerald Bruns's distinction[,] the "rhetorical" having "no greater ambition than to discover what can be said, in any given case." The rhetorical mode, which Bruns sees as characteristic of most literary criticism, is "more concerned with finding than with proving, is more speculative than analytical, more heuristic than polemical." It explores problems, relationships, patterns, without arriving at single minded or schematic theories. The rhetorician is a "public meditator."[19]

This meditator's task is not so much to say what the text means in some final and definitive way, but to loosen up what we think we know about a text. This is, it seems to me, very much like my statue of David

---

[16] Steiner, "Presences," 34.

[17] David Jobling, *1 Samuel* (Collegeville: The Liturgical Press, 1998) 3–27.

[18] Avivah Gottlieb Zornberg, *Genesis: The Beginning of Desire* (Philadelphia: Jewish Publication Society, 1995).

[19] Zornberg, *Genesis*, xi–xii, quoting Gerald Bruns, *Inventions: Writing, Textuality, and Understanding in Literary History* (New Haven: Yale University Press, 1982) 1–2.

metaphor: I tell you what I see from where I'm standing. She reads the text as a traditional Jew, standing in the midst of the traditional readings offered by the Jewish sages through the millennia as well as by contemporary thinkers. What she sees is Torah.

What is especially striking to me as a Christian is the way in which Zornberg feels free to delve into Midrash and pre-critical and non-critical rabbinic commentary. The parallel material for a Christian, the works of the Fathers of the Church, the early monastic writers, commentators, and homilists up to the dawn of the critical era in the last century, is frankly *terra incognita* for most commentators today. Augustine? Origen? The Sayings of the Desert Fathers? Gregory the Great? Bede? Bonaventure? Aquinas? None of these would be likely to appear in a contemporary Christian commentary. And we are the poorer for it. It is as if the first eighteen hundred years of Christian tradition has simply disappeared.[20] What to do today? Luke Timothy Johnson writes:

> Rather than a "right" reading of the text, therefore, we properly look for "responsible" readings, by which we mean interpretations that are both responsible to the text and responsible to the community of readers that is the church. Understood this way, the literal sense of the text is the indispensable instrument of discernment and decision-making in the community of faith, and historical criticism continues to play an indispensable role in maintaining the "otherness" of the text that protects it from manipulation.
>
> But not every reading of the text within the church is for deciding halakah. Much reading is for wisdom and delight. In such reading above all, the community as well as individual readers can enter into the imaginative world constructed not by this composition alone or that one, but by all the voices in the Bible and all the voices of faith that have also lived within the world imagined by the Bible. Allegory may no longer be to our taste, although we would be foolish (even as scholars) to declare we have nothing to learn from such brilliant readers as Origen and Augustine. Can our minds and hearts not still profit from the delicate inter-

---

[20] Luke Timothy Johnson engaged these issues while writing an article on the state of Catholic biblical scholarship. ("So What's Catholic About It? The State of Catholic Biblical Scholarship," *Commonweal* 125, 1 [1998] 12–6.) Although his focus was most particularly New Testament studies, what he said bears repetition here:

> Anyone who has worked seriously with patristic and medieval scriptural interpretation, for example, knows that it cannot simply be dismissed as aberrant; even at the level of the *sensus literalis*, one can gain at least as much insight from Bede as from the average recent homiletic commentary. But I am suggesting a more fundamental enlargement of vision, to include all the ways in which Scripture was actualized in the prayers, sermons, and spiritual teachings of the patristic and medieval church.

play of literal, moral, spiritual, and ecclesial dimensions of the "Parable of the Workers in the Vineyard" (Matt 20:1-16) found in Origen's Commentary on Matthew? Indeed, I wonder whether the purposeful playfulness found in some postmodernist readings of the Bible might not rightly claim a share in the noble heritage of allegory.[21]

This is a lengthy answer to the question I posed earlier: "Where am I standing?" A summary is probably in order. I stand in the midst of the Catholic Church and its ancient and modern traditions of biblical commentary. I am ordained for ministry in this Church, so have a preacher's sensibilities. I am a monk in this Church, so turn to scripture as the foundation of my daily life. But I am not divorced from the time in which I live and so must take seriously the skepticism with which contemporary literary theory regards fixed meanings in texts. Although I read the historical critics, I would describe myself, if I cannot simply borrow the term public meditator from Avivah Zornberg, as a reader—of admittedly moderate skill—of the final form of the text and one who is privileged to have an audience,[22] i.e., my interest is more in the canonical text and the details of literary craft encountered there than in the history of the text's development.[23] Perhaps I may call myself onlooker, eavesdropper, and conversation partner.

What Am I Seeing?

One must assume that whoever put the book of Genesis into the shape we now possess had sources, perhaps some written, perhaps some only oral. However, none survive. There are no rough drafts with which we can compare the final version to trace the development of the author's ideas. The documents known as J, E, D and P, scholarly reconstructions of various stages in the development of the final text, remain hypothetical. We can sometimes, with a certain reliability, trace

---

[21] Ibid., 16.

[22] Probably the best general study of the various models available for the interpretation of scripture that is contemporary with this book is John Goldingay's *Models for Interpretation of Scripture* (Grand Rapids, Mich.: Eerdmans, 1995). One should also read the slightly earlier book by James Barr, *Holy Scripture: Canon, Authority, Criticism* (Philadelphia: Westminster, 1983).

[23] A superlative survey of the history of the study of Genesis may be found in Robert Ignatius Letellier's *Day in Mamre, Night in Sodom: Abraham and Lot in Genesis 18 & 19* (New York: E. J. Brill, 1995) 1–29. The approach taken in this commentary would cause it to be among those labeled synchronic by Letellier.

the background of ideas or literary motifs that have made their way into the Bible. We seem to see an ancient Mesopotamian creation story called Enuma Elish behind Genesis 1, for example. But this line of investigation does not need to be continued here. There are many commentaries that may satisfy the curiosity of the reader who wishes to investigate these questions and issues.[24] Indeed, the literature on Genesis is so vast that one would hesitate to add to it at all were there not something interesting and new to say.

When I look at the book of Genesis, I see neither documents nor historical clues. I see a story. And in that story there are characters who act and are acted upon, who grow, change and develop. Yet, among all the brilliant and provocative commentaries[25] on Genesis, none reads the entire book as a story.[26] This is not to say that there are not extremely important studies of individual passages within the book, or sections of the book. Many of these will be referred to as we move through the commentary. However, as far as I know, there is no commentary that applies the tools of narrative analysis to the book as an integral whole. This is all the more surprising because of the extraordinary amount of fine work that has been done on the workings of biblical narrative.[27] The remainder of this Introduction will be devoted to a brief survey of some of the ways in which Hebrew narrative functions differently from the narrative traditions with which we are more famil-

[24] Among the classic commentaries are E. A. Speiser, *Genesis,* AB 1 (New York: Doubleday, 1962); Gerhard von Rad, *Genesis* (Philadelphia: Westminster, 1972); Claus Westermann, *Genesis 1–11: A Commentary, Genesis 12–36, Genesis 37–50* (Minneapolis: Augsburg, 1984, 1985, 1986).

[25] Again, the literature is huge, but the following are very much worth reading: Zvi Adar, *The Book of Genesis: An Introduction to the Biblical World* (Jerusalem: Magnes Press, 1990); Robert Alter, *Genesis: Translation and Commentary* (New York: Norton, 1996); Everett Fox, *The Five Books of Moses* (New York: Schocken, 1995).

[26] Although my readings differ considerably from his, one must credit Jack Miles and his book *God: A Biography* (New York: A. A. Knopf, 1995) for seeing that even God is a character whose development can be traced.

[27] Some of the key works are: Robert Alter, *The Art of Biblical Narrative* (New York: Basic Books, 1981); Shimon Bar-Efrat, *Narrative Art in the Bible* (Sheffield, England: Sheffield Academic Press, 1997); Adele Berlin, *Poetics and Interpretation of Biblical Narrative,* Bible and Literature 9 (Sheffield: Almond, 1983); Herbert Chanan Brichto, *Toward a Grammar of Biblical Poetics* (New York: Oxford University Press, 1992); George W. Coats, *Genesis: With an Introduction to Narrative Literature,* FOTL 1 (Grand Rapids, MI: Eerdmans, 1983); Jan P. Fokkelman, *Narrative Art in Genesis: Specimens of Stylistic and Structural Analysis* (Assen: Van Gorcum, 1975); David Gunn and Danna Nolan Fewell, *Narrative in the Hebrew Bible* (New York: Oxford University Press, 1993); Meir Sternberg, *The Poetics of Biblical Narrative: Ideological*

iar, especially the issues of meaning, mimesis, plot, structure, character, and point of view.

MEANING: NOT HOW IT WAS, BUT WHY IT IS

The modern Western mind turns to history in order to discover what some past moment was like, what happened then and there. The historical books of the Bible, certainly Genesis, have a very different concern. It is less important to these books to describe a past moment in a manner that we would regard as complete and objective than it is to explain why the writer's (and readers') present is as it is. In order to understand what these narratives mean, we modern readers must always remember that they were written so that their original readers would better understand the nature of their contemporary world, that their contemporary world is thousands of years distant from us, and that we are separated from it not only by time but also by language and culture. It might be helpful if we thought of ourselves as listening in on their conversation. The believer understands that God intended the conversation to be meaningful for us as well, but we are certainly not the principal audience the human authors envisioned. The concern of these books is fundamentally etiological (Greek: *aition*, "cause"), as the writers sought to explain the causes of the world in which they (not we) lived.

Any narrative is a form of representation. Just as a painting of an apple is not the real historical apple and may differ considerably from it, so too the persons depicted in the Bible are interpretations of possibly historical characters; they are not the characters themselves. Biblical narrative is thus best understood, according to a phrase that is used by some exegetes and must be carefully explained, as historicized prose fiction.[28]

Prose. Alone among the ancient peoples, Israel's national history was composed in prose. Sternberg has argued that this is due to a theological insight. Poetry is, by its nature, bound by rules that result in a regular, unchanging sequence of patterns. Israel's idea of God as One who freely intervenes in history in order to save those in need means

---

Literature and the Drama of Reading (Bloomington, Ind.: Indiana University Press, 1985). What follows in the remainder of this introduction is heavily dependent on all of these works. I certainly do not intend to give a full overview of techniques for narrative analysis of the Hebrew Bible. This is just a quick primer, which I hope will be useful to readers unfamiliar with the field.

[28] See Sternberg, *Poetics*, 23–35.

that this God must be free to do the unexpected. Such a God cannot be bound by the strictures of poetry, but must have the freedom of prose.

Historicized fiction. The stories found in the historical books of the Bible must either be fiction laying claim to history (i.e., purely imaginative renderings of the past without basis in fact) or history with a veneer of fiction (i.e., fundamentally reliable depictions of real past events with some reconstruction [e.g., conversations between characters] as necessary). Examples of both may be found because these books are complex interweavings of

a. Factual historical detail overlaid with legend (the crossing of the Red Sea in Exod 14:1–15:21);
b. Mythological lore (the Nephilim of Gen 6:1-4);
c. Etiological tales (Jacob wrestling with God in Gen 32:22-32);
d. Archetypal sagas of the nation's founders (the call of Abraham in Gen 12:1-9);
e. Folk tales of heroes and wonder workers (Samson in Judg 13:1–16:31);
f. Known historical figures with some element of reconstruction (David in 1 and 2 Samuel and 1 Kings).

MIMESIS: REPRESENTATION OR ILLUSTRATION?

Do these narratives represent the world of experience or illustrate the world of ideas? Illustrative characters (Adam and Eve, Cain and Abel) are really ideas dressed up as human characters in order to make a tale possible. Other characters (e.g., Moses) are more likely representative of the world of experience.

What ideas, then, do these stories illustrate? One of the most provocative readers of the Bible is the literary scholar and novelist Reynolds Price. In his book *A Palpable God*, he wrote:

> Any of the hundreds of separate tales in the Old and New Testament may be classed under one of those four types: *We are loved and needed by our Creator, We suffer but accept our fate, Our enemies and God's are rightly punished,* and lastly *God is sometimes veiled from our sight.*[29]

I agree with him. There is, after all, nothing further that a person of faith can say except these things about the relationship of God and hu-

---

[29] Reynolds Price, *A Palpable God* (New York: Atheneum, 1978) 23–4. Emphasis original.

manity: we are here because we are wanted; life is full of pain but we must endure and move on through it; an ultimate justice exists; and sometimes, perhaps most of the time, we are in the dark.

PLOT

A plot is the pattern of events in a narrative. Classically, these events are seen as linked by a chain of causality, such that the beginning of a story is some moment that is not caused by what precedes, the middle is caused by what precedes and causes what follows, and the end is that which is caused by what precedes but which causes nothing else. This is called scenic narrative and is typical of what we find in the Bible. There are rarely more than two characters in a biblical scene. A scene ends when a character leaves and another enters. A story, as opposed, say, to a report of events, requires some tension or conflict that needs resolution.

A plot has several moments that describe an arc of tension, i.e., there is no tension at the story's beginning; tension rises and falls back to a state of no tension:

> *Exposition:* the establishing of the situation in which conflict develops. Characters are introduced, but there is as yet no reason for them to interact. They are like actors on a stage as the curtain rises.
>
> *Inciting moment* (also called *the initiating action*): the event that brings the opposing forces into conflict. This is the spark that moves the characters from inaction to interaction.
>
> *Rising action* (also called *the complication*): the separate events that advance the conflict to the crucial point, at which the protagonist in the conflict takes, consciously or unconsciously, the action that determines the future course of things irrevocably. This latter action is called the turning point.
>
> *Falling action* (also called *the resolution*): incidents and episodes in which the force destined to be triumphant establishes its supremacy.
>
> *Conclusion:* the resolution of the conflict called forth by the inciting moment.

STRUCTURE

This material, part of the Western tradition of reading narrative since Aristotle, is familiar enough and does not require much elaboration.

However, notice does need to be given of narrative structures that are important in the biblical narrative tradition but much less well known to us. Jerome T. Walsh outlines these techniques, focusing on inclusions and symmetrical organizations; David Dorsey does an especially thorough job of describing ways in which literary structures may be identified and used for interpretation.[30]

Inclusion refers to some element that appears at the beginning of a passage and recurs at its end, thus marking its extent. The symmetrical organizations that appear in biblical narrative are much more complex, and where they occur in the book of Genesis they will be the subject of extended discussion. Here let me simply alert the reader to two techniques. Chiasm (often called concentric symmetry) is the name given to a narrative that takes the form ABCXC'B'A'. What this means is that elements in the first part of the story are paralleled in reverse order by elements in the second half. This technique is especially useful at indicating reversals, i.e., what developed in the first half of the story is reversed in the second half. The center, the turning point symbolized by an X here, is that element of the story which causes the reversal to take place. This will be clearer in the body of the commentary, so here a brief example will suffice. In the first half of the story of the building of the tower of Babel, the people of the earth come together and move upwards with their tower. In the second half they are sent down the tower and scattered. The turning point is the descent of God. This is a nice example of the sort of reversal this narrative structure is useful at illustrating.

When elements in the story are parallel, ABCA'B'C', the emphasis is not on the turning point and the reversal it initiates but rather on the individual elements in the story and the way the latter half echoes the former.

Things are rarely as neat and clean in narrative as these structures would seem to indicate. Often an otherwise neat symmetric structure has some element that makes it asymmetrical. In this case the reader's attention is drawn to the asymmetry itself, for it is the asymmetrical element that engages interest.[31] An important example is the story about Sarai in Pharaoh's court (Gen 12:10-20). As we will see, a neat chiasm is disturbed by the action of God. Important theological points, that God is always free to act and that God acts on behalf of the powerless, are made for us by means of narrative structure.

---

[30] Jerome T. Walsh, *Style and Structure in Biblical Hebrew Narrative* (Collegeville: The Liturgical Press, 2001); David Dorsey, *The Literary Structure of the Old Testament* (Grand Rapids, Mich.: Baker, 1999).

[31] Walsh, *Style and Structure*, 101–3.

However, I differ in at least one important way with these scholars. Both Walsh and Dorsey think that the structures they describe are somehow objective realities within the text and that they have discovered and described them. Are these structures really "in" the text we are studying? Has their author purposefully organized his material in this way so that we can discover it so many years later? I think not. These structures are generally speaking more in the exegete than in the text. In other words, whenever we study a text we necessarily organize our reactions in some manner. We note beginning and end, we find a middle point of high emotional drama and so on. Perhaps another metaphor will help.

Let us imagine a painting done on some large, flexible material, a sort of rubber sheet perhaps. If someone stands behind the sheet and pushes forward now here and now there, different parts of the scene will come into the foreground or recede into the background. These changes are not in the painting, but are results of someone choosing to foreground first this part and then another, someone choosing to say "What will happen if I look at this from this angle?" Similarly, in approaching a text, the exegete chooses to organize it somehow, saying, as it were, what happens if we choose to see this moment as central, and what will happen if we then choose to see that moment as not central but as part of a denouement or as a textual insertion by some editor?

CHARACTER AND CHARACTERIZATION

In general, a person's character is revealed in what is said or done, by the character, by other characters, or by the narrator. In other words, we come to know what characters in a story are like as we watch them interact with other characters, as we listen to what they say and what others say about them. In the Bible, one must pay special attention to what the narrator (i.e., the impersonal voice who is telling us the story) says about the person. There is very little attention given in the Bible to the inner lives of characters. This is a great contrast with the narrative tradition with which we are more familiar. Since we are usually denied access to their inner lives, we must take advantage of whatever external clues we are given.

It is best to be forewarned, though. The Bible proceeds oftentimes by a strategy of reticence or understatement. Perhaps this can best be explained if the reader thinks back to the earlier metaphor about porcelain miniatures. In that case, very little information is given to the viewer of the work of art. Hence, the viewer must be particularly careful to take in all of the details that are provided, in order to achieve the total effect of the piece. This is true in the Bible as well. There is very little description, for example; so when a character is described, whether that description be physical or moral, the reader must pay close heed. The biblical storyteller has several techniques at hand to accomplish characterization.

Characterization by naming. For most people reading this book, a name is simply a convenient label, one long used in the family perhaps, one associated with a favorite saint, or one that is currently popular. Whatever the case may be, we rarely give much attention to what a name means (at least after the books of baby's names are perused and put away). Such was not the case with the people of Israel, for whom names and their meanings were highly significant. Especially in the book of Genesis, the meaning of a character's name is key to understanding who the person really is. For example, "Adam" means "human being" and is also a pun on the Hebrew word for earth. Hence, we know that he is somehow intended to be representative of what it means to be human and at the same time a reminder of our mortality. "Eve" is related to the word for life and indicates her role as mother of all life. "Abel" means "puff of air." One is hardly surprised when Abel's insubstantial being is moved out of the story almost immediately. "Sarah" means "princess"; "Isaac" means "laughter." And on and on. When names are an important indication of who the character is, attention will be drawn to them. A rule of thumb—women's names often allude to some aspect of the natural world, e.g., Tamar = "palm tree," Deborah = "honey bee," Susanna = "lily." Men's names, by contrast, often contain a theophoric element, i.e., some reference to God: Michael = "who is like God?" Isaiah = "YHWH saves," etc.

Characterization by description.[32] Since we are dependent on narrative traditions, at least in film and on television, that are predominantly visual, the lack of attention given to the physical description of characters in the Bible is jarring at first. There is no hint of what Adam or Eve looked like, nor Abraham, nor Isaac, nor most of the others. When our attention is drawn to distinctive physical features, therefore, we must pay close attention. For example:

Esau's birth is described in this way: "The first [twin] came out **red**, all his body **like a hairy mantle**; so they named him **Esau**" (Gen 25:25). Red hair was apparently thought to connote strength, but hairiness was associated with boorishness. So, as soon as Esau is born, we know that he is strong but uncouth. His name, similar in sound to the

---

[32] See Bar-Efrat, *Narrative Art,* 47–92.

word for hair, and so meaning something like "Hairy," underlines this impression.

Jacob's first impression of the two women who would eventually become his principal wives was that "Leah's **eyes were lovely**, and Rachel was **graceful and beautiful**" (Gen 29:17). Here again, both names and descriptions are significant. Is Leah being damned with faint praise? Is she so unlovely that the stammering narrator is driven to say that, well, her eyes were nice? Is this the biblical version of "having a nice personality"? Her name, apparently related to a word for cow, according to some, would seem to indicate that this evaluation is correct. Homely, unmarriageable Leah, one thinks. As we will see, however, it is Leah, unloved by her husband perhaps, who is favored by God. Rachel, "ewe lamb" (Lambkins?), would seem to trump Leah with her beauty and grace and her very name. The reader will be curious to see whether she always lives up to the character her name and appearance imply.

One of the most powerful stories in the book of Genesis is that in which Tamar's life is described. In the following passage we watch her transform her character as she changes her clothes.

> . . . she put off her **widow's garments**, put on a **veil**, **wrapped herself up**, and sat down at the entrance to Enaim, which is on the road to Timnah. She saw that Shelah was grown up, yet she had not been given to him in marriage. (Gen 38:14)

Tamar leaves the confines of her father's house because she has decided to create a life and a future for herself. In a very real sense, she leaves the person she was, the widow, behind and becomes someone ambiguous and new. What she becomes is not easily identifiable. Her father-in-law thinks that she is a prostitute and approaches her. But people do not know what term to use for her, using both the regular secular word for a prostitute as well as that used for a so-called sacred prostitute. The story will receive lengthy attention later; suffice it to say here that a change in character is indicated by her change in clothes. Similar strategies will be seen in the stories of Jacob, when he dresses like his brother, and Joseph, where his changes of clothing track his ups and downs.

Attention given to social status, profession, or ethnic origin may also be useful in discerning character. Consider the following: "Now **Sarai, Abram's wife**, bore him no children. She had an **Egyptian slave-girl** whose name was **Hagar** . . ." (Gen 16:1).

Two things are immediately evident. These two characters embody the opposite ends of Israel's social scale. The wealthy wife, whose name means "Princess," seems a world apart from the slave who barely has a name. Hagar seems to be related to a verb that means "to dwell" or "to sojourn." It might well be that the author is intending a sort of pun here, giving Sarai's servant a name that is not really even a name, just a label that might mean something like "foreign girl."

Sometimes the narrator, always trustworthy and to be believed, simply tells the reader what a character is like.

> Now the serpent was **more crafty** than any other wild animal that the LORD God had made. He said to the woman, "Did God say, 'You shall not eat from any tree in the garden'?" (Gen 3:1)

> These are the descendants of Noah. **Noah was a righteous man**, blameless in his generation; **Noah walked with God**. (Gen 6:9)

> Now the people of Sodom were **wicked, great sinners** against the LORD. (Gen 13:13)

> Afterward his brother came out, with his hand gripping Esau's **heel**; so he was named **Jacob**. (Gen 25:26)

> So he said to him, "What is your name?" And he said, "**Jacob**." Then the man said, "You shall no longer be called Jacob, but **Israel**, for **you have striven** with God and with humans, and have prevailed." (Gen 32:27-28)

If the narrator is to be believed, how much more so God.

> Then the LORD said to Noah, "Go into the ark, you and all your household, for I have seen that **you alone are righteous** before me in this generation." (Gen 7:1)

> He said, "Do not lay your hand on the boy or do anything to him; for now **I know that you fear God**, since you have not withheld your son, your only son, from me." (Gen 22:12)

However, the narrator's intention is not always so explicit. Consider the following initial description of Laban.

> Rebekah had a brother whose name was Laban; and Laban ran out to the man, to the spring. As soon as he had seen the nose-ring, and the bracelets on his sister's arms, and when he heard the words of his sister Rebekah, "Thus the man spoke to me," he went to the man; and there he was, standing by the camels at the spring. (Gen 24:29-30)

One gets the impression, without having been told so in so many words, that Laban is greedy. He sees rich jewelry and runs right out the door to meet the man from whom it came. The narrator is careful to direct our attention to Laban's reaction to the jewelry, not to his sister's joy.

Similarly, after his brother steals Esau's blessing, we are given a sense of Esau's inner turmoil when the narrator calls our attention to the intensity of his lamentation.

When Esau heard his father's words, he cried out with an exceedingly great and bitter cry, and said to his father, "Bless me, me also, father!" (Gen 27:34)

Characterization by interior monologue. Interior monologue, i.e., a record of what is going on in the mind of the character, is rare in the Hebrew Bible, but not entirely unknown. Whether or not a particular instance of reported speech is intended to reflect interior monologue, however, can require a judgment on the part of a translator. Since the Hebrew probably says simply "he said" or "she said," the translator may have to decide from the context whether the character is speaking aloud.

Inner life told by narrator and other characters. Occasionally, the narrator will report that the character in question is speaking to himself or herself. This is important, of course, because it provides the reader with information about the character's future actions and/or motivation that is not available to the other actors in the story, thus placing the reader in a privileged position.

> Now Esau hated Jacob because of the blessing with which his father had blessed him, and Esau **said to himself**, "The days of mourning for my father are approaching; then I will kill my brother Jacob." (Gen 27:41)

> Then Jacob was greatly afraid and distressed; and he divided the people that were with him, and the flocks and herds and camels, into two companies, **thinking**, "If Esau comes to the one company and destroys it, then the company that is left will escape." (Gen 32:7-8)

Inner life shown by the same character. Theorists of narrative often make a distinction between "telling" and "showing." In the former case, the narrator will simply tell the reader what he or she is to know about some character or situation. This is held to be a less sophisticated method of storytelling because it requires less engagement on the reader's part. The narrator is doing the work that the reader would otherwise be required to do. For example, the narrator may simply have said of Adam that he was unable to take responsibility for his own actions and tried to shift the blame to the woman. The reader is drawn into the story more effectively when he or she must try to figure out the character's nature without assistance. For example, in Genesis 3:12 (The man said, "The woman whom you gave to be with me, she gave me fruit from the tree, and I ate"), Adam is shown to be shirking his responsibility for his act of disobedience, but the reader must conclude that without help from the narrator.

Prayer. A person can be assumed to be honest and straightforward in the speech with God that we call prayer. Oddly, prayer is not frequently reported in the Bible, so when it occurs we must observe the details of the prayer with care, for here too we learn more about who a character is. The following two prayers appear in the series of stories about Jacob. The first appears early on in the cycle, when Jacob has just fled from the murderous rage of his betrayed brother and is spending the night at the place he will name Beth-El, the House of God.

> Then Jacob made a vow, saying, "If God will be with me, and will keep me in this way that I go, and will give me bread to eat and clothing to wear, so that I come again to my father's house in peace, then the LORD shall be my God, and this stone, which I have set up for a pillar, shall be God's house; and of all that you give me I will surely give one tenth to you." (Gen 28:20-22)

The prayer reveals Jacob to be a self-centered dealmaker. This may seem no surprise, since Jacob has been a heel and a con-man ever since his birth. His name "heel," his duplicitous taking of his brother's birthright, his lie to his disabled father, his theft of his brother's blessing—all show us a man devoted to his own advancement. The charitable reader might well assume that in his most intimate of moments, when addressing his God, Jacob would be shown to be larger of heart. But such is not the case. Notice how Jacob's speech is full of "I" and "me." Notice that there is no expression of remorse for the damage done to his family. Nor is there any fear of God. Jacob coolly cuts a deal to his own advantage. "If God does thus and so for me, then I will acknowledge God."

This cool, self-absorbed dealmaker is transformed, at least a bit, by his subsequent experiences, living with his uncle Laban's family, marrying, and raising children. This is shown to the reader in the prayer Jacob makes upon his return, just before he meets his betrayed brother Esau again after a twenty-year hiatus.

> And Jacob said, "O God of my father Abraham and God of my father Isaac, O LORD who said to me, 'Return to your country and to your kindred, and I will do you good,' I am not worthy of the least of all the steadfast love and all the faithfulness that you have shown to your servant, for with only my staff I crossed this Jordan; and now I have become two companies. Deliver me, please, from the hand of my brother, from the hand of Esau, for I am afraid of him; he may come and kill us all, the mothers with the children. Yet you have said, 'I will surely do you good, and make your offspring as the sands of the sea, which cannot be counted because of their number.'" (Gen 32:9-12; NRSV, modified)

A certain awe and gratitude mark this second prayer, as well as a recognition that God is the source of blessings that Jacob enjoys. Perhaps most striking, and evocative of a change in Jacob, is the cry for salvation not only for himself but also for the rest of his family. This concern for family well-being is hardly imaginable in the earlier Jacob who manipulated his family for his own well-being, not theirs.

Characterization by contrast. We can see things more clearly when they are viewed against a contrasting background. This use of contrast is especially important in Genesis. We have already seen that a later version of Jacob strongly contrasts with an earlier. But contrasts are of various kinds. We view Abraham in contrast with Lot, Sarah in contrast with Hagar, Jacob in contrast with Esau, Rachel in contrast with Leah. In all of these cases, and many more that we will look at in detail throughout the book, we discover what a person is like, what strengths he or she possesses as well as what weaknesses. Characters' actions, as well as their more enduring traits, may be contrasted as well.

> So **Lot** chose for himself all the plain of the Jordan, and Lot journeyed eastward; thus they separated from each other. **Abram** settled in the land of Canaan, while Lot settled among the cities of the Plain and moved his tent as far as Sodom. Now the people of Sodom were wicked, great sinners against the LORD. (Gen 13:11-13)

In this instance, Lot chooses what appears, although the appearance is superficial, to be better, so revealing himself as a selfish character. To his selfishness is added a lack of moral insight, since he is shown to move into the neighborhood of Sodom. The following verse (Gen 13:13) is what is called a frame-break. The narrator speaks directly to the audience, telling us what we need to know in order to understand the implications of the character's action fully. Lot, we are told, is doing a foolish thing, by putting himself in proximity with great danger. Lot's foolishness will, of course, be an important theme in the book, but here it appears for the first time. Abram by contrast has generously allowed his nephew the first pick of suitable grazing land and is content to take land that is perhaps less lush but is morally more secure.

It might be that the contrast we are shown is with the expected norm of behavior for a person of a particular station. A good example occurs in Genesis 16:4: "He went in to Hagar, and she conceived; and when she saw that she had conceived, **she looked with contempt on her mistress**." The narrator shows us that Hagar is acting in a way that a slave, even though she is now some sort of secondary wife, ought not to behave (see Prov 30:23b). From her earlier position of imposed and enforced servility, she is now able to look down on the woman who was once her mistress because she has been able to do what the mistress was unable to do, conceive a child.

However, Sarai also behaves in a way that contrasts with what she should do. In Genesis 16:6 we read, "But Abram said to Sarai, 'Your slave-girl is in your power; do to her as you please.' Then **Sarai dealt harshly with her**, and she ran away from her." As we will see when we look at this passage in more detail, the verb translated here as "dealt harshly" seems to imply that Sarai beat Hagar viciously. The contrast here, although the history of slavery shows us what a vain expectation it is, is with the humane behavior that one might expect from one in a position of power over one weaker than she.

Characterization: summary. The storyteller of the Hebrew Bible had at hand a variety of ways to effect characterization. These techniques offer a sort of ascending ladder of reliability, moving from a report of what someone says or does up through a direct statement on the part of the narrator. The following list shows this ladder of ascents more clearly.

> Report of actions
> Appearance
> Gesture
> Posture
> Costume
> One character's comment on another
> Direct speech by character
> Inward speech
> Narrator's statement.[33]

Literary theorists have some other language with which they characterize the complexity of characters in a particular narrative. They speak of a continuum of character types that range from flat to round.[34] The flat character is just that, a person without any depth or complexity, merely a function of the plot, e.g., the servant who opens the door. But a character who changes and develops, growing in complexity all the while, gradually being fleshed out, comes eventually to be known as a rounded character. Some use an alternative set of labels, which are explained in the accompanying table.

---

[33] Alter, *Biblical Narrative*, 116.

[34] The distinction originated with E. M. Forster. For more on flat and round characters see his *Aspects of the Novel* (New York: Harcourt, Brace & Company, 1927) 65–75.

Agent	Type	Full-fledged
This character is merely a function of the plot. Nothing is known about the character except what is necessary for him or her to function.	This character possesses a limited and stereotyped range of traits and represents the class of people with these traits.	This character possesses a broader range of traits (not all of which belong to the same class of people). More is known about the character than is strictly necessary for his or her function in the plot.

While this language is useful, readers of the Bible disagree whether there are any complex, rounded, or full-fledged characters to be found there. Since characters are introduced and disappear so rapidly, some think that they cannot really approximate an actual person. But a careful examination of details will show characters of real complexity and depth; this is an art of miniaturization.

POINT OF VIEW

Point of view may be understood by thinking of the narrator as a movie director. Viewing the action through the camera's eye, we look where our attention is directed and see only what the narrator allows us to see. So, for example, in the story of Abraham and the binding of Isaac (Genesis 22) we are not shown Sarah and know nothing, at least while the story is still being told, of her reaction to the events depicted therein.

This understanding of point of view, in which it refers to visual experience (i.e., we are actually seeing something), can be expanded by adding at least two additional types that refer to other sorts of perception: conceptual point of view and interest point of view. Conceptual point of view comes into play when we view the action of the story through someone else's worldview or ideology. That is, there is no reference to the physical act of sight but to the ways in which facts and impressions are filtered through another's attitudes. When one speaks of interest point of view, one is neither referring to sight or to the mind. The phrase is a synonym for "as far as X was concerned."

In his classic treatment of these terms, Seymour Chatman gives the following examples:

Literal point of view: From John's point of view, at the top of Coit Tower, the panorama of the San Francisco Bay was breathtaking.

Conceptual point of view: John said that, from his point of view, Nixon's position, though praised by his supporters, was somewhat less than noble.

Interest point of view: Though he didn't realize it at the time, the divorce was a disaster from John's point of view.[35]

SUMMARY

It is my task as an exegete to tell my readers what I see from where I am standing. In the preceding pages I have tried to tell you some of the things that make me who I am, where I am standing, and what it is that I see. It is now my task to turn from these words of introduction to the commentary itself. Do not expect too much: it is never possible to see everything, and I will not manage to do so here. The treatment of each narrative section will differ, as sometimes plot, sometimes character, sometimes point of view, sometimes traditional commentary will engage my interest. The result may seem unsystematic and idiosyncratic. Be that as it may, it is nonetheless what I see from where I stand. Finally, with Wendell Berry, may I pray:[36]

> Heavenly Muse, Spirit who brooded on
> The world and raised it shapely out of nothing,
> Touch my lips with fire and burn away
> All dross of speech, so that I keep in mind
> The truth and end to which my words now move
> In hope. Keep my mind within that Mind
> Of which it is a part, whose wholeness is
> The hope of sense in what I tell. And though
> I go among the scatterings of that sense,
> The members of its worldly body broken,
> Rule my sight by vision of the parts
> Rejoined. And in my exile's journey far
> From home, be with me, so that I may return.

---

[35] Seymour Chatman, *Story and Discourse: Narrative Structure in Fiction and Film* (Ithaca: Cornell University Press, 1978) 151–3.

[36] Wendell Berry, *Remembering* (San Francisco: North Point Press, 1988) frontispiece.

Part One

STORIES ABOUT BEGINNINGS
GENESIS 1–11

Chapter 1

THE STORY OF THE CREATION OF ALL THAT IS

Genesis 1:1–2:3

Is This a Story?[1]

God saves. God is always savior. The Bible begins with a story that recounts the creation out of nothing, by the one eternally existing God, of all that exists. Among God's creations is Adam/Humanity, the image and likeness of the Creator. The characters of God and Humanity, which do not change throughout the rest of this very complex but nonetheless unified collection of books, are established here at the beginning. God saves from the sterility of meaningless lifelessness, and Adam/Humanity is called to the same task, in relationship with each other and with God. When Humanity finally achieves its goal, history draws to a close, according to Christian belief, at the Parousia with which the Christian version of the Bible ends.

This creation story serves as a sort of prologue for the entire Bible, introducing characters and themes, serving, as it were, as the inciting moment for the plot that develops in all the books that follow. It is not, however, the first of two creation stories, as is often said to be the case. As we shall see, the creation story in Genesis 1:1–2:3 is followed, in Genesis 2:4–3:24, by a story of a different genre entirely wherein the beginnings of human life and culture are explained.

---

[1] In much of what follows the contributions of Jean-Louis Ska, S.J. (of the Pontifical Biblical Institute in Rome) to the study of Genesis will be evident. This most subtle of exegetes introduced me to the literary study of biblical texts in a course on Genesis 1–11 in 1986. My debt to him and his work is profound.

It must be said that Genesis 1:1–2:3 is an unusual story, that it even seems to lack elements that are essential for a story. There is no tension, no plot, just a sequence of events. If it is the major thesis of this commentary that Genesis may be best read and understood by approaching it as a story, it is necessary first of all to address this fundamental question. Is this opening sequence a narrative? And if it is not, what is it? In his book *Genesis: With an Introduction to Narrative Literature*, George Coats says:

> If ancient Near Eastern myths lie behind this unit, it is nonetheless clear that the unit is no longer myth. . . . Nor can the unit properly stand as a tale: It develops no plot; there is no arc of tension, no resolution of crisis. The dominant structural characteristic, an enumeration of days with a specific sequence of events in each day, destroys any story quality by its regular progression and suggests the unit has more in common with genealogy, even with hymns or wisdom tradition, than with tale. . . . It thus seems most appropriate to label the unit a REPORT, a genre that communicates events for the sake of the communication, not for the sake of building interest or developing plot.[2]

Coats disputes the narrative quality of this text on a very narrow basis; as far as he is concerned, it lacks plot, which he identifies with the development and resolution of tension. That there is character and characterization in Genesis 1 he does not deny. He makes no mention of complex and varied points of view or of the fact that there is a narrator present in the text who engages in a very particular kind of omniscient narration.

However, these elements of story are very much part of Genesis 1:1–2:3. The passage does teach a great deal about the person and nature of God, right from the initiatory verb *bārāʾ*.[3] God alone, throughout the Hebrew Bible, enjoys the prerogative of the sovereign, effortless, creative power denoted by this word. The point of view adopted by the omniscient narrator here is as wide-angle as possible, what Genette calls "zero-focalization."[4] In order to gain the reader's trust that this is

---

[2] George Coats, *Genesis: With an Introduction to Narrative Literature*, FOTL 1 (Grand Rapids, Mich.: Eerdmans, 1983) 47.

[3] As with most topics relating to Genesis, the literature on this verb is enormous. Here I will mention only the basic reference works: Ernst Jenni and Claus Westermann, *Theologisches Handwörterbuch zum Alten Testament*, Band I (Munich: Chr. Kaiser, 1984) s.v. ברא; Francis Brown, S. R. Driver and Charles A. Briggs, *A Hebrew and English Lexicon of the Old Testament* (Oxford: Clarendon, 1972) s.v. ברא.

[4] Gérard Genette, *Figures III*, Collection Poétique (Paris: Éditions du Seuil, 1972) 206.

how it really was, the narrator does not focus on any particular field. Rather, everything is shown, everything is told.

We have, then, character, characterization, a storyteller who is omniscient and assures us of his omniscience by adopting a very particular point of view. We have a series of events that take place over a period of time. But do we have plot? First, a few words about plot in general, what it is, and what it requires; then we will return to the text at hand to see how it compares.

The study of plot is not a fashionable enterprise among literary scholars, who have been, for a long time, much more interested in the development of character. That characters have to do things, that those things take place in time, and that inevitably and unavoidably that sequence of events in time cannot be entirely free of plot, is taken as one of the pitfalls of the writer's trade.

Discussions of plot begin with a bow in the direction of Aristotle, for whom it was central, then make mention of, say, Henry James and E. M. Forster, and then peter out fairly rapidly. A few representative words:

Edward J. O'Brien: "Plot is merely a means to an end."[5]

Henry James: "What is incident but the illustration of character?"[6]

This denigration of plot is a fairly recent phenomenon. Aristotle saw plot as the very stuff of which narrative was made.[7] That a story has a beginning, middle and end; that the scenes of a plot are causally

---

[5] *The Short Story Case Book* (New York: Farrar & Rinehart, 1935).

[6] *The Art of Fiction* (London: De Wolfe and Fiske, 1884).

[7] Aristotle states his views in *Aristotle's Poetics,* trans. S. H. Butcher (Boston: Hill and Wang, 1989):

On the necessity of plot: "I propose to treat of Poetry in itself and of its various kinds, noting the essential quality of each, to inquire into the structure of the plot as requisite to a good poem." (Part I).

On the causal linkage of the parts of plot: "These principles being established, let us now discuss the proper structure of the Plot, since this is the first and most important thing in Tragedy. Now, according to our definition Tragedy is an imitation of an action that is complete, and whole, and of a certain magnitude; for there may be a whole that is wanting in magnitude. A whole is that which has a beginning, a middle, and an end. A beginning is that which does not itself follow anything by causal necessity, but after which something naturally is or comes to be. An end, on the contrary, is that which itself naturally follows some other thing, either by necessity, or as a rule, but has nothing following it. A middle is that which follows something as some other thing follows it. A well constructed plot, therefore, must neither begin nor end at haphazard, but conform to these principles" (Part VII).

related internally while not causally related to their context; that the moments of plot may be conveniently labeled exposition, development, turning point, resolution, and conclusion—this is what we would glean from a study of plot. And we would realize that the question has not moved forward greatly since the days of Aristotle. Yet these apparent commonplaces will prove to be most salient in what follows.

In recent years there has been a modest revival of interest in this topic. In particular, Peter Brooks has contributed a most important book to the discussion: *Reading for the Plot: Design and Intention in Narrative*.[8] What follows is largely dependent on this book.

A story may be told without reference to the place of its telling, or the location of its being told. However, it is not possible to tell a story without indications of the time of telling in relation to the time of its being told. The use of verb tenses, and their relation to one another, necessarily give us a certain temporal place in relation to the story.[9]

> We approach a story as a story precisely because it takes place over a period of time. Confronted with a sequence of events in time, a reader, as part of his "competence" animates a certain sense-making process. Barthes calls this "the passion for meaning." It is a desire to organize, to structure, the intention of time and activity. Narrative begins with the arousal of desire, a kind of irritation which demands to be told, is moved forward with desire, and is told as a result of desire. Yet that telling is never, except in the dullest of tales, straightforward. Rather it is full of detours, tricks and surprises. Action takes place because someone wants to do something. I am told what those actions were because someone wants me to know. They tell it in a particular fashion, so that a particular range of meanings will be elicited. Yet that range of meanings may far exceed what the original teller of the tale intended, or could have conceived. New readers are always approaching the text with new competencies, new questions, new desires. "Language can mean more than it says."[10]

Where does the reader first look for meaning? Brooks suggests, somewhat paradoxically, that meaning is to be found in the story's end.

> The very possibility of meaning plotted through sequence and through time depends on the anticipated structuring force of the ending: the interminable would be the meaningless, and the lack of ending would jeopardize the beginning. . . . [It is those endings] which will retrospectively give them the order and significance of plot.[11]

[8] New York: Vintage Books, 1984.
[9] Ibid., 21.
[10] Ibid., 56.
[11] Ibid., 93–4.

As the reader works through a text to its end, attention is necessarily given to repeated elements. Brooks maintains that an event gains meaning by repetition.[12] This is so because there is no true repetition. Each repetition, because it appears in a new context, is essentially a new statement, and thus gives new insight. For our purposes here in the consideration of Genesis 1, I will only partly agree. Just as an author may underline the importance of some aspect of the story by means of repetition, equally powerful use may be made of a single isolated statement or event.

Brooks is particularly provocative in his treatment of the subplot. It is the wrong choice of meaning dangled before the reader, the falsely attractive detour that will lead to a dead end. Yet the author must build these in, moving back and forth between plot and subplot, between meaning and frustration, to draw the reader forward, to tantalize, to suggest possibilities.

Source critics tell us that Genesis 1 is part of the Priestly Document, composed by a member of the exiled people of Israel, or one of the recently returned exiles, in order, at least in part, to serve as a polemic against the cult of Babylon. All of that is inferred, however, and the story is told without any of it being made explicit to the reader. A story it is, but a very unusual sort of story. It has a character, God (and for reasons that we will see there can only be one character); it has a sequence of causally linked events; and there is a beginning and an end of activity. So I think it is appropriate to call it a story.

The storyteller has to confront two difficulties. The first difficulty is that there was no one to witness and narrate the events to be described. Since God has yet to create anyone else, there is no other character available to be the narrator, so the author has to make the narrator as unobtrusive as possible. This means telling the story in the "third person," even though, in the story world, there is not even a second person alongside of God.

The other problem facing the storyteller is that if God is God there cannot be any conflict. Otherwise God would not really be God. Yet there has to be some conflict for the story to engage a reader's interest. How does the storyteller solve this dilemma?

Creating a very minimal opposition solves the problem. God is opposed by—faces—nothing. God confronts nothingness. That is the tension, the opposition. There is neither another person, nor another God, nor even a great monster to oppose him. What confronts God is an utter blank, "without form and void." The storyteller shows the reader what nothing is like by creating a picture of a blank.

[12] Ibid., 99.

Why bother with this when another approach was available simply by telling the story in a different fashion? For example, in Proverbs 8:22-31 personified Wisdom is created first and then acts as eyewitness to the rest of God's creative acts. Indeed, there are a number of creation stories in the Bible;[13] with the exception of Genesis, they tend to be told in the first person, by God's Wisdom, the instrument with which God created the world. Choosing in Genesis 1 to avoid that device, this storyteller must convince the reader that this account can be trusted; to achieve this, the storyteller creates the impression that everything is being told, that nothing is being held back. Therefore the narrator has to be omniscient. The dry, objective tone of reportage in which the reader is told everything that happened in the sequence in which it happened creates trust. We come to believe that this cool, detached voice is objective and reliable.

On the other hand, the storyteller is not unaware of the need to engage the reader's interest. There are three ways this story can arouse interest: its ideas might engage the reader, its patterns can appeal to the senses, or it can touch one's sympathies. The first thing a storyteller can do to arouse interest is to engage the intellect, to focus attention on the ideas that are being told, to make one wonder what this all means. How am I to understand it? What really is going on here? Hence, an intellectual engagement. Secondly, a storyteller can keep the reader interested by creating a very strong pattern. If a pattern is started, a reader wants to see it played out to its conclusion. Or the storyteller can involve the sympathies of the reader, making one character sympathetic and another unsympathetic. One wants to see what happens to both.

All three of these things happen in Genesis 1. The author engages our ideas and our intellect by making us wonder, "How did the world come to be?" He engages our pattern-seeking interest by using days: "How many days will God use?" By presenting the story in a very rhythmic fashion he catches us up in the rhythm and makes us want to know how long that rhythm is going to continue. The author also engages our sympathy. That is, one wants to see God succeed with the task that God sets out to do.

God confronts an empty chaos of meaninglessness. This nothingness or meaninglessness is put into its proper place. The meaningless chaos is turned into an ordered universe. God then gives it a name and continues to separate and name its component parts. Light is

---

[13] See, e.g., Exodus 15; Isaiah 40–42; 45; Hab 3:8; Psalms 18; 19; 24; 29; 33; 68; 93; 95; 104; Job 38–41; Sirach 43; 2 Esdras 6.

placed over here, darkness over there. God names what has been separated. Then God calls our attention to humanity. But we get ahead of ourselves.

How Is the Story Structured?

One can organize this text in a variety of ways, i.e., we can look at it from a variety of perspectives, each of which brings something not previously well seen into sharper focus. Indeed, one suspects that there are as many structures of the chapter as there are commentaries about it. As we saw in the Introduction, these structures are not so much objective descriptions of something that is really inherent in the text as they are heuristic devices that help us to organize the text in some way so that we can understand it and react to it.

Genesis 1 and *Enuma Elish*

The time called the Babylonian Exile (587–539 B.C.) was, paradoxically, one of the most theologically and literarily creative in Israel's history. It was then that concepts the later tradition simply takes for granted were born. In Babylon, for example, Israelite thinkers finally formulated the ideas of monotheism (Isaiah 40–55), individual moral responsibility (Ezek 3:16-21), and vicarious atonement (Isa 52:13–53:12). In Babylon, Tanakh[14]—what Christians call the Old Testament—began to achieve the shape in which we have it today.

The heart of Babylonian religion was the annual New Year Festival, when the statue of Marduk, King of the Gods, was taken from his temple in the center of Babylon and paraded through his city, so that he could see the city and bless it for the coming year. During this weeklong festival, the Babylonian Creation Story, *Enuma Elish* ("When from on high . . .") might well have been recited and acted out.

The following table has, on the left-hand side, an outline of the principal moments of *Enuma Elish*. For each of these assertions about the nature of divinity and the universe, Israel provided a rejoinder. These, the elements of Genesis 1, are listed in the right-hand column.

---

[14] An acronym that serves as the name for the Hebrew Bible, Tanakh combines the first letters of Torah (Law), Neviim (Prophets), and Ketuvim (Writings).

Enuma Elish (I-VI, ca. 2000 B.C.)	Genesis 1:1–2:3 (ca. 500 B.C.)
The gods are created from Apsu (Fresh Water) and Tiamat (Salt Water, Tortoise).	God is eternal and uncreated.
Marduk is selected as King of the gods. He uses words for magic purposes. His task is to slay Tiamat.	God creates out of nothing, effortlessly separating and distinguishing merely by use of effective words.
Marduk's chariot is drawn by Killer, Relentless, Trampler, and Swift, with poisonous teeth. He arms himself with Smiter and Combat and is wrapped in terror and fearsomeness.	No combat.
Tiamat's body is split in two; the upper section serves as sky, and the lower section as dry ground.	The sky is a thin layer of beaten metal; earth is merely dry ground.
The stars are gods, seated on platforms.	Stars are merely lights, signs to tell the passage of time.
Kingu revolts, is slain and his blood and bones are used for the creation of Humanity.	Adam/Humanity is created in the image of God.
Humans are created as slaves for the gods.	Adam/Humanity is given dominion over the earth.

Organized in this way, Genesis 1 is a rejoinder to *Enuma Elish*. Using the template of a story that was both widely known and believed, the author of Genesis 1 describes the same known universe but endows it with a very different theology and anthropology. One eternally existing and uncreated God creates everything without any expenditure of effort. Into a universe that is not founded on the remains of dead and defeated gods and goddesses but is simply an inanimate platform, God places a likeness of the divine person to rule the universe in God's stead. There is one God, not many warring gods. Humanity is good, free, and godlike, not mere slave creatures. Time is holy, not to be feared.

THREE DAYS PLUS THREE DAYS PLUS ONE DAY

To approach this passage as a story is not to deny that there are other ways of organizing it, which draw our attention to other facets of its meaning. Some exegetes remark that the description of the consecutive days grows longer. Thirty-one and thirty-eight words suffice for the first two days, whereas the next three days are nearly double that (sixty-nine, sixty-nine and fifty-seven words) and the last creative day is fully 149 words. "This structuring technique conveys the impression of ever-increasing variety and profusion."[15]

There is also a real parallelism between the first and second three-day blocs, which conveys both orderly progression, and the special, set-apart nature of the seventh day, the Sabbath.[16]

> A. Light
> > B. Sea and sky
> > > C. Dry land
> A'. Luminaries
> > B'. Fish and birds
> > > C'. Land animals and humans
> > > > D. Sabbath

Yet another version draws our attention to the creation of separate realms and their inhabitants.[17]

> A. First day: <u>light</u> (1:3-5)
> > B. Second day: <u>firmament</u>, called <u>sky</u>, divides the <u>waters</u> (1:6-8)
> > > C1. Third day: sea and <u>earth</u> (1:9-10)
> > > C2. Third day: <u>plants</u> (1:11-13)
> A'. Fourth day: <u>lights</u> (1:14-19)
> > B'. Fifth day: fish in the <u>waters</u> and birds in the <u>firmament</u> of the <u>sky</u> (1:20-23)
> > > C1'. Sixth day: animals of the <u>earth</u> (1:24-25)
> > > C+. Sixth day: humankind (1:26-28)
> > > C2'. Sixth day: <u>plants</u> for food (1:29-31)

---

[15] David Dorsey, *The Literary Structure of the Old Testament* (Grand Rapids, Mich.: Baker, 1999) 49.

[16] Umberto Cassuto, *A Commentary on the Book of Genesis, Part I: From Adam to Noah,* trans. Israel Abrahams (Jerusalem: Magnes, 1961) 1–17.

[17] Jerome T. Walsh, *Style and Structure in Biblical Hebrew Narrative* (Collegeville: The Liturgical Press, 2001) 37. The underlined words show repetitions that link the two parts of the chapter.

ELEMENTS OF A PLOT

For our purposes in arguing that the section is best understood as a story, the following division of the text into the elements of a plot will lead to a more detailed commentary on the individual sections. Note, by examining the left-hand column in the following figure, that the same material may be organized in slightly different ways. There is no essential contradiction here; the left-hand column may be understood to provide a sort of summary of the action of the story at various points.

Exposition (1:1-2)	
Development (1:3-30)	Meaningless nothing becomes an ordered universe by means of God's separating and naming (1:3-19). The ordered universe is filled with life, culminating in the creation of Adam/Humanity, by means of God's creating and blessing (1:20-31).
Turning point (1:31)	
Conclusion (2:1-3)	From the Human, there is a return to God, who sanctifies (2:1-3).

Commentary

EXPOSITION: 1:1-2

While the first sentence of the Bible is relatively straightforward in Hebrew, it possesses a subtle ambiguity that makes it difficult to translate. It can be rendered in the classical fashion, with an implicit relative clause, or, with the inclusion of v. 3, as one sentence. Witness the following examples.

The King James Version and Its Descendants

Classical
[1]In the beginning God created the heaven and the earth.
[2]And the earth was without form and void; and darkness was upon the face of the deep.
And the Spirit of God moved upon the waters.
[3]And God said, "Let there be light"; and there was light. (KJV, 1611)

Classical
[1]In the beginning God created the heavens and the earth. [2]The earth was without form and void, and darkness was upon the face of the deep; and the Spirit of God was moving over the face of the waters. (RSV, 1952)

Implicit relative clause
[1]In the beginning when God created the heavens and the earth, [2]the earth was a formless void and darkness covered the face of the deep, while a wind from God swept over the face of the waters. (NRSV, 1991)

The Vulgate and Its Descendants

Classical
[1]In principio creavit Deus caelum et terram.
[2]Terra autem erat inanis et vacua, et tenebrae erant super faciem abyssi, et Spiritus Dei ferebatur super aquas. (VG, 1592)

Classical
[1]Au commencement, Dieu créa le ciel et la terre. [2]Or la terre était vague et vide, les ténèbres couvraient l'abîme, l'esprit de Dieu plânait sur les eaux. (Bible de Jérusalem, 1956)

Classical
[1]In the beginning God created the heavens and the earth. [2]Now the earth was a formless void, there was darkness over the deep, and God's spirit hovered over the water. (Jerusalem Bible, 1966)

Implicit relative clause
[1]In the beginning, when God created the heavens and the earth, [2]the earth was a formless wasteland, and darkness covered the abyss, while a mighty wind swept over the waters. (New American Bible, 1970, 1990)

Genesis 1:1-3 as one sentence
[1]Lorsque Dieu commença la création du ciel et de la terre, [2]la terre était déserte et vide, et la ténèbre à la surface de l'abîme; le souffle de Dieu plânait à la surface des eaux, [3]et Dieu dit: «Que la lumière soit!» Et la lumière fut. (Traduction Oecuménique de la Bible, 1979)

Translations in the Jewish Tradition
Classical [1]In the beginning God created / the heavens and the earth. [2]As for the earth, it was without form or life, / and darkness was upon the face of the Deep; but the Spirit of God / was hovering over the face of the waters.[18]

Classical
[1]In the beginning God created the heavens and the earth.
[2]—Now the earth had been wild and waste
    darkness over the face of Ocean
    breath of God over the face of the waters—[19]

Genesis 1:1-3 as one sentence [1]When God began to create heaven and earth—[2]the earth being unformed and void, with darkness over the surface of the deep and a wind from God sweeping over the water—(New Jewish Publication Society Version, 1985)
Scholarly translations
Classical [1]In the beginning God created the heavens and the earth. [2]The earth was still a desert waste, and darkness lay upon the primeval deep and God's wind was moving to and fro over the surface of the waters.[20]
Implicit relative clause [1]When God set about to create the heaven and earth—[2]the world being then a formless waste, with darkness over the seas and only an awesome wind sweeping over the water—[21]

Why such variety? The first two words of the Bible, *běrē'šît bārā'*, present the translator with a conundrum. *běrē'šît* (see, for example, Jer 26:1) means the beginning of something, e.g., the harvest, and not "first" in some absolute sense. Such an expression does exist in the Hebrew Bible, (*bāri'šonâ;* for example, Gen 13:4) but it is not used here.

---

[18] Cassuto, *Genesis. Part I: From Adam to Noah*.

[19] Everett Fox, *In the Beginning: A New English Rendering of the Book of Genesis* (New York: Schocken, 1983).

[20] Claus Westermann, *Genesis 1–11: A Commentary*, trans. John J. Scullion (Minneapolis: Augsburg, 1984).

[21] E. A. Speiser, *Genesis*, AB 1 (Garden City, N.Y.: Doubleday, 1962).

The implication seems to be that what is being described is the first of a series of creative acts rather than some absolute beginning of things and that God may have created other things before those described here. Some suggest that the creation of the Law or of the angels might be hinted at here. Many feel that the text says that God created the universe out of pre-existing chaotic matter, not out of nothing and that the doctrine of *creatio ex nihilo* is a theological assertion not necessarily founded in this biblical text.

What does God do? God creates. The word "create" here is *bārā'*.[22] *bārā'* means to expend no energy, to make something without any effort, without any work involved. In the entire Bible only God is the subject of the verb, so it seems to capture some part of God's own character. Therefore, when God makes he does it completely freely and effortlessly. God is an uncreated, genderless, powerful God creating without any energy at all.

The author does not use the personal name for Israel's God, YHWH; he simply uses a generic term, "God" (*'ĕlōhîm*). Seemingly, he wants to avoid any sort of narrow identification between this story and Israelites' national concerns.

What exactly does he do? He creates the heavens and the earth. This is a merismus, a figure of speech that describes a totality by naming polar opposites. "Heavens and earth" means all of creation. God creates everything in the face of what sort of opposition—what does God confront? "Empty void" *(tōhû wābōhû)* conveys the sense of a sterile nothingness.[23] "Darkness on the face of the abyss" *(ḥōšek 'al-pĕnê tĕhôm)* conveys a similar idea of a world where God is not present.[24]

The author draws a picture of a world that features none of the distinctions that are important to us and necessary for being, just an empty pit of water and darkness and wind. There was no life, no up, no down, neither space nor time, a desert in which there are no paths. Lacking a vocabulary to express nothingness, he sets a scene where he gives us a picture that negates everything positive instead. Into the nothingness come a first positive hint of life, *rûaḥ 'ĕlōhîm*. Depending on context *rûaḥ* can mean wind, breath, soul, spirit; and *'ĕlōhîm* can mean divine, of God, or simply indicate a superlative construction. Translations, then, can range from "the spirit of God" to "a mighty

---

[22] The verb is most common in Isaiah 40–55, so-called Second Isaiah (for example, 40:26, 28).

[23] *tōhû wābōhû*, see also Isa 34:11 and Jer 4:23. More often, *tōhû* appears alone as in Isa 45:18 or Ps 107:40 (a desert where there are no paths).

[24] *ḥōšek*, see Ps 88:7, 13, 19 [English 88:6, 12, 18].

wind." The translator's choice has as much to do with theological pre-conceptions about what is going on as with the words involved. Having introduced the character of a single God who acts effortlessly to confront a cosmos of chaotic, meaningless nothing, I suggest that we have in these first two verses a picture of creation of everything out of nothing. And so the stage is set for the story's development.

DEVELOPMENT: 1:3-30

Over the next six days, there are eight creative acts by God, first to create the physical environment and then to fill it with life. God orders, names, and distinguishes, putting things where they belong, blessing, and filling the now ordered and blessed world with life.

The first to the fourth days (1:3-19): Chaos becomes an ordered world—God separates and names. God said, God saw, God separated, God called. In vv. 3-5 an orderly rhythm of language and repetition is introduced. The effect is to create a certain wonder in the reader about how the pattern will be completed. The unexpected word order of God's evaluation of the first creative act is emphatic, showing how pleased God is with what has been done: "God saw the light, that it was good" *(wayyar³ ³ĕlōhîm ³et-hā³ôr kî-ṭôb)*. With creation of the light time becomes possible, and so begins the succession of days.

On the second to the fourth days (vv. 6-19) the verb "separates" appears four times as God separates the waters above the dome (a word related to "beaten metal") from those beneath it (vv. 6-7), day from night (v. 14), and light from darkness (v. 18). God creates space on the second day and on the third day gives the first hint of eventual life in the world with the sprouting forth of vegetation. Everett Fox captures the near poetry of the original: "Let the earth sprout forth with sprouting growth, plants that seed forth seeds, fruit trees that yield fruit, after their kind (and) in which is their seed, upon the earth."[25]

The fourth day is of especial importance. It is the middle of the week, the longest work, and on this day God completes what was begun on the second day by putting lights in the firmament, so the formula of approval, missing from the second day, appears again here, "And God saw that it was good." The lights are not named because they are not astral deities but simply lamps with three functions: to give light, to rule, and to separate. The liturgical calendar with its times and seasons is now possible. Humanity's contingency is also underlined here. How-

---

[25] Everett Fox, *The Five Books of Moses* (New York: Schocken, 1995) 14.

ever powerful Humanity's rule may appear, even the human is subject to things beyond his or her control.

In the first four days God accomplishes several things. The basic conditions of life, time, space, and food are now in place. God has "separated" things that are different and put them where they belong. Life is conditional on obedience to time.

The fifth and sixth days (1:20-31): The ordered world is filled and peopled—God creates and blesses. On the fifth day the world, which has been devoid of living things until now, begins to fill with life, starting with birds and sea monsters *(tannînim)*—which are mere creatures and not contestants with God in a cosmic battle, as they are elsewhere (e.g., Isa 27:1; 51:9). Both fowl and denizens of the sea are blessed with the ability to carry on their own lives: "Be fruitful. Be many. And fill the earth." This is the first occurrence of the motif of blessing.

The sixth day sees the creation both of the animals and of humanity. The former are not blessed, since there seems to be only one blessing for each realm, air, water and land.

The last of God's creative acts is the creation of Humanity *(ʾādām,* Gen 1:26-30). This story does not envisage the creation of a single primal pair (although that is not incompatible with it) but rather the creation of all of Humanity, male and female, at the same time. There are several points of interest in this passage.

Why does God say "Let *us* make . . ."? The Hebrew word translated "God" *(ʾĕlōhîm)* is a masculine plural noun, but is ordinarily treated as a singular. Some suggest that this is an instance of the so-called plural of majesty, but that is unknown in Hebrew.[26] It can hardly be a remnant of polytheism in a text opposed to polytheism. There seems no hint elsewhere in this chapter of a committee of divine counselors that might be at work here. In short, there is no good and entirely convincing explanation. One possibility is that God is speaking internally in a sort of deliberative language, "*Let's* make . . ." (cf. Gen 11:7).

What does it mean to be created in the image of God?[27] Do we bear a physical resemblance to God? Hardly likely if both male and female

---

[26] P. Joüon, *Grammaire de l'hébreu biblique* (Rome: Pontifical Biblical Institute, 1923) §114e, note.

[27] See the masterful excursus on this subject in Westermann's *Genesis 1–11,* 147–55. One should note that the NRSV is not entirely consistent with the MT at this point. The translation reads "in the image of God he created them" whereas the Hebrew has a singular direct object ". . . he created him." That this is understood to refer both to male and female is indicated in the next line ". . . male and female he created them." Both "image" *(ṣelem)* and "likeness" *(dĕmût)* are used in cultic contexts.

are created in the divine image and the story is told in the context of Israel's famously aniconic religious system. Or perhaps we bear a spiritual resemblance to God? One thing is clear, our author avoids the term *mîn* ("kind, species") in speaking about humanity. While there are many sorts of animals and plants, there is only one sort of humanity. As a result, while the Israelites had many political and ethnic dislikes, what we know as racism was impossible for them. The idea that there is only one sort of humanity flows from their monotheistic conception of God. If there is only one God, and only one image of God present in all people, there can be only one sort of humanity, not many kinds. This also explains why human life is sacred and cannot be taken unjustly (Gen 6:8).[28]

Humanity is given the one blessing[29] that pertains to the earth: "Be fruitful and multiply, and fill the earth and subdue it; and have dominion over the fish of the sea and over the birds of the air and over every living thing that moves upon the earth" (Gen 1:28). Like the other living creatures humanity is given the power to procreate and so possesses at least a reflection of the divine power to give life. To that is added the blessing of subduing and having dominion over the world. This might well mean, especially given the context of blessing, to lead, to guide, or to tend (as a flock).[30] To be in God's image means to be blessed with the responsibility of ruling the world in such a way that it is the ordered, good, life-giving place that God intends it to be. Perhaps an analogy will make the point better. God : Universe :: Humanity : World. As God is to the entire universe—the One who creates a good, blessed, nonviolent place where life is possible and order reigns—so Humanity is to be to the world. We live up to this responsibility when we make the world good, live in just nonviolence, and render the blessed life possible here.

The book of Wisdom, which is part of the canon of Scripture for some Christians, including Catholics, adopts this reading of the text when it says:

For the former see Ezek 7:20; 16:17; 23:14; Num 33:27; 2 Kgs 11:18 (= 2 Chr 23:17); Amos 5:26; 2 Sam 6:5, 11; Pss 39:7; 73:20; Gen 5:3; 9:6. For the latter see Ezek 1:5, 13, 16, 22, 26, 28; 8:2; 10:1, 10, 21, 22; 23:15; 2 Kgs 16:10; 2 Chr 4:3; Isa 40:18; Dan 10:16; Ps 58:5; Isa 13:4; Gen 5:1, 3.

[28] For a very different reading, see Phyllis A. Bird, "'Male and Female He Created Them': Gen. 1:27b in the Context of the Priestly Account of Creation," *Harvard Theological Review* 74 (1981) 129–59.

[29] For "blessing" see Isa 65:8-9; Hag 2:18-19; Gen 9:1; 12:2-3; 17:16, 20; 27:27-29.

[30] See, for example, 1 Kgs 3:7-9; 5:4 [English 4:24].

> God of our ancestors, Lord of Mercy,
> who by your wisdom have made the universe,
> and in your wisdom have fitted human beings
> to rule the creatures that you have made,
> to govern the world in holiness and saving justice,
> and in honesty of soul to dispense fair judgment. . . . (Wis 9:2-3)

TURNING POINT: 1:31

We have become used, during the account of the six days of crea-tion, to the rolling parallel cadences our author has used to link one day to the next. We have seen, too, that the first three days are linked with the last three days as the stage of world is first set and then filled. Genesis 1:31 indicates that the sequence is ending and that something else is about to happen. God inspects all that has been made and it is very good. What, we wonder, can happen next?

CONCLUSION: 2:1-3

The seventh day: God is present in the world in time—God blesses a day. God can be found in time. The community of exiles who heard this text and who were without a place to worship God learned that no particular place was needed in order to find God. They could find God wherever they were, in the holiness of Sabbath.

A number of linguistic and thematic links to the whole of Genesis 1 converge in these three verses: the verbs "to create" *(bārāʾ)* and "to make" *(ʿāśâ)* are found throughout the section and serve to tie the end with the beginning *(ʿāśâ:* 1:7, 16 [2x]; 1:25, 26, 31 [3x]; 2:2-3 [3x]; *bārāʾ):* 1:1, 21, 27; 2:3). The verb "to bless" *(brk)* also appears here for the final time (1:22, 28; 2:3).

Just as the first three days were marked by separation and naming and the second three days by creating and blessing, the concluding section of the creation story is marked by the verb "to sanctify" *(qdš).*

Characterization

We have moved from a sterile chaos, by means of God's effortless creative activity, to a universe that is good, ordered, nonviolent, and full of blessing. This is a universe where God can be found in time and in rest. We have been shown that the world was exactly as God wanted it to be because the narrator tells us repeatedly "and it was so" *(wayhî kēn)*. We will see these themes play out in the chapters that follow, as the world God created is, sadly, transformed by human action into the world we know.

So far the story only has one character, who is revealed to us by his action. We have learned that God is one, acting alone, and uncreated. In a word, God is transcendent in this story, able to create a universe by word alone. Although referred to with grammatically masculine language, he does not act in concert with a female deity, but creates simply by fiat. There is no gendered action here, but the action of a Being who transcends the limitations of gender. His motivation can only be inferred from his activity. There must be some aspect of the divine being that desires community, that needs to share itself. This God is not content to rest in eternal isolation but must make things to bless, to which some part of the divine being can be given and shared. Nothing has been hidden from those of us privileged to be onlookers, no secrets remain to be ferreted out. All is open, and all is good. A desire to share the blessings of order, creativity, and life seems to motivate this God, as well as a desire to encounter his creation not in some predetermined place but in time. Even though we are subject to the conditions of time, it is nevertheless in time that we encounter God.

Nor does God jealously hold on to a solitary exercise of power. Rather, dominion is given to all humanity as a blessing. The one God can be seen in all people, male or female, of any race. We live that image when we are to the world as God is.

I said at the beginning of this chapter that God is always savior. Here he has saved the raw materials of the universe from sterile futility. In the next chapter, God will save humanity from itself and in so doing reveal yet more of the divine person.

Genesis 1:1–2:3 in the Tradition

The early chapters of Genesis were, according to a recent scholarly evaluation, the most influential parts of the Old Testament in the development of Christian theology.[31] Many early Christian commentators

---

[31] This commentary would be unwieldy if even a modest attempt were made to incorporate all the riches of the precritical interpretative traditions of Judaism and Christianity. This sample of a few especially important or provocative texts will, I hope, whet the reader's appetite to delve into this unfamiliar material. See further

wrote on the days of creation, some returning time after time to the same texts with fresh insights. Augustine, for instance, wrote no less than five times on the text. Given its fundamental importance in both Judaism and Christianity, it will not be possible to do more than very broadly hint at some key issues that attracted these early commentators.

Christian commentators were very much taken by Genesis 1:26-27, the creation of humanity in the image and likeness of God. Customarily they distinguished between the two. The second-century theologian Origen wrote:

> In recording the first creation of man, Moses before all others says, "And God said, Let us make man in our own image and likeness." Then he adds afterwards, "And God made man; in the image of God made he him; male and female made he them, and he blessed them." Now the fact that he said "he made him in the image of God" and was silent about the likeness points to nothing else but this, that man received the honor of God's image in his first creation, whereas the perfection of God's likeness was reserved for him at the consummation. The purpose of this was that man should acquire it for himself by his own earnest efforts to imitate God, so that while the possibility of attaining perfection was given to him in the beginning through the honor of the "image," he should in the end through the accomplishment of these works obtain for himself the perfect "likeness."[32]

It is our task, then, as humans to choose to live well enough, to live in accord with the divine image, that we become the likeness of God. Gregory of Nyssa expresses the same idea in these words:

> "Let us make man in our image, after our likeness." We possess the one by creation; we acquire the other by free will. In the first structure it is given to us to be born in the image of God; by free will there is formed in us the being in the likeness of God. . . . "Let us make man in our image": Let him possess by creation what is in the image, but let him also become

---

James L. Kugel, *The Bible as It Was* (Cambridge, Mass.: Belknap, 1997); idem, *Traditions of the Bible* (Cambridge, Mass.: Harvard University Press, 1998); Andrew Louth, *Genesis 1–11*, Ancient Christian Commentary on Scripture: Old Testament I (Downers Grove, Ill.: InterVarsity, 2001); and especially Avivah Gottlieb Zornberg, *Genesis: The Beginning of Desire* (Philadelphia: Jewish Publication Society, 1995).

[32] *On First Principles*, 3.6.1, quoted in Louth, *Genesis*, 30. Readers may find that readily available translations of these authors sound almost hopelessly outdated, especially in their use of "Man" and "he" to refer to both men and women. I can only hope that, given the importance of the texts in question, the reader will be willing to look beyond the antique language of the translations.

according to the likeness. God has given the power for this. If he had created you also in the likeness, where would your privilege be? Why have you been crowned? And if the Creator had given you everything, how would the kingdom of heaven have opened for you? But it is proper that one part is given to you, while the other has been left incomplete: this is so that you might complete it yourself, and might be worthy of the reward which comes from God.[33]

Gregory goes on to explain that the word "image" is a comprehensive way of describing all of the gifts that God gave to humanity.

God creates man for no other reason but that God is good; and being such, and having this as his reasons for entering upon the creation of our nature, he would not exhibit the power of his goodness in an imperfect form, giving our nature some of the things at his disposal and grudging it a share in another: but the perfect form of goodness is here to be seen by his both bringing man into being from nothing and supplying him with all good gifts. But since the list of individual good gifts is a long one, it is out of the question to apprehend it numerically. The language of Scripture therefore expresses it concisely by a comprehensive phrase, in saying that man was made "in the image of God," for this is the same as to say that he made human nature participant in all good; for if the Deity is the fullness of good, and this is his image, the image finds its resemblance to the archetype in being filled with all good.[34]

These writers are well aware of the dignity with which this conception endows the human person. To quote Gregory of Nyssa one final time:

Thus human nature, created to rule the world because of his resemblance to the universal King, has been made like a living image that participates in the archetype by dignity and by name. He is not clothed in purple, scepter and diadem, for these do not signify his dignity (the archetype himself does not possess them). But in place of purple he is clothed with virtue, the most royal of garments. Instead of a scepter, he is endowed with blessed immortality. Instead of a royal diadem, he bears the crown of justice, in such a way that everything about him manifests royal dignity, by his exact likeness to the beauty of the archetype.[35]

It is in beauty, dignity and goodness that we were created, and we can, if these Fathers of the Christian Church are at all sensitive and

---

[33] *On the Origin of Man,* in Louth, *Genesis,* 33.
[34] *On the Creation of Man,* 16.10, in Louth, *Genesis,* 34.
[35] *On the Creation of Man,* 4, in Louth, *Genesis,* 34.

right in their reading, return to that dignity by the exercise of our free will. But why do we need to return? What became of the very good world that God saw when his work was finished? If the story has begun so well, we know that it continues sadly. And so we turn to the next part of the story and discover that we freely chose to disorder the world, to live not in regal dignity but in disobedience to the one in whose image we were so hopefully made.

Chapter 2

THE STORY OF THE CREATION OF
MAN AND WOMAN, THE PARADISE IN WHICH
THEY LIVED AND THAT THEY CHOSE TO LOSE,
AND THE SIN THAT ENSUED

Genesis 2–3; 4

Which World Are We in Now?

Before we begin our analysis of the next complex of stories, something needs to be said about the transition from the narrative world of Genesis 1 to the very different world depicted in Genesis 2:4–4:26.

That a new unit begins in Gen 2:4 is clear on several counts. David Dorsey lists six.

1. The *tôlĕdôt*[1] formula in 2:4 suggests a new beginning.
2. The account of the seventh day of creation in 2:1-3 heralds the end of a unit in that the number *seven* generally represents completeness.
3. The content of 2:1-3 declares the completion of the creative task recounted in 1:1-31.

[1] This word, derived from a root that means "to give birth," is notoriously difficult to translate adequately. The NRSV uses "generations." In his new commentary, Richard Elliott Friedman suggests "record" (*Commentary on the Torah* [San Francisco: HarperSanFrancisco, 2001] 16). It appears ten more times in Genesis after 2:4 (5:1; 6:9; 10:1; 11:10; 11:27; 25:12; 25:19; 36:1, 9; 37:2). Opinion about its purpose, if any, is varied. Friedman (*Torah*, 16) suggests that it always introduces a list or story about family history and that it functions to tie the whole book together as a continuous narrative rather than simply a collection. This is probably correct, but since most readers encounter Genesis in translation, where this word functions much less powerfully, I will take less note of it here.

4. Genesis 2:4-25 neither represents an eighth day nor further describes the seventh, signaling that the series that began in 1:3 is finished.
5. The shift in divine name, from "Elohim" to "Yahweh Elohim," in 2:4-25 suggests a new unit.
6. Shifts in *topos* (now Eden), characters (now Adam and his family), mood (from tranquility to discord), storytelling technique (from narrative with no dialogue to narrative carried primarily by dialogue), etc., likewise signal the initiation of a new narrative unit.[2]

Older commentaries would attribute this new beginning to the appearance of a new source, Genesis 1 being part of the Priestly narrative (P) and Genesis 2–3 part of the Yahwist (J). That may well be the case, but this commentary is interested in the final form of the text, not its composition history. One also frequently hears that there are two creation stories in Genesis. This is an imprecise way of describing these two stories. Genesis 1, properly speaking is a creation story (like Prov 8:22-31) since it describes how everything in the universe came to be. It is better to think of Genesis 2–3 as a story that describes the origin of human life and culture. It appears uninterested in the act of creation itself, since there is no hint of how the dry plain on which the Garden was planted came to be there. Its interest, rather, is in people, how they live, and why they behave in certain ways. The story contains numerous etiologies, explanations of the origin of various cultural practices. Why are there genders, both men and women? Why do they marry? Why do they wear clothes? Why do people fear snakes? Why does it hurt for humans to bear children? Why is there sexual desire? Why is it difficult to earn a living? The story also ponders larger issues. Why is there good and evil? Why is there death? Why is there distrust between people? Why do we hide from each other? Why do we communicate so poorly? Why isn't this Paradise?

Still, it is clear to almost any reader that the narrative of Genesis 1 has been left behind. What might be less clear is why the story of Adam and Eve in Genesis 2–3 is connected to the story of Cain and Abel and the mini-narrative of Lamech in Genesis 4. Walsh sees two "threads" connecting them and making them one narrative bloc that can be analyzed as a single piece. The Man is formed from the soil (2:7) but is condemned to eke out a living from it only with difficulty (3:17-18). His son Cain continues to till the soil (4:2) but finally is alienated from it (4:11-12). The word *ʾădāmâ* appears eight times in Genesis 2–3,

---

[2] *The Literary Structure of the Old Testament* (Grand Rapids, Mich.: Baker, 1999) 49.

six times in Genesis 4, and is almost absent elsewhere in Genesis 1–5. The second connection stems from the Man's name.

> Throughout the story of the Garden of Eden the male character is called *hā'ādām*, literally, "the human being," not simply *'ādām*, the proper name "Adam." The same is true at 4:1. From that point on, however, the form *'ādām* appears without the article (Gen 4:25, 5:1-5).[3]

The same characters, the same scenes, the same issues: For all of these reasons it is fitting to treat Genesis 2:4–4:26 as a unit in several panels.

Commentary: Genesis 2–3

THE STORY OF THE CREATION OF MAN AND WOMAN, THE PARADISE IN WHICH THEY LIVED AND THAT THEY CHOSE TO LOSE

The Story of the Garden of Eden falls into two panels, the second of which is marked by the introduction of a new character, the serpent, in Genesis 3:1 and by a change in mood from the joy of intimacy to foreboding. Genesis 2:4b-25 tells the story of the Garden (2:4a serves as a sort of title for the whole complex), and Genesis 3:1-24 tells the story of the Fall and the Expulsion. The narrative structure of the two panels can be described with the language of traditional narrative analysis in this way.

Panel 1	Panel 2
Exposition: 2:4b-6	Exposition: 3:1a
Development: 2:7-22a	Inciting moment: 3:1b
a) The man and the garden (2:7-17)	Complication: 3:2-8
b) Looking for a partner (2:18-22a)	Turning point: 3:9-11
Turning point: 2:22b	Resolution: 3:12-19
Resolution: 2:23-25	Conclusion: 3:20-24

Viewed in this way, the two stories lead the reader from a consideration of what is not good for a human (isolated loneliness) to what is good for a human (communion in dialogue), through the loss of communion and, finally, to a state not unlike the isolated loneliness with which we began.

[3] Jerome T. Walsh, *Style and Structure in Biblical Hebrew Narrative* (Collegeville: The Liturgical Press, 2001) 177–8.

Another way of structuring the text shows us a rather different perspective. Walsh divides the section into seven concentrically arranged scenes:[4]

A. 2:4b-17: *hāʾādām* is placed in the garden
Theme: Creation of *hāʾādām* Characters: YHWH God (active); *hāʾādām* (passive) Locale: the earth outside the garden, moving into the garden

B. 2:18-25: Character relationships are established in harmony
Theme: creation of woman and animals; relationships among creatures Characters: YHWH God (active); *hāʾādām* (gives names); animals, woman (passive) Locale: unspecified location in the garden

C. 3:1-5: The snake makes statements to the woman
Theme: dialogue about eating the fruit Characters: snake ("the cleverest of the animals"), woman Locale: in the garden, not at the center

D. 3:6-7: The woman and her husband eat of the tree
Theme: narrative about eating the fruit Characters: the woman and her husband Locale: center of the garden

C': 3:8-13: YHWH God asks questions of *hāʾādām*
Theme: dialogue about eating the fruit Characters: YHWH God, *hāʾādām*, the woman Locale: in the garden, not at the center

B': 3:14-21: Character relationships are reestablished, but with disharmony
Theme: punishment of all creatures; hostile relationships among them Characters: YHWH God (active); *hāʾādām* (gives names); woman, snake (passive) Locale: unspecified location in the garden

A': 3:22-24: *hāʾādām* is driven from the garden
Theme: expulsion of *hāʾādām* Characters: YHWH God (active); *hāʾādām* (passive) Locale: inside the garden, moving to the earth outside the garden

---

[4] Walsh, *Style and Structure*, 21–22; see also idem, "Genesis 2:4b–3:24: A Synchronic Approach," *Journal of Biblical Literature* 96 (1977) 161–77.

This arrangement has an advantage over others because it captures the wholeness of the section and because it helps us focus on movement and obedience/disobedience—from outside the garden to its center and then back outside again, and from the giving of the command in Scene A to disobedience in Scene D to repercussions in Scene A'. We will see later that such movement is an important motif in the book and may well help us understand the ultimate meaning of the passage in question. But it seems from the start that part of what this passage teaches is that central (Scene D) to the way Humanity chooses to live in the world is disobedience. Can it be that we prefer disobedience to Paradise?

In what follows I will comment on each scene, pointing out some of the more important literary features.

A. 2:4b-17: *hāʾādām* IS PLACED IN THE GARDEN

Creation is sterile because there is no one to bring it to life: *wĕʾādām ʾāyin laʾăbōd ʾet-hāʾădāmâ* (Gen 2:5); literally, "there was no *ʾādām* to work the *ʾădāmâ*." So God fashioned an *ʾādām* (using a verb *yṣr* which means "to sculpt" in modern Hebrew) from the dust of the *ʾădāmâ*. In the previous story we were told that Humanity was created in the image of God. Here we are shown the same thing, as God breathes a life-giving breath into the man. The difference between telling in Genesis 1 and showing in Genesis 2 is not merely a change in narrative technique. The change is utilized to make an important theological point. This seems to be a very different God from the one acting in Genesis 1:1–2:3. There, God was transcendent and removed from physical contact with the creation, which was effected by word alone. Here God, called Yʜᴡʜ God to indicate that a different aspect of characterization comes into play, acts as potter, shaping the clay into the desired result. Thus the human bears the imprint of God and lives with the breath of God within.

What is this Human? Biologically male? Such would seem to be the case, since he is certainly grammatically male. Recent exegetes have suggested that the Human is neither male nor female, but inclusive of both until the Woman is built out of his side.[5] The argument is based, at least in part, on the fact that the Hebrew word for "biological male" (*ʾîš*) is not used until after the building up of the Woman. A like idea occurred to biblical commentators long before our day. Consider, for instance, Ephrem the Syrian in his *Commentary on Genesis:*

---

[5] See Phyllis Trible, "A Love Story Gone Awry," in *God and the Rhetoric of Sexuality*, Overtures to Biblical Theology (Philadephia: Fortress, 1978) 72–165.

Then Moses said, "Male and female he created them," to make known that Eve was already inside Adam, in the rib that was drawn out from him. Although she was not in his mind she was in his body, and she was not only in his body with him but also in soul and spirit with him, for God added nothing to that rib that he took out except the structure and adornment. If everything that was suitable for Eve, who came to be from that rib, was complete in and from that rib, it is rightly said that "male and female he created them." (1.29.2)

The Human, still quite alone, was placed in a garden that God had planted in Eden,[6] full of trees beautiful and nourishing as well as two other trees, one known as the Tree of Life[7] and the other as the Tree of the Knowledge of Good and Bad. The former tree disappears from the story until the very end. It is the latter tree that looms large both in the story and in the biblical religions, especially Christianity.

Why did God forbid the consumption of its fruit on pain of death? There are several possibilities: God desired to withhold ethical knowledge from Humanity, making humans dependent on commandments; God desired Humanity to remain without the knowledge of sexuality, pleasure and pain, life and death; since Good and Evil are an example of merismus meaning something like "everything," God was commanding Humanity not to attempt universal knowledge. Yet others feel that the command is purely arbitrary, that God might equally well have forbidden something else just as long as Humanity realized that they were subject to divine command and not free to act at will.

The text does not say which of these possibilities, or perhaps some other, is meant here, but we can reason our way to some conclusions. When the serpent approached the woman and offered the fruit to her she already possessed ethical knowledge. She knew that her action would be wrong. If she already knew the nature of evil and possessed the ability to make moral choices, the tree's meaning must be something other. At any rate, knowledge of such sort is hardly a sin, but a good thing to be desired. Too, the sort of utter intimacy described in Genesis 2:23-25 makes it hard to imagine that Man and Woman were not physically intimate, and Genesis 4:1 ("and the Man knew his wife Eve"; *wĕhāʾādām*

---

[6] Fox translates this as *Land-of-Pleasure* (*The Five Books of Moses* [New York: Schocken, 1995] 19). For other appearances of *ʿēden*, see Gen 2:10, 15; 3:23, 24; 4:16; Isa 51:3; Ezek 28:13; 31:9, 16, 18; 36:35; Joel 2:3; Sir 40:27. Similar language is used elsewhere: *gan-yhwh* ("the garden of YHWH") appears in Gen 13:10; *gan-ʾĕlōhîm* ("the garden of God") in Ezek 28:13; 31:8. Paradise (*pardēs*, a Persian loan-word) appears in Cant 4:13; Qoh 2:5 and Neh 2:8.

[7] See also Prov 3:18; 11:30; 13:12; 15:4.

yādaᶜ ʾet-ḥawwâ ʾištô) seems to indicate a continuation rather than an initiation of sexual knowledge between the husband and wife.

My suggestion is that the phrase refers to universal knowledge. Humanity is commanded not to try to become like God and know all things. For in doing so they will lose what is distinctive about their humanity, their very conditionality and limitation, and so die.[8]

B. 2:18-25: CHARACTER RELATIONSHIPS ARE ESTABLISHED IN HARMONY

For the first time, a note of hesitancy appears in the text. So many times already the goodness of creation has been proclaimed that one is jarred to read: Then the LORD God said, "It is not good that the man should be alone; I will make him a helper as his partner" (Gen 2:18).

The Hebrew words translated in the NRSV as "helper as his partner" (*ᶜēzer kĕnegdô*) are deceptively simple.[9] *ᶜēzer* means "help," "support," "aid," or "succor." But it is a special kind of help in that it comes from God, is personal rather than spiritual, and one receives it when facing the danger of death, which one will overcome if one receives this sort of help.[10] What danger faces the Human? Solitude. Only solitude for the Human has been declared by God to be not good (*lōʾ-ṭôb hĕyôt hāʾādām lĕbaddô*, Gen 2:18a). The story teaches that solitude, loneliness, is a condition that will cause the human to die. The solution is for God to help, but it must be a help which is *kĕnegdô*, "appropriate" or "fit" (RSV). Literally, the word means something like "in front of him," indicating that the sort of help that will save the Human from the death of solitude must be something that is at one and the same time suitable but different; a nuance of opposition is built into the description of the help needed.[11] The NRSV attempts to find a translation that captures both the personal aspect of this kind of help and the difference involved and settles on "his partner."

---

[8] Note that the verb form of the prediction of death (*môt tāmût*) means that death will follow as a punishment but not necessarily immediately. It does not imply immediate execution. See Gen 20:7; Num 26:65; Judg 13:22; 1 Sam 14:39, 44; 2 Sam 12:14; 14:14; 1 Kgs 1:4, 6, 16; 8:10; Jer 26:8; Ezek 3:18; 33:8, 14.

[9] Any treatment of this passage must make mention of the classic studies by Phyllis Trible, "Depatriarchalizing in Biblical Narrative," *Journal of the American Academy of Religion* 41 (1973) 30–48, and "A Love Story Gone Awry" (see note 5 above).

[10] See Exod 18:4; Deut 33:7, 26, 29; Hos 13:9; Pss 20:3; 33:20; 70:6; 89:20; 115:9, 10, 15; 121:1, 2; 124:8; 146:5; Dan 11:34.

[11] The Maharal of Prague in his commentary to Rashi, *Gur Aryeh*, elaborates on this explanation.

> This explanation contains a profound truth. The male and female respectively represent two opposites. If man is worthy they merge into a single whole.

Friedman adds an importantly different perspective.[12] He notes
that the same root can mean strength, since *ʿēzer* appears in parallel
with *ʿōz*, "strength" in Psalm 46:2, and the names Azariah ("The LORD is
my help") and Uzziah ("The LORD is my strength") refer to the same
king in 2 Kings 14:21 and 2 Chronicles 26:1. The result is that a richer
biblical image of Woman develops. She is not merely a helpmeet for
Man; it becomes evident that she and he both are created in God's
image and that they possess corresponding strengths.

A series of trial and error attempts follows. The Human shows mas-
tery over the other living things by naming them. But, since they are
made from scratch just as the Human was, there is no recognizable
kinship between them. They are not suitable helps.

God puts the Human to sleep,[13] draws out a rib, and, from the only
human stuff available, builds up into the world what humanity will
need in order to survive. God introduces difference, real gender distinctions, maleness and femaleness. These corresponding strengths
will give humanity what it needs in order to live. The Human recognizes the rightness of fit and speaks for the first time. The first human
words are a poem in praise of Woman:

> The human said:
> This-time, she-is-it!
> Bone from my bones,
> Flesh from my flesh
> She shall be called Woman/ *Isha*
> For from Man/ *Ish* she was taken.[14]

Aside from praising Woman, the poem explains a fact of the Hebrew language, the similarity between the words for Woman (*ʾiššâ*)
and Man (*ʾîš*.)[15] One might well read what follows just as an etiology

---

In all cases two oppositions merge to form a single whole when they are worthy
i.e., when the Almighty who makes peace between opposites links and joins
them. But when they are not worthy the fact that they are opposites causes her
to be "against him." See Nehama Leibowitz, *Studies in Bereshit*, 4th ed. (Jerusalem: World Zionist Organization, 1981) 13.

[12] Friedman, *Torah*, 19.

[13] The word used (*tardēmâ*) indicates a state of deep receptivity for an encounter
with the divine. See Gen 15:12; 1 Sam 26:12; Isa 29:10; Job 4:3; 33:15.

[14] Fox, *Moses*, 20.

[15] The word for "woman" sounds like a feminine form of the word for "man." In
reality *ʾiššâ* is derived from an entirely different root (*ʾnš*). The intended pun makes
more sense in the Septuagint, which reads "out of *her* man" (*ek tou andros autēs*, Hebrew: *ʾîšâh*).

for marriage, but it is not merely that. It speaks to the moment, nearly universal in human experience, of finding another person with whom one shares such an intense kinship and intimacy that, in meeting the other, one feels as though a hitherto lost and unknown part of oneself is being discovered, that two people seem to share, in some mysterious fashion, a single personhood. And so, having found what has been missing, one desires both to know the difference of the undiscovered other and to enjoy the unity that makes life possible.

Their communion is total and their intimacy unbarred. This is indicated by their nakedness and lack of shame. Nothing hid them from each other,[16] so they are vulnerable without inferiority, needing no protection from the other. Shame, which they do not yet feel, is the guilt of the condemned (Ps 6:11) or of the defeated enemy (Ps 83:17-19; Mic 3:7; 7:16). Thus, in this first moment of coexistence in Eden, there is partnership without any sense of victor and vanquished, openness without fear. In writing of his deceased wife, Eugenio Montale suggests that if, even in this no longer Paradise world, such intimacy is possible, one can only imagine, and mourn, what was lost.[17]

> Your arm in mine, I've descended a million stairs at least.
> And now that you're not here, a void yawns at every step.
> Even so our long journey was brief.
> I'm still en route, with no further need
> of reservations, connections, ruses,
> the constant contempt of those who think reality
> is what one sees.
> I've descended millions of stairs giving you my arm,
> not of course because four eyes see better.
> I went downstairs with you because I knew
> the only real eyes, however darkened,
> belonged to you.

C. 3:1-5: THE SNAKE MAKES STATEMENTS TO THE WOMAN

This gentle idyll is short-lived however. At first glance there seems to be a sharp disjunction between the worlds of Genesis 2 and Genesis 3, but the two are linked together by a homonym, two words which sound alike although they mean different things and come from different

---

[16] See Isa 20:1-6; 2 Sam 10:4; Isa 47:2-3; Jer 13:22; Ezek 16:36-37; Hos 2:5, 12; Amos 2:16; Mic 1:8; Nah 3:5

[17] Eugenio Montale, *Satura 1962-1970*, trans. William Arrowsmith (New York: W. W. Norton, 1998) 25–7.

roots. The Man and Woman are naked (*ărûmmîm*) whereas the snake is sly (*ārûm*). Desirous of real wisdom, the couple mistakenly thinks that the snake's slyness[18] is what they seek. The pun continues when, expecting to open their eyes with new wisdom, they discover only that they are without clothing, simply naked (*ʿêrummîm*).

The serpent does not ask questions of the woman, as most translations, including the NRSV, imply ("Did God say, 'You shall not eat from any tree in the garden'?"). Rather he makes incorrect and incomplete statements to her, which she endeavors to correct.[19] And then, having drawn her into dialogue, he lies to her and tells her only part of what he seems to know. They cannot become like God, because in doing so they will die.

D. 3:6-7: THE WOMAN AND HER HUSBAND EAT OF THE TREE

Even the center of this tragedy has its center marked for the reader.

> So when the woman saw
> that the tree was good for food,
> that it was a delight to the eyes,
> that the tree was to be desired to make one wise,
>> she took of its fruit and ate; and she also gave some to her husband,
>>> who was with her,
>> and he ate.
> Then the eyes of both were opened,
> and they knew that they were naked;
> and they sewed fig leaves together and
> made loincloths for themselves.[20]

Speech, with which the appearance of human communion had been marked, is here absent. They do not speak to each other because now they know that they need to hide from each other. The bad thing they

---

[18] The word implies a certain conniving cleverness, a craftiness that can get a job done without worrying too nicely about its morality.

[19] Fox (Fox, *Moses*, 21) refers to the snake's words as an example of aposiopesis, an uncompleted phrase that leaves someone else to complete the speaker's thoughts. See also Gen 14:23; 21:23; 26:29; 31:50.

[20] "The first couplet, almost verbless, depicts the woman standing before the tree, mulling over the advantages of acting. The last couplet, with four verbs equally distributed in each half-line, tolls the inexorable knell of the wages of sin. Between them stands a single line, charged with verbs, in which first the woman, then her husband, succumb to the snake's charm." Walsh, *Style and Structure*, 23.

have learned is that they are not to be trusted, if not with God's gifts, then certainly not with each other. God is conspicuously absent as his creations freely work out their destiny and make it clear that they prefer a world in which they have chosen to disobey. Disobedience is central to the text, to their relationship with God, and reverses everything they have known until now. The disobedience is on the part of both Man and Woman. He is with her and participates without persuasion. The snake speaks to the woman using plural forms, indicating that he is targeting both Man and Woman.

C': 3:8-13: YHWH GOD ASKS QUESTIONS OF *hāʾādām*

God returns to the scene and with him come speech and the need to take responsibility. The response of the Man and the Woman is fear, knowing themselves untrustworthy and in the wrong. So, having started to hide from each other, they hide from God as well. Man and woman try to evade responsibility, blaming the other (so far gone is the utter openness of 2:25!).

B': 3:14-21: CHARACTER RELATIONSHIPS ARE REESTABLISHED, BUT WITH DISHARMONY

Both serpent and ground are cursed, but the humans, however heavy their punishment, are not cursed. It seems that the snake had told only part of the truth: that they would know bad but not that acts have consequences. The interest in vv. 14-21 is etiological: why snakes do not have legs, why people fear snakes, why childbirth hurts, why there is sexual desire, why men dominate women, why work is burdensome, why people die.

It should be noted that these, especially male dominance, are the undesired realities of a sinfully disordered world. Our author is attempting to explain the mysterious realities of the world in which he (or she) lived. Why are there such improbable and undesirable realities as one gender dominating the other? For the author, it was evidence that the world is not the way it ought to be. And one might add, it remains evidence that the world is not the way it ought to be. A sign of this dominance is the Man giving a name to the Woman, as he had earlier to the animals. Yet this act of domination is softened by the name given, *ḥawwâ*, a feminine form of the word "life."

Having shown them the consequences of their choice, God acts to save them by making them clothes. The garment given them is special, however. A *kuttōnet* is always worn by one in authority[21] showing that, however diminished their standing, they still act with divine authority.

A': 3:22-24: *hāʾādām* Is Driven from the Garden

Just as in Genesis 1, God appears here again as the one who brings order, who separates what should not be mixed. The Man and Eve, his wife, are no longer to be trusted and so are expelled into the world. They can no longer simply approach the Tree of Life. God's words to the Man have come true; they have died to the paradise they knew and must now choose a new life outside.

Characterization

God gives the Man and the Woman a command. But why? Does he desire to test them? That the God of Genesis tests people will become evident later on (Gen 22:1), but this part of God's character is present here at the beginning of the story as well. God tests, evaluates the results, and then doles out consequences.

Man and Woman choose not to live in Eden. Why is there evil in the world? Because we chose it and brought it with us.

In the Tradition

No detail of this story has escaped the notice and careful attention of commentators, modern or ancient. Here is a sample, along with suggestions for further reading.

Why did God allow Man and Woman to be tempted? Was it fair, knowing that they were so utterly naïve? Augustine did not have an answer to the question that he found entirely convincing, but he inclined toward the idea that there is no virtue without the possibility of sin, and that God uses the example of the sinner to instruct the virtuous.

> If someone asks, therefore, why God allowed man to be tempted when he foreknew that man would yield to the tempter, I cannot sound the depths of divine wisdom, and I confess that the solution is far beyond

---

[21] Gen 37:3, 23, 31-33; Exod 28:4, 29-30 . . . [15 x in all]; 2 Sam 13:18-19; 15:32; Isa 22:21; Job 30:16; Cant 5:3.

my powers. There may be a hidden reason, made known only to those who are better and holier than I, not because of their merits but simply by the grace of God. But insofar as God gives me the ability to understand or allows me to speak, I do not think that a man would deserve great praise if he had been able to live a good life for the simple reason that nobody tempted him to live a bad one. For by nature he would have it in his power to will not to yield to the tempter, with the help of him, of course, "who resists the proud and gives his grace to the humble" (1 Peter 5:5). Why then, would God not allow a man to be tempted, although he foreknew he would yield? For the man would do the deed by his own free will and thus incur guilt, and he would have to undergo punishment according to God's justice to be restored to right order. Thus God would make known his will to a proud soul for the instruction of the saints in ages to come. For wisely he uses even bad wills of souls when they perversely abuse their nature, which is good.[22]

Why tunics made from fig leaves? Irenaeus sees it both as a sign of human repentance and an opportunity for divine mercy.

Now "the fear of the Lord is the beginning of wisdom" (Ps 110:10). The understanding of transgression leads to penitence, and God extends his kindness to those who repent. For [Adam] showed his repentance in making a girdle, covering himself with fig leaves, when there were many other trees that would have irritated his body less. He, however, in awe of God, made a clothing that matched his disobedience. . . . And he would no doubt have kept this clothing forever, if God in his mercy had not clothed them with tunics of skin instead of fig leaves.[23]

The early Palestinian monastic writer Dorotheus of Gaza reaches the opposite conclusion and sees Adam as stiff-necked and unrepentant.

Again, after Adam had done wrong God gave him a chance to repent and be forgiven, and yet he kept on being stiff-necked and unrepentant. For God came to him and said, "Adam, where are you?" instead of saying, "From what glory are you come to this? Are you not ashamed? Why did you sin? Why did you go astray?"—as if urging him simply to say, "Forgive me!" But there was no sign of humility. There was no change of heart but rather the contrary. He replied, "The wife that you gave me"—mark you, not "my wife"—"deceived me." "The wife that *you* gave me," as if to say, "this disaster *you* placed on my head." So it is, my brethren, when a

---

[22] *On the Literal Interpretation of Genesis*, 11.4.6, in Andrew Louth, *Genesis 1–11*, Ancient Christian Commentary on Scripture: Old Testament I (Downers Grove, Ill.: InterVarsity, 2001) 80.

[23] *Against Heresies*, 3.23.5, in Louth, *Genesis*, 82.

man has not the guts to accuse himself, he does not scruple to accuse God himself. Then God came to Eve and said to her, "Why did you not keep the command I gave you?" as if saying, "If you would only say 'Forgive me,' to humble your soul and be forgiven." And again, not a word! No "forgive me." She only answered, "The serpent deceived me!"—as if to say, if the serpent did wrong, what concern is that to me? What are you doing, you wretches? Kneel in repentance, acknowledge your fault, take pity on your nakedness. But neither the one nor the other stooped to self-accusation, no trace of humility was found in either of them.

And now look and consider how this was only an anticipation of our own state! See how many and great the evils it has brought on us—the self-justification, this holding fast to our own will, this obstinacy in being our own guide.[24]

Many writers considered the question of the culpability of Eve and, with few, if any, exceptions, found her more deeply guilty than Adam and therefore the cause of humanity's later misery. In the late biblical book Sirach, one reads, "From a woman was sin's beginning, and because of her, we all die" (Sir 25:24), and this sets the tone for most of what follows.

The *Apocalypse of Moses,* for instance, says:

Adam said to Eve, "Why have you brought destruction among us and brought upon us great wrath, which is death gaining rule over all our race?"

"Oh evil woman! Why have you brought destruction among us?"[25]

But the judgment is not entirely negative, even among the ancient commentators. Notice how *Abot de R. Natan* seizes upon a crucial detail in the text.

The text says, "And God commanded Adam, saying, 'Of the tree of the knowledge of good and evil you shall not eat, for in the day that you eat of it you shall die' (Gen 2:17)." But Adam did not choose to tell God's words to Eve exactly as they had been spoken. Instead he said to her, "God said, 'You shall not eat of the fruit of the tree which is in the midst of the garden, neither shall you touch it, lest you die' [as per Gen 3:3]." Whereupon the wicked serpent said to himself, "Since I am unable to trip up Adam, let me go and try to trip up Eve." He went and sat down next to her and started talking with her. He said, "Now you say that God has forbidden us to touch the tree. Well, I can touch the tree and not die, and

---

[24] *Spiritual Instruction,* I, in Louth, *Genesis,* 87.

[25] *Apocalypse of Moses* 14:2; 21:6, in James L. Kugel, *Traditions of the Bible* (Cambridge, Mass.: Harvard University Press, 1998) 101.

so can you." What did the wicked serpent then do? He touched the tree with his hands and feet and shook it so hard that some of its fruit fell to the ground . . . Then he said to her, "[You see? So likewise] you say that God has forbidden us to eat from the tree. But I can eat from it and not die, and so can you." What did Eve think to herself? "All the things that my husband have told me are lies" . . . Whereupon she took the fruit and ate it and gave it to Adam and he ate, as it is written, "The woman saw that the tree was good to eat from and a delight to the eyes" [Gen 3:6].[26]

Accordingly, the guilt of the Woman is less than the guilt of the Man, for it was he who lied and so rendered his wife vulnerable to temptation. Evil entered into the world not with her misdeed but with his, for he failed to trust her.

Some contemporary writers have taken a new approach, seeing in Eve not the cause of Original Sin but a brave and innovative actor who, unlike her passive husband, was willing to dare new things and bring us into a world of new opportunities as a result.

In the biblical text, the words "sin" and "fall" do not appear, but "expel" does occur. Expulsion is one phase of giving birth: the fetus is expelled from the mother's body where all that is necessary for life has been provided. It is after the expulsion that life begins—work, exertion, and sexuality.[27]

Similarly, Barbara Grizzuti Harrison's "A Meditation on Eve" in *Out of the Garden* says:

When Eve bit into the apple, she gave us the world as we know the world—beautiful, flawed, dangerous, full of being. . . . Even the alienation from God we feel as a direct consequence of her Fall makes us beholden to her: the intense desire for God, never satisfied, arises from our separation from him. In our desire—this desire that makes us perfectly human—is contained our celebration and our rejoicing. The mingling, melding, braiding of good and mischief in every human soul—the fusion of good and bad in intent and in art—is what makes us recognizable (and delicious) to one another; without it—without the genetically transmitted knowledge of good and evil that Eve's act of radical curiosity sowed in our marrow—we should have no need of one another . . . of a one and perfect Other . . . Eve's legacy to us is the imperative to desire.[28]

---

[26] *Abot de R. Natan*, A., ch. 1, in Kugel, *Traditions*, 102–3.

[27] Dorothee Sölle, *Great Women of the Bible in Art and Literature* (1993), quoted in Bill Moyers, *Talking about Genesis: A Resource Guide* (New York: Doubleday, 1996) 43.

[28] In Moyers, *Talking about Genesis*, 43. See also David J. A. Clines, "What Does Eve Do to Help? And Other Irredeemably Androcentric Orientations in Genesis

The final word on this still developing tradition comes from contemporary Israeli author Avivah Gottlieb Zornberg, who considers the words of the Vilna Gaon.

> The Gaon says simply, "Everyone flees from the presence of God; no one wants to stand in His presence." . . . No one, says the Gaon, chooses to be; it is normal to decompose, to evade the demands of a whole consciousness. Unlike the phenomena of nature, man cannot be shocked into being, by fear, by Necessity, by the fiat of God. His is a more complicated story. It is the story of the quest for *amidah,* for a solid reality on which to base his life. Adam could not hold his position long: "things fall apart; the center cannot hold." And in his failure to be, the whole world loses solid specification.[29]

Adam could not bear to stand before God, and fled in fear. But God does not desire that we simply stand there.

> To stand in the presence of God is not, then, to be static: It is a kind of dance, invisible to the naked eye. Neither rigidity nor chaos is God's desire of man. What He desires is the human response of transformation. Erich Neumann writes: "For Satan as antithesis to the primordial living world of transformation is rigidity . . . but at the same time he appears as its opposite, as chaos. . . . The smooth, undifferentiated fixity of the one is inseparable from the molluscous, undifferentiated chaos of the other. . . . In the creative sphere, they give rise to a third term, which embraces and transcends them both, and this is form. . . . [that] is menaced from both sides, by sclerosis and by chaotic disintegration."[30]

Commentary: Genesis 4

THE SIN THAT ENSUED

Although Genesis 2–3 describe a transgression against a divine command and so become the biblical basis for the later Christian doctrine of Original Sin, the word "sin" only appears for the first time in Gene-

---

1–3," in *What Does Eve Do To Help? And Other Readerly Questions to the Old Testament* (Sheffield, England: JSOT Press, 1990) 25–48; and Carol Meyers, *Discovering Eve: Ancient Israelite Women in Context* (New York: Oxford University Press, 1988).

[29] *Genesis: The Beginning of Desire* (Philadelphia: Jewish Publication Society, 1995) 24.

[30] Ibid., 33.

sis 4 (*ḥaṭṭā't*, Gen 4:7, in a passage famously difficult to translate). Here too appear for the first time themes that will become important in the rest of the book, especially rivalry between brothers, displacement of the elder by the younger, and disjunction between generations.

STRUCTURE

Cassuto divides the chapter into six paragraphs.[31] A division of the chapter according to the traditional moments of the plot yields quite similar results. Note that the whole chapter is tied together in a number of ways. In 4:1-2a and 4:25 the birth formula is repeated, Seth takes the place of Abel, and YHWH's name is mentioned. There is an increase of violence throughout (vv. 8, 15, 24), and the verb "to kill" appears five times (vv. 8, 14, 15, 23, 25).

1. The birth of Cain and Abel (4:1-2)	Exposition (4:1-2)
2. The murder of Abel by Cain (4:3-8)	Inciting moment (4:3-4) Complication (4:5-8)
3. The sentencing of Cain (4:9-16)	Turning point (4:9a) Resolution (4:9b-16)
4. The genealogy of Cain (4:17-22) 5. The song of Lamech (4:23-24) 6. The birth of Seth and Enosh (4:25-26)	Conclusion (4:17-24, 25-26)

EXPOSITION: 4:1-2

It is Eve who more vigorously asserts her presence in the world outside Eden. Although it is Adam who "knows" her, she proclaims that she has created a man in the same way as YHWH (*qānîtî 'îš 'et-Yhwh*, 4:1) and names him Cain (*qayin*, "Smith") in a way that both foresees his alienation from the land and creates a similarity in sound with the verb *qānîtî*. The stage is set with the birth of Cain's brother Abel— "Breath," a name that hints at his insubstantial nature, which is not to remain long in the world.

---

[31] Umberto Cassuto, *A Commentary on the Book of Genesis, Part I: From Adam to Noah*, trans. Israel Abrahams (Jerusalem: Magnes, 1961) 178–9.

Beyond this it should be noted that it is the woman, again asserting her creative vitality, who pronounces the name of God for the first time and proclaims that she participates with God in the act of creation.

INCITING MOMENT: 4:3-4; COMPLICATION: 4:5-8

The offering of sacrifice becomes complicated when God does not accept Cain's. While there is doubtless an echo here of the tension between herdsman and farmer, the reasons the story gives for Cain's rejection is that Abel exercised his free will and brought the best, with the implication that Cain did not choose but simply took what was at hand. Other explanations have been offered: the soil from which the crops grew was cursed; Abel found an outlet in the bloodletting of the sacrifice for the violence inherent in all human beings, Cain had no such outlet and so killed his brother instead; God prefers the younger to the older; or this is part of the unknowable mystery of God's election. To Cain's anger God responds with a poem (highlighting the importance of what is being said by the adoption of this heightened speech form):

> Why are you incensed,
>   and why is your face fallen?
> For whether you offer well,
>   or whether you do not,
> At the tent flap sin crouches
>   and for you is its longing
>   but you will rule over it. (Gen 4:6-7)[32]

To whom does God speak? Not to Abel, to warn him, nor to the absent parents to tell them of the tragedy about to occur. Rather God chooses to speak to Cain, attempting to save him from the sin of fratricide that he is about to commit. He invites Cain to choose (as he did not do in selecting what he sacrificed). Again, the text reminds us of God's fundamental nature of savior, as well as of human freedom, and implies that all sin is somehow fratricide. Cain does not respond to God, even in the evasive way his parents did when interrogated by God in Eden. Simply ignoring God, Cain invites[33] his brother into a field. The field has long intrigued commentators. Friedman shows how this small detail connects the various fratricides in the Old Testament, starting

---

[32] Robert Alter, *Genesis: Translation and Commentary* (New York: Norton, 1996) 17.

[33] Cain's words to Abel are missing from the MT, probably as the result of a scribal error.

with this first instance and ending with Solomon's execution of his brother Adonijah (1 Kgs 2:25). Fratricide recurs in the stories of Jacob and Esau, Joseph and his brothers, Abimelech (who kills seventy brothers in Judges 9), Israel and Judah (2 Sam 2:26-27), and David's sons Absalom and Amnon (2 Samuel 13–14). In these stories, the reader is reminded over and over of events occurring in fields (2 Sam 14:6; Gen 25:17, 29; 37:7, 19-20; Judg 20:13, 23, 28; 21:6).[34] In this way, the primal sin is recalled over and over throughout the history of Israel.

Cain's motive for killing his brother is not made explicit in the text, possibly because there was not one discrete thing that lay behind the violence. Rather Cain objected to the entire fact of Abel's existence. The repetition of the word "brother" seven times in the story (vv. 2, 8 [2x], 9 [2x], 10, 11) underlines that it is brother-ness itself that is at play here. Cain did choose after all, but he chose to remain in an undifferentiated world where relation and brotherhood play no role. Cain prefers anonymous aloneness to relationship.

TURNING POINT: 4:9a; RESOLUTION: 4:9b-16

This section can be subdivided according to speaker: in vv. 9-12 God speaks and Cain replies, and in vv. 13-16 Cain speaks and God replies. The judge intervenes in v. 9a, inquiring after Abel. God's question in v. 10 repeats 3:13; again God gives someone the chance to tell the truth and once again is disappointed. Like his parents before him, Cain tries to deny responsibility. Cain's punishment completes the process of human alienation from the earth begun in Genesis 3:17-19 but with a subtle nuance. Whereas before the ground was cursed, it is now the cursed ground which curses Cain. Cain, in his reply to God, does not repent but claims that the punishment is too great for him to bear. In a gesture of protection parallel to the giving of tunics in 3:21, God marks Cain in some way that will protect him, and he departs from God's presence to live in the east, in the land of Nod ("Wandering").

CONCLUSION: 4:17-24, 25-26

The appearance of Cain's wife is something of a surprise since the reader is aware only of Adam, Eve, Cain, and the now deceased Abel (but cf. 5:4). The end of Genesis 4 describes the origin of urban life and

---

[34] Friedman, *Torah*, 27.

the increase in violence. One is left with a sense of the ambiguity inherent in life. From a murderer descend music and skill in metalworking.

The poem of Lamech, a song of victory sung by a man to his wives, lacks narrative context but is a carefully crafted poem in line with the norms of Hebrew poetic parallelism. He seems to be saying that he has not only taken revenge on a man who wounded him, he has even killed a boy who merely hurt him. Violence, brought into the world by Cain, increases and becomes ever more senseless.

The Man and Eve beget another child to replace the one they have lost. Their grandchild is named Enosh, a word that means "man." It was in his time that Eve's custom of calling on the God YHWH became general. Monotheism thus, at least in this version of Israel's story, predates the revelation to Moses in Exodus 3.

In the Tradition

In some texts, Cain, when asked by God where Abel is, attempts to turn the tables on his divine questioner and say that the ultimate responsibility lies with God. Consider this version from the Midrash:

> As soon as the Holy One blessed be He said unto him: "Where is thy brother Abel?" Cain replied: "I do not know. Am I my brother's keeper?" Thou art the keeper of all creatures; notwithstanding, thou dost seek him at my hand? To what may this be compared? To a thief who stole articles by night and got away. In the morning the gatekeeper caught him and asked him: Why did you steal the articles? To which the thief replied: I stole but I did not neglect my job . . . You however, your job is to keep watch at the gate, why did you neglect your job? Now you talk to me like that? So, too, Cain said: I did slay him because thou didst create in me the evil inclination. Thou are the keeper of all; yet me Thou didst allow to slay him? Thou it was that didst slay him; for hadst thou accepted my sacrifice the same as his, I would not have been jealous of him.[35]

In various versions of this story Cain's complaint is dismissed by calling to mind the free will with which the Human has been endowed at creation. But we dare not dismiss this so casually, because Cain makes an important point in the developing characterization of God. It may well be that Humanity is created free, but the God who demands that they care for each other seems to be shirking his responsibility. Should

---

[35] Midrash *Tanḥuma*, in Leibowitz, *Bereshit*, 49.

he not also be watching over Abel, lest he be killed? Should he not also be watching over Cain, preventing him from doing such an evil? Or does freedom really bring with it such a heavy burden of responsibility? What was the mark of Cain? Ambrose says that he is marked by his slavery to sin, that henceforth he belongs to sin as surely as any slave belongs to an owner:

> Like a slave, Cain received a mark and he could not escape death. Thus is the sinner a slave to fear, a slave to desire, a slave to greed, a slave to lust, a slave to sin, a slave to anger. Though such a man appears to himself free, he is more a slave than if he were under tyrants.[36]

Finally, any number of writers have commented on the ambiguity of urban life. Robinson Jeffers' poem "The Purse-Seine" (1937) will help us to ponder this aspect of the story:[37]

> Our sardine fishermen work at night in the dark of the moon;
>   daylight or moonlight
> They could not tell where to spread the net, unable to see the
>   phosphorescence of the shoals of fish.
> They work northward from Monterey, coasting Santa Cruz; off New
>   Year's Point or off Pigeon's Point
> The look-out man will see some lakes of milk-color light on the sea's
>   night-purple; he points, and the helmsman
> Turns the dark prow, the motorboat circles the gleaming shoal and
>   drifts out her seine-net. They close the circle
> And purse the bottom of the net, then with great labor haul it in.
>   I cannot tell you
> How beautiful the scene is, and a little terrible, then, when the crowded
>   fish
> Know they are caught, and wildly beat from one wall to the other of
>   their closing destiny the phosphorescent
> Water to a pool of flame, each beautiful slender body sheered with
>   flame, like a live rocket
> A comet's tail wake of clear yellow flame; while outside the narrowing
> Floats and cordage of the net great sea lions come up to watch, sighing
>   in the dark; the vast walls of night stand erect to the stars.
>
> Lately I was looking from a night mountain-top
> On a wide city, the colored splendor, galaxies of light: how could I help
>   but recall the seine-net

---

[36] Ambrose, *Letter to Priests*, 54, in Louth, *Genesis*, 108.

[37] Robinson Jeffers, "The Purse-Seine," in *The Collected Poetry of Robinson Jeffers*, vol. 2: *1928–1938*, ed. Tim Hunt (Stanford: Stanford University Press, 1989) 517–8.

Gathering the luminous fish? I cannot tell you how beautiful the city
    appeared, and a little terrible.
I thought, We have geared the machines and locked all together into
    interdependence; we have built the great cities; now
There is no escape. We have gathered vast populations incapable of free
    survival, insulated
From the strong earth, each person in himself helpless, on all dependent.
    The circle is closed, and the net
Is being hauled in. They hardly feel the cords drawing, yet they shine
    already. The inevitable mass-disasters
Will not come in our time nor in our children's, but we and our children
Must watch the net draw narrower, government takes all our powers—
    or revolution, and the new government
Take more than all, add to kept bodies kept souls—or anarchy, the
    mass-disasters.

These things are Progress;
Do you marvel our verse is troubled or frowning, while it keeps its
    reason? Or it lets go, lets the mood flow
In the manner of the recent young men into mere hysteria, splintered
    gleams, crackled laughter. But they are quite wrong.
There is no reason for amazement: surely one always knew that
    cultures decay, and life's end is death.

A Note on Genesis 5

THE ONGOING GENEALOGY OF HUMANITY

This commentary focuses on the narrative material in the book and such is lacking here. Suffice it to say that the chapter reprises material from Genesis 1 on the creation of humanity in the image of God and serves to separate the stories of the first humans from the Flood, which follows in Genesis 6–9. It has also been suggested that this is an alternative version of the events recounted in Genesis 1–4. At the beginning, humans are said to have lived tremendously long lives, which then decline to the Mosaic limit of 120 years. Most of the antediluvians approach a millennium, but as mortals, never attain it. Noah, for instance, becomes a father at 500, halfway to the unattainable millennial goal.

The only hint of narrative here is the enigmatic reference to Enoch, who "walked with God." This intrigued later readers and gave rise to the apocryphal books known as 1 and 2 Enoch, but what the phrase means is not clear.

To modern Western readers (one presumes) for the most part, this sort of material seems strange, the stuff of amateur sleuths interested in genealogy, and one can hardly imagine how it would have been composed or used. Thomas Mann, in his *Joseph and His Brothers*, sets a likely scene, which helps us to imagine how these lists functioned, as the young Joseph and his elderly father recite their memories of their family:

> "Well know I of Hanoch, who was of the first tribe of men, son of Jared, who was son of Mahalaleel, who was son of Cainan, who was son of Enos, who was son of Seth, who was son of Adam. Such was Hanoch's birth and tribe back to the beginnings. But the son of his son's son was Noah, the second first man, and he begot Shem, whose children are black but comely, of whom Eber came in the fourth remove, so that he

was the father of all the children of Eber and of all the Hebrews, and our father . . ."

This was well-known fact, there was nothing new in what he said. Every member of the tribe and race had the succession at his tongue's end from early childhood, and the old man was only taking occasion to repeat it and bear witness to it in conversation. Joseph understood that the talk was now to turn "fine"; that they were now to indulge in "fine language"—in other words, in conversation which no longer served the purpose of a practical exchange of ideas of intellectual discussion, but consists in the mere relation and utterance of matters well-known to both speakers: in recollection, confirmation, and edification, a kind of spoken antiphony, such as the shepherds in the field exchanged round their evening fires, beginning: "Knowest thou? Well I know."[1]

---

[1] Trans. H. T. Lowe-Porter (London: Vintage, 1999) 73–4. Originally published as *Joseph und Seine Brüder* in four volumes: 1. *Die Geschichten Jakobs* (S. Fischer, 1933); 2. *Der Junge Joseph* (S. Fischer, 1934); 3. *Joseph in Ägypten* (Bermann-Fischer, 1936); *Joseph, Der Ernährer* (Bermann-Fischer, 1943).

Chapter 3

THE STORY OF THE GREAT FLOOD AND THE COVENANT THAT ENSUED

Genesis 6–9

How Is the Story Structured?

The *tôlĕdôt* formula at Genesis 5:1 indicates to the reader that a fresh sequence of stories is beginning. Even were that not the case, the cast of characters, the setting, and the thematic concerns of Genesis 6–9 are all radically different from the preceding chapters.

The story of human misdeeds prior to the Great Flood, then the Flood itself and its aftermath describe God's undoing of creation and its subsequent rebirth in a modified form. The story's antiquity[1] and composite nature are both clear to all those who study it. While our concern here is not with the pre-biblical history of the text, some notice must be taken of its composite nature.

Of course, the story of the Flood makes sense as a unity: God becomes aware of human evil and decides to destroy humanity. Noah, the only just person of his age, is commanded by God to build an ark. When it is completed, Noah, his family, and representatives of all the animals of the earth enter in. The flood begins, and everything on earth perishes except for those in the ark. When the flood ends and the earth dries out, Noah and those with him in the ark can come out. God guarantees the continued existence of life.

---

[1] For those interested in the connections between the biblical Flood story and its ancient Near Eastern provenance in the Gilgamesh Epic, the commentary of E. A. Speiser, *Genesis*, AB 1 (Garden City, N.Y.: Doubleday, 1962) is a good place to begin. He does a fine job of outlining the similarities and differences between the two tales.

So much is clear to any reader. But even beginners notice difficulties:

1. The reason for the flood: the perversity of the human heart (6:5) or the corruption of all living things and the presence of violence (6:11-12, 13);
2. God's commands to Noah: to take with him a pair of each type of animal (6:19-20) or seven pairs of clean animals and one pair of unclean animals (7:2);
3. The length of the flood: forty days and forty nights (7:4, 12) or a whole year (7:6, 11; 8:13, 14);
4. The nature of the flood waters: a great rain (7:12; 8:2b) or a cosmic cataclysm due to the opening of the springs of the deep and the heavenly cataracts (7:11; 8:1-2a);
5. Leaving the ark: after sending out various birds (8:6-12) or because of a command from God (8:15-17);
6. The divine names: YHWH *(yhwh)* or God *(ʾĕlōhîm).*

Most exegetes feel that two stories, which can be reconstructed more or less completely and which stem from different documents, have been combined in the final canonical form of the text.

		A	B
1.	The evil of humanity	6:5	6:11-12
2.	God decides to destroy the universe	6:7	6:13
3.	The announcement of the flood	7:4	6:17
4.	The order to enter the ark	7:1	6:18
5.	The command concerning the animals	7:2	6:19-20
6.	The aim: to save them from the flood	7:3	6:19
7.	Entering the ark	7:7-9	7:13-16
8.	The beginning of the flood	7:10	7:11
9.	The rising of the waters	7:17	7:18
10.	The destruction of all living things	7:22-23	7:20-21
11.	The end of the flood	8:2b	8:2a
12.	The waters recede	8:3a	8:3b, 5
13.	Preparations for leaving the ark	8:6-12	8:15-17
14.	God promises never to send another flood	8:20-22	9:16-17

In version A the cause of the flood is humanity's evil. God, called by the name Yʜwʜ in this version, orders Noah to take seven pairs of clean and one pair of unclean animals into the ark. The flood, the result of torrential rain, lasts forty days and nights; the flood ends when the rain ceases. Noah leaves the ark and offers a sacrifice of (apparently clean) animals. Yʜwʜ smells the odor of the sacrifice, resigns himself to the evil in the human heart, and promises never to destroy humanity again by means of a flood.

In version B God is called by the name ʾĕlōhîm, "God." The cause of the flood is less specific; the earth has become corrupt and there is violence everywhere. God commands Noah to build an ark and bring into it one pair of each kind of animal. The chronology of this version is remarkably precise, with dates and a calendar that correspond to the life of Noah. The flood is a result of the deeps and the heavenly cataracts opening, reversing the cosmology of Genesis 1. At the end of the flood, after the waters have receded, God blesses Noah and his family, gives them permission to eat meat and makes a covenant with Noah. The rainbow is a sign that God will never destroy the earth by means of a flood again.

There are difficulties with this reconstruction,[2] neither version being complete, but there seems no doubt that two rather different stories about the same general course of events have been combined here. Does a unity nevertheless result? Yes. Witness the following concentric arrangement, which points us right toward what is central.[3]

A	6:9-10	*Genealogical note* —Noah's three sons enumerated —Noah's righteousness
	B	6:11-12	God sees (*rāʾâ*) that the earth (*hāʾāreṣ*) is ruined (*šāḥat*) —all flesh (*kol-bāśār*) has ruined (*šāḥat*) its way
		C	6:13-22 God's instructions to Noah in light of his coming destruction of life on earth —directions regarding the food (*ʾoklâ*) that they may eat (*ʾākal*)

----

[2] For the difficulties, and for much of what has preceded, see Jean-Louis Ska, *Introduction à la lecture du Pentateuque: Clés pour l'interprétation des cinq premiers livres de la Bible*, Le livre et le rouleau 5 (Brussels: Éditions Lessius, 2000) 90–7.

[3] David Dorsey, *The Literary Structure of the Old Testament* (Grand Rapids, Mich.: Baker, 1999) 52. See similar attempts by B. W. Anderson, "From Analysis to Synthesis: The Interpretation of Genesis 1–11," *Journal of Biblical Literature* 97 (1978) 23–9 and G. J. Wenham, "The Coherence of the Flood Narrative," *Vetus Testamentum* 28 (1978) 336–48. Both of these authors locate the center of their concentric structures at 8:1 "But God remembered Noah. . . ."

D	7:1-9	**They enter the ark** at God's command —Noah takes "<u>clean</u> <u>animals</u> and [clean] birds"		
	E	7:10-16	*Flood begins, ark is closed* —<u>after seven days</u> —<u>forty days</u>	
		F	7:17-20	*Waters rise* —series of clauses depicting prevailing waters —<u>mountains</u> *(hehārîm)* <u>are cov-ered</u> and ark is borne over them
			X	7:21-24	**CLIMAX: All life on land dies**; only Noah and those with him are spared

		F'	8:1-5	*Waters recede* —series of clauses depicting receding waters —<u>mountains</u> *(hehārîm)* <u>are uncovered</u> and ark rests on one of them
	E'	8:6-14	*Flood ends, ark's window is opened* —<u>after seven days</u> —<u>forty days</u>
D'	8:15-22	**They exit the ark** at God's command —Noah takes some "<u>clean</u> <u>animals</u> and clean birds" and offers them to God
C'	9:1-7	**God's instructions to Noah** in light of his renewal of life on earth —directions regarding <u>food</u> *(ʾoklâ)* that they may <u>eat</u> *(ʾākal)*
B'	9:8-17	**God promises never again to ruin** *(šāḥat)* **the earth** *(hāʾāreṣ)* —God will never again ruin *(šāḥat)* all flesh *(kol-bāśār)* —God will see *(rāʾâ)* the rainbow
A'	9:18-19	*Genealogical note* —Noah's <u>three sons</u> enumerated

Unit B is tied together by the repetition of *ʾet* and the fourfold repetition of *hāʾāreṣ*.
Unit B' is tied together by the repetition of *ʾet* and the fourfold repetition of *hāʾāreṣ*.[4]

---

[4] See Dorsey, *Literary Structure*, 52.

This scheme omits 6:1-8. These verses, while outside the formal structure of the flood narrative, serve as a prelude to it by showing the terrible condition that humanity and the entire world were in before God intervened. The marrying of the sons of God and human women, a motif widely found in such stories of primeval time,[5] is objectionable to God because it represents a mixing of things that should be separate, a transgression of the separation God effected in Genesis 1. The Nephilim (from the verb that means "to fall"; hence, the "fallen ones") are the "sons of God" who have sexual relations with human women.

Immediately preceding the flood story the author has placed God's motivation. Notice the contrast between the human and divine hearts. The hearts of humanity are evil (6:5), in marked contrast with God's, which is grieved (6:6). God's grieving heart is described with a word from the same root (*ʿṣb*) that was used previously to describe Eve's birth pangs in Genesis 3:16 (*ʿiṣṣĕbônēk*), the burden of the Man's toil in Genesis 3:17 (*bĕʿiṣṣābôn*), and the toil from which Noah is to relieve humanity in Genesis 5:29 (*ûmēʿiṣṣĕbôn*). This use of repetition serves to focus our attention on the pain that humanity has brought upon itself and that which it has caused in the heart of God. Humanity's contribution to the story thus far is pain, and so God regrets having made humanity. How can God regret what he has done? Could God, all-knowing and all-seeing, not foresee the consequence of his creative acts? What does this passage say about the developing characters of God and Humanity in this story?

Just as one wonders about God's grieving heart, repetition is skillfully used as well to focus attention on Noah, who will bring relief (5:29). The name Noah (*nōaḥ*) is understood to mean "Comfort" (5:29). The consonants "n" and "ḥ," from which the name is formed, are used repeatedly throughout the rest of the section: "this one will comfort us" (*yĕnaḥămēnû*, 5:29); "he regretted" (*wayyinnāḥem*, 6:6); "I regret" (*niḥamtî*, 6:7); "Noah found favor" (*wĕnōaḥ māṣāʾ ḥēn*, 6:8); "and the ark rested" (*wattānaḥ*, 8:4); "pleasant smell" (*ʾet-rêaḥ hannîḥōaḥ*, 8:21). Through the use of these two repetitive devices the reader comes to expect that in the story that follows divine and human relief will be found for the grief of humanity, caused by humanity.

While much of the remainder of the story is told from Noah's point of view (the reader is, as it were, experiencing the events along with Noah and through Noah's eyes) there are at least two important

---

[5] See Speiser, *Genesis*, 44–6.

exceptions, 6:5 and 6:12. In 6:5, God sees *(wayyar² yhwh)*, and the reader sees with him, identifying with his experience. This privileged entry into God's own self is further heightened by the interior monologue that the reader hears in 6:7 when God speaks *(wayyō²mer yhwh)*. Since God is alone, the speech reported must be interior, especially since the reader is invited into the heart of God in 6:6. In this way, the reader knows what is in God's heart, overhears these deepest concerns. (On 6:12, see below.)

Commentary: Genesis 6:9–9:19

A. 6:9-10: Genealogical Note

Why mention that Noah was righteous and blameless *in his generation*? Why draw this contrast when, after all, it is not clear when else Noah could have been righteous and blameless. Some have seen it as a way of heightening Noah's achievement; i.e., given the milieu in which he was forced to live it is even more remarkable that he was such an exemplary individual. Others read it in exactly the opposite fashion; Noah was blameless by comparison with the folks in whose midst he lived but was otherwise rather ordinary. The word "blameless" *(tāmîm)* is rather frequent and often used elsewhere to refer to a sacrificial animal that is suitably and unambiguously without fault (e.g., Lev 1:3, 10). The same approbation seems to be the case here, especially since such a strong link is made with Enoch, who in 5:24 is also said to have walked with God *(wayyithallēk ḥănôk ²et-hā²ĕlōhîm)* as did Noah in 6:9 *(²et-hā²ĕlōhîm hithallek-nōaḥ)*.

B. 6:11-12: God Sees the Earth's Ruin

This section draws the reader back into God's interior, using God's literal point of view to understand the nature of God's complaint against humanity. The word "behold" *(hinnēh*, present in the RSV but sadly omitted in the NRSV) serves as an important marker for a shift in point of view. One is, all of a sudden, transported into the divine character's mind, seeing what he sees and so identifying more closely with the character's experience (cf. Gen 24:63).

What God sees is corruption (from the root *šḥt*, "ruin"). The word appears five times in Genesis 6:11–13:17 and with some frequency in prophetic texts,[6] where it means "to become ruined," "spoiled," "no longer fit for an intended use." What has rendered humanity so unfit is ubiquitous violence *(ḥāmās)* upon the earth.[7] Thus, the sin that threatens the very being of creation is a human sin—what one person, or nation, does to another.

C. 6:13-22: GOD'S INSTRUCTIONS

In v. 13 the point of view shifts from God to Noah, as God lets Noah in on what has been occurring in God's own heart. Repetition functions importantly in this verse. The same root *(šḥt)* that was used to describe the corruption of the earth by humanity is here used by God to say how he will destroy the earth. Since humanity has ruined the earth, God will bring ruin upon it.

Instructions for the building of the ark follow. It is important to note that the ark is not an ordinary boat. The word itself *(tēbâ)* is unusual, appearing elsewhere in the Old Testament only in Exodus 2:3 and 5 to describe what the infant Moses was sheltered in when his mother placed him in the river to be discovered by the daughter of Pharaoh.

The ark is rectangular, with three floors. It has been suggested that it serves as a microcosm of the universe—with the four sides representing the directions, the three floors representing underworld, earth and heaven, and the human and animal occupants serving as a sample of all the living things to be destroyed.[8] In the instructions and subsequent building of the ark there is already a beginning of God's reconstruction. The microcosm is ordered exactly as God wants it to be. Corrupted creation is outside; within, all is as it should be for obedient creatures. At the same time, God tells Noah both his plans for the total ruination of all the already ruined earthly life (v. 17) and his plans for restoration (v. 18).

---

[6] E.g., Isa 1:14; Jer 6:28; 13:7; 18:4; Ezek 16:17; 20:44; 23:11; 28:17, etc.

[7] Note that it is only the earth, the realm of human habitation, that is so corrupted, not the seas. As a result the oceans and sea creatures escape destruction, and responsibility for the disaster of corruption due to violence is placed even more firmly with humanity. For *ḥāmās* see Isa 53:9; 60:18; Jer 6:7; 20:8; 22:3; Ezek 7:23; 28:16; 54:9; Joel 4:19; Amos 3:10; Mic 6:12; Hab 1:3; 2:8, 17; etc.

[8] A cubit was the length of a person's forearm, about 17–18 inches. The wood cannot be identified. The meaning of the word *ṣōhar*, ordinarily translated as "skylight," "window" or "roof," is unclear since the word appears only this one time.

After the transgression of the Man and the Woman in Eden, God protected them by giving them leather garments (3:21) and made it clear that they could never regain their former way of life. Similarly, when Cain went away from the presence of the LORD, never again to experience the life he had before his sin, he went marked with God's protective sign. With an increase in human evil, God's reaction is to increase both punishment and succor. The first couple lost Eden but were given garments. Cain lost the very ground on which he toiled, but his very person was marked as protected. Here, all flesh will lose its very creation, but God will bind himself to a new humanity with a covenant. Genesis 6:18 is the first occurrence of this word (it appears nearly thirty times in the remainder of Genesis alone) that will loom so large throughout the rest of the Bible and come to define the divine-human relationship. Rather than depart from the creation that has so badly and so often disappointed him, this God binds himself ever more closely to it.

Noah is to take representatives of all animal life and a store of food. This too is a hint of what is to come, for God will allow humanity, hitherto vegetarian, to eat meat after the flood.

D. 7:1-9: They Enter the Ark

The beginning of this section reflects the composite nature of the canonical text. Here the command is to take ritually pure animals, those suitable for sacrifice and also fit for human consumption once humans are allowed to eat meat, and a pair of ritually impure animals. Noah is perfectly compliant, and God's microcosm of a restored world is completed.

E. 7:10-16: The Flood Begins, the Ark Is Closed

The date on which the flood begins is carefully noted. However, the chronology of the flood is immensely complicated.[9] Consider first the plethora of dates.

---

[9] See Niels Peter Lemche, "The Chronology of the Flood," *Journal for the Study of the Old Testament* 18 (1980) 52–62; L. Michael Barré, "The Riddle of the Flood Chronology," *Journal for the Study of the Old Testament* 41 (1988) 3–20.

7:4	For in seven days I will send rain on the earth for forty days and forty nights.
7:10	And after seven days the waters of the flood came on the earth.
7:11	In the six hundredth year of Noah's life, in the second month, on the seventeenth day of the month . . .
7:12	. . . forty days and forty nights . . .
7:17	. . . forty days on the earth . . .
7:24	. . . one hundred fifty days (i.e., five months) . . .
8:1, 3, 4	. . . one hundred fifty days (i.e., on the seventeenth day of the seventh month) . . .
8:5	. . . in the tenth month, on the first day of the month . . .
8:6-7	At the end of forty days (i.e., on the tenth day of the eleventh month) . . .
8:10-12	He waited another seven days . . . Then he waited again another seven days (i.e., thrice seven days).
8:13	In the six hundred first year, in the first month, the first day of the month . . .
8:14	In the second month, on the twenty-seventh day of the month (i.e., twelve months and ten days after the beginning of the flood) . . .

The flood seems to last for twelve (probably lunar) months and ten days for a total of 364 days. At its end, since his birthday coincides with the first day of the new year, Noah will be 601 years old, at the beginning of his seventh century.

God, in a note that is both remarkably anthropomorphic and indicative of divine concern and protection, closes the door behind all those living beings who have entered the ark. God remains outside to confront the remnant of ruined creation and to ruin it in turn.

F. 7:17-20: The Waters Rise

Two verbs, "increase" and "swell," alternate in this section, coupled with modifiers to give a sense of mounting waters that overwhelm everything on earth. Fox's translation captures the way the clauses in this section convey the swelling of the waters:

The Deluge was forty days upon the earth.
The waters increased [*wayyirbû*] and lifted the Ark, so that it was raised above the earth;
the waters swelled [*wayyigbĕrû*] and increased exceedingly [*wayyirbû mĕʾōd*] upon the earth, so that the Ark floated upon the face of the waters.
When the waters had swelled exceedingly, yes, exceedingly [*gābĕrû mĕʾōd mĕʾōd*] over the earth, all high mountains that were under all the heavens were covered.
Fifteen cubits upward swelled [*gābĕrû*] the waters, thus the mountains were covered.[10]

X. 7:21-24: CLIMAX

We reach the center of the tale, God's irreversible ruining of the ruined creation before he creates anew. In vv. 21-23 there are echoes of Genesis 1 as, one by one, each of the sorts of creatures God made dies. An unusual phrase appears in v. 22, in which the first two words are essentially synonyms: "the breath of a breath of life" (*nišmat-rûaḥ ḥayyîm*). Explanations for this vary. Some suggest that it refers to the smallest hint of life, i.e., even the tiniest of creatures, but it seems rather to be an allusion to Genesis 1:2 where, in the midst of chaos, the breath/spirit of God was a hint of the life to come. Here it is a reminder of God's withdrawal of his spirit, his breath, from this creation. Without the divinely vivifying presence, all die. Again, repetition of the verb underlines the destruction: "He blotted out. . . . were blotted out." All was obliterated except for Noah and those with him who were, for five months, the only living things on earth.

F'. 8:1-5: THE WATERS RECEDE

The flood ends in the same order in which it began, with words that cannot fail to call to mind the story of Creation: "wind" in 8:1 and 1:2, waters receding in 8:2 and 1:6-8, the dry ground of the earth appearing in 8:5, 14 and 1:9-10. God has unmade and now will set about making anew, saving creation from itself as an act of love for Noah. That Noah is central to God's concern is highlighted in 8:1, "And God remembered Noah." The new order of creation is anchored in the memory of God and founded on the covenant of which God is ever mindful. The phrase will occur elsewhere in Genesis. In 9:15-16 God pledges to re-

---

[10] Everett Fox, *The Five Books of Moses* (New York: Schocken, 1995) 38.

member the covenant. Later, in 19:29 God remembers Abraham and saves Lot for Abraham's sake. In 30:22 God remembers Rachel and she becomes pregnant. To be remembered by God is to be the object of God's saving and life-giving concern. So too here in Genesis 8:1, the world is recreated for the sake of Noah, the sole righteous person.

E'. 8:6-14: The Flood Ends, the Ark's Window Is Opened

Little by little the waters recede as the occupants of the ark wait and test to see how far the waters have gone down. Finally the ground *(hāʾădāmâ)* is dry and humanity can once more step into the world.

D'. 8:15-22: They Exit the Ark

Creation took place by God's word, and so re-creation takes place at God's word. Obedient to the divine command, the microcosm, which God spared for the sake of Noah, emerges from the ark into a world washed clean. Noah's first act is one of worship. It takes place on a mountaintop, where divine and human realms are as close as can be.

God savors the smell of the sacrifice but does not eat it, unlike the gods of Mesopotamia. The sacrifice is pleasing in odor *(hannîḥōaḥ)*, allowing a pun on the name Noah, so that the one whom God found pleasing offers pleasing worship. This animal sacrifice must call to mind the unacceptable sacrifice of Cain. Even though God accepts this one, he will still warn humanity about the dangers of violence, which this act of worship does nothing to lessen.

In an echo of 6:6, God again speaks to himself (8:21-22) recognizing that there is something in humanity that is inherently flawed, that cannot be changed, but that God will not destroy again on that account. All of this takes place as interior monologue. God does not tell Noah what he has learned about the unconquerable evil of humanity. Could it be that he knows humanity could not bear such self-knowledge? Regardless of the true inner nature of humanity, God pledges to allow time, and the liturgical cycle, to continue.

C'. 9:1-7: God's Instructions

God restores human dominion over creation in an echo of Genesis 1:27-28. But this new blessing is importantly different from its predecessor. God gives humanity an outlet for its violence. God acts to rein in that violence as well. In 9:6 God forbids the taking of human life by a human. The passage is also arranged concentrically to stress its importance:[11]

> The one who sheds / the blood / of a human being / /
> for a human being / his blood / shall be shed.
> (*šōpēk / dam / hāʾādām // bāʾādām / dāmô / yiššāpēk.*)

God's words continue, "for in his own image God made humankind" —yet another reference back to the creation story of Genesis 1, by which God explains that the divine image in which humanity has been created precludes the taking of human life.

B'. 9:8-17: God Promises Never Again to Ruin the Earth

Here God makes with Noah the first of the four covenants on which the biblical understanding of the divine/human relationship is based. This first covenant is between God and all creation and promises security. The three subsequent covenants are between God and the people he has chosen for his own, the descendants of Abraham and Sarah. The covenant with Abraham (Genesis 15, 17) promises the land to his descendants and makes YHWH the God of Israel. The covenant at Sinai (Exodus 20, Deuteronomy 5) provides structure to the relationship, commands that order human life in relation to God. The covenant with David promises that a king descended from David will rule over Jerusalem and Israel (2 Samuel 7).

The rainbow, which brings to mind a warrior's bow, but pointed away from earth and made a thing of beauty, will always serve as a reminder of the covenant and the peace it promises and demands. Never again will all flesh be ruined—at least not by God.

A'. 9:18-19: Genealogical Note

The flood story ends as it began with a listing of Noah's sons. And yet nothing is as it began. As the concentric structure indicates, everything has been reversed. Violence is channeled, although not rooted out. Creation is bound by covenant to God. The isolation of humanity and the world in which humanity lives is no more. Once again God

---

[11] Jerome T. Walsh, *Style and Structure in Biblical Hebrew Narrative* (Collegeville: The Liturgical Press, 2001) 28. See also his reasoning for changing the usual translation "by a human being" to "for a human being."

has responded to human evil by committing himself yet more firmly to humanity. No longer is just one person marked out for God and saved from violence; violence is forbidden and all of creation is seen as special, covenanted, in God's sight. Because of the covenant God will overlook the violence that dwells within. And so the flood ends with humanity unchanged but more deeply cherished.

In the Tradition

Both Jewish and Christian commentators are aware of the ambiguity with which Noah's righteousness is described. According to the midrash:

> "Noah was a righteous man, blameless in his generation" [Gen 6:9]. R. Judah and R. Nehemiah disagreed on this verse. R. Judah said: in *his generation* he was righteous; had he lived in the generation of Moses or the generation of Samuel, he would not have been considered righteous . . . R. Nehemiah said: if even *in his generation* he was a righteous man, had he lived in the generation of Moses or Samuel, how much more of a righteous man would he have been.[12]

The Christian Jerome would have agreed with R. Judah.

> It says specifically "in his generation," so as to show that he was not just according to absolute justice, but that by the standards of justice of his generation he was just.[13]

What was the sin that caused God to decide to destroy creation? Augustine speaks only of wickedness in some general sense.

> Somebody may say to me, "Was Adam, created by God as the first man in the original state of the world, condemned for lack of faith or for sin?" It was not incredulity but disobedience that was the cause for his condemnation and the reason why all his posterity are punished. Cain too was condemned, not for lack of faith but because he killed his brother. Why need I seek further proof when I read that this whole world was condemned not for incredulity but for wickedness.[14]

---

[12] *Genesis Rabbah* 30:9, in James L. Kugel, *Traditions of the Bible* (Cambridge, Mass.: Harvard University Press, 1998) 187.

[13] Jerome, *Questions in Genesis* 6:9, in Kugel, *Traditions*, 187.

[14] Augustine, *Christian Life* 13, in Andrew Louth, *Genesis 1–11*, Ancient Christian Commentary on Scripture: Old Testament I (Downers Grove, Ill.: InterVarsity, 2001) 130.

Others were more ready to identify the sin more specifically, generally as some sort of sexual immorality.

> Because the sons of Seth were going in to the daughters of Cain, they turned away from their first wives whom they had previously taken. Then these wives, too, disdained their own continence and now, because of the husbands, quickly began to abandon their modesty, which up until that time they had preserved for their husbands' sake. It is because of this wantonness that assailed both the men and the women that Scripture says, "All flesh corrupted its path."[15]

But was sexual misbehavior alone enough to warrant universal destruction? Or was it a symptom of a more widespread transgression against the natural order? The latter is reflected in the New Testament Epistle of Jude, which teaches that angels overstepped the boundary between the human and divine realm and reaped their own punishment as a result: "And the angels who did not keep their own position, but left their proper dwelling, he has kept in eternal chains in deepest darkness for the judgment of the great Day" (Jude 6).

Why a flood instead of some other manner of destruction? The New Testament saw in the flood a prefiguring of the cleansing waters of baptism (1 Pet 3:20-21) or the cataclysm at the end of time (e.g., Matt 24:37-39). Some Jewish commentators also took up the idea of the flood as purification.

> When the Creator took it in mind to cleanse the earth by means of water and decided that the soul [symbolized by the earth] should be purged of its unmentionable evil deeds and have its uncleanness washed away in the manner of sacred purification. . . .[16]

Both Christians and Jews also found in the covenant with Noah a sort of universal natural law that impinges on all people.

> He [God] concluded three covenants with Noah: First, that they [his descendants] not eat blood, another of retaliation, that He would seek out [avenge] their blood from animals, another, that a murderer be killed.[17]
>
> The descendants of Noah were commanded [to keep] seven commandments, [those] concerning [the establishment of a set of] laws and [forbidding] idolatry and cursing with the name [of God] and forbidden unions and murder and theft and eating a limb from a living animal.[18]

---

[15] Ephrem the Syrian, *Commentary on Genesis* 6.3.3, in Louth, *Genesis*, 130.

[16] Philo, *The Worse Attacks the Better*, 170, in Kugel, *Traditions*, 189.

[17] Ephrem the Syrian, *Commentary in Genesis* 6:14, in Kugel, *Traditions*, 226.

[18] Tosefta, *Abodah Zarah* 8:4.

Commentary: Genesis 9:18-29

NOAH'S DRUNKENNESS

This brief, unlovely tale tells us that the ground is still a source of alienation. Here Noah is alienated from himself, and his son Ham becomes alienated from his family. The world is still a dangerous place where some forces and experiences are better left alone.

It is possible to apply the standard language of plot analysis here.

Exposition: 9:18-20
Complication: 9:21-23
Turning point: 9:24
Resolution: 9:25-27
Conclusion: 9:28-29

What is the origin of the enmity between the people of Israel and the Canaanites? They were culturally and linguistically similar yet commanded by God to stay apart. The answer is found here in Ham's misbehavior. It is not clear what the misdeed is, whether castration, sexual penetration, or merely immodestly viewing Noah's nakedness. But it is clear that slavery, servitude, is a result of sin and not intended by God as part of the design of the world.

IN THE TRADITION

Canaan, the son, is cursed rather than Ham, the father, who actually sinned. This has perplexed commentators. Justin Martyr finds a solution in Ham's blessing before the flood.

> In the blessings with which Noah blesses his two sons, he also curses his son's son. For the prophetic Spirit would not curse that son himself, since he had already been blessed by God, together with the other sons of Noah. But since the punishment of the sin was to be transmitted down to all the posterity of the son who laughed at his father's nudity, he made the curse begin with the son's son.[19]

---

[19] *Dialogue with Trypho* 139, in Louth, *Genesis*, 158.

A Note on Genesis 10
THE ONGOING GENEALOGY OF HUMANITY

There is no narrative material in Genesis 10, so we will not tarry long in discussing it. It begins with the standard *tôlĕdōt* formula with which the final editor of Genesis marked the beginning of a new complex of genealogy and tales. It shows that humanity continues to be fruitful and to multiply. However, the purpose of this chapter, the so-called Table of Nations, is a good deal more ambitious than previous genealogies. In Robert Alter's words:

> In keeping with the universalist perspective of Genesis, the Table of Nations is a serious attempt, unprecedented in the ancient Near East, to sketch a panorama of all known human cultures—from Greece and Crete in the west through Asia Minor and Iran and down through Mesopotamia and the Arabian Peninsula to northwestern Africa.[1]

However, note does need to be taken that the way in which humanity spread, and language developed, is at odds with the story told in Genesis 11, which follows immediately. It is to that story, with its structure, etiologies, and role in furthering the characterization of humanity and God that we now turn.

---

[1] Robert Alter, *Genesis: Translation and Commentary* (New York: Norton, 1996) 42.

65

Chapter 4

THE STORY ABOUT BABEL

Genesis 11:1-9

Commentary

Genesis 11 consists of two parts. The first (11:1-9) is the story of the Tower of Babel, which explains the origin of the various human languages. Since all people were descended from the family of Noah, linguistic diversity required some explanation. This is followed in Genesis 11:10-32 by another genealogy in which Abram, his family, and their troubles are introduced.

Robert Alter says that this chapter turns language itself into a game of mirrors.[1] With a severely restricted vocabulary (*śāpâ*, "language," appears five times in these few lines) and using a highly symmetrical narrative device, the story is about the origin of language diversity. This is an aspect of human culture that we do not understand terribly well in our own day, so the curiosity of the Israelite, heightened by the unitary nature of human descent from Noah, is understandable.

Many remark on the story's symmetry. We will examine three possible structures to see which works best, from which we are able to derive the most insight.

The story may be organized according to traditional plot structure language:

> Exposition: 11:1-2
> Complication: 11:3-4
> Turning point: 11:5-6
> Resolution: 11:7-8
> Conclusion: 11:9.

---

[1] Robert Alter, *Genesis: Translation and Commentary* (New York: Norton, 1996) 47.

In this case, to call 11:5-6 a turning point is almost literally true, since God comes down just as humanity is trying to go up. But as useful as this description of the story may be it misses a number of features that are especially prominent in the Hebrew.[2]

a) Inclusion:

> v. 1: "The whole earth was of one language" (*wayhî kol-hā᾽āreṣ śāpâ ᾽eḥāt*).
>
> v. 9: "There YHWH confused the language of all the earth" (*šām bālal yhwh śĕpat kol-hā᾽āreṣ*).
>
> cf. also v. 6: "YHWH said, 'Behold, they are one people and all have one language . . .'" (*wayyō᾽mer yhwh hēn ῾am ᾽eḥād wĕśāpâ ᾽aḥat lĕkullām*).

b) Repetition of language relating to the themes of unity and scattering:

> v. 1: "The whole earth was of one language, one [set of] words" (*wayhî kol-hā᾽āreṣ śāpâ ᾽eḥāt ûdĕbārîm ᾽ăḥādîm*).
>
> v. 4: "lest we be scattered upon the face of all the earth" (*pen-nāpûṣ ῾al-pĕnê kol-hā᾽āreṣ*).
>
> v. 6: "Behold, they are one people and all have one language" (*hēn ῾am ᾽eḥād wĕśāpâ ᾽aḥat lĕkullām*).
>
> v. 8: "And YHWH scattered them from there upon the face of all the earth" (*wayyāpeṣ yhwh ᾽ōtām miššām ῾al-pĕnê kol-hā᾽āreṣ*).
>
> v. 9: "for there YHWH confused the language of all the earth" (*kî-šām bālal yhwh śĕpat kol-hā᾽āreṣ*), "and from there YHWH scattered them upon the face of all the earth" (*ûmiššām hĕpîṣām yhwh ῾al-pĕnê kol-hā᾽āreṣ*).

c) Repetition of language relating to the theme of decision-making:[3]

> v. 3: "Come, let us make bricks and bake them thoroughly" (*hābâ nilbĕnâ lĕbēnîm*).
>
> v. 4: "Come, let us build for ourselves . . ." (*hābâ nibneh-lānû*).
>
> v. 7: "Come, let us go down and confuse . . ." (*hābâ nērĕdâ wĕnābĕlâ*).

d) Repetition of the theme of "name" (*šēm*) and "there" (*šām*):

> v. 2: ". . . and they settled there" (*wayyēšĕbû šām*).

---

[2] What follows is largely drawn from Chapter I, "Genesis 11:1-9," in J. P. Fokkelman's *Narrative Art in Genesis: Specimens of Stylistic and Structural Analysis* (Assen/Amsterdam: Van Gorcum, 1975) 11–45.

[3] Note also the alliteration between *lbn*, "to make bricks," *bnh*, "to build," and *bll*, "to confuse."

v. 4: "... and let us make a name for ourselves" (*wĕnaʿăśeh-lānû šēm*).

v. 7: "... and let us confuse there their language" (*wĕnābĕlâh šām śĕpātām*).

v. 8: "And YHWH scattered them from there" (*wayyāpeṣ yhwh ʾōtām miššām*).

v. 9: "Therefore they called the name of that place Babel for there ... and from there ..." (*ʿal-kēn qārā*) *šĕmāh bābel kî-šām ... ûmiššām*).

The inclusion shows what the story is about; unity is transformed into disunity. The repetitions function in a similar way, to highlight the desire for unity and its frustration, that the two actors in the story (God and humanity) are working to opposite purposes and that the name (i.e., reputation) they expect to achieve is entirely different from the name they do achieve ("Babel," i.e., "Confusion").

It is clear that vv. 1-4 describe human activity and vv. 5-9 describe God's activity. But is it better to view the story as two parallel sets of actions or as a reversal, God reversing humanity's actions?

The two possibilities can be schematized as follows:

Symmetrical parallels:

    A. v. 1: one language and one [set of] words (*šāpâ ʾeḥāt ûdĕbārîm ʾăhādîm*)

      B. vv. 3, 4: Let us ... (*hābâ* + cohortative)

        C. v. 4: let us build (*nibneh*)

          D. v. 4: let us make a name (*naʿăśeh šēm*)

            E. v. 4: lest we be scattered over the face of the earth (*pen-nāpûṣ ʿal pĕnê hāʾāreṣ*)

    A'. v. 6: one people and one language (*ʿam ʾeḥād wĕšāpâ ʾaḥat*)

      B'. v. 7: let us ... (*hābâ* + cohortative)

        C'. v. 8: they stopped building (*wayyaḥdĕlû libnōt*)

          D'. v. 9: its name Babel (*šĕmāh bābel*)

            E'. v. 9: scattered them over the face of the earth (*hĕpîṣām ʿal-pĕnê kol-hāʾāreṣ*)

While this structure shows how the actions of God and humanity are parallel to each other, viewing the passage as a concentric structure highlights the reversal: what humanity does, God undoes.

Concentric structure:

> A. v. 1: all the earth was of one language (*kol-ā᾿āreṣ śāpâ ēḥāt*)
> > B. v. 2: there (*šām*)
> > > C. v. 3: and they said to one another (*wayyō᾿měrû ᾿îš ᾿el-rē῾ēhû*)
> > > > D. v. 3: let us make bricks (*hābâ nilběnâ lěběnîm*)
> > > > > E. v. 4: let us build for ourselves (*nibneh-lānû*)
> > > > > > F. v. 4: a city and a tower (*῾îr ûmigdāl*)
> > > > > > > X. v. 5: YHWH came down to see (*wayyēred yhwh lir᾿ōt*)
> > > > > > F'. v. 5: the city and the tower (*᾿et-hā῾îr wě᾿et-hammigdāl*)
> > > > > E'. v. 5: which the people had built (*᾿ăšer bānû běnê hā᾿ādām*)
> > > > D'. v. 7: come . . . let us confuse (*hābâ . . . wěnābělâ*)
> > > C'. v. 7: so that they will not understand each other's speech (*᾿ăšer lō᾿ yišmě῾û ᾿îš šěpat rē῾ēhû*)
> > B'. vv. 8, 9: from there (*miššām*)
> A'. v. 9: the language of all the earth (*šěpat kol-hā᾿āreṣ*)

Human beings still fail to follow God's command to fill the earth. Rather, they try to come together, challenge their earthly finitude, and approach God's own dwelling. So after all this time humanity has not advanced significantly over the time of Adam and Eve in the Garden of Eden. Still the humans disobey. But God is still savior and comes down to save humanity from itself.

Much in this story is lost in translation, since it is so highly dependent on untranslatable puns:

> And how is translation to cope with the episode of Babel? *Migdal* is not, primarily, a "tower." It is a "great" or "exceeding" object with its "head in the heavens." Most likely, the inference is that of a giant idol. The edge of blasphemy throughout the narrative, however, turns on the synonymy between the verb "to make," used for the building of the Tower, and the term of "divine creation." The puns are the crux, and untranslatable: the Hebrew root *balal* signifies "to mix," "to confound," "to disperse." But it can also be read as another echo of "Babel": as *nebelah*, meaning destruction. And of the great translators of Babel, only Luther sees that *safah* is not only "language" or "speech," but the actual tongue (*einerlei Zunge und Sprache*).[4]

---

[4] George Steiner, "A Preface to the Hebrew Bible," in *No Passion Spent* (New Haven: Yale, 1996) 60. Although Steiner does not mention it, the root *nbl* from which *něbēlâ* is derived also gives us the word for "fool."

The story shows a number of biases—against the artificial temple mountains of Mesopotamia, against urban life, against Bablyon. The name Babel is understood here to mean "confusion" but more probably means "Gate of God." This is the Mesopotamia from which the people of Israel will spring, through Abraham. Yet it is repudiated already.

In the Tradition

While many writers of the pre-critical era wrote extensively on this chapter, much of what they had to say strikes a modern reader as foreign. These early writers speculated, for example, on the size of the tower builders and decided, generally, that they must have been a race of giants to attempt such a feat. They wondered what language this single humanity spoke and decided that it must have been Hebrew.

At least one commentator, Saint John Chrysostom in his *Homilies on Genesis*, provides us with material for pondering. He is concerned with God's motivation for confusing human speech. In short, he teaches that God acts to save humanity from itself.

> This in fact is the way the Lord is accustomed to behave. . . . So when the people in the present case, who had been dignified with similarity of language, used the privilege given them for evil purposes, he put a stop to the impulse of their wickedness through creating differences in language. "Let us confuse their speech," he says, "so that they will be unable to understand one another's language." His purpose was that, just as similarity of language achieved their living together, so difference in language might disperse them.[5]

George Steiner, the contemporary literary critic, also provides insight into the text in his "A Preface to the Hebrew Bible."

> *Davar* can signify "thing," "fact," "object," "event," as well as the speech-acts of "saying," "commandment" and "revelation." The word appears for the first time in Genesis 11:1 (where it is often translated, with misleading connotations, by *logos* or *verbum*). This first appearance led midrashic commentators to suppose that the initial ten chapters of Genesis transpire in some pre-discursive context. Speech goes unfulfilled, as

---

[5] John Chrysostom, *Homilies on Genesis*, in Andrew Louth, *Genesis 1-11*. Ancient Christian Commentary on Scripture: Old Testament I (Downers Grove, Ill.: Inter-Varsity, 2001) 169.

in the "monologues" of Adam and Eve. *Vayyomer qayin el hevel ahiv*: "Cain said to his brother Abel." But we are *not* told what he said. Noah has no dialogue with God. *Davar*, in its full speech-sense, evolves around and is aborted at Babel. Henceforth mankind chatters in a host of closed, mutually incomprehensible tongues: *devarim*.[6]

One need only mention that the mutually incomprehensible languages which separate us from each other are not only the world's natural languages. We chatter with blithely mutual incomprehension quite happily while speaking the same language as well; such is the division, indeed the *nĕbēlâ*, that Babel wrought.

---

[6] Steiner, "Preface," 59.

A Note on Genesis 11:10-32
THE ONGOING GENEALOGY OF HUMANITY
(Abram, his family, and their troubles introduced)

A fundamental shift begins to occur in the ongoing story of humanity, which changes from a universal history to the history of one man and his family. The shift does not take place in a random fashion, however. There were ten generations from Adam to Noah, who begot three sons (Genesis 5). There are now ten generations from Shem to a father, Terah, who begets three sons. Lifespans shrink, but not in a random fashion. From the birth of Shem's son to Abram's migration to Canaan is 365 years, a year of years.[1]

The stately progression of generations stumbles at one point when there appears the laconic notice, "Now Sarai was barren; she had no child" (Gen 11:30). And so the next stage of humanity's relationship with God begins. Having failed to relate fruitfully to all of humanity, God narrows his focus to one man and his family. God chooses Abraham, and so all people will know salvation.

Sarai and her inability to conceive is central to everything that follows; this is highlighted by the way in which this bloc of genealogy is put together. Sarai's inability to conceive is located in the middle of 11:27-32, while Abram and his family live in Ur before she and her husband Abram are taken by Terah to dwell in Haran.

---

[1] Robert Alter, *Genesis: Translation and Commentary* (New York: Norton, 1996) 48.

73

Summary

THE NARRATIVE STRUCTURE OF GENESIS 1–11

We noted earlier that the Flood Story of Genesis 6–9 is a story of un-creation and re-creation. This is part of a more complex series of parallels between Genesis 1–6 and Genesis 6–9.[1]

A. Narrative: creation (1:1–3:24)
    B. Narrative: sin and curse of the son (4:1-16)
        C. Genealogy: the origins of culture (4:17-26)
            D. Genealogy: from Adam to Noah and Shem (5:1-32)
                E. Narrative: blurring the divine-human boundaries (6:1-4)
A'. Narrative: re-creation by flood (6:5–9:19)
    B'. Narrative: sin and curse of the son (9:20-29)
        C'. Genealogy: the origins of nations (10:1-32)
                E'. Narrative: blurring the divine-human boundaries (11:1-9)
            D'. Genealogy: from Shem to Terah and Abram (11:10-26)

The parallels between the sections labelled A and A' in the scheme have long been noted. What is done in A is systematically reversed in A'. The sin of the son of the primal parents is the focus of B and B'. Both C and C' are genealogies but neither focuses on one family. D traces the ten generations from Adam to Noah, ending with his three sons, whereas D' traces the ten generations from Noah to Terah and ends

---

[1] Jerome T. Walsh, *Style and Structure in Biblical Hebrew Narrative* (Collegeville: The Liturgical Press, 2001) 112.

75

with his three sons. E and E' describe humanity's attempts to blur the distinction between the divine and the human.

As Jerome Walsh rightly points out, transposing E' and D' has a powerful effect.[2] Attention is shifted away, at the last moment, from the transgression at Babel to the infertility of Abram and Sarai. It is as though the text were telling us to look away from the sterility of the past, for something new is about to happen. Read otherwise, one might think that all of the first history of humanity has ended in the infertility of Abram and Sarai. Humanity has reached a point of such division from God that they can no longer fulfill the first commandment and practice the first blessing; to be fruitful and multiply. What will God do?

[2] Ibid.

Part Two

STORIES ABOUT THE TROUBLED FAMILY CHOSEN FOR BLESSING

GENESIS 12–50

Introduction
CHOOSING WHERE TO STAND

How should we best approach the remainder of the book? Most commentaries still call it the "Patriarchal History" or something very similar. In so doing, these commentators tell us to be mostly aware of the stories about the male patriarchs of the people of Israel. Everyone else necessarily recedes a bit into the background, so that their lives and travails become a bit of an addendum to the main action.

Why call it anything? There are certainly no titles given in the MT or the LXX, the two most important ancient language versions on which all modern translations are based. Titling the stories seems to be an occupation of modern commentators. But a name is important because it helps us to organize our reactions to what we are reading. It lets the reader know where the commentator is standing. Readers are then free to join me where I stand or not, or in their own way to select another perspective that better suits them. I will call these latter chapters of the book "Stories about the Troubled Family Chosen for Blessing."

Consider other options.

II. The Abraham Saga (11:10–25:26)
    A. Genealogy (11:10-32)
    B. Narrative (12:1–22:19)
    C. Death Reports (22:20–25:26)
III. The Isaac Saga (25:19–37:2)
    A. Narrative (25:19–35:15)
    B. Death Reports (35:16–37:2)
III. The Jacob Saga (37:1–50:26)
    A. The Joseph Novella (37:1–47:27)
    B. Death Reports (47:28–50:26)

This version[1] creates the impression in the reader that the latter part of Genesis is almost entirely about these three patriarchs, that they are

---

[1] George W. Coats, *Genesis: With an Introduction to Narrative Literature*, FOTL 1 (Grand Rapids, Mich.: Eerdmans, 1983) 28–9. To be fair, what I have presented here are only the major headings of a very complex structure.

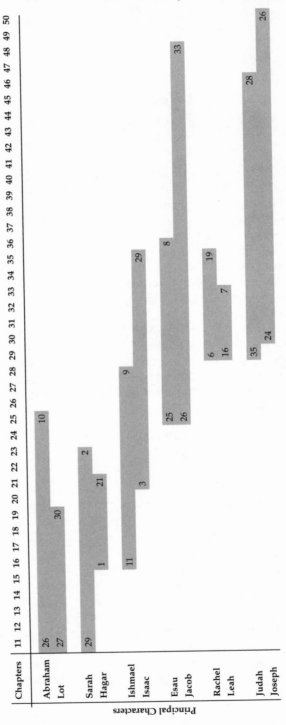

Figure 1: Interrelationships among the Principal Characters of Genesis 12–50

treated more or less equally in the book and that there is a certain appreciable symmetry to the treatments.

A different impression arises when one reads the following.

> It is easy to distinguish, among the stories about the patriarchs, narrative blocs which possess their own characteristics: the Abraham cycle (12–25); some traditions about Isaac (26); the Jacob cycle (25; 27–35) and the Joseph story.[2]

The impression of neat symmetry disappears. Isaac, far from being the dominant figure for a quarter of the book is merely the subject of some traditions that appear in a single chapter. Joseph stands on his own as one of the patriarchs, although one senses that there is a difference between the section in which he is dominant, a "story," and the "cycles" of Abraham and Jacob.

One final example:[3]

Abraham and the Promise of a Son (Gen 12:1–21:7)

The Life of Isaac: Strife between Older and Younger Brothers (Gen 21:8–28:4)

Jacob's Exile and God's Protection and Blessing (Gen 28:5–37:1)

Joseph and His Brothers (Gen 37:1–50:26).

This approach is much more subtle. The impression of symmetry between the various sections is gone, and it is clear that different parts of the book build on what has gone before, adding new themes and characters. But it is still about patriarchs; it still gives the impression that when a fresh patriarch appears on the scene his predecessor, and those who appeared in that part of the book, are gone. There is still, in short, the impression that there are four tales, or cycles of tales, about four men who lived and strove and built a relationship with God in relative isolation from each other and from others who were living at the same time as they.

Yet the reality is a good deal more complex. The accompanying chart shows when the book's principal characters are introduced to the story and when they leave the story. The latter is not always easy to determine. The death of some characters is noted, while others (e.g., Leah) simply disappear after a certain point. Some might quibble with

---

[2] Jean-Louis Ska, *Introduction à la lecture du Pentateuque: Clés pour l'interprétation des cinq premiers livres de la Bible,* Le livre et le rouleau 5 (Brussels: Éditions Lessius, 2000) 291.

[3] David Dorsey, *The Literary Structure of the Old Testament* (Grand Rapids, Mich.: Baker, 1999) 55–60.

a detail or two, but the chart makes clear that the latter part of the book of Genesis is not at all a neat succession of four series of tales. These people—their lives, their relationships with each other and with God —overlap and interrelate.

Viewing the patriarchs in such isolation also causes one to miss one of the most important characterization devices in the book. The principal characters, as is evident from Figure 1, are presented in pairs. We come to know and understand the character of Abraham better when we view him over against Lot; their lives are importantly parallel. So too with the book's other major characters: Sarah and Hagar, Ishmael and Isaac, Esau and Jacob, Rachel and Leah, and, finally, Judah and Joseph.[4] This is not to say that all of the characters are treated in this way—Rebekah, for instance, seems to have no such partner—but this pairing of parallel characters remains an important and overlooked aspect of the book. Nor is this the only device the final author/editor had at hand. What emerges is a complex portrait, not only of four important men in the history of Israel but of a troubled family, which YHWH has, nonetheless, chosen for blessing.

If the book is, in reality, a complex interweaving of ideas, themes, lives, and relationships, a commentary on the book must have some sort of practical organization. By way of unhappy compromise, I have chosen to divide what follows into four main chapters, interrupted by an essay on the nature of the character of God in Genesis 12–25.

> Genesis 12–25: In the Time of the First Generation
> God as a Developing Character in Genesis 12–25
> Genesis 25–28: In the Time of the Second Generation
> Genesis 28–35: In the Time of the Third Generation
> Genesis 36–50: In the Time of the Fourth Generation

But let the reader be aware that this is only a compromise and that, in the commentary, there will be shifts back and forth to examine the pairings that are important tools for characterization. In addition, there will be an excursus on a theme that deserves more attention and more extended development than can be done in the body of a commentary, namely, the autonomy of the female characters.

---

[4] Interestingly, this approach is also followed, with very different results and for a very different theological purpose, by Karl Barth in his *Church Dogmatics* (Edinburgh: T. & T. Clark, 1957) II/2, § 35.2, pp. 340–409, especially p. 355.

Chapter 5

IN THE TIME OF THE FIRST GENERATION

Genesis 12–25

How Is the Story Structured?

The story of the people chosen by God for blessing, the family descended from Abraham and Sarah, begins in Genesis 11:27. The death of Sarah is recorded in Genesis 23:2 and that of Abraham follows in Genesis 25:10, but by that time the focus has already shifted to the second generation of the chosen family. Ishmael has found a wife (Gen 21:21) and established a family line of his own, not chosen by God but vigorously free (Gen 25:12-18). A search for a wife for Isaac, the chosen son of Abraham and Sarah, the one to whom the promises of blessing and possession of the land descend, begins in Genesis 24:2 and bears fruit when Rebekah agrees to marry Isaac (Gen 24:28).

There have been a number of attempts to organize the material in Genesis 12–25, to demonstrate the literary structures at play there. The idea that these chapters are somehow organized around a center that gives them a structural and thematic unity seems widespread. Three examples will suffice. George Coats[1] offers a structure (beginning at 11:10, concluding at 22:19 and schematized as ABCDD'C'B'α-B'βA'), the complexity of which reflects the growth of the traditions about Abraham and his family but which is ultimately centered in the final form of the biblical text on the giving of the covenant in Genesis 15–17.

---

[1] George W. Coats, *Genesis: With an Introduction to Narrative Literature*, FOTL 1 (Grand Rapids, Mich.: Eerdmans, 1983) 97–8.

Although his arrangement of the various passages involved is quite different, Jerome Walsh nevertheless agrees that the center of this section of the book is to be found in Genesis 15:1–16:16 and 17:1–18:15. In the former YHWH promises progeny to Abram, makes a covenant with him and Ishmael's birth is announced. In the latter YHWH promises progeny to Abraham, makes a covenant with him and Isaac's birth is announced. These two blocs form the center of a concentric pattern that extends from YHWH's command to Abram to leave his home (12:1) to the command to sacrifice his son in Genesis 22.[2]

David Dorsey takes a rather different approach. He too begins at Genesis 12:1, but concludes with the birth of Isaac in Genesis 21:1-7. He finds the center of the section to be in Genesis 17:1-21, where Abram and Sarai's names are changed, circumcision is instituted, and the promise of a son is repeated.[3]

Of course, these three readings are all perfectly correct in some sense, especially if one views these chapters as principally about Abraham and his desire for a son. If that is the case, then everything is indeed centered on that quest. But if we choose to stand in a slightly different place, a different perspective emerges, one in which these stories are suddenly less about a sonless man wanting a son than they are about God, the nature of God, and the way God relates to humanity.

Consider the following structure, which is both concentric and not, and which results from deciding not to focus on Abraham (with, almost involuntarily, the idea somewhere in mind that these chapters are "The Abraham Cycle" and as such *should* be focused on him) but on God.

In his treatment of this section, Walsh notes there is no counterpart for the birth of Isaac.[4] Thus, there is a fundamental asymmetry to the whole section. In this Walsh is correct. But the asymmetry plays out rather differently than Walsh sees.

The substance of life before (11:27-32)
    A. Near obedience, but failure to sacrifice what was asked (12:1-8)
       B. YHWH acts to free Sarai (12:9–13:1)
          C. Abram and Lot settle (13:2-18)
             D. Evil is vanquished by Abram (14:1-24)

---

[2] Jerome T. Walsh, *Style and Structure in Biblical Hebrew Narrative* (Collegeville: The Liturgical Press, 2001) 89–90.

[3] David Dorsey, *The Literary Structure of the Old Testament* (Grand Rapids, Mich.: Baker, 1999) 56.

[4] Walsh, *Style and Structure*, 90, n. 6.

E. YHWH acts and commits himself to a covenant (15:1-21)

    X. YHWH saves Hagar and her child (16:1-15)

E'. Abraham acts and commits himself to a covenant (17:1-26)

  D'. Evil is vanquished for Abraham's sake (18:1–19:29)

   C'. Lot settles (19:30-38)

    B'. YHWH acts to free Sarah (20:1-18)

!!!. YHWH acts freely to create a life and to free; dwellers and sojourners (21:1-34)

A'. Obedience, and the sacrifice of what was asked (22:1-19)

The substance of life afterwards (22:20–25:10)

God calls Abram in Genesis 12:1, and they finish speaking to each other in Genesis 22:18. Abraham had already lived a long life before his encounter with God and would continue to live for decades after the events of Genesis 22, remarrying and raising another family. God, it seems, does not regard these events as central to the divine task. So the beginning and end of divine speech mark the beginning and end of the structure above (A and A'). In B and B' YHWH acts to free Sarah, showing that freedom, especially for those not able to free themselves, is key to the way God acts in the world. Where Lot chooses to dwell (contrasting it with choices Abraham makes) is an important part of the ongoing parallel characterization of Lot and Abraham that is such a large part of this section's purpose. As an important element it is introduced early on and pointedly resolved (C and C'). Abraham is called to act as a blessing and complies with this call in Genesis 14 (D) and Genesis 18–19 (D'). No reader could so misread these chapters as to doubt that progeny and covenant are central to their project. So the dual covenants, with their attendant promises, are very nearly at the center of this arrangement (E and E'). In the former God commits himself to the pact with Abram, and in the latter Abraham acts to show that he, too, is committed.

In Genesis 16, we reach the center of the divinely centered plot of Genesis 12–25. Here God shows concern for the alien, those without structures of family support. One of the most important literary leitmotifs of the Old Testament is the concern that is demanded for the alien, the orphan, and the widow.

> You shall not wrong or oppress a resident alien, for you were aliens in the land of Egypt. You shall not abuse any widow or orphan. If you do abuse them, when they cry out to me, I will surely heed their cry. (Exod 22:21-23)

This striving on behalf of the weak and defenseless comes to be identified with justice itself and is built into Israel's Law, as is seen in the citation from Exodus, in the Prophets (e.g., Isa 1:17: "learn to do good; seek justice, rescue the oppressed, defend the orphan, plead for the widow . . ."), and in the Writings:

> Do not remove an ancient landmark or encroach on the fields of orphans, for their redeemer is strong; he will plead their cause against you. (Prov 23:10-11)

> O LORD, you will hear the desire of the meek; you will strengthen their heart, you will incline your ear to do justice for the orphan and the oppressed, so that those from earth may strike terror no more. (Ps 10:17-18)

> Give justice to the weak and the orphan; maintain the right of the lowly and the destitute. Rescue the weak and the needy; deliver them from the hand of the wicked. (Ps 82:3-4)

> I delivered the poor who cried, and the orphan who had no helper. The blessing of the wretched came upon me, and I caused the widow's heart to sing for joy. (Job 29:12-13)

This is such a powerful theme in Scripture that any attempt to list all the instances would be nearly impossible. In fact, one reads that doing justice is all that God desires.

> He has told you, O mortal, what is good; and what does the LORD require of you but to do justice, and to love kindness, and to walk humbly with your God? (Mic 6:8)

Doing justice for the helpless is central to Israel's life with God from its very beginning as seen in this arrangement. God does justice (see Ps 7:6-11) for Hagar, the alien, scorned and abandoned by her husband and father of her child.[5]

---

[5] For an extended treatment of this theme, see the Excursus "Outsiders: The Use of Location, Movement and Concentric Structure to Highlight the Autonomy of Female Characters (Genesis 38; 1 Samuel 25; 2 Samuel 11; 2 Samuel 13)." In *The Names of God: Poetic Readings in Biblical Beginnings* (New York: Oxford University Press, 1998), Herbert Chanan Brichto discusses this passage in detail (see especially pp. 213–6). He argues that Hagar's subsidiary status (and that of her son) is marked by her being addressed by YHWH's angel rather than YHWH himself. Nor does she use the divine name, as Sarah does. However, she herself says that it is YHWH who speaks to her: "So she named the LORD who spoke to her, 'You are El-Roi'"

But, as Walsh rightly notes, the second half of the pattern contains an asymmetrical unit. In Genesis 21 God brings a number of threads to a conclusion. Isaac is born, against all expectation. Hagar finds freedom outside of Abraham's world in a free life with her son.[6] And Abraham finds a home, finally beginning to be at home in the land he has been promised. For God everything is wrapped up at this point. He has created life for Abraham and Sarah; he has freed the enslaved, given a home to the homeless. There remains only the question of Abraham's obedience. Having begun with only partial obedience, will Abraham finally obey?

These chapters then, when read from this perspective, teach us what is central to God's way of being in the world. Called to be a blessing, Abraham wasn't. So God was. Central to God's way of being in the world is salvation—creating a place for Hagar, the alien, the homeless woman—for central to God's way of being in the world is justice. The God who commanded it later, whose prophets preached it and whose sages taught it, could not have acted otherwise from the very beginning.

God acts as a replacement father in these chapters. After Terah dies, YHWH appears to Abram, to Isaac after the death of Abraham, to Jacob after he leaves his apparently dying father. God never appears in the stories about Joseph, in keeping with the theme of divine distance from human activity found in those stories but does give Joseph special insight needed to survive.

Finally, that life is orderly and meaningful is an article of faith for these tales. This is conveyed in various ways that are not immediately apparent to the reader. The ages of Abraham, Isaac, and Jacob are clearly intended to play an important role in conveying this theme. Abraham lives 175 years ($7 \cdot 5^2$), Isaac for 180 years ($5 \cdot 6^2$) and Jacob for 147 years ($3 \cdot 7^2$). Abraham lives seventy-five years in the lifetime of his father and

---

(Gen 16:13, *wattiqrā' šēm-yhwh haddōbēr 'ēleyhā 'attâ 'ēl rŏ'î*). Fuller comment on this passage, and what may well seem like an entirely fanciful misreading, will follow below. Here it will suffice to note that Hagar is the only woman in Genesis to speak to God, indeed, to give God a name. Surely this is a narrative device bestowing on this character extraordinary privilege.

[6] It should be noted that in this incident Hagar speaks to YHWH, thus using the name (I am who I am) that God gives himself, a name that "suggests free choice and unhindered power" (Richard Clifford, "Exodus," *The New Jerome Biblical Commentary*, ed. Raymond E. Brown, et al. [London: Chapman, 1990] 47).

seventy-five years in the lifetime of his son. Jacob and Joseph both spend twenty years away from their fathers.[7]

Commentary

A. 12:1-8: NEAR OBEDIENCE, BUT FAILURE TO SACRIFICE WHAT WAS ASKED

Genesis 12–13 consists of one lengthy story about Abraham and other members of his family and has a number of interesting narrative features. Lot is introduced as a character whose blunders and short-comings will stand in decided contrast to Abraham. At 12:6 and 13:7 there are two examples of "breaking frame," where the narrator intrudes into the story to give the reader information that is not immediately pertinent to the developing story but is meaningful to the reader. It is structurally complex in that, embedded within the larger story, there is a tale about God and Sarai in Egypt. This latter is a good example of what Robert Alter calls a type scene.[8] In 12:17ff; 13:7, and 13:10 are three interesting manipulations of point of view. The first is a good example of so-called interest point of view. It is not in Pharaoh's interest to keep Sarai in his house. The others are less easy to classify. Genesis 13:7 describes the emotional atmosphere between two groups of herdsmen. This is a conceptual point of view. The last example is a fine example of irony in point of view. The plain where Sodom is located seems, in Lot's view, to be a fine place to live. Readers know otherwise, and our evaluation of Lot and his opinions heads downhill.

The beginning and end of the section are clearly marked. The section is preceded by the genealogical list in Genesis 11; and it is followed by Genesis 14 where, in a story with an entirely different narrative texture, Abram appears not as a landless wanderer but rather as the leader of a considerable army campaigning to protect the feckless nephew Lot. With these external boundaries, chapters 12 and 13 are held together internally by the same characters appearing throughout and by a chain of causality that links the three episodes.

The bloc can be described in various fashions:

---

[7] Everett Fox, *The Five Books of Moses* (New York: Schocken, 1995) 51.

[8] "[T]he writer invokes a fixed sequence of narrative motifs, familiar as a convention to his audience, while pointedly modifying them in keeping with the needs of the immediate narrative context." Robert Alter, *Genesis: Translation and Commentary* (New York: Norton, 1996) 52.

Inciting Moment (12:1-4b)	Near obedience, but failure to sacrifice what was asked (12:1-8)	
Development (12:4c–13:4)	YHWH acts to free Sarai (12:9–13:1)	A. A trip to the Negeb (12:9) 　B. Descent into Egypt (12:10) 　　C. Abram addresses his wife (12:11-13) 　　　D. His prediction comes true: her beauty is seen (12:14-15a) 　　　　X. The woman in Pharaoh's house (12:15b) 　　　D'. His prediction comes true: it goes well with him (12:16) 　　**!!!. The free Action of YHWH (12:17)** 　　　C'. Pharaoh addresses Abram (12:18-19) 　　B'. Ascent out of Egypt (12:20) 　A'. A trip to the Negeb (13:1)
	Abram and Lot settle (13:2-18)	
Turning point (13:5-7)		
Resolution (13:8-17)		
Conclusion (13:18)		

YHWH speaks to Abram, as he is known at this point in his life, without any indication that Abram has known or worshiped this God before. The first words spoken to Abraham are mysterious, or at least grammatically unusual: *lek-lĕkā*. This phrase occurs only one other time in the Hebrew Bible, at Genesis 22:2, when God speaks to Abraham for the last time.[9] It is an unusual form of the imperative of the verb "to go" that grammarians call an ethical dative[10] and means, in this instance, something like "You must go!" Much has been made of the phrase in the Jewish interpretative tradition particularly,[11] since it can also be understood to mean, "Go for yourself" or "Go to yourself." This is the first human journey that is not a punishment but is undertaken to secure a blessing. That Abram went is noted in 12:4a, which serves as an inclusion to mark the end of the passage's inciting moment.

---

[9] See Josh 22:4 for a similar (plural) form and Cant 2:10, 13 for a feminine version. Walsh suggests the translation "Get yourself going!" Walsh, *Style and Structure*, 49.

[10] See G-K §119s: ". . . to give emphasis to the significance of the occurrence *for* a particular subject"; see also §135i.

[11] No one has written more powerfully on this text than Avivah Gottlieb Zornberg in *Genesis: The Beginning of Desire* (Philadelphia: Jewish Publication Society, 1995) 72–96.

There are two other important elements to examine within the inciting moment. Abram is commanded to leave three things: country, kindred, and his father's home. Thus, he is to leave behind the past, everything and everyone familiar to him, all the previous supports and influences he has known, and to depend on God alone. These three leave-takings are increasingly intense. While it is hard to leave the part of the world with which one is familiar, it is clearly harder to leave one's clan with all of the complex, long-established relationships one would find there. Finally, Abraham is commanded to leave behind those closest to him. All that is past must be left behind, however wrenchingly. Modern readers, accustomed as we are to ease of travel and communication and to the very idea that family is something to be left behind when outgrown, might not feel the same emotional tug as Abraham would have felt. Northrop Frye says, "We belong to something before we are anything. . . ."[12] If Abram leaves behind all that to which he belongs, will he *be* anything any longer?

Does he comply? Does he take the chance of no longer belonging to the family of Terah so that he might become part of the family of YHWH? The plot really begins to develop when, in Genesis 12:4b, it is made known to the reader that he is only partially obedient; that instead of leaving all behind he takes his nephew Lot with him. Before that point, however, God tells Abram what awaits him, the blessing of progeny and land. This must appeal to the childless Abram, who has already wandered from his birthplace to Haran.

God's first promise to Abram is a land, a place where he can be rooted in the world.[13] The divine speech that follows (Gen 12:2-3) contains seven elements:

1. I will make of you a great nation, and
2. I will bless you, and
3. make your name great, so that
4. you will be a blessing.
5. I will bless those who bless you, and
6. the one who curses you I will curse; and
7. in you all the families of the earth shall be blessed.

---

[12] Northrop Frye, *Words with Power: Being a Second Study of the Bible and Literature* (New York: Harcourt, Brace, Jovanovich, 1990) 17.

[13] One writer says that the central question of the Bible is not "emancipation but rootage, not meaning but belonging, not isolation from others but placement between the generation of promise and fulfillment." Walter Brueggemann, *Place as Gift, Promise and Challenge in Biblical Faith* (Philadelphia: Fortress, 1977) 187.

This series, or its near equivalent, is repeated four times, in four other moments of revelation: to Abraham when he receives the three guests before the destruction of Sodom (Gen 18:17-18), in the blessing after Abraham obediently prepares to offer Isaac (22:16-18), when God first appears to Isaac (26:2-4), and when Jacob first encounters God at Bethel (28:10-14). As such it serves as a description of how Abraham and his descendants are to be in the world.

Each clause adds something to the developing picture. The first implies numerous progeny to the still childless Abram; with that will come material prosperity (clause 2), joined by the esteem due to one of superior character (clause 3). As a consequence of his own blessing, Abram's task in the world will be to bring to others what he himself enjoys (clause 4). Those in solidarity with the blessed Abram will enjoy what he enjoys (clause 5), but those who oppose him will experience the opposite of blessing (clause 6). Finally, the blessing of Abram will spread throughout the world (clause 7).

Abram departs but cannot bring himself to sever all ties with his past. Although God told him to leave all behind, his nephew Lot comes with him.

Typically the Bible shows little interest in what happens on a journey, so Abram and his entourage arrive in Canaan seemingly as soon as they leave Haran. Once in the land they journey to what was probably a shrine associated with a particular tree at Shechem in the middle of the country. There YHWH, who had previously spoken to Abram without appearing to him, does appear to him and makes explicit the promise of the land. Lest the reader misunderstand the implications of this promise the narrator breaks into the story to remind us that the land is not uninhabited. There are Canaanites in the land. What implications this has for Israel are not made clear, but it seems that God, having chosen the family of Abram for blessing, will give them a land that already belongs to someone else. In response, Abram builds an altar. The patriarchs of this chosen family never participate in any existing cult, always building new altars or rebuilding old ones. Nor do they ever worship outside the Promised Land. It is not at all clear what is done with the altar, but there is no mention of sacrifice. He continues to travel through the land, going some twenty miles south to Bethel, where he builds another altar and invokes YHWH's name.

B. 12:9–13:1: YHWH ACTS TO FREE SARAI

The central part of this first section of the story of the first generation is the story of YHWH's action to free Sarai. Two different versions of the same type-scene appear later in the book: 20:1-18, where Abraham tries the same ruse with Abimelech, king of Gerar, and 26:1, 6-11, where Isaac and his wife Rebekah attempt the same ruse yet again with the same long-suffering Abimelech.

This story causes problems for commentators because of Abraham's apparent lie.[14] Was it a case of the end—the survival of both—justifying the means, since the alternative would have meant death for Abram at least? Was it a great lie that serves to underline Abram's fallible humanity? More probably, as Alter points out, the story provided an opportunity to create a series of parallels between the experiences of Abram and the later Israel of the Exodus. The danger to Abram's continued existence is Egypt and Egypt's Pharaoh, as will later be the case as well. In both cases, plagues bedevil the Egyptians.[15] Genesis 12:12 echoes Exodus 1:22; in both cases the life of females endangers the life of males.

> . . . they will say, "This is his wife"; then they will kill me, but they will let you live. (Gen 12:12)
>
> Every boy that is born to the Hebrews you shall throw into the Nile, but you shall let every girl live. (Exod 1:22)

However, the passage has a powerful theological message as well, one that is communicated by the use of an asymmetrical narrative structure. As is typical of such structures, the latter half is a reversal of the first half, so the relatively poor and endangered Abram and wife go down into Egypt, where Abram saves his life at the expense of his wife's freedom. Enriched, as he had predicted, they go up out of Egypt. His two predictions come true. However, what he had not predicted was God's free action, when YHWH afflicted Pharaoh with great plagues and he decided to let Sarai go.

This is the first instance we have in Genesis of what will become an important biblical motif. When a woman is trapped inside a building or a relationship, she is unfree and God acts to save her.[16] In this par-

---

[14] Genesis 20 clarifies the situation insofar as Sarah is identified as Abraham's half-sister. See further comments there.

[15] In Genesis, the author uses alliteration to good effect (although it is not clear in the NRSV), saying that "YHWH plagued Pharaoh with great plagues" *(waynaggaʿ yhwh ʾet-parʿōh nĕgāʾîm gĕdōlîm).*

[16] For an extended treatment of this motif see the Excursus "Outsiders: The Use of Location, Movement and Concentric Structure to Highlight the Autonomy of Female Characters (Genesis 38; 1 Samuel 25; 2 Samuel 11; 2 Samuel 13)."

ticular example, Sarai is defined by her identification as Abram's wife/woman.[17] This changes in 12:13 when Abram asks her to identify herself as his sister. It is further modified when she becomes simply "the woman" who is beautiful and taken into Pharaoh's house. Thus robbed of her individual identity, she is robbed of her freedom until God acts to free her. Pharaoh piles up all the names that have been given to her, wife, sister, wife, wife, suffixed with the Hebrew particle that denotes she belongs to Abram. She who was trapped in a mesh of relationship language was then trapped in a house without any identity, just a woman. Freed by God, she returns to her previous status. It should be noted that Abram, who did not act to free her but, rather, put her into servitude, will, in Genesis 14, act decisively to save his nephew Lot. After her release she is still identified in terms of her relationship to man but is, at least, no longer a nameless woman in a harem. Pharaoh's last words to Abram are a mocking reminder of the first words God spoke to him: *qaḥ wālēk*. So, now enriched by his lie, Abram, his still nameless and voiceless wife, and his nephew Lot return to the Promised Land.

C. 13:2-18: ABRAM AND LOT SETTLE

When Abram and his entourage return they realize that the land is unable to support the entire company if it remains together, especially since (as the frame break in 12:7 reminds us) they are hardly alone in the land. Abram, couching his request in polite terms, asks Lot to choose where he would like to live.

The remainder of the chapter is important in the ongoing characterization of Abram and Lot. Abram allows Lot to choose first and the latter is seduced by the relative lushness of the Jordan Valley. His point of view, both literal and interest, marks the remaining verses. Lot, confused creature that he is, thinks the Valley is like the garden of God, apparently not noticing or not understanding the presence of Sodom and Gomorrah. Abram generously allows him the first and superficially more attractive choice, and Lot uses it to set up his tent "near Sodom" (Gen 12:12). Three times the narrator mentions Sodom and its dangers. Much will follow from that fateful choice.

Pointedly, after Lot's departure, the land is explicitly promised to Abram, and he is asked by God to walk through it and take possession. Here we see another contrast between Abram and Lot. Lot raised his

---

[17] The word for "wife" and "woman" is the same in Hebrew.

eyes and saw only the morally dangerous valley with its cities. Abram raises his eyes (12:14) and has a comprehensive view of the whole land. There is no record of his response to God's speech, but fortified by this promise Abram settles near Hebron.

In the Tradition

Avivah Gottlieb Zornberg, working with texts as diverse as Midrash Rabbah and Henri Bergson's essay "The Idea of Nothing," considers the motivation for all human action. We experience an absence that compels us to seek a presence.

> "Every human action has its starting-point in a dissatisfaction, and thereby in a feeling of absence."
> The "human action" of Abram and Sarai begins in this absence. The midrash expresses this paradox of generation as follows: "Wherever it is written '*Ein la*—there is not,' there essentially is." A similar comment is made on the poignant leitmotif of absence in Lamentations: *ein la menaḥem*—"there is none to comfort her" (1:2); *ein av*—"we have become orphans, fatherless" (5:3). In the latter case, Midrash Rabbah refers to the paradigm of Esther, who is fatherless and motherless, and therefore is nurtured to a singular sensibility of absence and hope (Esther 2:7). What is suggested here in this first human experience of *ein* is a new and difficult mode of being and having: absence leads a man and a woman to travel far in search of a realization of self that comes effortlessly to those who preceded and surrounded them.[18]

D. 14:1-24: EVIL IS VANQUISHED BY ABRAM

Genesis 14 can be easily summarized. Lot, furthering his characterization as feckless and incompetent, is taken captive by four kings on campaign. Abram, leading his own men, puts them to flight, rescues Lot, and gets booty. He gives a tithe to Melchizedek, the priest-king of a city named Salem, and keeps nothing for himself. The story's narrative structure is similarly straightforward:

---

[18] Zornberg, *Genesis*, 74. Compare the words of Anatole France, "All changes, even the most longed for, are melancholy. For what we leave behind us is a part of ourselves. We must die to one life before we can enter another."

Exposition: 14:1-11
Inciting moment: 14:12
Turning point: 14:13
Resolution: 14:14-15
Conclusion: 14:16
Epilogue: 14:17-20

Most of the chapter is taken up with exposition (14:1-11), describing the actions and dispositions of the four attacking kings. Abram becomes involved when, in 14:12, his feckless nephew Lot is taken captive along with his possessions. Lot's fate moves in a more positive direction when Abram is alerted (14:13). Backed by a somewhat surprising 318 armed retainers—surprising since in the previous chapter he seems to be accompanied only by family, herdsmen, and livestock—Abram routs Lot's captors and drives them back beyond Damascus. Lot is rescued along with all of his goods and so the story concludes.

An epilogue introduces the hitherto unknown figure of Melchizedek, a king and priest who worships a god named El Elyon (ordinarily translated "God Most High"). Abram gives him a tithe but takes nothing at all for himself, rejecting the idea that he could be at all beholden to the king of Sodom who offers him part of the booty. However, in giving a tithe to the priest of El Elyon he identified his own god, YHWH, with this hitherto unknown deity.

In contrast to the stories that have gone before, this story is relatively secular. None of the kings or places named is readily identifiable. Abram appears not as the timid supplicant before Pharaoh but as a man of considerable power, with his own private armed force. Where did this story come from, and why is it here?

Historical-critical commentaries will inform the interested reader about the possible origin of this story. However, I would argue that whatever its origins it is placed here because it serves an important role in the ongoing characterization of Lot and Abram. The former appears typically passive and helpless. On the contrary, Abram, secure in the land promised to him, is decisive and courageous. The man of peace can fight if need be and so appears a man loyal to family, unconcerned with material reward, and disdainful of Sodom. Lot remains passive and helpless, as he will always be. Sodom, personified here in its king, appears as grasping and selfish. This will be important in our reading of Genesis 18–19. In short, Abram is already starting to be a blessing of peace, living up to his vocation by God.

It is the epilogue, with the appearance of Melchizedek, the god El Elyon, and the identification of YHWH with this God, that requires some comment. According to Robert Alter[19] El is the name of the sky god in the Canaanite pantheon, and Elyon is the name of an associated deity. The two are ordinary Hebrew words as well, simply meaning God Most High. In giving them this sense, i.e., reading them as ordinary Hebrew words used to name God, Abram is able to identify the God he worships with Melchizedek's deity.

The name Melchizedek means Righteous King, and it is this figure that has most interested the tradition. In Genesis 14 itself precious few details are provided about him. He offered some food, blessed Abraham, and was given a tithe. The latter two elements liken him to the priests of the much later Jerusalem Temple. To further that identification he is called a priest of God Most High. But how could he be a priest of a not yet existing Temple and a member of a hereditary priesthood whose founder, Levi, has not been born yet? The name appears only one other time in the Old Testament, in Psalm 110, and it is to that psalm that biblical readers looked for clarification. Psalm 110:1-4 will provide some context.

> [1]The LORD says to my lord, "Sit at my right hand until I make your enemies your footstool." [2]The LORD sends out from Zion your mighty scepter. Rule in the midst of your foes. [3]Your people will offer themselves willingly on the day you lead your forces on the holy mountains. From the womb of the morning, like dew, your youth will come to you. [4]The LORD has sworn and will not change his mind, "You are a priest forever according to the order of Melchizedek."

The difficulty lies in v. 4, which can also be understood to mean "You are a priest forever by my order, O Melchizedek." Thus God is the one who appointed Melchizedek to his priesthood, so he comes to be regarded as a heavenly or angelic figure.[20]

Another way of reading the problematic passage found favor among Christians. Psalm 110 was given a christological interpretation. The "lord" of v. 1 was understood to refer to Christ and, in accordance with the Greek translation of the Old Testament, the Septuagint, v. 3 was understood to refer to Christ's preexistence.[21] The priesthood, then,

---

[19] Alter, *Genesis*, 61.

[20] James L. Kugel, *Traditions of the Bible* (Cambridge, Mass.: Harvard University Press, 1998) 280.

[21] In the Septuagint, the psalm is numbered 109. Verse 3 reads, *meta sou hē archē en hēmera tēs dynameōs sou en tais lamprotēsin tōn hagiōn ek gastros pro heōsphorou exegennēsa se.* According to A. Pietersma this should be translated:

was Christ's and helped Christians understand how Christ's death could both be the final and ultimate sacrifice and he could be the one who offered the sacrifice. This is the understanding found in the New Testament Letter to the Hebrews, where Melchizedek figures prominently (Heb 5:1-10; 7:1-4, 26-28).[22] In short, the bread and wine he offered prefigured the Eucharist, and his non-levitical priesthood prefigured both the priesthood of Christ and the ministerial priesthood of the Catholic tradition of Christianity.[23]

E. 15:1-21: YHWH ACTS AND COMMITS HIMSELF

Genesis 15–17 forms the heart of the stories about the first generation of the family God has chosen. The two covenants—Genesis 15, God committing himself in the covenant between the pieces, and Genesis 17, Abraham committing himself and his male descendants in the covenant of circumcision—bracket Genesis 16. In this central story God commits himself to the weakest and those without support. It is as if God says, in Genesis 16, that regardless of his choice of Abram's family, the weak and the poor are central to God's concern.

The beginning and end of the first covenant are clearly marked. It is separated somewhat ambiguously and indeterminately from what precedes by the briefest of expositions in Genesis 15:1a, "After these things" (*ʾaḥar haddĕbārîm hāʾēlleh). The implication is that the events recounted in Genesis 15 happen some time, but not a terribly long time, after the events of Genesis 14. Genesis 16 begins with a notice of Sarai's childlessness, and so a new story begins.

Rule is yours on the day of your power
among the splendor of the holy ones.
From the womb, before the morning star, I brought you forth.

See Albert Pietersma, *A New English Translation of the Septuagint and the Other Greek Translations Traditionally Included under that Title. The Psalms* (New York: Oxford 2000)

[22] See Daniel Harrington, "Hebrews," *The New Collegeville Bible Commentary* (Collegeville: The Liturgical Press, forthcoming) for an excellent exposition of these texts.

[23] In the Rite for the Ordination of a Priest in the Roman Catholic Church, while the newly ordained priest is being vested in the stole and chasuble, garments appropriate to his ministry, Psalm 110 is chanted with the antiphon "Christ the Lord, a priest forever in the line of Melchizedek, offered bread and wine." International Commission for English in the Liturgy, "Ordination of a Priest," *Rites of the Catholic Church*, vol. 2 (New York: Pueblo, 1980) §28.

Genesis 15:1 plays on the ambiguity of the Hebrew word *dābār*, which can mean thing, event, or word. "After these things" *(děbārîm)*, "a word/thing/event *(dābār)* from Y<small>HWH</small>" came to Abram. The phrasing sounds like the prophets, whose oracles often begin, "the word *(dābār)* of Y<small>HWH</small> came to me." In this way the narrator associates Abram in the readers' minds with those later religious figures in Israel. The vision makes clear why Abram has remained safe from the depredations of raiders, in contrast to his nephew Lot, and provides a connection, however tenuous, with Genesis 14. Y<small>HWH</small> is Abram's protection, his shield.

The section is, for all of its brevity, rather more complicated than appears at first. There are two dialogues between God and Abram, the first at night and the second at sundown (we will consider the odd order of time references below). The first reiterates the promise of a son and the second the promise of land. Is this, then, one long and extended experience or two? It can be neatly described as a story in the analysis that follows, so it seems best to consider the whole as one indissoluble event where Abram is caught up in the presence of God.

> First dialogue (at night): the promise of a son
> > Exposition: 15:1a
> > Development: 15:1b-5
> > Turning point: 15:6
> Second dialogue (at sundown): the gift of land
> > Resolution: 15:7-16
> > Climax: 15:17
> > Conclusion: 15:18-20

Both dialogues have the same three elements. In both cases God's speech begins "I am . . . ," calling to mind the divine speech at Mount Sinai (Exod 20:1). Other elements of the theophany, fire and awe, will also serve to call to mind the later Sinai encounter, linking this covenant with that one. God makes a promise to Abram, who is apprehensive. God, by word and symbol, allays Abram's misgivings.

> a. Divine self-identification and promise (15:1 // 15:7)
> b. Abram's apprehension (15:2-3 // 15:8)
> c. Reassurance by word and symbolic action (15:4-5 // 15:9-21)

The author uses a variety of other narrative devices to good effect as well. In particular, the reader is invited to take part in Abram's experience, and so to identify with him, by the use of the word "behold" *(hinnēh)*.[24]

---

[24] This word is translated in the R<small>SV</small> either as "behold," or sometimes "lo," but has sadly and inexplicably been left out of the N<small>RSV</small>. Translating it might result in a

And behold *(wĕhinnēh)* the word of the lord came to him, "This man shall not be your heir; your own son shall be your heir." (15:4)

As the sun was going down, a deep sleep fell on Abram; and lo *(wĕhinnēh)*, a dread and great darkness fell upon him. (15:12)

When the sun had gone down and it was dark, behold *(wĕhinnēh)*, a smoking fire pot and a flaming torch passed between these pieces. (15:17)

The first instance, 15:4, places us inside Abram's mind as God responds to him. It seems that the vision with which the chapter begins is continuing, so that we experience it along with Abram. The second instance places us again within Abram's mind and allows us to experience with him the dread of God approaching. Finally, we see with him the fire pot and the brazier, which are the appearance of God. In these three instances, we zoom in on Abram. Otherwise the reader remains rather remote from the action that is unfolding.

With these narrative devices in mind, let us examine other elements of the tale. The first dialogue has a close but not immediate connection with the story of the four kings and Abram's refusal of booty. They will not bother him because of YHWH's protection. He will not require the proffered booty, because God is preparing a better reward for him. For the first time, Abram speaks back to God, complaining about his continued childlessness. His patience is wearing thin because, after all, he had left, wandered, been endangered, all without complaint. Abram plans, but has not yet acted on his plans, to adopt a faithful servant to provide for care when he and Sarai grow old. The repetition of "And Abram said" at the beginning of v. 3 implies a gap, that Abram had waited a bit for a reply from God, but none had been forthcoming. He repeats the same complaint, and God responds with another promise of descendants as numerous as the stars.[25]

---

version that sounds somewhat stilted or unlike contemporary English usage, but it would allow the reader dependent on translation to be aware of this important narrative device.

[25] In 13:16 the number of progeny was likened to the dust of the earth. This forms a nice comparison that brings to mind the opening chapters of Genesis. As God created heaven and earth, so Abram's progeny will be as numerous as the stars of the heavens and the dust of the earth. YHWH's creative aspect was evoked explicitly in chapter 14, where YHWH was identified with the creator god El Elyon (see 14:19, 22). As Creator of heaven and earth, YHWH can do the lesser thing of creating descendants for Abram.

The clear turning point of the story is 15:6: "And he believed the Lord, and he reckoned it to him as righteousness" *(wĕheˀĕmin bayhwh wayyaḥšĕbehā lô ṣĕdāqâ).* What is not clear is why Abram believed, what belief means in this context, why God reckoned this to him as righteousness, and what exactly righteousness means here.

One will look in vain here for a definition of faith. This is a fine example of the narrative device of showing rather than telling: the reader is shown, in Abram, what faith is. The root *ˀmn* means "to believe," "to have faith." It can be used in Qal, Niphal, or Hiphil. The root occurs numerous times in the Hiphil.

> The general sense of the word in the *Hipˁil* is "to be firmly set in/on something." With the preposition *b* it means to have confidence (1 Sam 29:12), and with the preposition *l* it seems to mean "to hold something to be true," "to believe" (Gen 45:26). Three significant passages occur with the *Hipˁil*. The first is Gen 15:6, "And [Abraham] believed in Yahweh and He counted it as righteousness in him." . . . In these instances the sense of *trusting* and having confidence is most noticeable.[26]

In Abram then we *see* what it means to have faith; it means to trust in relationship even when trust seems unwarranted. But why did he believe? Because he chose to trust. In the ongoing testing that is Abram's life, we begin to see growth and development in the character. The one who was only partially obedient in Genesis 12 has made progress. This progress is what God perceives and so credits him with righteousness.[27] Perhaps most concisely, "faith" can be seen to mean mutual trust. Abram trusts that Yhwh will give him progeny. In response Yhwh trusts that Abram will remain faithful to him. The moment makes most sense if, as this commentary argues, Abram is not seen as perfectly obedient at the moment of his call but as growing in his faith. This moment, then, marks a milestone in mutually developing trust. Abram allows himself to trust God, and God allows himself to trust Abram.

The second dialogue is thematically and structurally similar to the first. Again there is a word of divine self-identification, followed by Abram's apprehension and Yhwh's reassurance. The event recounted here occurs at sundown, so it cannot follow immediately upon the first

---

[26] Joseph P. Healey, *ABD*, s.v. "Faith (Old Testament)."

[27] This is one of the most widely used and significant concepts in the Bible (there are 523 uses of the root *ṣdq* in the OT), and no brief treatment here can do it justice. A good place to begin a serious study of the concept in both Testaments is J. J. Scullion's article "Righteousness (Old Testament)," *ABD* 5:724–36.

dialogue. One must assume that Abram is, through night and the following day, somehow caught up in God's presence.

Again, God's self-identification calls Sinai and the Exodus to mind. There, YHWH brings Israel out of Egypt, a place of slavery; here, YHWH brings Abram from Ur to the land where he will finally be at home. This event is, along with the Exodus, then, one of the pivots on which Israel's history will turn.

In response to Abram's question ("How am I to know . . . ?") YHWH makes a covenant with him, one that involves self-imprecation. Abram was instructed to secure certain animals and to prepare them as directed.[28] He is then overcome by *tardēmâ*, the deep sleep that is preparatory for meeting God (cf. 2:21). Dread and awe (which the reader also experiences by means of the shift to Abram's point of view in 15:12) accompanies the approach of this God, who then speaks to Abram and predicts the future of Abram's offspring. There will be three stages of suffering followed by three stages of redemption, as the following table makes clear. Again, aided by the shift in point of view, the reader experiences Abram's emotions.

Three stages of suffering (15:13)
1. Alienation from the Promised Land
2. Enslavement
3. Oppression
Three stages of redemption (15:14-16)
1. Judgment on oppressor
2. Exodus
3. Settlement of Promised Land[29]

The cutting of the covenant proper then ensues. The idea behind the rite is that the one who fails to deliver what has been contracted calls down upon himself the fate of the slaughtered animals. What is remarkable, and ultimately mysterious, about this experience is that it is God who calls down the potential curse upon himself, as he appears in symbols reminiscent of the theophanies at Sinai in Exodus 3 and 19. What this can mean is not at all clear, but it shows that God's commitment to the family of Abram has reached a new level. A seemingly small grammatical point shows how deeply felt God's commitment is.

---

[28] The Hebrew idiom "to make a covenant" is literally "to *cut* a covenant" and is reflected in the practice described here.

[29] The list of inhabitants in 15:19-21 does not accord with any known historical period. The list of peoples serves to remind Abram that the gift of the Land is made with full knowledge that others live there when the promise is made.

Moshe Weinfeld shrewdly observes that for the first time the divine promise—compare 12:1-3; 12:7; 13:14-17; 15:4-5—is stated with a perfective, not an imperfective verb—that is, as an action that can be considered already completed. This small grammatical maneuver catches up a large narrative pattern in the Abraham stories: the promise becomes more and more definite as it seems progressively more implausible to the aged patriarch, until Isaac is born.[30]

X. 16:1-15: YHWH SAVES HAGAR AND HER CHILD

Despite its centrality to the story of the first generation of God's chosen family, the story of Hagar is told in a simple and straightforward fashion without recourse to elaborate structuring mechanisms. It is divided into three sections, Hagar with Abram's household (16:1-6), Hagar with YHWH in the desert (16:7-14), and a conclusion (16:15-16). Similarly, the plot of Genesis 16 is easy to describe, as the following chart makes clear:

Section 1: Hagar with Abram's Household (16:1-6)
  Exposition: 16:1
  Development: 16:2-5
  Turning point: 16:6
Section 2: Hagar with YHWH in the Desert (16:7-14): Resolution
Section 3: Conclusion (16:15-16)

The exposition sets the scene in a very subtle fashion. Sarai is no longer described as unable to have children (compare Gen 11:30, "Now Sarai was barren; she had no child"—*wattĕhî śāray ʿăqārâ ʾên lâh wālād*). More ambiguously, the reader is simply told that she—literally—had not borne to him [children] (*wĕśāray ʾēšet ʾabrām lōʾ yālĕdâ lô*, 16:1). There seems to be a hint there that what follows is neither necessary nor correct. And there are other hints as well that the actions of Abram and Sarai are not what God willed. In the preceding chapter, God had been relatively talkative with Abram. In this chapter, God is silent, except for the extended dialogue with Hagar. When had God been silent before? When humanity acts in a way contrary to God's will, e.g., in Genesis 3, when the Man and the Woman transgressed God's command, and in Genesis 4, when Cain brought his brother into the field.

---

[30] Alter, *Genesis*, 66.

In this way, our author sets a scene that renders what follows as both unnecessary and unwilled by God.

There are other actors in this story, principally of course Hagar, and she too is introduced right at the beginning and carefully characterized. Her name is possibly related to the Hebrew verb "to dwell" (*gwr*) and could mean something like the Fugitive or the Foreign Girl. She is a slave who belongs to Sarai[31] as her property. In the first verse then we have described for us the two poles of social reality; Sarai is the wealthy wife of a powerful man, and Hagar the essentially nameless piece of property. The reader will be well advised to see to whom God chooses to speak.

The story begins to develop when Sarai laments her God-caused childlessness to her husband. This is the first time that the reader has heard her voice, and her suggestion is not entirely unreasonable. After all, she had not been named in the covenantal promise, so maybe some other mother was intended. Her words contain a pun which depends on the similarity in sound between the verb "to build" *bnh* and the word "son" *bn*. She tells her husband to take Hagar so that she (Sarai) might be "built-up/sonned" through her. Quite pointedly, Abram listens to her voice (not God's), and that will get him into trouble. God is conspicuously absent from these machinations. Yet the arrangement described here was apparently a commonplace in the ancient Near East. What is remarkable is that Abram had not previously taken another wife, albeit of secondary status, to provide himself with an heir. This is taken by some to indicate a special bond of affection between Abram and Sarai.

Verse 3 begins with a frame-break, which refers to the length of time Abram had already lived in the Promised Land. That ten years had already passed gives us an insight into the sense of increased anxiety and frustration on the part of Abram and Sarai as the couple, old when we first met them, continue to age beyond a point where one might expect them to bear. It places this event in the real world, unlike the previous covenant, which happened almost outside of time; it also recalls the ten generations from Adam to Noah and the ten generations from

---

[31] *šipḥâ* is sometimes translated "maidservant," which gives a rather more genteel tone to her status than the text warrants. Once Hagar becomes Abram's "wife," (16:3, *ʾiššâ*, literally, "woman"), her social status should rise from being Sarai's *šipḥâ* to being Abram's *ʾāmâ* ("maid," or "concubine"). Yet throughout the chapter she continues to be referred to, by Sarai, by Abram, and even by the angel, as Sarai's *šipḥâ*. By contrast, in chapter 21, where she is definitively wronged by being sent away from Abraham's household, the narrator regularly reminds us of the status she deserves by calling her Abraham's *ʾāmâ*. Once she has left Abraham's family entirely, neither term is applied to her.

Noah to Babel. The gap in time also makes clear to the reader that Abram is not acting out of an uncontrollable passion but at Sarai's insistence. It is important to note that Hagar's status changes and that she is referred to in v. 3 as Abram's wife (literally, his "woman").

Unlike Sarai, Hagar conceives immediately and is rude to her former mistress. In anger (although the entire messy situation is her own fault), Sarai demands action from Abram. Note that Hagar loses her name at this point. In line with the "outsider" motif Hagar has become trapped in the tent in which Abram took her to his bed and trapped in her status. She is just a slave again, although she had been a wife. Trapped, God will free her.

And so we reach the turning point of the story. Abram is strangely passive and refuses to become involved (in stark contrast to his reaction to Lot's abduction). Sarai deals harshly with "her" (now Hagar is simply a feminine suffix), so she flees *(brḥ)*. The root *ʿnh* means "to humble," "to mishandle," "to afflict." It is used to describe Israel's condition in Egypt before the Exodus (Exod 1:11-12),[32] and Israel is expressly forbidden to act in this fashion in Exodus 22:21-23.

> You shall not wrong or oppress a resident alien, for you were aliens in the land of Egypt. You shall not abuse any widow or orphan. If you do abuse them, when they cry out to me, I will surely heed their cry.

Hagar is now outside of Abram's household. God's angel speaks to her and calls her by name and station. Her world (and that this story is set in the real world is underlined by the naming of the spring where the conversation takes place) cannot yet afford her true freedom. There is also an important shift in point of view from that of Sarai to that of the angel under whose gaze the scene in the desert unfolds.[33] But who is the angel?

Carol Newsom, writing in *ABD,* offers such a fine analysis of this passage and the question that it is worth quoting her at some length:

> In Gen 16:7, for example, when Hagar has run away from Sarai's cruel treatment, the text says that "a *malʾāk yhwh* found her by a well in the wilderness." The two converse and the narrator again identifies the one who speaks with Hagar as a *"malʾāk yhwh"* in vv. 9, 10, and 11. But the words which the *malʾāk yhwh* speaks in v 10 ("I will multiply your de-

---

[32] Hagar's situation is described in language that is identical to Israel's in Egypt. Israel *fled (brḥ,* Exod 14:5), like Hagar to the wilderness.

[33] The story shows an interesting series of shifts in point of view: Sarai (16:1-4a, 5-6); Hagar (16:4b, 13); the angel (16:7-12); the narrator (16:14-16).

scendants . . .") appear rather to be the first person speech of Yahweh himself. In the following verse, however, the *mal'āk yhwh* again speaks of Yahweh in the third person. Yet v 13 begins "Hagar called the name of Yahweh who spoke with her 'You are a God of seeing' . . ." The end of the verse is textually corrupt but is probably to be translated "I have indeed seen God after He saw me." The apparent interchangeability of the *mal'āk yhwh* and Yahweh cannot be resolved by assuming a clumsy merging of two traditional stories. The same ambiguity occurs in many narratives (e.g. Gen 21:15-21; 22:11-12; 31:11-13; Exod 3:2-6; Judg 6:11-24). Numerous suggestions have been put forward to account for this peculiar feature (e.g. that the *mal'āk yhwh* is a sort of hypostasis of the deity; that a functional identity exists between messenger and sender; that the phrase *mal'āk yhwh* is a late pious interpolation; that the alternation between Yahweh and *mal'āk yhwh* has to do with point of view; etc.). . . . But the explanation that seems most likely is that the interchange between Yahweh and *mal'āk yhwh* in various texts is an expression of a tension or paradox: Yahweh's authority and presence in these encounters is to be affirmed, but yet it is not possible for human beings to have an unmediated encounter with God. . . . Hagar is correct—she has seen God. But the narrator is also correct that the one who appeared to her was a *mal'āk yhwh*. The unresolved ambiguity in the narrative allows the reader to experience the paradox.[34]

The son Hagar is to bear will have a name that recalls this event, for she is to name him Ishmael ("God hears"). His wild freedom[35] will be a consolation for the years when she knew only harsh servitude. Hagar too will be the mother of innumerable progeny.

It is to be assumed that Hagar returned to Abram's household and that, like Tamar in Genesis 38, she once again took up the limited role her society provided for her. Once there she bore her son and Abram named him, thereby legitimating him. The final note of the story returns to Abram's age, so as to remind us of the pressing passage of time. Genesis 17 will take up his story again, but Genesis 16 is Hagar's chapter, and she, in a fiercely paradoxical fashion, is central to what seems otherwise to be Abram and Sarai's story. Power and its abuse are never central to God's story. A woman like Hagar is, for "He raises up the poor from the dust; he lifts the needy from the ash heap, to make them sit with princes and inherit a seat of honor" (1 Sam 2:8).

The simplest meaning of the name that Hagar gives to the being she encountered is "God Who Sees Me." This is a fitting name, for prior to this moment it seems that no one has ever seen her. Essentially

---

[34] *ABD*, s.v. "Angels."
[35] Apparently the wild ass or onager cannot be domesticated.

nameless, she was simply a tool to create a son. It was only God who saw her. Hagar's position of privilege can hardly be overestimated. Like Abram she received a promise of progeny. Like Israel she underwent an Exodus towards freedom. Like Moses she sees God. And why? Because God is justice, and she stands for those for whom God has special concern, the foreigner, the orphan, and the widow.[36]

This story ends with the most prosaic of notices, the location of the well at which the event took place. This serves to root the story once again in the real world and remind us readers that these people are not merely characters in a story and that the world described here is not merely a narrative construct. In this real world in which we live, this is how God acts.

E'. 17:1-26: ABRAM ACTS AND COMMITS HIMSELF

Bracketing the story of Hagar are the two stories of covenant making between Abram and YHWH. Whereas in Genesis 15 YHWH acted to commit himself, here God asks for a like commitment from Abram, and the promises made so often become concrete. In the interim thirteen years have passed. We have absolutely no idea what happened during that time, but Abram and Sarai are still childless as a couple.

Suddenly, without any warning, Abram experiences a series of revelations. The old promise of a son is reaffirmed but this time with a date. Abram and Sarai are given new names and Abraham is ordered to circumcise himself and to institute the practice for all his descendants.

> [W]e must address the really remarkable amount of repetition in the first fourteen verses. The term *bᵉrît* "promise, covenant-sign" appears ten times. The reciprocal aspect of covenant, the *betweenness*, appears four times; the single-vector aspect of *bᵉrît*, as from God to man or from man to God . . . appears almost a dozen times. Abraham, as the individual with whom God is establishing His pact, is featured seven times; five times the covenant is with both Abraham and his posterity. The emphasis on posterity appears eleven times: five times under the rubric *ʾaḥărey*, three times under the rubric *lᵉdōrōt*, and three times under *ʿôlām*.[37]

---

[36] Hagar stands, in fact, for all three groups. As an Egyptian in Abram's household, she represents the alien. Bereft of the support and refuge provided by one's extended family, she represents the orphan. Repudiated by her "man" and driven from his home (see ch. 21), she is effectively a widow. (I am grateful to Jerome T. Walsh for this suggestion.)

[37] Brichto, *Names of God*, 226; italics original.

The issue of the chapter, circumcision as the outward sign of an individual's acceptance of the obligations of the covenant between God and the progeny of Abraham, is presented in the first half. In the second half there is a blessing for Sarai, now Sarah, a prediction of the future of Ishmael and of the birth of Isaac. The result of this analysis is that the story is seen to fall into four parts, the second two in parallel to the first two.

A. Abraham, the father of nations and kings (vv. 1-8)
B. The law of circumcision set forth (vv. 9-14)
A'. Sarah, the mother of nations and kings (vv. 15-22)
B'. The law of circumcision carried out (vv. 23-27)

The story is almost entirely dialogue, so it is important to pay careful attention to what elements of narration are found in it. In the narration we are given a number of details, Abram's age, that he fell on his face twice (vv. 3, 17), and that he laughed on the second occasion. The details of circumcision follow in vv. 22ff.

Yet the dialogue also contains important details. Abraham still has doubts but keeps them to himself in a very rare example of interior monologue (v. 17b). He speaks to God only once (v. 18) when he pleads for Ishmael.

A plot for the story can be described in this fashion:

Exposition: 17:1a
Development: 17:1b-16
Turning point: 17:17-18
Resolution: 17:19-22
Conclusion: 17:23-27

The exposition is as brief as possible. The simple mention of Abram's age tells us that thirteen years have passed since the events recounted in Genesis 16, but also hints to the reader that, whatever else Abram, Sarai, Hagar, and Ishmael have been doing in the interim, tension and anxiety must have increased as well. We realize also, without needing to be told, that Ishmael will now be thirteen years old, a young man to whom Abram, sonless for so long although desiring a son, must necessarily have grown attached. The relationship between Hagar and Sarai, never serene, must also have grown more complicated with the passing of years and the maturation of Hagar's son. Against the backdrop of all of this drama, the story of the covenant of circumcision begins.

Another name for God, the third along with YHWH and El Elyon, is introduced as the story unfolds. The meaning of *ʾēl šadday* is not at all clear. It appears in parallel with Elyon in a number of texts (Num 24:16; Ps 91:1; and Gen 49:25). In both the Septuagint and the Vulgate[38] it was translated as "Almighty," a usage that has continued in modern translations, if only for want of one that is more precise. Whatever the name actually meant etymologically, the text that best enlightens it for us is Exodus 6:3:

> I appeared to Abraham, Isaac, and Jacob as God Almighty, but by my name "The LORD" I did not make myself known to them.
>
> *wā'ērā' 'el-'abrāhām 'el-yiṣḥāq wě'el-ya'ăqōb bě'ēl šadday ûšěmî yhwh lō' nôda'tî lāhem.*

The purpose of the text from Exodus is to identify the experience of Israel's ancestors with that of the generation that would experience the Exodus. The revelation of the name YHWH does not invalidate prior religious experience, and hence the religious experience of the Hebrew people and their ancestors prior to the revelation of God's name in Exodus 3 remains their heritage. Abraham and those descended from him had a legitimate knowledge of God. It is as though God said to Moses, "They called me *'ēl šadday,* and you call me YHWH, but I am and have always been the same God."[39]

God tells Abram to walk before him, as an obedient subject before his king, and to be blameless *(tāmîm).* In this way, the covenant between king and subject is given a moral content and objective, and a clear contrast is made with Noah, the only other character in the book to whom this word is applied. Noah was said to be blameless only among his generation, i.e., his blamelessness was only relative to the rest of the world's population. Abram, on the contrary, is to be blameless in some absolute fashion. Abram responds with awe and submission, and the promise of fatherhood is reiterated.

So far, none of this is startlingly new, and one might wonder what Abram, whose interior thoughts are related later in the chapter, was thinking at this point. But the change in name is new. In reality "Abram" and "Abraham" are simply variants of the same name, the second a slightly longer form than the first, but this story invests the change with great significance.[40] Throughout the books, names have carried a

---

[38] To be precise, the LXX translates the term merely as *ho theos sou* ("your God") in Gen 7:1. The VG uses *"deus omnipotens,"* i.e., "Almighty God."

[39] See Martin Rose, *ABD,* s.v. "Names of God."

[40] Abram is told by God that he will be father to a multitude (or mass) of nations *'ab hămôn gôyim.* Why the name Abraham? How does "Abraham" convey that

person's meaning. Adam was Humanity and Eve became the Mother of the Living. Abel was just an evanescent presence and Cain the first human creation. Seth was a replacement. Noah gave comfort. And so forth. The change in name here is intended to convey a real change in Abram's identity. So, just as his people is to be made great, his name is "made great," i.e., lengthened.[41]

The promise Abraham has been hearing since Genesis 12, and the divine commitment to fulfilling that covenant, which God made in Genesis 15 on the basis of the trust Abram expressed, now demand an active response from Abraham. God commands circumcision for all the males in Abraham's family and possession. This is the first commandment specifically made to this people, and it involves a practice that was neither invented by them nor native to them.

Abraham clearly knows what circumcision is and needs no instruction on the performance of the rite, as would be expected given the time and place in which he lived. Even in Israel its antiquity is so great that it comes to be associated with the founding father. Most Semites (with the exclusion of Babylon and Assyria) were accustomed to it, and in Egypt at least the priests were circumcised. According to Exodus 4:25 a stone knife was used even later in Mosaic times, long after such an implement would have been an anachronism in Israel. Only the circumcised could participate in the Passover sacrifice before the Exodus (Exod 12:43-48), and only those circumcised were regarded as suitable mates for Israelite women (Gen 34:14-17). As this final example shows, the practice was almost always associated with puberty and preparation for marriage. Israel adopted the custom but transformed it in a fundamental way. Moving it to the eighth day after birth deprived it of its connection with rites of passage into puberty and marriage. It became a mnemonic sign of an individual's relation to the covenant people and his desire (or more precisely the desire of his parents for him) to be so related.[42]

---

meaning better than "Abram"? Nahum Sarna explains that Abraham (*ʾBRHM* in the consonantal writing system used in Hebrew) can be read as a sort of acronym for "Father of a Multitude of Nations" (*ʾaBiR Hamon goyiM*, literally, "Mighty One [of a] multitude [or, mass] [of] peoples"). See *Genesis, The JPS Torah Commentary* (Philadelphia: Jewish Publication Society, 1989) 124. To change a name, whether through marriage or religious profession, is, then or now, a powerful means of adopting a new identity.

[41] With the exception of Isaac, whose name was given him by God, the fathers of this family all have a change of name; Abram becomes Abraham, Jacob becomes Israel and Joseph becomes Zaphenath-paneah (Gen 41:45).

[42] Robert G. Hall, *ABD*, s.v. "Circumcision."

Sarai is given a blessing and a new name, Sarah, as well. Like Abraham's, this is really the same name in a slightly different version, and no explanation of its meaning is given.[43] What is new is that God tells Abraham explicitly that Sarah is to be the mother of the covenant-continuing son and so blesses her with a blessing that will allow her to become mother of nations and of kings of different peoples.

What will Abraham do? It is upon his response that the success of God's attempt to save humanity rests. So it is correct, in our analysis of the plot, to see that development continues until this point. So far all we have are words from God, familiar enough in the main, which we have heard many times. Abraham has heard these or similar promises for a long time already. He has partially obeyed, but then he brought Lot with him (Genesis 12); he has been moved to trust (Genesis 15) but then he did not trust, took matters into his own hands, and listened to a voice other than God's, and Ishmael was born. So tension rises to this point as we wait to see what Abraham will do.

So the key verses, on which all turns and which are remarkable for their subtle use of repetition and allusion, are reached in vv. 17-18.

> Then Abraham fell on his face and laughed, and said to himself, "Can a child be born to a man who is a hundred years old? Can Sarah, who is ninety years old, bear a child?" And Abraham said to [the] God, "O that Ishmael might live in your sight!"
>
> *wayyippōl ʾabrāhām ʿal-pānāyw wayyiṣḥāq wayyōʾmer bĕlibbô hallĕben mēʾâ-šānâ yiwwālēd wĕʾim-śārâ hăbat-tišʿîm šānâ tēlēd; wayyōʾmer ʾabrāhām ʾel-hāʾĕlōhîm lû yišmāʿēʾl yihyeh lĕpāneykā.*

But Abraham had already fallen on his face in 17:3 and, since he never rose from that position, we must assume that he is still prostrate before God. What the author is doing is drawing our attention to Abraham's persistent only-near obedience. In 17:1-2, he was told:

> When Abram was ninety-nine years old, the LORD appeared to Abram, and said to him, "I am God Almighty; walk before me [literally, 'before my face'], and be blameless. And I will make my covenant between me and you, and will make you exceedingly numerous."
>
> *wayhî ʾabrām ben-tišʿîm šānâ wĕtēšaʿ šānîm wayyērāʾ yhwh ʾel-ʾabrām wayyōʾmer ʾēlāyw ʾănî-ʾēl šadday hithallēk lĕpānay wehyēh tāmîm; wĕʾettĕnâ bĕrîtî bênî ûbênekā wĕʾarbeh ʾōtĕkā bimʾōd mĕʾōd.*

---

[43] Both names mean "Princess." Sarai differs from Sarah only in having an older feminine ending.

How did then Abram respond to God's command to face him and be blameless? In 17:3, "He fell on his face, so God spoke to him [again] saying . . ." *(wayyippōl ʾabrām ʿal-pānāyw waydabbēr ʾittô ʾĕlōhîm lēʾmōr).* In other words, when God told Abram to face him he—Abram—did not listen, did not walk in God's way. His posture should bespeak worshipful obedience. Instead it bespeaks the opposite. In 17:17-18, Abraham is still in that posture of not listening to the God who is addressing him. He is distracted, laughing to himself about the silly things this divinity says to him. The narrator indicates that Abraham is not really attending to God of the covenant in 17:18 when the definite article *(hā)* is included before the word *ʾĕlōhîm.* The latter, when used without the definite article, is a proper name for God in Hebrew just as in English. However when the definite article is used it becomes simply a generic word for any deity or divinity. YHWH told Abram to face up to him and act obediently (17:1-2), but Abram did not (17:2), still preferring seemingly pious near-obedience. God speaks to him again (17:3b-16), and still Abraham does not listen. So whomever Abraham thinks he is talking to, the narrator tells us readers, it is not the covenant God but simply Abraham's mistaken notion of who *the* god he relates to might be. Abraham cannot be bothered to listen to God; Abraham is too busy talking to himself.

In his lack of trust he refuses God's offer of a future contrary to Abraham's will and suggests that the appropriate posture between the two be that God walk before him, be obedient to him, and do his will. All of this reflects the thirteen years of silence during which Abram would have come to think of Ishmael as his son, indeed the only son he was ever likely to have, and would have come to love him.

How will this be resolved? Will God obey Abraham or will Abraham obey God? God's nature as savior is clear in the future he describes for Ishmael; he too will sire twelve tribes. But the child of promise will be Isaac/Laughter, to be borne in a year by the elderly Sarah. God does not wait for a reply: "When he finished speaking to him, God[44] went up from Abraham" (AT, *waykal lĕdabbēr ʾittô wayyaʿal ʾĕlōhîm mēʿal ʾabrāhām).* This creates yet another contrast with Genesis 15. There God and Abram were both present when God committed himself in the covenant between the pieces. Here God departs and leaves Abraham to obey (or not) in his absence. In that divine absence, Abraham obeys and circumcises all the males in his household.

---

[44] Without the definite article, to indicate that it is really God and not Abraham's imagination of what the divinity might be like who is being spoken of here.

The skillful use of repetition has revived an important theme in the narratives about this first generation: how obedient they are, or are not, to the divine vocation given them. In this chapter we see God acting in a manner consistent with his character since the beginning of the book. God saves. Here God saves Abraham from his own persistent near-obedience. He saves Ishmael from the ignominy of becoming no longer beloved, a second or disinherited son. He promises to save Sarah from her childlessness.

The family, in the person of Abraham, needs further testing to help them to obedience. Sarah's opinion needs to be heard about the son still to be born to her. We are prepared for Genesis 18–19 and are curious whether Abraham will walk before God and be perfect. Our hopes are not high when, in the very next verse, we read that Abraham is sitting in the opening of his tent.

D'. 18:1–19:29: Evil Is Vanquished for Abraham's Sake

C'. 19:30-38: Lot Settles

At the end of one of his cases, "The Naval Treaty," Sherlock Holmes says:

> The principal difficulty in your case . . . lay in the fact of there being too much evidence. What was vital was overlaid and hidden by what was irrelevant. Of all the facts which were presented to us we had to pick just those which we deemed to be essential, and then piece them together in their order so as to reconstruct this very remarkable chain of events.[45]

Sherlock Holmes and his case may seem far removed from the Jordan Plain and the fate of Sodom. But there is an affinity between the two situations. An overabundance of detail has obscured what is essential and important about both narratives. In this case, investigations concerning the nature of the sin of Sodom have tended to blur the reality that the sexual sin is only one of several sins of Sodom and that it is a relatively minor element of the text. These two chapters are about the characters Abraham and Lot and YHWH.[46] The reader sees Abraham

---

[45] Arthur Conan Doyle, "The Naval Treaty," in *The Memoirs of Sherlock Holmes* (London: Penguin Books, 1950) 233.

[46] Perhaps the most thorough study of this section of Genesis to appear recently is the very fine monograph by Robert Ignatius Letellier, *Day in Mamre, Night in Sodom: Abraham and Lot in Genesis 18 & 19* (E. J. Brill: Leiden, 1995).

more clearly because he is viewed in comparison to Lot and YHWH. The reader comes to understand these characters better because each of them is viewed against the backdrop of other characters' behavior. None of them stands in isolation, none of them has meaning in isolation. Until that essential foundation is accepted, all exegesis of this section must go awry.

Delimitation of the Text. While there is no particular difficulty in discerning the end of this block of narrative at 20:1, given the change of scene and character involved at that point as Abraham transfers to Gerar, the beginning is rather more problematic. The difficulty is twofold. The setting appears to be the same as that of Genesis 17, the desert tent of Abraham. At least some of the characters are the same, Abraham and his wife Sarah. Indeed, the topic of discussion, the prediction of the birth of a son for Abraham and Sarah is the same as in the preceding scene. Abraham, the principal figure of Genesis 18, is introduced in the first verse of the chapter simply by the pronoun "him," without an explicit mention of his name. The same theme, same setting, same characters, and lack of explicit introduction would seem to indicate that at least the opening scenes of Genesis 18 are a continuation of Genesis 17. To be sure, critics have long pointed out that the latter is part of the Priestly document, while the chapters at hand are largely the work of the Yahwist. But according to their final form, the level with which we are concerned here, the two seem to merge together almost imperceptibly.

A number of schemes have been proposed in order to deal with the quandary. Classic Jewish exegetes, in the persons of the Rashbam and the Rambam, taught that 18:1 was merely the title of the following story. The Ramban, approaching the text from another angle, discounts the importance of the chapter division and sees 17 and 18 as parts of a continuous story.[47] This accounts for the lack of identification for Abraham.

---

[47] Many classical Jewish scholars are known traditionally by acronyms. Rabbi Solomon bar Isaac is known as RaSHI; he lived at Troyes in France from 1040 to 1105, and is renowned for his works on biblical and Talmudic interpretation, Hebrew grammar, and Jewish Law. Abraham ben Meir is known as Ibn Ezra. He was born in Spain in 1089 and traveled widely before his death in 1164. He was a scholar who wrote on Hebrew grammar, biblical interpretation, philosophy, and astronomy as well as ethics and poetry. Rabbi Moses ben Maimon, or Maimonides, is known as RaMBaM. He was born in Cordoba in Spain in 1135 and spent much of his life in Egypt, where he died in 1204. He was a physician but also the most influential Jewish writer of the Middle Ages, contributing works on biblical and legal interpretation and ethics. Rabbi Samuel ben Meir is known as RaSHBaM. He was the grandson and student of Rashi and lived from 1083 to 1174. Like his grandfather he commented on biblical and legal texts.

The theophany to Abraham, described in 18:1a is not, then, the beginning of a new narrative block but rather the conclusion of the one already begun. Two different incidents are being described, according to this way of analyzing the text. In the first, the circumcision of Abraham is concluded by a visitation from YHWH, described in 18:1a ("YHWH appeared to him by the oaks of Mamre"). Subsequently, starting in 18:1b, the second incident begins with the arrival of the three visitors. This approach completely avoids one of the chief enigmas of the text as it is ordinarily read, i.e., the question of the relationship between YHWH, the three men of Genesis 18, and the two angels of Genesis 19.[48]

It seems simpler, and more true to the text, to say that 18:1 introduces a new block of narrative. It is clearly not entirely separate from what precedes; Abraham need not be reintroduced to readers who know who is meant. But that 18 and 19 form a coherent, relatively self-contained whole may be demonstrated in a variety of fashions.

Genesis 18 and 19 are neatly framed by a reference to Abraham's perceptual point of view. In 18:2 his point of view is established by the typically Hebrew use of "and behold" *(wĕhinnēh)*. The reader, placed inside the mind of Abraham with this technique, looks out through his eyes and sees the three men who have without warning materialized in front of him. Similarly, in the only other use of this particular technique in these chapters, the same word occurs in 19:28 to invoke Abraham's perceptual point of view again. In this latter instance, Abraham returns to the place from which he and YHWH had looked over the Plain to observe Sodom. Once again, the reader is placed inside Abraham's mind and looks with him over the destruction that has taken place in the intervening hours. In this fashion, the arrival, the discussion, the activity, and the aftermath of the three visitors has taken place under the gaze of Abraham.

---

[48] This has proved to be an insoluble riddle to scholars throughout the centuries. In addition to the solution offered here, that there is no problem because there were two visits, a host of others have been proposed. The three were angels sent with separate tasks, e.g., to minister to Abraham as he recovered from his circumcision, to judge Sodom, and so forth. The three were YHWH and two attendant angels. Difficulties are as numerous as solutions. So to the last mentioned solution it has been countered that it would not be dignified for YHWH and attendants to be lumped together. It is perhaps best to think, with von Rad, that there is no rational and neat solution to the question. Somehow YHWH is present in all three of the visitors. (Gerhard von Rad, *Genesis* [Philadelphia: Westminster, 1972] 204). What is probably most important about the number three is that in Genesis 19 it becomes two. Although YHWH is present in the three, the narrator wants the reader to be very certain that YHWH never entered the sinful city but is waiting to destroy it with fire and brimstone from the sky.

There is also a series of time references within these two chapters that, while internally specific in referring to this particular sequence of events, is vague with reference to their external context in Genesis 17 and 20. All the action described here takes place within an eighteen-hour period. Abraham is encountered at noon (18:1). The angels arrive at Sodom in the evening (19:1), where they remain until morning of the next day (19:15). By the time they reach Zoar with the reluctant Lot and his company, dawn has arrived (19:23). Early the same morning Abraham returns to his lookout to see what has transpired during the night (19:27-28). In contrast to this fairly tight system of internal time references, the chapter division between Genesis 17–18 makes no indication as to what amount of time may have passed between Abraham's circumcision of Ishmael and the men of his household and Abraham's midday repose. Nor is there, in the division between Genesis 19–20, any indication of the passage of time. Internally tightly bound, and only loosely placed in context, these two chapters stand together.[49]

Yet there is more to the argument, which will also tie 19:30-38 more firmly to this arrangement. In Genesis 18–19 the characters move, first toward, and then away from, Sodom. The men arrive in 18:2, and, having rested with Abraham and promised the birth of a son a year hence, they set out for Sodom, toward which they have looked, accompanied part of the way by Abraham (18:16, 22). Abraham draws near to YHWH as they discuss the fate of the righteous minority among a wicked majority. At the end of this dialogue (18:33), YHWH leaves and Abraham returns to his tent. Where YHWH goes is not revealed to the reader, arousing curiosity and raising the level of tension.

The two angels arrive that evening at Sodom (19:1), from which they depart the following morning (19:16f). Lot will accompany them only as far from the city as Zoar (19:21). Zoar proving unsatisfactory to him, he continues away from Sodom to dwell in a cave (19:30), where he remains. Movement toward and away from Sodom defines the section. Reinforcing this general movement, and concluding the piece, is the return of Abraham on the morning subsequent to his visitation to the place at which he had challenged YHWH's justice.

However, there is one final bit of narrative technique that, although extremely subtle, makes this whole section snap neatly shut. In 18:19 YHWH decides to disclose his intentions to Abraham. After all, Abraham has been known by him precisely so that he may "observe the way of YHWH." As the two angels arrive at Sodom, Lot beseeches them to turn aside to his house, that they may return to "their way" early the next

---

[49] See Walsh, *Style and Structure*, 180–1.

morning. Early the next morning (19:27) Abraham returns and observes what YHWH has done, observes the "way" YHWH has of dealing with injustice. Finally, the daughters of Lot (19:31) decide to lie with their father because no one will come in to them "in the way of all the earth." The author plays most cleverly in these instances on the ambiguity of the Hebrew word "way" *(derek)*. To observe "the way of YHWH" is to act with justice. Yet YHWH's way also leads to Sodom, where, as Abraham observes from the hilltop, the punishment of injustice is severe. Having learned little from their experience, the daughters of Lot still seek the way of all the earth rather than the way of YHWH.

Characters, point of view, time, motion, and theme all serve to bind Genesis 18–19 tightly together. These elements of the narrative are dependent on a variety of literary elements of the text. Another line may be developed from a purely theoretical point of view. Fundamental to the traditional understanding of narrative is that there be a causal connection between its constituent scenes. Where causality obtains, there is narrative. Where causality fails, a new narrative begins. Between the scenes of Genesis 18–19, there is most evidently a chain of causality. Because Abraham sees the men approach, he offers them hospitality. Having been grandly feted, they offer a gift in return before their departure. Having looked upon Sodom, YHWH broaches the purpose of this visit to Abraham and so forth. There is, though, no such connection between the circumcisions with which Genesis 17 concludes and the action in Genesis 18. Nor is there any necessary causal connection between the conclusion of Genesis 19 and Abraham's journey toward the Negeb with which Genesis 20 begins. This tight chain of causality, divorced from its surroundings, further heightens the coherence of the two chapters. Some indications have already been given as to the movement of plot in these chapters, but a more detailed consideration will follow.

The Plot.

Panel A. With Abraham, Where All Is as It Should Be
Exposition: 18:1
Development: 18:2-32
    First scene: 18:2-15: hospitality (v. 16: "look toward Sodom")
    Second scene: 18:17-21: YHWH's quandary (v. 22: "went toward Sodom")
    Third scene: 18:23-32: Abraham's quandary
Turning point 18:33: YHWH and Abraham part

Panel B. With Lot, Where All Is Amiss
Resolution: 19:1-21
    First scene: 19:1-3: hospitality

Second scene: 19:4-11: the sin of Sodom
Third scene: 19:12-15: Lot dithers
Fourth scene: 19:16-22a: escape
  (etiological frame break: 19:22b)
Fifth scene: 19:23-26: destruction
Conclusion: 19:27-29
Epilogue: 19:30-38

As is so often the case in the study of Hebrew narrative, reticence on the part of the author betrays authorial intention. In other words, the author highlights or underlines what is important for the development of his thought as much by what is not said as by what is said. In considering the development of the various moments of the plot in this particular block, that general principle holds especially true.

These two chapters serve as two panels, each highlighting one of the main characters and, at the same time, showing the reader two alternative ways of being in the world. With Abraham, all is as it should be in human society. It is a society solicitous for those in need, whether a need that may be met by the ordinary courtesies of Near Eastern hospitality or a more radical need that requires intercession in the face of divine wrath. This is not to say that it is a world without difficulties or doubts. The reaction of Sarah to the (overheard) announcement of the guests that she would bear a son indicates that humanity is fully rounded among these characters. Alternatively, in the world of Lot, all is awry. Hospitality is better intentioned than carried out, violence is done to the guest, and family members experience hostility rather than solidarity. In contrast to the honest world of Abraham, Lot's world is twisted and wrong.

The exposition (18:1) sets the scene and in so doing informs the reader of important information that remains unknown to Abraham until 18:23, when he seems to intuit the identity of his visitor. The narrator shares this omniscience with the reader from the beginning but leaves Abraham and Sarah to react as they would normally to the arrival of visitors with stupendous news of both good and evil.

Tension begins to grow as soon as Abraham lifts his eyes and sees three men standing before him. The narrator is careful to inform us that it is noon, the hottest part of the day, when normally travelers would not be abroad. The reader is not told, however, what Abraham might make of that surprising fact. The narrator is not averse to recounting interior speech (cf. 18:12; 18:17-19) but wants the reader to begin to wonder, as Abraham must have, who these men were, where they had come from, and what their goal was. All of those questions remain hidden within Abraham as he goes toward them to show elaborate courtesy.[50] His generous welcome, relatively long by the standards set in previous chapters for speeches of Abraham, is answered in a brusque, if not to say churlish, way by his visitors. Regardless, narrative time is allowed to slow as an ornate meal is prepared. The narrator underlines Abraham's haste (18:6, 7), his generous hospitality (18:6, 7, 8), and his patient solicitude while the guests refresh themselves. In all this time, there passes no question regarding origin or destination, nor any word of identification. Business is allowed to wait while the amenities are served.

This first scene, thus, allows tension to build in the reader by the relaxed use of slowed narrative pace and reticence. Even after the meal, it is not Abraham who breaks the silence but the visitor, and he in a rather unexpected manner. His prediction of the birth of a son for Sarah is surprising for any number of reasons; neither her existence nor her childlessness is known to the visitor. The narrator has to intrude, in fact, in order to inform, or at least to remind, the reader that that is the case. Sarah's reaction is not unduly surprising in that she is elderly and the visitors can know nothing of her. YHWH's (for the visitor has been explicitly identified to the reader, at least, in 18:10) reaction to her laughter must serve to raise tension even further, for it becomes apparent that YHWH knows what is passing within the minds of those to whom YHWH speaks. YHWH is even able to repeat her inmost thoughts in rather more polite speech, certainly disconcerting Sarah. This insistence causes Sarah to try to cover up, and she lies in order to save face. Her lie is brusquely dismissed.[51]

During all of this Abraham is silent. Here we encounter the Hebrew narrator at his most reticent. We know nothing of Abraham's thoughts, reactions, doubts, or beliefs. He is content merely with telling the guests where his wife is. After that point he lets on nothing. That questions surely arise in him, and in the mind of the reader, we may be certain, because the narrator has planted them there. In 18:11, we have already been told that this whole business of a son is humanly impossible. Abraham has, by now, heard the promise of a son with some frequency and, as he grew older, with increasing improbability. Why then is he silent? From exasperation? From disbelief? Or might he be silent, the reader wonders, because it is dawning on him that these visitors are

---

[50] Again von Rad makes an elegant point when he notes the "subtle double meaning" of Abraham's phrase, "If I have found favor" (Rad, *Genesis*, 207). It is also useful to note that Lot's introduction is slightly different. This careful use of near, but not quite exact, repetition serves to underline the unusual courtesy of Abraham's proposal.

[51] Note the use of the woman as a "negative figure of contrast" (Rad, *Genesis*, 208) in Job 2:9; Tob 2:14; 10:4f.

not ordinary, that what has long been known to the reader (18:1) is becoming apparent even to him.

18:16 serves an extremely important function in the development of this plot. It serves as a marker to introduce the principal theme that will concern the remainder of the narrative. The men move out from the camp of Abraham, looking toward Sodom, accompanied by Abraham. Verbs of motion carry the plot along, as indicated above in the section on delimitation of the text. The men arrived at Abraham's camp, and now they continue their movement toward Sodom. The first mention of the doomed city at this point is surprising to the reader. This is not, after all, simply another announcement of birth to Abraham. Nonetheless, no mention has been made as yet as to why Sodom is of particular interest. Abraham's silence remains somewhat discomfiting. Why has his garrulousness been transformed into silence? The second scene (18:17-21) differs from the first in that it has only one character, YHWH, who does nothing but speak. Interior monologue is presented rarely in Hebrew narrative, although it is clear that the narrator's omniscience can make us privy to it. In two previous instances, interior monologues of YHWH have been reported, Genesis 6:5-7 and 11:6-7, that have to do with the decision to destroy. In the former case, YHWH decides to destroy the world with the Flood, while the latter case has to do with the scattering of the peoples who were building the Tower of Babel. The typical restraint is abandoned here, underlining the importance of what YHWH has to think about. But it should be noted that what YHWH says interiorly and what he says aloud to Abraham are markedly different.

Speaking interiorly, YHWH alludes to an intimate past relationship with Abraham and the latter's possible future. The intimacy of their relationship is indicated by the verb used to describe it. "To know," as Rashi points out (cf. Ruth 2 and Exodus 33), indicates knowledge and understanding, in fact, love. YHWH prepares a moment of instruction for Abraham, instruction in the meaning of justice, righteousness, and the observing of YHWH's way. None of this is made known to Abraham, as the narrator continues to allow the reader to share in privileged information. Rather, YHWH simply describes an eventual destination to Abraham. Even the intention to destroy is left implicit. The Midrash sees in 18:20 a subtle clue that indicates what the sin of Sodom will be.[52]

---

[52] The Midrash interprets the nature of the sin of Sodom in a way very different from that of many modern readers, and yet one that makes a serious effort to account for a very real difficulty with the way "the sin of Sodom" appears in the rest of the Hebrew Bible. Isaiah (1:10; 3:9) considered the sin of Sodom to have been maladministration of justice. Ezekiel (16:49), rather differently, identified it with pride, excess of food, and luxury. Jeremiah (23:14) uses the label to condemn adultery,

18:22 serves as another marker, drawing the action ever nearer to Sodom. This time, however, Abraham and YHWH remain left behind. Textual traditions differ at this point. Whether Abraham stands before YHWH (blocking the way?) or YHWH stands before Abraham (in the posture of one willing to be taught?) really does not affect the result. These two remain behind because they have things to discuss. Their discussion takes place on a height in view of the city, which lies unaware that its fate is being debated. The veil of non-identification notwithstanding,

---

lying, and lack of willingness to repent. The Midrash exploits an accident of grammatical gender to combine all of these in a charming story. In Gen 18:20, the Hebrew reads "the outcry of it (lit. "her") is very great." "Outcry" is a technical term for the cry for help of one who has suffered a great injustice. The antecedent is doubtless Sodom and Gomorrah, which, since "city" in Hebrew is feminine in gender, require the use of the feminine pronoun. It is this feminine reference which led to the creation of a story to account for it. The line was read to refer to "the cry of that young woman." Who was she? According to the *Pirkei de Rabbi Eliezer* 25:

> They issued a proclamation in Sodom, saying: "Everyone who strengthens the hand of the poor and the needy with a loaf of bread shall be burnt by fire!" Pelotit the daughter of Lot was wedded to one of the magnates of Sodom. She saw a certain very poor man in the streets of the city and her soul was grieved on the account. What did she do? Every day when she went out to draw water she put in her pitcher all kinds of provisions from her house and she sustained that poor man. The men of Sodom said: How does this poor man live? When they ascertained the facts they brought her forth to be burnt by fire. She said: Sovereign of all the worlds! Maintain my right and my cause at the hands of the men of Sodom! And her cry ascended before the throne of glory. In that hour the Holy One blessed be he said: "I will go down and see whether they have done altogether according to her cry which is come unto me?—and if the men of Sodom have done according to the cry of that young woman, I will turn her foundation upwards and the surface downwards."

Nehama Leibowitz, in writing on this passage, says:

> The Midrash wishes to emphasize two points. First, what exactly constituted the wickedness of Sodom? What form has such wickedness to take to warrant the total destruction of the city? The answer given by the Midrash to this question is—social iniquity—even of a passive and not an active form . . . But the height of their wickedness lay not in the activities of individual transgressors but in the fact that such iniquitous behaviour was clothed with a cloak of legality, raised to the level of a social norm. (*Studies in Bereshit*, 4th ed. [Jerusalem: World Zionist Organization, 1981] 173)

Regardless of the unscientific nature of such exegesis, it shows that the sin of Sodom is not easily, if at all, to be identified with homosexuality. That is too facile and does not account for all of the biblical evidence. Judged by that criterion the sages of the Midrash were more advanced than we.

Abraham now makes clear that he knows full well to whom he is speaking. In contrast to the elaborate prostration with which he greeted the unknown visitors, Abraham approaches YHWH to instruct YHWH in his (Abraham's) understanding of justice (18:25). Yet it is really YHWH who is instructing Abraham even as Abraham tests YHWH.

The third scene of the first panel (18:23-32) serves to bring the developing narrative tension to its highest point, at which some shift must be made, the narrative taking some particular line. Without having been told, Abraham knows that unrighteousness at Sodom will call for its destruction. He "draws near" to speak to YHWH. Rashi points out that "draw near" can appear in three contexts: war (2 Sam 10:13), reconciliation (Genesis 44), and prayer (1 Kings 18). It is for all of these that Abraham steps forth and musters all his resources, gentle and hard, love and fear, mildness and boldness, to wage a prayerful war for the reconciliation of YHWH and the people of Sodom. YHWH begins by saying that Sodom will be spared if there are fifty righteous in the city. Couching his interventions in carefully respectful speech, Abraham eventually elicits YHWH's promise that, if ten righteous, people should be found at Sodom, it will be spared.[53] This, as Abraham tells YHWH (18:25b), is only right.

So, at long last, and in a rather untypically leisurely fashion, the climax or turning point of the story is reached at 18:33. There is nothing left to say. YHWH is now committed to a particular course of action. Destruction of the unrighteous or their salvation along with the righteous; one or another of these YHWH is now resolved to do. Therefore, the two part to go their separate ways.

From this height of tension, things begin to resolve themselves. The second panel, wherein the reader sees that all is twisted in the world of Lot in the city of Sodom, consists of three parts: resolution, conclusion, and epilogue. The resolution has five scenes, each of which describes another aspect of this city's pallid virtue, vicious inhospitality, lack of fruitfulness, and merited destruction. A conclusion (19:27-29) closes the whole by returning the reader to Abraham's viewpoint. This restores the level of tension to where it was when we first entered this narrative bloc. As Abraham was alone and at rest in 18:1, so too he is alone and in thoughtful repose in 19:28. His interior processes have been kept opaque to us throughout, and the narrator sticks with this strategy to the end. We know nothing of how he reacts as a person. Finally an epilogue (19:30-38) completes the sad portrait of Lot.

---

[53] The repetition of "in the city" is taken by some commentators to imply that a purely private piety will not suffice, that the righteousness that will save the city must be known publicly.

Immediately after the climactic 18:33, the motion verbs that have been describing a process of drawing nearer to Sodom cease. In 19:1, the two travelers, now identified as angels, arrive. Previously the visitors were to be identified with YHWH, but that is no longer the case. YHWH does not enter Sodom but sends angels to do the work of investigation.

The resolution begins with a scene of hospitality that is both like and unlike that encountered earlier. Lot never quite gets anything right. Having invited the travelers to his home, he offers them only water as refreshment after the night, in direct contrast to Abraham (18:4). They agree to his offer only after strong urging. This contrasts with their reception of Abraham's hospitality. In that instance they accepted, albeit rather brusquely, whereas in this case they have to be urged. The contrast between the two occasions continues to develop. Abraham's elaborate preparations and meal contrast vividly with Lot's feast of unleavened bread.

The second scene (19:3-11) further complicates the picture of disordered hospitality in Sodom. Only a perverse mockery of hospitality could tolerate the sort of activity that is described in these verses. The sin of Sodom that God intended to investigate is portrayed here in all its detail. But it would be quite wrong to think that the sin of Sodom was only what took place before the house of Lot. In fact, several sins are described here. The attempted gang-rape (19:5) is followed by the pandering offer of virgin daughters (19:8). In succeeding scenes, Lot's sons-in-law mock him, and Lot refuses to believe what the angels have to say (19:16). Over and over, hospitality is mocked. Lot is not identified as righteous nor does he act in a righteous manner. He is saved only because of Abraham (19:29).

Thus, the first three scenes of Genesis 19 (19:2-3, 3-11, 12-15) describe different aspects of Sodom's sinfulness. The general allusions to Sodom's evil in Genesis 13:13; 14:21-24 and Genesis 18 are thus made concrete in this description of evil and its passive acceptance.

Lot's ineffective dithering (19:12-15) finally frustrates his would-be saviors to such an extent that they seize him and bring him out of the city. In Genesis 18 a movement was seen toward Sodom. At this point a movement begins away from Sodom. However, where the former was purposeful and committed, this latter is shown as fitful and half-hearted. The fourth scene of the resolution (19:16-22a) focuses on Lot's unwillingness to depart from the place of evil. Even when he flees and is directed to flee toward the mountain where he would certainly find safety with Abraham, he refuses. His diffident behavior finally causes the angels to concede to him a place in Zoar. The narrator uses three nominal sentences, in which the emphatic subject comes first, to slow down the pace of narration. The sun rises, Lot arrives in Zoar, fire and brimstone fall; there is a certain leisure to the recital. The narrator then (19:22b-23) breaks frame to add an etiological explanation of the place name. Finally, YHWH, who has never visited Sodom, destroys it (19:24-26), and the wife of Lot, caught up in the general maelstrom, serves as a metonymic symbol of the wasted whole.

Narrative tension, which has been moving the piece along throughout these two chapters, is now very nearly spent. Genesis 18 was an examination of whether destruction would become inevitable. Genesis 19 showed the reader that it was clearly both inevitable and necessary. With the orientation once more in 19:28 to Abraham's point of view the story has reached its end. However, there is one point left hanging. Genesis 18 had raised the question of fruitfulness. Genesis 19 finally dismisses Lot and his crew by raising once again the same issue. The author does it in a way that will quite eliminate any residual sympathy for these erstwhile inhabitants of the destroyed city.

The epilogue (19:30-38), with its description of manipulation, drunkenness, and incest serves not only to skewer some of Israel's traditional enemies. In the context of the development of this story it underlines the fact that even the people who were saved from the conflagration are well beyond the pale of what is acceptable. They continued to move away from Sodom (19:30), but not toward Abraham. Lot has always done the wrong thing, when he managed to act at all. First he chose the Jordan plain and its superficial attractions, despite the presence of Sodom. He offered his daughters to a predatory crowd. He had to be carried away from his own destruction and was not even satisfied then. The author is working to create one final masterly stroke in this use of verbs of motion to and away from Sodom. Lot continues on the move but ends up drunk in a cave. There he incestuously begets sons. Like Abraham, he says nothing when sons for him are discussed. Unlike Abraham, he cannot, for he is drunk and unconscious. The contrast could neither be more powerful, nor more damning.

Point of View. The role of Abraham's perceptual[54] point of view in framing this section ("and behold . . . ," 18:2; 19:28) has already been noted. However, that is not the only framing device to which the narrator (and hence the implied author) has recourse in these chapters. Abraham's perceptual point of view is itself contained within a yet more inclusive ideological point of view. In 18:1 the narrator informs the reader that it is YHWH with whom Abraham will be dealing in the

---

[54] The discussion of point of view that follows here is dependent in large measure on the work of Seymour Chatman, *Story and Discourse: Narrative Structure in Fiction and Film* (Ithaca: Cornell University Press, 1978) 151–3.

ensuing scenes. This information is withheld from Abraham. Similarly, immediately after Abraham beholds the destruction of Sodom and Gomorrah, the narrator once again reminds the reader that all that has happened has taken place by means of YHWH's activity. Lot was saved, not as a result of his own worth but of Abraham's. This information, as far as the reader knows, is also withheld from Abraham.

Genesis 19:29 has long proved something of an enigma to exegetes. Its language seems more reflective of the Priestly tradition—e.g., the use of *ʾĕlōhîm* ("God") instead of YHWH—than the Yahwist tradition, to which the rest of this block is typically assigned. Equally out of place, given the lack of connection between Abraham and Lot in the rest of the story, is the note that Lot was saved for Abraham's sake, that God "remembered" Abraham. The word "remember" is a *Leitwort* in Genesis. That is to say, it appears in similar contexts in a variety of stories, thus linking them together thematically. "Remember" is used in a similarly charged sense in Genesis 8:1; 9:15, 16; 30:22; 40:14, 23; 42:9. In each instance, existence hangs upon memory. Whether a covenant is remembered, an infertile mother is remembered, or an unjustly imprisoned slave begs to be remembered, the precariousness of human existence is connected to memory. In using this device at this point in this particular narrative, the narrator establishes an ideological framework within which the entire story takes place. YHWH is present and active among human beings (18:1); human existence hangs on YHWH's memory (19:29). Abraham's role in God's memory is unique. For his sake, God saves the otherwise unremarkable. Thus, a double frame surrounds this piece: God : Abraham :: Abraham : God. Within the ideological framework, Abraham's activity takes place, and the final prediction of the birth of Abraham's son is made. It should also be noted that this device neatly excludes Lot's incestuous behavior with his daughters; this latter falls, as it were, outside the divine perspective.

The first scene of the first panel (18:2-15) is told from Abraham's interest point of view. He addresses the (to him) unknown visitors with a request that they stay with him, if he has found favor in their sight. It is for him, then, a confirmation of his righteousness that they agree to stop awhile in his home. Similarly, it is in his interest that he bear a son, as is predicted in 18:10. Note, however, that in neither case does Abraham exploit this situation for his own advantage. It is, in the first part, in his interest to serve others. In the second part, where he might be expected to exclaim joyfully at the birth of a son, or at least to react somehow, he remains enigmatically silent. For others, he works diligently, while for himself he seeks nothing. Thus, telling this part of the tale from Abraham's interest point of view supports the idea that, for him, self-interest is service for another.

The perceptual point of view is reintroduced in 18:16, the marker between scenes. This serves to introduce the question of Sodom into the piece and continues the process of movement towards it.

The following scene, wherein YHWH's dilemma is recounted by way of interior monologue, is ideological or conceptual in its point of view. A possible course of action is considered as part of an overall conceptual system of divine-human relationship. That Abraham's task is to do righteousness and justice, observing the way of YHWH, fits neatly with what has already been observed of him in this chapter. So far, the ideological perspective, that Abraham's task in life is to serve as a source of goodness, has been borne out. YHWH is perplexed about whether this should be made explicit to Abraham in the context of the destruction that is about to occur.

Once again, 18:22, the marker between this scene and the next, reintroduces a perceptual point of view. Sodom still looms in the distance, and our characters continue to draw nearer to it. This process is momentarily halted as Abraham and YHWH break stride with the others and remain where they are, talking. Ideology is once again the perspective through which the action is viewed during the conversation (18:23-32) that describes Abraham's quandary, his perplexity at a seemingly unjust act on the part of a just God.

The narrator's perceptual point of view brings the action to its highest point of tension in the turning point at 18:33. YHWH and Abraham part, each going in opposite directions, while the reader ponders the possible outcomes.

The narrator introduces the first scene of the second panel (19:1-3) with a use of point of view which matches that with which Genesis 18 begins. Perceptual point of view is used to set the scene and then interest point of view determines Lot's appeal to the two angels to stay in his home. Lot's interests continue to be uppermost in the near riot that follows. Only the intervention of the angels can keep Lot from sacrificing his young daughters to the rapacity of the crowd. In contrast to Abraham, Lot is willing to sacrifice others' interests in favor of his own. The next several scenes are all told from the viewpoint of Lot's interests, as he can neither convince his family of the gravity of the situation nor rouse himself to take effective action. Abraham's vitality in service for others is paralleled by Lot's vacillating buffoonery.

Perceptual point of view is used by the narrator in 19:15, 16, 23 to orient the reader to the unremitting process of divine destruction. As Lot dithers, time passes and necessary action fails to be taken. Finally, the angle of perspective offered to the reader pulls back to its widest possible vantage point as in 19:24-28 the ultimate destruction takes place and is beheld by Abraham. As already noted, this last is put into its ideological place by 19:29.

Lot's daughters, acting now on their own interest because of the fruitless passivity of their father, act as they see fit. Lot, unconscious, is at his most passive. However, their interests and those of YHWH have diverged so far that they give birth to enemies of YHWH's people. The caustic ideological point of view with which the whole section ends in 19:37-38 dismisses these offspring from the people of Abraham's line and places them firmly outside of YHWH's compass.

Repetition. There is no true repetition in these two chapters, but there are several instances where a motif introduced in Genesis 18 is alluded to in Genesis 19 or has a variation played on it. The first is the location of the two encounters. Abraham sits in the desert (18:1), while Lot is in the city, previously identified as a wicked place (13:13). Abraham's visitors were three in number (18:2), while Lot receives only two (19:1). This difference, which could have been so easily avoided by the editor, highlights the absence of one of Abraham's visitors. The reader remembers that YHWH and Abraham are still debating the fate of a righteous minority (and hence, at least indirectly, of Sodom) even as Lot greets his guests. The two greetings are similar, but Lot reverses the customary offering of refreshing water until the next morning (19:2). The text gives no clue whether this is mere social ineptitude or a scheme to hide their presence from the townspeople, as some medieval exegetes thought. The descriptions of the two meals are very tellingly different. Narrative time slows in 18:6-8 in order, paradoxically, to linger over Abraham's haste. He busily prepares a superb meal, and the narrator allows the reader to savor the preparations. Contrarily, Lot's preparations and service both are conveyed in a mere half verse (19:3b). The only detail offered is the unleavened bread, a quickly prepared food that hardly matches Sarah's cakes of the finest flour. In both panels there is skeptical or mocking laughter. Sarah laughs at the thought of her dried-up old body growing fruitful once more (18:12). Lot's sons-in-law mock their father-in-law. The distinction here is between a promise too incredibly good to be believed, yet it is true, and a man too incredibly silly to be believed, yet he is right.

Most importantly, Abraham intercedes for righteous people unknown to him and is willing to tolerate the continued existence of evil for their sake (18:23-32). In this section there is a certain type of repetition as well. Each of Abraham's intercessions combines petition with some supplicatory or self-disparaging formula. Lot shows concern only for himself (19:20), and that only when bodily carried away from danger.

The uses of repetition between these two chapters point over and over again to the theme noted above, that with Abraham all is as it should be, while with Lot all is amiss.

There is another aspect of repetition that should be noted. The annunciation of the birth of a child to Sarah is only one of several such announcements to previously infertile women in Genesis and in the entire Hebrew Bible. George Coats suggests that this instance may be profitably compared with 2 Kings 4:8-17. Such a comparison reveals a certain pattern to this type of story, the elements of which would be "(1) recognition of the problem, (2) annunciation (birth, name, destiny, although this series may not be stated in full), (3) expression of doubt, and (4) fulfillment of the annunciation."[55] In Genesis 18, not all of these are present, for several reasons. The most important is that no author must slavishly follow such a pattern. To do so would be intolerably dull. Also, the focus of this particular narrative bloc is less on the annunciation of the birth of Isaac than it is on the question of Abraham's intercession for Sodom. The former recedes behind the latter.

Characterization. For the most part, the characters encountered in these two chapters are agents, props who simply move the plot along. This is true particularly of the divine visitors. Nothing is known of them, nor need be known of them, other than that they accomplish their purpose and advance the story. The various members of the family of Lot, his wife, daughters, and sons-in-law, may also be included in this category. They serve as foils for Lot's buffoonery and passivity and have no depth in themselves.

There is little that is admirable about Lot. In fact, he seems to serve almost as a mirror image of the thoroughly admirable Abraham. In line with the overall narrative strategy in Genesis of creating double portraits in order to make the details of a characterization more readily apparent by the resulting contrasts, Lot is pictured here as increasingly passive, a mediocrity. He was dazzled by the fertile fields of the Jordan plain and grabbed them when offered, despite the proximity of the fateful city. At that time he was pictured as a rich man (Gen 13:10-13). He was captured by the eastern kings (Genesis 14) and had to be rescued by his uncle Abraham. His riches are not heard of again, and in Genesis 19 he seems to be a simple householder in Sodom.

In Sodom his weaknesses become increasingly apparent. Although he welcomes the two angels, his hospitality does not come up to the mark of Abraham's. But that offer of hospitality is his high water mark, and from that point on an increase in passivity and comic buffoonery comes to characterize him. He offers his daughters to the rapacious crowd, is unwilling to convince his family of their danger, and is unable to take effective steps even to save himself. Instead of fleeing to the

[55] Coats, *Genesis*, 138.

heights where safety with Abraham was to be found, he settles (momentarily) in an insignificant village. Yet even there he does not feel safe and continues to wander farther and farther from Abraham and his God until he ends up an unconscious, intoxicated, manipulated object. This portrait of moral and psychological decay is set in contrast to that of Abraham.

If indeed Genesis 18:1 describes a private theophany to Abraham that precedes the arrival of the guests, as some medieval exegetes maintained, it is noteworthy that Abraham did not remain in a state of mystic exaltation but hurried to serve his guests. This will be the hallmark of the portrait of Abraham that is drawn in these two chapters. He is unfailingly, vigorously, active. He is solicitous not for his own needs or pleasures but for those of others. The needy, whether travelers or the righteous in danger of destruction, benefit from his labors.

His eagerness to serve is immediately evident. Words expressing haste and eagerness recur over and over in Genesis 18:2, 6, and 7. His situation, the righteous man in the midst of an unrighteous generation, has invited comparisons with Noah. The comparison generally hinges on Noah's lack of intercession for those around him. The Zohar says of the two:

> And Abraham drew near and said, Wilt thou also destroy the righteous with the wicked? (18:23)—said R. Yehudah: Who hath seen a father as compassionate as Abraham? Come and see: Regarding Noah it is stated (6:13) "And God said to Noah, the end of all flesh is come before me; . . . and behold I will destroy them from the earth. Make thee an ark of gopher . . ." And Noah held his peace and said naught, neither did he intercede. Whereas Abraham, as soon as the Holy One blessed be He said to him: "Because the cry of Sodom and Gomorrah is great and because their sin is very grievous I will go down and see . . ." Immediately, as it is stated, "and Abraham drew near and said: Wilt thou also destroy the righteous with the wicked?"[56]

Energy as opposed to passivity, weightiness in God's view as opposed to silliness in human view, intercession as opposed to self-concern—all of these characterize Abraham. Lot, in particular, has served as an other, a foil for the narrator of these chapters, with which to highlight the strengths of Abraham. Abraham will continue to develop while Lot, having served his narrative purpose and given birth to enemies of Israel, will fade from view.

---

[56] Leibowitz, *Bereshit*, 181.

B'. 20:1-18: Yhwh Acts to Free Sarah

Genesis 20 comes as a surprise to the reader because it presents Abraham in an old and still unfavorable light. It is a surprise that Abraham tries the tired ruse of lying about his relationship to his wife once again (and hints that it has been used other times as well). Even if they are really half-siblings, the half-truth is hardly to be distinguished from a lie, because either way his wife is placed in a position of moral danger from which God must rescue her. But coming as it does immediately after Abraham's intercession for the righteous people of Sodom, where he quite literally walked before God, it is disconcerting to see him now act in a manner less than righteous and yet be identified by no less than God himself as a prophet.

In all of these ways, the story functions to further the characterization of Abraham and of God. In the latter case, for instance, it shows that God continues to act consistently as savior. It shows God, in particular, committed to saving women trapped inside relationships that hinder them. God still acts to free them and to bring them outside.

There is no doubt that one is intended to read this present story against the backdrop of Genesis 12:9–13:1. It is loosely tied to its immediate context but works well in the overall arrangement of Genesis 12–25 to show us God's consistency and Abraham's need for the further testing and development that will follow in Genesis 21–22. The "there" of 20:1, from which Abraham moves his family, must be the place near Mamre where Abraham had previously settled, near which he overlooked the destruction of Sodom. In order to remove himself from that place and its association with human unrighteousness and divine justice, Abraham moved. But he moved toward the Negeb, thus necessarily recalling 12:9, where he did the same thing. Similarly, 12:10 is recalled in the wordplay between "sojourned" and Gerar (*wayyāgor bigrār*; literally, "and he sojourned in Gerar").[57] Irony is introduced—along with a narrative tension that will not be resolved until Genesis 21—because in the same sentence he is said to "settle" (*yšb*) there, but he cannot "settle" while he is still an alien sojourner. This passage is not entirely divorced from its setting because the theme with which Genesis 20 ends (Yhwh's reversal of the inability of the women of Abimelech's household to bear children) leads smoothly

---

[57] There is an untranslatable pun embedded here. If one recalls that *gēr* means "an alien residing on sufferance in the midst of a people other than his own," the phrase says something like "he was a *gēr* in Gerar."

into the beginning of Genesis 21 (Yhwh's reversal of Sarah's inability to bear children).[58]

> For the Lord had closed fast all the wombs of the house of Abimelech because of Sarah, Abraham's wife. The Lord dealt with Sarah as he had said, and the Lord did for Sarah as he had promised. (Gen 20:18–21:1)[59]

Abimelech appears again in Genesis 21 and really does allow Abraham to settle and begin to possess the land so long promised to him and his family.

Genesis 20 is particularly well analyzed by George Coats,[60] and his structure is used here. Note that the turning point of the story is 20:7; the threat of death against Abimelech is the highest possible point of tension and the one that moves the story toward its resolution.

1. Itinerary (v. 1)
2. Complication (v. 2)
   A. Abraham's plan (v. 2a)
   B. Consequences (v. 2b)
3. Denouement (vv. 3-16)
   A. Divine intervention speech (v. 3)
   B. Self-defense (vv. 4-5)
   C. Divine response (vv. 6-7[61])
      i. Acquittal (v. 6)
      ii. Instructions (v. 7a)
      iii. Threat (v. 7b)
   D. Execution of instructions (vv. 8-16)
      i. Report to royal household (v. 8)
      ii. Abimelech's accusation (vv. 9-10)

---

[58] It is also an important link in the ongoing theme of fertility and infertility.

> [W]e have the implausible promise of a son to the aged Sarah; then a whole people is wiped out; then the desperate act of procreation by Lot's daughters in a world seemingly emptied of men; and now an entire kingdom blighted with an interruption of procreation. The very next words of the story . . . are the fulfillment of the promise of progeny to Sarah. (Alter, *Genesis*, 96)

[59] The sentence structure of Gen 21:1 indicates a break in the sequence of the narrative, and could quite properly be translated as comparing two contrasting events: "For Yhwh had closed fast all the wombs of the house of Abimelech because of Sarah, Abraham's wife, but with Sarah Yhwh dealt as he had said, and for Sarah Yhwh did as he had promised."

[60] Coats, *Genesis*, 149–50.

[61] 20:7 serves as the turning point of the story.

   a. First accusation (v. 9)
   b. Second accusation (v. 10)
   iii. Abraham's response (vv. 11-13)
   a. Fear (v. 11)
   b. Sister-brother (v. 12)
   c. Explanation of plan (v. 13)
   iv. Restoration (vv. 14-16)
   a. General report (v. 14)
   b. Abimelech's invitation to Abraham (v. 15)
   c. Abimelech's explanation to Sarah (v. 16)
   4. Conclusion (vv. 17-18)

Unlike its parallel in Genesis 12, this story does not use an asymmetrical version of a concentric structure. God's freedom of action is indicated, though, in the dreams and lengthy dialogue with which Abimelech and God communicate,[62] God being free to communicate with whom he will, just as YHWH spoke to Hagar, whether or not they are part of the chosen family. This contrasts with the parallel story in Genesis 12 where the reader never knows how Pharaoh found out the truth about Sarai. This freedom of God is further highlighted by placing the dream and dialogue right at the beginning of the story, before God speaks to Abraham. This is not to say that the warning given the king of Gerar is not stark. In the vivid translation of the RSV, God says to him "Behold, you are a dead man. . . ."

Abimelech's reply, in which he declares his innocence and that of his people, is interesting and deserving of some attention because it is a mini-catalogue of Hebrew words for blamelessness. At the center of this catalogue, the word that Abimelech chooses to describe the nature of his "heart," i.e., his inmost person, is the word *tām*. In this whole encounter it is he, the outsider, who possesses integrity. It was Abraham who was called by God to possess this characteristic as central to his being in Genesis 17:1 *(tāmîm)* but Abimelech who possesses it in this instance, as even God recognizes in 20:6.[63]

---

[62] Note that the divine name YHWH is not used when Abimelech and God communicate but rather the generic name "God" *(ʾĕlōhîm)*. YHWH is the God worshiped by this family and not known by this name to outsiders. Nor does Abimelech call him by that name although this is not clear from most translations. The title "Lord" with which Abimelech speaks to God in 20:4 does not translate YHWH but the Hebrew *ʾădōnāy*, a common noun that serves as a term of respectful address to a superior.

[63] But what Abimelech has to say to God is more subtle still, as Alter recognizes when he says:

"O Lord, will you kill a **righteous** people?" (20:4b: *ʾădōnāy hăgôy gam-ṣaddîq tahărōg*)

". . . in the **integrity** of my heart" (20:5b: *bĕtām-lĕbābî*)

". . . and in the **innocence** of my hands" (20:5b: *ûbĕniqyōn kappay*)

"I[64] know that in the **integrity** of your heart . . ." (20:6a: *ʾānōkî yādaʿtî kî bĕtām-lĕbābĕkā*)

Despite God's recognition of Abimelech's integrity[65] and the way in which God has protected him from inadvertent sin, Sarah must be returned lest Abimelech die. Or is it Sarah? Sarah's name appears five times in the tale (vv. 2 [twice], 14, 16, 18). Her name disappears when Abimelech takes her (v. 2) and reappears (v. 14) when she is restored to Abraham. Five occurrences may seem like rather a lot in such a brief tale, but words describing her and her relationship to Abraham are a

---

This phrase, which might also be construed "slay a nation with the innocent," sounds as peculiar in the Hebrew as in translation. . . . The apparent deformation of idiom has a sharp thematic point. "Innocent" *(tsadiq)* is the very term Abraham insisted on in questioning God as to whether He would really slay the innocent together with the guilty in destroying the entire nation of Sodom. If the king of Gerar chooses, oddly, to refer to himself as "nation," leaning on the traditional identification of monarch with people, it is because he is, in effect, repeating Abraham's question to God: will not the Judge of all the earth do justice? (*Genesis*, 93)

[64] Note that the use of the Hebrew pronoun "I" *(ʾānōkî)* is not required except for emphasis. So God does not grudgingly admit Abimelech's integrity but asserts it emphatically.

[65] In commenting on this passage, Meir Sternberg says of Abimelech, "And if the king remains an injured party, sexual scruple has nothing to do with it. His spirit was willing enough, only the flesh was weak" (*The Poetics of Biblical Narrative: Ideological Literature and the Drama of Reading* [Bloomington, Ind.: Indiana University Press, 1985] 316). This is a surprising and disturbing sentence. It second-guesses God's moral evaluation of Abimelech. After all, if Abimelech married Sarah he had every right to have intercourse with her. He was prevented from doing so because, entirely unbeknownst to him, Sarah was already married and so unavailable to him. To imply some rapacious sexual appetite held in check only by God goes beyond what the text says. There is no unmasking of the king to be done. The text says, simply and clearly, that he and his people were blameless and recognized as such by God. Blame is to be assigned here only to Abraham. Also troubling is Sternberg's allusion, witting or not, to Matt 26:41, "Stay awake and pray that you may not come into the time of trial; the spirit indeed is willing, but the flesh is weak." Jesus, bereft of company the night before he dies, laments that his friends are not strong enough to wait with him for his betrayal. This is far afield indeed from rapacious sexual appetite.

great deal more numerous: wife[66] (vv. 2, 3 *[bĕʿūlat]*, 6, 11, 14), sister (vv. 2, 5, 12), brother (vv. 5, 13, 16), daughter (v. 12 [twice]), father (vv. 12, 13), mother (v. 12), woman (v. 3), husband (v. 3 *[bāʿal]*). Thus there are seventeen references to Sarah in terms of her relationship to Abraham and only five references to her own name. In a crucial verse, 20:6, she is not even a noun but, in the Hebrew, merely a suffix to a preposition: "to her" *(ʾēleyhā)*. This is very much in line with the ongoing leitmotif in Genesis (and other books of the Hebrew Bible) of God acting on behalf of women trapped inside relationships and robbed of their freedom as a result.[67]

The turning point is reached in 20:7 with God's blunt ultimatum. Regardless of Abimelech's innocence in the matter, the person of Sarah is untouchable for him and must be returned. The alternative, using an intensive form of the Hebrew infinitive, is that Abimelech and all those associated with him will surely die *(môt tāmût)*. Thus God's speech to Abimelech begins and ends with the possibility of his death but is centered on his innocence, with the seemingly paradoxical result that both the possibility of his death (as well as that of all his people) and his innocence are emphasized.

Verses 8-16 describe Abimelech's compliance with God's will for him. As Coats points out,[68] its general shape is similar to 12:18-19 but much expanded. Of particular interest in this latter part of the chapter is Abraham's response to Abimelech's accusation. He acted as he did, he says, because Gerar is a place where the fear of God is not to be found. Clearly, Abimelech has acted in such a way as to put the lie to that accusation. But Abraham goes on, getting lamer and lamer.

> [I]n his self-defense speech Abraham pleads innocence in calling Sarah his sister (v. 12). But whether historically husbands might pass wives off as sisters or not, in this story Abraham's designation of his wife as his sister leads to the crisis. It is a deceptive deed, and as a consequence, the appeal is almost comic, at least lame. It bespeaks loss of relationship between Abraham and his wife. Indeed, the appeal to wandering from the

---

[66] In Hebrew, the word most ordinarily used for "wife" is the word for "woman" *(ʾiššâ)*. In 20:3, the author distinguishes between the woman *(ʾiššâ)* Abimelech took (but with whom he has as yet been unable to consummate a marriage because of God's prohibition) and her status as another's man wife by using the less usual word *bĕʿūlat*, "wife." This is a feminine passive form of the word *baʿal*, "lord," "husband," and means "a woman who belongs to a husband."

[67] It should be noted too that in this verse, the name "God" is not used but rather the generic "the Deity" *(hāʾĕlōhîm)*.

[68] Coats, *Genesis*, 150.

protection of the father's house into various dangers wherever they might arise may suggest that Sarah warmed various beds. But the lame quality of the self-defense here is that, in Abraham's words, the cause of it all was God: "And God caused me to wander. . . ." Abraham's appeal in effect passes responsibility first to physical relationship to Sarah, then to relationship with God (→ Genesis 2–3).[69]

Abraham emerges from the crisis richer than before, with the honor of his wife exonerated. This was true in the earlier version of this story as well. There are two important differences. He is given the right to dwell wherever he wants—and this despite his dishonorable behavior to Abimelech. He even comes to be regarded as a figure of religious authority because as a prophet he must intercede for Abimelech and his family in order for them to be healed. This has not happened before and, coming as it does in the wake of the incident at Sodom, both defines a prophet as one who intercedes for others and shows that Abraham has somehow been changed by that event—at least in God's eyes.

The end result of this is a complicated and subtle theological point as well as a contribution to Abraham's ongoing characterization. It remains true that God chooses Abraham not because of some discernible perfection but *in spite of* his human imperfections. This presents the reader with a striking counterbalance to Genesis 18, where Abraham was seemingly a paragon of human perfection. But the reality is more complicated than that. He is both the person who can intercede for the righteous of an evil city and the man who can expect the worst of a patently God-fearing man. Abraham acts dishonorably in this incident but remains the chosen prophet whose intercession is necessary for life. Abraham needs still to grow into the person who is obedient to God's will for him because he is still not acting with as much integrity as Abimelech, the outsider.

!!! 21:1-34 YHWH ACTS FREELY TO CREATE A LIFE AND TO FREE;
DWELLERS AND SOJOURNERS

This, the penultimate chapter in Genesis 12–22, the part of Genesis that focuses on the relationship between God and Abraham, is deceptively

---

[69] Ibid. This very perceptive point should be held in mind in Genesis 21, where Abraham disapproves of Sarah's decision to drive Hagar and Ishmael away and then especially in the subsequent story in Genesis 22 when Abraham, without a word to his wife, takes their son away to be sacrificed, immediately after which Sarah dies.

simple in its construction. It seems to be merely a concatenation of three brief incidents: the birth of Isaac, the sending away of Hagar and Ishmael, and the covenant with Abimelech.[70] But some oddities occur to the reader straightaway. Many scholars agree that Genesis 12–25 is strongly symmetrical, even if they would describe a very different symmetrical structure than has been adopted in this commentary. But however the section is arranged, the birth of Isaac does not fit, and the resulting asymmetry requires some explanation. Consider Walsh's explanation:

> One climax of this dramatic plot is the birth of Isaac, the child of the promise, in 21:1-7, which is emphasized by having no corresponding subunit in the Abraham story. . . .
> This asymmetry can also be read intratextually, as a lack in the first sequence rather than a surplus in the second. The principal counterpart to Isaac in the Abraham story is Ishmael: their birth announcements are structurally parallel, and Ishmael is the potential rival for Isaac's role as the heir of the promise (see, for instance, Gen 17:18-21; 21:10-11). Ishmael's birth is recounted very briefly at the end of the subunit announcing his destiny (16:15-16). Isaac's could have been narrated similarly, for example with an editorial aside following Sarah's words in 18:15, something like "But Sarah conceived and bore a son in due season, according to the word of YHWH." By deferring the notice of Isaac's birth for three chapters the narrator prolongs dramatic tension about the promised heir, and by expanding the account to a full scene, complete with dialogue, he demonstrates Isaac's preeminence over Ishmael, whose birth warrants no comparable scene.[71]

Indeed, if the book is a history of the life of Abraham, for whom the lack of progeny was the central issue that guided all the decisions he made, this analysis is correct.[72] But if we as readers choose to stand in such a way that God and not Abraham is central to our vision, a radically different perspective emerges, as we have seen already. What is central to this vision is the saving nature of God, who graciously chooses to save Abraham and Sarah from childlessness and who makes covenants with them (Genesis 15, 17) but for whom the stranger and

---

[70] It seems not at all helpful to regard the chapter as three independent stories. They are much too brief to stand alone, and both chapters 20 and 22 are clearly coherent on their own.

[71] Walsh, *Style and Structure,* 106–7.

[72] It is clear that this is the way most commentators approach the chapter; witness, for example, George Coats's title for Genesis 21, "Birth of Isaac, 21:1-21" (*Genesis,* 152), although the birth of Isaac takes up only one half verse (21:1a).

her plight are central (Genesis 16).[73] If Genesis 12–25 is, then, primarily a theological text which uses the backdrop of the life of the first generation of the chosen family to proclaim the nature of God, the asymmetry evident here has a different purpose, one indicated by the title given to this section. Here God acts freely to create life, to free those without freedom, to give a home to some of the homeless, but to leave others as sojourners.

The chapter falls into three sections. In the first, the birth of Isaac and his circumcision on the eighth day are recounted (vv. 1-8). Subsequently Hagar and Ishmael are driven away because of Sarah's jealousy (but with God's permission). Freed in this way, they find a home in which to dwell (vv. 9-21). Finally Abraham makes a covenant with Abimelech and finds a place to sojourn (vv. 22-34). Why separate the first and third parts? Might it not have been clearer to combine them? Then the situation of Abraham and the situation of Hagar would have been neatly parallel:

birth of Isaac → settlement

departure of Ishmael → settlement.

This more complicated tripartite structure, in which Hagar and her son appear in the center, surrounded by covenantal acts of Abraham, calls to mind the larger structure of the entire section, as the following shows.

---

[73] In a fine recent article entitled "Hagar and Ishmael as Literary Figures: An Intertextual Study" (*Vetus Testamentum* 51 [2001] 219–42), S. Nikaido ponders an important issue:

> Therefore, birth narratives have two main functions: first, to indicate the special nature of the hero himself, and, secondly, to tell the story of the heroic deeds of the hero's mother or father.
>
> Given the dual function of these narratives, a question arises regarding the story of Hagar and Ishmael: Why is so much attention focused on them—two separate stories (Gen. xvi J and xxi 8-21 E)—when they are clearly the antagonists, the adversaries of Sarah and Isaac (Gen. xxi 10)? Since they are not the central characters, what could be the rationale for such a detailed presentation of their story?

There are many excellent insights in this article, but one way to answer Nikaido's question is found in the thesis adopted here, that Hagar and Ishmael are—at least in a very important sense—central. The centrality of Hagar and Ishmael is, if anything, made more sure by Nikaido's comparison of the many parallels between the ordeal of Hagar and Ishmael in Genesis 16 and 21 and that of Abraham and Isaac in Genesis 22.

15:1-21: YHWH acts and commits himself to a covenant	21:1-8: Covenant of circumcision carried out
16:1-15: YHWH saves Hagar and her child	21:9-21: God saves Hagar and her child
17:1-26: Abraham acts and commits himself to a covenant	21:22-34: Abraham acts and commits himself to a covenant

These parallels emerge:

(1) In Genesis 15 Abraham trusted that God would provide him with a son. // In Genesis 21, the son is finally born and circumcised in accord with the covenant between God and Abraham.

(2) In Genesis 16 Hagar is driven away but is spoken to by YHWH, who foretells a future for her son. // In Genesis 21 Hagar is driven away but is spoken to by God, who foretells a future for her son.

(3) In Genesis 17 Abraham makes, and witnesses to, a covenant with God. // In Genesis 21 Abraham makes, and witnesses to, a covenant with Abimelech.

Two themes emerge. In both cases, it is Hagar and her son who are central, even though God does not covenant with them and Ishmael is not the son of promise. It is to Abraham and Isaac that the election and the promise belong. This seems to be a paradox, and for us as readers it doubtless is, because we cannot see as God sees. But it is nonetheless a true reading: the family of Abraham is the chosen family and the recipient of God's promises, but always at the heart of who God is and of the way God relates to the world is justice, care of the foreigner, the orphan, and the widow. So, central to every story in which God is a character are Hagar and Ishmael, or someone like them. In no way does this change God's choice of Abraham and his descendants. Rather both are true at the same time.

When we turn to vv. 9-21, where God saves Hagar and her son, we see that it too can be arranged in a sort of concentric fashion, such that the jealousy and complaint with which the section begins are reversed and transformed into care. Sarah complains and demands the ouster of her son's rival (A), but God cares for the rejected one and, with Hagar as the agent, provides a future for the one who has been rejected (A'). The father (B) and mother (B') are both deeply distressed by the plight of their son. God speaks to both father (C) and mother (C') to assuage their grief and guide their actions. Abraham sends them away (D, using the verb *šlḥ*) while Hagar casts her son away (D', using the near homonym *šlk*). In the center—demonstrating to us how far we have not come since Genesis 16—is Hagar, once again alone and desperate in the wilderness with her son. However, in accord with the leitmotif of the outsider that we have seen time and again, it is once she is outside the household of Abraham, outside of her identity there as slave, that she encounters God who describes a future for her wherein she is pointedly no longer either slave or wife but free to arrange a life for herself and her son.

> A. Sarah's complaint (21:9-10)
> B. The father's distress (21:11)
> C. God speaks to Abraham (21:12-13)
> D. Sent away (*šlḥ*; 21:14a)
> X. Hagar in the wilderness (21:14b)
> D'. Cast away (*šlk*; 21:15)
> B'. The mother's distress (21:16)
> C'. God speaks to Hagar (21:17-18)
> A'. God's care (21:19-21)

The outsider motif is also marked, as we have seen, by the way in which the woman is referred to—heavily marked by relationship language and much less so by her own name. In this instance, it is worthwhile examining how both Hagar and Ishmael are referred to in the course of the chapter.

Surprisingly, since his fate is so central to this chapter, Ishmael is never mentioned by name. Rather, the narrative refers to him "by different terms in accordance with the various attitudes to Ishmael."[74] Sarah sees the son of Hagar the Egyptian (v. 9); to Abraham, he is "his son" (v. 11); for Hagar, he is "the child" (vv. 14, 15); to God he is "the youth" (*hannaʿar*, vv. 17, 20[75]).

The situation with Hagar is more complex. In the space of twelve verses, she is referred to twenty-one times: Hagar the Egyptian (v. 9); Hagar (vv. 14, 17 [twice]); female slave (*ʾāmâ*; vv. 10 [twice], 12, 13); his mother (v. 21); her (as direct or indirect object; vv. 10, 14 [twice], 17, 19); she (as subject of a verb; vv. 14, 15, 16 [three times], 19 [twice]). For most of the passage she is simply a grammatical particle, but how she is referred to also helps to show how she is viewed. To Sarah, she is the foreigner, the slave, the mother of the rival. To Abraham, she is Hagar.

---

[74] Shimon Bar-Efrat, *Narrative Art in the Bible* (Sheffield, England: Sheffield Academic Press, 1997) 37.

[75] The word refers to a young unmarried man. Its use by God here indicates Ishmael's still unmarried state. It should be noted that although Ishmael's name is not used, it is certainly alluded to in 21:17 ("and God heard," *wayyišmaʿ ʾĕlōhîm*).

God speaks of her as the female slave, but when the angel of God speaks to her, she is addressed by name—the only time that happens in the story. The last notice taken of her in the book (outside of the genealogy in 25:12) is when she is called "his mother," and we are told that she secured a wife for her son from Egypt. In this way God begins to fulfill his promise that Ishmael will also be a great nation. Acting independently, outside of the network of relationships into which she was tied in the household of Abraham, she—and her son—will be free.

Covenant of circumcision carried out (21:1-8). The birth of Isaac, so often promised and long awaited, is somewhat surprisingly accomplished in a mere half-verse. Although Hebrew narrative style is laconic, the importance of the event is highlighted by the use of several lines of what may be described as poetry, or at least heightened and formal speech. The first verse of the chapter is typical of the parallel pattern of intensification characteristic of Hebrew poetry.[76]

> Now YHWH took account of Sara as he had said,
> YHWH dealt with Sara as he had spoken.
>
> *wayhwh pāqad ʾet-śārâ kaʾăšer ʾāmar*
> *wayyaʿaś yhwh lĕśārâ kaʾăšer dibbēr*

So, in accord with God's promise, Sarah conceives and bears Isaac. As commanded, Abraham circumcises his new son and calls him by the name that God had already chosen for him. Sarah's announcement of the birth is also poetic in style and shows an interestingly ambiguous use of language.

> And Sarah said:
> Laughter has God made me
> Whoever hears will laugh at (for?) me[77]

---

[76] Fox, *Moses*, 87.

[77] Alter, *Genesis*, 97. He goes on to say:

> The ambiguity of both the noun *tseḥoq* ("laughter") and the accompanying preposition *li* ("to" or "for" or "with" or "at me") is wonderfully suited to the complexity of the moment. It may be laughter, triumphant joy, that Sarah experiences and that is the name of the child Isaac ("he-who-laughs"). But in her very exultation she may feel the absurdity . . . of a nonagenarian becoming a mother. *Tseḥoq* also means "mockery," and perhaps God is doing something to her as well as for her. (In poetry, *tseḥoq* is often linked in parallelism with *laʿag*, to scorn or mock, and it should be noted that *laʿag* is invariably followed by the preposition *lĕ* as *tsaḥaq* is here. All who hear it may laugh, rejoice, with Sarah, but the hint that they may also laugh at her is evident in her language.

wattōʾmer śārâ
ṣĕḥōq ʿāśâ lî ʾĕlōhîm
kol-hāššōmēaʿ yiṣḥaq-lî

She continues—again using poetically heightened language (21:6, *millēl*, "uttered," is used only in poetry)—to extol her surprise and wonder. All seems well and happy, but the fear of ridicule embedded in the text continues to bother the reader. Will this family, so long riven by fraught emotions, really continue so placidly? Will there be any recurrence or echo of the haughtiness that Hagar showed when she became pregnant with Ishmael?

God saves Hagar and her child (21:9-21). Genesis 21:9 is not entirely clear, although the NRSV ("But Sarah saw the son of Hagar the Egyptian, whom she had borne to Abraham, playing with her son Isaac") removes the difficulty by adopting the reading of the LXX[78] so that it is not apparent to the reader of the translation. The Hebrew simply says that "Sarah saw the son of Hagar the Egyptian whom she had borne to Abraham laughing" *(wattēreʾ śārâ ʾet-ben-hāgār hammiṣrît ʾăšer-yālĕdâ lĕʾabrāhām mĕṣaḥēq)*. The word *mĕṣaḥēq* ("laughing") is clearly a reference to the name of Sarah's son *yiṣḥāq*. But there is no hint of who or what the object of Ishmael's laughter might be. Various translations try to capture the ambiguity in one way or another. Friedman uses "fooling around," which is actually a very good choice; it captures in English the same salacious tone the verb has elsewhere in the Pentateuch and can help us to understand the fierce nature of Sarah's subsequent anger.[79] Fox uses an elision ("laughing . . .") to indicate that an object of the verb seems to be missing.[80] However, it is Alter who has the best reading, one that is true to the text without emendation and offers us an insight into Sarah's mind and emotions.

> The same verb . . . meant "mocking" or "joking" in Lot's encounters with his sons-in-law and . . . elsewhere in the Patriarchal narratives refers to sexual dalliance. . . . Some medieval Hebrew exegetes, trying to find a justification for Sarah's harsh response, construe the verb as a reference to homosexual advances, although that seems far-fetched. Mocking laughter would surely suffice to trigger her outrage. Given the fact, moreover, that she is concerned lest Ishmael encroach on her son's

---

[78] In the LXX Gen 21:9 reads *idousa de Sarra ton huion Agar tēs Aiguptias hos egeneto tō Abraam paizonta meta Isaak tou huiou autēs.*

[79] Richard Elliott Friedman, *Commentary on the Torah* (San Francisco: HarperSanFrancisco, 2001) 71.

[80] Fox, *Moses*, 89.

inheritance, and given the inscription of her son's name in this crucial verb, we may also be invited to construe it as "Isaac-ing-it"— that is, Sarah sees Ishmael presuming to play the role of Isaac, child of laughter, presuming to be the legitimate heir.[81]

This rings absolutely true and helps us also to understand why Ishmael is called "son of Hagar the Egyptian." When Sarah looks at Ishmael, she does not see the teenaged son of her husband, half-brother to her own son, whose very being is the result of her action and who has been a part of her family for many years. All she sees is Hagar. She remembers the humiliation she suffered at Hagar's hands (Gen 16:4) and finds that the time is ripe to wreak her revenge. So, robbing them of any shred of identity, refusing to name them or admit any relationship between these two boys, she demands that the slave and her son be driven out.

In 21:11, Abraham is understandably upset because this evil deed will rob him of his son. In 21:12-13, Abraham is reassured that he may listen to Sarah's voice (the reader remembers the disastrous effects of listening to Sarah's voice—as opposed to God's—in Genesis 16). This looks forward to the latter part of the episode where Hagar listens to the voice of God.

There are a number of parallels between 21:14-21 and Genesis 22, the story of the binding and near-sacrifice of Abraham's other son, Isaac. Ordinarily this story is read in light of that one, as though the latter were prior or somehow more important. Perhaps it would be better, and certainly truer to the order of the text, to read Genesis 22 in light of this story, so that Hagar and Ishmael can better be seen as central to the developing plot of the book.

Both begin identically, referring to Abraham's rising: "And Abraham rose in the morning" (*wayyaškēm ʾabrāhām babbōqer,* 21:14; 22:3). They then proceed to describe necessary items being placed on Hagar's and Isaac's backs.[82] Although in the case of Ishmael, Abraham (and the reader) knows that this son will survive and prosper, Hagar and her son know nothing of this. To them, a long trek in the desert with only the meager provisions that can be carried on one's back probably seems very much like a death sentence.[83] In neither case does Abraham attempt to plead with God, as he did for any righteous people who

---

[81] Alter, *Genesis,* 98.

[82] The narrator seems to have lost track of Ishmael's age in this chapter. The "child" whom Abraham puts on Hagar's back, and whom she later "casts" under a bush, is around sixteen years old (see 16:16; 21:5; and 21:8)!

[83] See Nikaido, "Hagar," 224.

might have been in Sodom. In both cases, a voice from heaven calls out to them just as they face the death of their sons (Gen 21:17: "And an angel of God called to Hagar from heaven," *wayyiqrāʾ malʾak ʾĕlōhîm ʾel-hāgār min-haššāmayim;* Gen 22:11: "And the angel of YHWH called to him from heaven," *wayyiqrāʾ ʾēlāyw malʾak yhwh min-haššāmayim*). If one broadens the comparison to include Hagar's desert test in Genesis 16, both Abraham and Hagar give the sites where they encountered God a name relating to seeing, using the verb *rāʾāh*.

Nikaido[84] offers the following table to compare the two:

Hagar	Abraham	
Angel calls from heaven; the rescue of Ishmael	Angel calls from heaven; the rescue of Isaac	Gen 21:17-18; 22:11-12
Solemn journey; send off with "bread and waterskin"	Solemn journey; send off with "wood, fire and knife"	Gen 21:14; 22:3, 6
Naming speech: *ʾēl-rŏʾî, bᵉʾēr laḥay rŏʾî*	Naming speech: *yhwh-yirʾeh, bᵉhar yhwh yērāʾeh*	Gen 16:14; 22:14
"God opened her eyes and she saw a well"	"Abraham looked up and saw there a ram"	Gen 21:19; 22:13

Finally, it should be pointed out that in being separated from his home, Ishmael becomes associated with other biblical heroes who suffer the same fate: Moses, Joseph, Jacob, David, Esther.[85] In all of these stories, the separation allows the hero to flourish.

Despite all the parallels between the plight of Hagar in Genesis 16 and 21 (to say nothing of the parallels with Genesis 22) there is one striking difference between Hagar's first and second trials. In the first case, God's angel found her by a well (16:7) whereas in the latter, God heard the boy's voice (21:17), although she, not he, is quoted in the text. Why this difference? Perhaps because in Genesis 21 the boy is now old enough to provide for his mother, so God deals with him as head of the household.

The central part of the chapter ends with a note that Ishmael, cared for by his mother, grew, became a man, had a place where he dwelled, and married the woman "his mother" selected for him.

---

[84] Ibid., 229.
[85] Ibid., 233.

Abraham acts and commits himself to a covenant (21:22-34). The final portion of this chapter seems misplaced to some, but it is an important counterpoint to the notice of Ishmael's settling. After Hagar's first expulsion, Abraham made a covenant with God. After this second expulsion, he makes a covenant with Abimelech. True, this provides an etiology, an explanation, for the name of the place most closely associated with Abraham, Beer Sheba, i.e., the "well of the seven," or the "well of the oath." But surely one must wonder whether all is exactly as God would want it with Abraham. Maybe he *should* have pleaded with God over Hagar and Ishmael's fate. Maybe he should *not* have made a covenant with Abimelech. After all, what did he gain thereby? He is still a sojourner in the land, just as he has always been, and Ishmael—rejected, not pleaded for—is settled. Maybe Abraham needs to be tested so that God can see who he really is at this point—so that God can see if he really is willing to throw away sons so easily.

A'. 22:1-19: Obedience and the Sacrifice of What Was Asked

Many, at least those who have learned the biblical languages as adults or near adults, know Genesis 22[86] as the first unadulterated passage of biblical Hebrew at which they were allowed to try their hands as readers and translators of the Bible. It is deceptively easy, with only a few of the lexical and syntactical difficulties that so delight the writers of commentaries. The story is simple: Abraham hears a divine voice telling him to sacrifice Isaac at the end of a journey. He complies absolutely with the command, and is stopped from killing his son only by another voice, which tells him to desist because it is evident that he fears God. But nearly everyone who reads this story reacts to it in some visceral fashion that implies it is not simple at all.[87] It looms large in the

---

[86] The Christian tradition generally refers to the events recounted in this chapter as the Sacrifice of Isaac. However, the Jewish tradition refers to it as the Akedah, i.e., the Binding of Isaac, since Isaac is bound but not sacrificed.

[87] Of course all who read this chapter as a work of literature are beholden to the classic treatment that appeared in Erich Auerbach's study *Mimesis* (Princeton: Princeton University Press, 1953). My own debt to this classic study will be evident in all that follows. Other classic treatments worthy of study include Gerhard von Rad, *Das Opfer des Abraham* (Munich: C. Kaiser, 1971); Henning Graf Reventlow, *Opfere deinen Sohn: eine Auslegung von Genesis 22*, Biblische Studien 23 (Neukirchen: Neukirchener Verlag, 1968); and George W. Coats, "Abraham's Sacrifice of Faith," *Interpretation* 27 (1973) 389–401. The great historical-critical commentaries, von Rad, Westermann, Speiser, all have penetrating insights to offer and are also well worth careful study.

Jewish mind because of its daily recitation as part of the morning service. Although heard less frequently in the Catholic liturgical tradition—being read only on the Second Sunday of Lent (Year B) and on Thursday of the Thirteenth Week of the Year (Year I)—it occupies a very prominent place in the Easter Vigil. During this lengthy nighttime service of waiting and anticipation for the arrival of Easter, Genesis 22:1-19 is the second of seven Old Testament readings, which the congregation hears and ponders immediately following the account of creation in Genesis 1. Also, Christians know the event through its inclusion in the Letter to the Hebrews.

> By faith Abraham, when put to the test, offered up Isaac. He who had received the promises was ready to offer up his only son, of whom he had been told, "It is through Isaac that descendants shall be named for you." He considered the fact that God is able even to raise someone from the dead—and figuratively speaking, he did receive him back. (Heb 11:17-19)

Herewith a very brief and unsystematic sampling of, mostly, modern writers, to show how varied reactions are to this tale.

> As to Genesis 22, how is moral understanding, on a human scale, be it that of Maimonides, of Kant, of Kierkegaard, formidably penetrating as these are, to cope with the *Aquedah,* the story of the sacrifice of Isaac? None but an evil demon can ask of a father to sacrifice his only son (so Kant); solely the true, omnipotent God can ask of a father to sacrifice his only son (so Kierkegaard). How could Abraham "forgive" God for the unspeakable suffering inflicted upon him during the three days journey to Mount Moriah? How could Isaac endure his father after the aborted offering?[88]

The Parable of the Old Man and the Young

> So Abram rose, and clave the wood, and went
> And took the fire with him, and a knife.
> And as they sojourned both of them together,
> Isaac the first-born spake and said, My Father
> Behold the preparations, fire and iron,
> But where the lamb for this burnt-offering?
> Then Abram bound the youth with belts and straps,
> And builded parapets and trenches there,
> And stretched forth the knife to slay his son.

---

[88] George Steiner, "A Preface to the Hebrew Bible," in *No Passion Spent* (New Haven: Yale University Press, 1996) 66.

When lo! An angel called him out of heaven,
Saying, Lay not thy hand upon the lad,
Neither do anything to him. Behold,
A ram, caught in a thicket by its horns;
Offer the Ram of Pride instead of him.
But the old man would not so, but slew his son,
And half the seed of Europe, one by one.[89]

"Many people say that this story means that sometimes it is necessary to make a sacrifice for God," my master began. "A terrible sacrifice, if need be. And on one level they are right. Abraham was willing to kill his son. Then there are some people who say that it is wrong of God to have asked this of a man. And wrong of the man to have agreed. Maybe they are right. I sometimes believe so myself. But here is the secret . . ." Uncle lowered himself across the table so that his face was but a foot from Judah's. His eyes were flashing. Lifting a finger to his lips, he whispered, "Do not forget that Isaac means, 'he laughed.' That is the proof we need to be sure that the Torah is speaking metaphorically, in riddles of a very particular sort. Isaac is not Abraham's son in this world. He is a kind of son inside Abraham himself. He is a child made up of Abraham's laughter and sorrow, anger and tenderness, fears and dreams. And what was God asking from Abraham? That he be willing to give these up. That he be willing to give up his innermost emotions and thoughts, his dearest possessions. That he untie the knots of his mind. That he extinguish part of himself. And why? So that a door might open inside him through which God could enter. Dearest Judah, the story is asking you to open yourself to God and nothing more." Uncle reached out to tousle his nephew's hair, then twisted his nose. "God loves you so much that he is willing to tell a terrible story and have you think bad of Him. All this so that you may one day meet Him inside yourself. He wants to be able to hug you, nothing more. Okay?"[90]

The will of a hideous demon; the expression of someone who wants a hug. . . . Surely, one thinks, they must have been reading different stories. But, no, it is this one story that evokes reactions so fiercely different.[91] Elsewhere in this commentary I have tried to explore my own understanding of how the passage functions as part of the scheme by which our author effects the characterization of God and Abraham. Here I will comment largely on the narrative techniques used.

[89] Wilfred Owen, killed in action in 1918.
[90] Richard Zimler, *The Last Kabbalist of Lisbon* (Woodstock, N.Y.: Overlook, 1998) 130.
[91] A fascinating take on this exercise, and one that all students of the passage would do well to read and ponder, is Reynolds Price's study of four works of art by Rembrandt all based on the story. It was published in *Things Themselves: Essays and Scenes* (New York: Atheneum, 1972) 260–9.

It is no exaggeration to say that this chapter is the best exemplification of Hebrew style. There is no concern for the physical details—just how old is Isaac? where was Sarah? where is Moriah? Nor is there easy access into the inner lives of the characters—why did God test Abraham? how did Abraham and Sarah feel? Isaac? Gaps are used to great effect—what did they talk about in the course of the journey? or as they walked up the mountain with the implements for sacrifice but without a victim? This stripped down narrative technique allows the reader to focus very narrowly on what God and Abraham will do. The plot is clear and straightforward:

Exposition: 22:1a
Inciting moment: 22:1b-2
Development: 22:3-10
Turning point: 22:11
Resolution: 22:12-14
Conclusion: 22:15-19

The narrator is omniscient and trustworthy, even if not as entirely forthcoming as the reader would like. He tells us that what follows is a test, which most commentators take to be a hint to readers that Abraham will not kill his son. However, on the evidence of his life to this point, Abraham seems quite willing to dispose of inconvenient members of his family, especially when the request is from God. In Genesis 12 he left nearly his entire family and never looked back. Twice he disposes of Sarah, and twice he disposes of Hagar, once while pregnant and again with his adolescent son Ishmael. Apparently he finds it all too easy to pass this test. How would this time be any different? This is a fine example both of narratorial reticence and of gapping.

The author uses point of view cleverly as well. To mention here only its most obvious form, perceptual point of view, the reader is left agonizingly behind as father and son draw off together in Genesis 22:8, unable to hear the unimaginable continuation of their conversation: "Abraham said, 'God himself will provide the lamb for a burnt offering, my son.' So the two of them walked on together."

Dialogue is relatively sparing as this example itself shows, but sharply pointed. Witness Abraham's response to God in 22:1, the laconic (and untranslatable) *hinnēnî*. Literally this means "Behold me" but has the sense "Here I am." Nor does Abraham speak more expansively after God's demand is heard. Strangely, he says nothing at all, neither to agree nor to demur. The dialogue between Abraham and Isaac in 22:7 is the only time they speak. One might wish for more.

Pace is also an important part of the chapter's technique. During a three-day journey Abraham would have had plenty of time to ponder what has been asked of him, to regret it, and to plead for a change. How does he know where to go during that time? The relatively long description of the building of the altar in 22:9 serves to heighten tension and increase amazement.

Finally, as we have seen before, the links between this chapter and many of those before are dense and serve to tie all of Abraham's life together. Especially worthy of attention are the complex links between this chapter and the one immediately preceding, and other links between the lives of Abraham's two sons.[92]

The birth and naming of the two sons are nearly identical both in the vocabulary and in the word order used to describe the events.

Ishmael	Isaac
Hagar **bore Abram a son;**	Sarah conceived and **bore Abraham a son** in his old age, at the time of which God had spoken to him.
and Abram named his son, whom Hagar **bore,** Ishmael. (16:15)	**and Abraham named his son** born to him, **whom** Sarah **bore** him, Isaac. (21:2-3)
wattēled hāgār lĕʾabrām bēn	*wattahar wattēled śārâ lĕʾabrāhām bēn lizqūnāyw lammôʿēd ʾăšer-dibber ʾōtô ʾĕlōhîm*
wayyiqrāʾ ʾabrām šem-bĕnô ʾăšer-yālĕdâ hāgār yišmāʿēʾl	*wayyiqrāʾ ʾabrāhām ʾet-šem-bĕnô hannôlad-lô ʾăšer-yālĕdâ-lô śārâ yiṣḥāq*

Both stories begin with God telling Abraham to take some action regarding his son. The imperfect form of the verb "to say" is used in the two scenes that describe God speaking to him.

---

[92] See Curt Leviant, "Parallel Lives: The Trials and Traumas of Isaac and Ishmael," *Bible Review* (April, 1999) 20–5, 47. See also pages 107–9 in Karel Deurloo, "The Way of Abraham: Routes and Localities as Narrative Data in Gen. 11:27– 25:11," in *Voices from Amsterdam*, ed. Martin Kessler (Atlanta: Scholars, 1994) 95–112; and Karel Deurloo, "Because You Have Hearkened to My Voice (Genesis 22)," in the same work, pp. 113–30.

But God **said** to Abraham, "Do not be distressed because of the boy and because of your slave woman; whatever Sarah says to you, do as she **tells you**, for it is through Isaac that offspring shall be named for you." (21:12)	He **said**, "Take your son, your only son Isaac, whom you love, and go to the land of Moriah, and offer him there as a burnt offering on one of the mountains that I shall show [lit: "**tell**"] **you**." (22:2)
wayyō᾽mer ᾽ĕlōhîm ᾽el-᾽abrāhām ᾽al-yēraᶜ bĕᶜêneykā ᶜal-hannaᶜar wĕᶜal-᾽ămātekā kōl ᾽ăšer tō᾽mar ᾽ēleykā śārâ šĕmaᶜ bĕqōlâh kî bĕyiṣḥāq yiqqārē᾽ lĕkā zāraᶜ	*wayyō᾽mer qaḥ-nā᾽ ᾽et-binkā ᾽et-yĕḥîdĕkā ᾽ăšer-᾽āhabtā ᾽et-yiṣḥāq wĕlek-lĕkā ᾽el-᾽ereṣ hammōrîyâ wĕhaᶜălēhû šām lĕᶜōlâ ᶜal ᾽aḥad hehārîm ᾽ăšer ᾽ōmar ᾽ēleykā*

As already noted, both stories use identical vocabulary to describe the beginning of the fateful days. In addition, the verbs "to take," "to put," and "to go" appear in both accounts.

So Abraham rose early in the **morning**, and **took** bread and a skin of water, and gave it to Hagar, **putting** it on her shoulder, along with the child, and sent her away. And she **went**, and wandered about in the wilderness of Beer-sheba. (21:14)	So Abraham rose early in the **morning**, saddled his donkey, and **took** two of his young men with him, and his son Isaac; he cut the wood for the burnt offering, and set out and **went** to the place in the distance that God had shown him. (22:3)
wayyaškēm ᾽abrāhām babbōqer wayyiqqaḥ-leḥem wĕhēmat mayim wayyittēn ᾽el-hāgār śām ᶜal-šikmâh wĕ᾽et-hayyeled wayšallĕḥehā wattēlek wattētaᶜ bĕmidbar bĕ᾽ēr šābaᶜ	*wayyaškēm ᾽abrāhām babbōqer wayyaḥăbōš ᾽et-ḥămōrô wayyiqqaḥ ᾽et-šĕnê nĕᶜārāyw ᾽ittô wĕ᾽ēt yiṣḥāq bĕnô waybaqqaᶜ ᶜăṣê ᶜōlâ wayyāqom wayyēlek ᾽el-ham-māqôm ᾽ăšer-᾽āmar-lô hā᾽ĕlōhîm*
	Abraham **took** the wood of the burnt offering and **put** it on his son Isaac, and he himself **took** the fire and the knife. So the two of them **went** on together. (22:6)
	wayyiqqaḥ ᾽abrāhām ᾽et-ᶜăṣê hāᶜōlâ wayyāśem ᶜal-yiṣḥāq bĕnô wayyiqqaḥ bĕyādô ᾽et-hā᾽ēš wĕ᾽et-hamma᾽ăkelet wayyēlĕkû šĕnêhem yaḥdāw

Whereas wood and fire are key to the sacrifice in the Isaac story, it is the polar opposite to fire—water and the lack thereof— that is the potential cause of death in the Ishmael account. So we see Abraham splitting wood for the sacrificial fire in the Isaac scene and, in the Ishmael story, carrying the jug of water that will soon run out. Both stories use the same Hebrew verb, *va-yikach* (took), to show Abraham grasping the object that symbolizes the "sacrifice" of each son. In both stories, Abraham puts (*yasem* and *sam*) the objects—wood for Isaac, water for Ishmael—on or near the intended victim.[93]

In both cases the endangered child accompanies a parent to the place where he will die. Both tales describe the final preparations for death, using similar-sounding verbs *(wayyišlaḥ; wattašlēk)* to describe the potentially death-dealing parental act.

When the water in the skin was gone, she **cast** the child under one of the bushes. (21:15)	Then Abraham **reached out** his hand and took the knife to kill his son. (22:10)
wayyiklû hammayim min-haḥēmet **wattašlēk** *ʾet-hayyeled taḥat ʾaḥad haśśîḥim*	**wayyišlaḥ** *ʾabrāhām ʾet-yādô wayyiqqaḥ ʾet-hammaʾăkelet lišḥōṭ ʾet-běnô*

Abraham sees the fateful mountain "from afar" (22:4; *mērāḥōq*) while Hagar sits "afar" (21:16; *ḥorḥōq*) so that she will not be able to see her son die. Exactly at the last possible moment, a heavenly voice saves each boy.

Then the angel of God **called** to Hagar **from heaven**. (21:17)	Then the angel of the LORD **called to** him **from heaven**. (22:11)
wayyiqrāʾ malʾak ʾĕlōhîm ʾel-hāgār min-haššāmayim	*wayyiqrāʾ ʾēlāyw malʾak yhwh min-haššāmayim*

The verb *nś* appears in both accounts. In the Ishmael tale, Hagar, sitting afar from the soon-to-die boy, "lifts up" (21:16; *wattiśśāʾ*) her voice and weeps, whereas in the Isaac tale Abraham "lifts up" (22:13; *wayyiśśāʾ*)

---

[93] Leviant, "Lives," 22.

his eyes and sees the ram. After the danger is past, the angels speak to the parents, using the words "fear," "listen," "God," and "voice."

Do not **fear**, for **God** has **heard** the **voice** of the boy. (21:17)	that you **fear God**, . . . because you have obeyed (lit., "**heard**") my **voice**. (22:12, 18)
ʾal-tîrĕʾî kî-šāmaʿ ʾĕlōhîm ʾel-qôl hannaʿar	*kî-yĕrēʾ ʾĕlōhîm ʾattâ . . . ʿēqeb ʾăšer šāmaʿtā bĕqōlî*

Both angels make a point of speaking of "hand" and "boy" as they save the children.

. . . lift up **the boy** and hold him fast with **your hand**. (21:18)	Do not lay **your hand** on the **boy**. (22:12)
śĕʾî ʾet-hannaʿar wĕhaḥăzîqî ʾet-yādēk bô	*ʾal-tišlaḥ yādĕkā ʾel hannaʿar*

The next verse in each account describes what is made available by God as an alternative to death. The parent's "eyes" are either lifted up or opened, each "sees" the life-saving alternative and "goes" to fetch it.

Then God opened **her eyes** and she **saw** a well of water. She **went**, and filled the skin with water, and gave the boy a drink. (21:19)	And Abraham looked up (lit: "lifted up **his eyes**") and **saw** a ram, caught in a thicket by its horns. Abraham **went** and took the ram and offered it up as a burnt offering instead of his son. (22:13)
wayyipqaḥ ʾĕlōhîm ʾet-ʿêneyhā wattēreʾ bĕʾēr māyim wattēlek wattĕmallēʾ ʾet-haḥēmet mayim wattašq ʾet-hannāʿar	*wayyiśśāʾ ʾabrāhām ʾet-ʿênāyw wayyarʾ wĕhinnēh-ʾayil ʾaḥar neʾĕḥaz bassĕbak bĕqarnāyw wayyēlek ʾabrāhām wayyiqqaḥ ʾet-hāʾayil wayyaʿălēhû lĕʿōlâ taḥat bĕnô*

After his rescue, each boy is promised to be the source of abundant life, although the key word "blessing" does not appear in the promise relative to Ishmael.

I will make a great nation of him. (21:18b)	I will indeed **bless** you, and I will make your offspring as numerous as the stars of heaven and as the sand that is on the seashore. (22:17a)
kî-lĕgôy gādôl ʾăśîmennû	*kî-bārēk ʾăbārekĕkā wĕharbâ ʾarbeh ʾet-zarʿăkā kĕkôkĕbê haššāmayim wĕkaḥôl ʾăšer ʿal-śĕpat hayyām*

Nonetheless, as Leviant points out:

> There is a fascinating crisscrossing of blessings regarding Ishmael's posterity on one side and Abraham and Isaac's on the other. As if to further accent the equality of Ishmael and Isaac, an angel of the Lord earlier spoke the same words to Hagar—"I will make your descendants numerous" (Genesis 16:10)—that the angel now speaks to Abraham. And the promise of a "great nation" *(goy gadol)* that is made to Ishmael here and also earlier (Genesis 17:20) has previously been made to Abraham (Genesis 12:2 and 18:18). Continuing his remarks to Hagar, the angel (Genesis 16:10) uses the very same words, "they shall be too numerous to count" *(lo yisafar me-rov)* regarding Ishmael's descendants that Jacob uses in referring to God's promise to him (Genesis 32:13). Moreover, the phrase "multiply exceedingly" is used for both Abraham's posterity and for Ishmael's. "I will multiply thee exceedingly"—*ve-arbeh otcha bi-me'od me'od* (Genesis 17:2)—for Abraham; and "I will multiply him exceedingly"—*ve-hirbeiti oto bi-me'od me'od* (Genesis 17:20)—for Ishmael.[94]

There are yet other parallels. Abraham sojourns at Beer Sheba, where Ishmael faced his trial. Both parents give names to the sites where they faced the possible deaths of the children, and both names have the verb "to see" as an element. The lives of the two are spent quietly but take very different routes, Ishmael living as a desert hunter married to an Egyptian and Isaac dwelling quietly married to his cousin. However their deaths are described in identical words.

And he **breathed his last and died, and was gathered to his people**. (25:17)	And Isaac **breathed his last and died, and was gathered to his people**. (35:29)
wayyigwaʿ wayyāmot wayyēʾāsep ʾel-ʿammāyw	*wayyigwaʿ yiṣḥāq wayyāmot wayyēʾāsep ʾel-ʿammāyw*

[94] Ibid., 25.

The chapter, and the exposition, begins with the phrase "After these things . . . ," which not only places these events chronologically subsequent to those which precede but also suggests that they are causally related as well, i.e., that these events flow from what precedes as consequence from cause. We have already seen the numerous parallels between the two, but a question still arises. Why a test? The word is used only this one time in Genesis and, with only thirty-seven occurrences, is not very frequent in the rest of the Hebrew Bible. A survey of some of these instances will help us create an idea of what is meant by such a divine test.[95]

Sometimes the tests are of Israel (e.g., Exod 15:25; 16:4; 20:20; Deut 8:2, 16; 13:4; 33:8; Judg 2:22; 3:1, 4). In 2 Chronicles 32:31 Hezekiah is tested, and the Psalmist is tested in Psalm 26:2. Are the people, whether individually or corporately, loyal and obedient to God? Do they love God wholeheartedly and walk in God's ways? Do they trust that God will fulfill the promises made to God's people? The test, if successful, works both ways; both parties learn that the other is trustworthy.[96] In short, they need to know whether they are mutually trustworthy. In this particular instance, of course, the reader knows that Abraham is being tested, but he does not.

Complications begin as soon as God—not identified here as YHWH, this personal name of God not appearing until much later in the tale— calls out to Abraham.[97] This latter responds "Here I am,"[98] implying

---

[95] Normal Hebrew word order is inverted in this first sentence for emphasis. Additionally, the word "God" is preceded by the definite article. According to E. A. Speiser this is also for emphasis, indicating that God had some special objective in mind (*Genesis*, AB 1 [New York: Doubleday, 1962] 162). Brichto takes a very different approach. He identifies the article as the *hē* of abstraction, meaning something like Heaven. He also points out that the voice who speaks to Abraham is not identified, merely the third masculine singular form of the verb, and it is for the reader to connect the voice with Heaven. This raises yet more ambiguities for the reader. Is it really God that tested Abraham? Was the voice he heard really God's or that of another? Or even Abraham's own voice? Maybe the whole thing was "The Madness of Father Abraham" (Brichto, *Names of God*, 280).

[96] Marsha M. Wilfong, "Genesis 22:1-18," *Interpretation* 45 (1991) 393–4.

[97] The LXX has "Abraham, Abraham. . . ." The repetition nicely parallels the angel's repetition later in the chapter and also the repetition of Moses' name when he encounters YHWH on Mount Horeb in Exodus 3.

[98] Biblical Hebrew lacked words that were straightforward equivalents to "Yes" and "No" in modern English. This very common word (more than 180 occurrences in the Hebrew Bible), which literally means "Behold me," sometimes means no more than "Yes." However, it frequently means that the one addressed is attentive and able to obey. That is the case here.

that he is present, willing, and able to do God's will. In one of the Bible's most famous sentences, God says, "Take your son, your only son Isaac, whom you love, and go to the land of Moriah, and offer him there as a burnt offering on one of the mountains that I shall show you."

Each element of the sentence warrants comment. The command sounds more brusque in translation than the original *(qaḥ-nāʾ)* warrants. This is a polite request, something more like "Would you take . . . ," and a request, moreover, that at least according to some commentators[99] could be declined without difficulty. Perhaps even the appearance of being able to avoid the test was part of the test, but Abraham might well have missed this subtlety, so shocking will the next words have been:[100] "your son[101] *(ʾet-binkā)*, your only son *(ʾet-yĕḥîdĕkā)*, whom you love[102] *(ʾăšer-ʾāhabtā)*, Isaac *(ʾet-yiṣḥāq)*." But of course Abraham has two sons, so what can God mean? Rashi, the great medieval Jewish commentator, includes in his commentary on Genesis a famous midrash that this sentence is actually one half of a dialogue between Abraham and God.

> *"Thy son"*: (Abraham) said to Him, "Two sons have I." (God) said to him, "Thine only son." (Abraham) said to Him, "This one is an only son to his mother and the other is an only son to his mother." (God) said to him, "Whom thou lovest." (Abraham) said to Him, "Both of them do I love." (God) said to him, "Isaac." (Sanh. 89)[103]

The midrash points to an especially perplexing element of this sentence. Why is there the threefold qualification of Isaac, one element of which ("your only son") is factually incorrect? The midrash teaches that God leads Abraham patiently toward the final revelation of God's plan. Is there another way to approach the difficulty?

As I argue elsewhere in this commentary, this chapter functions as part of an inclusion, a bracketing device, around the central part of Abraham's life with God. As such, this first sentence of his test—the last

---

[99] Rashi, *The Pentateuch and Rashi's Commentary: A Linear Translation into English,* trans. Abraham ben Isaiah and Benjamin Sharfman (Brooklyn: S. S. & R. Publishing, 1949) vol. 1, *Genesis:* 199.

[100] Typically, English translations like the NRSV change the word order of the original, with a result like ". . . your son, your only son Isaac, whom you love . . ." This may yield a more typical English word order but it loses the tension of the original which builds gradually toward the revelation of the name of the intended victim.

[101] The reader notices that the words "father" and "son" recur frequently in the chapter, far more often than is required for sense. We are never allowed to forget that this is a father and son.

[102] This is the first time the word "love" appears in the Bible.

[103] Rashi, *Pentateuch,* 199.

time God speaks to him—mirrors the first time God spoke to him. There, too, he was commanded to undergo a leave-taking that was threefold and coupled with the phrase *lek-lĕkā:* "Go from your country and your kindred and your father's house. . . ." The reappearance of this phrase here (the only other time the phrase occurs in the Bible), plus the three-fold qualification of Isaac, leads scholars to associate the two. Just as Abraham had to go "for himself" in that instance, he must go "for himself" here, and in order to do so he must take his son and give him to God. But in neither case does Abraham know where he is going. There God told him to go to the land "that I will show you" (12:1), while here the command is to go to the otherwise unknown land of Moriah and offer him on "one of the mountains that I will tell you." Is the name Moriah significant? Scholars are divided on the real meaning of the name, but it is at least alike in sound to the verb *r'h,* "to see" (in the Qal) or "to reveal" (in the Niphal). Since seeing and revelation play such a large part later in the chapter, this reading makes sense. Abraham is told then to make his way to the Mountain of Revelation, where he will see indeed. The enormity of this command can hardly be overstressed. Abraham is asked not only to kill his son but also to commit a real sort of suicide, since his hope of blessing and of the promises would die with Isaac, no matter how great a nation Ishmael might become.

How does Abraham respond? With silence. Was he angry, serene, trusting, despairing, planning an escape? Did he toss and turn during a sleepless night? We have no way of knowing. There is no insight into Abraham's interior life; all we have is a sequence of verbs: he rose, saddled, took, cut, set out, went, looked up, and saw.

The narration remains enigmatic. When did God show him the land? Was the revelation Abraham received from God ongoing, such that he knew where to go because God was leading him along, and he looked up and saw Mount Moriah when God told him to? He looked up after three days—a time period universally commented upon—during which he must have had time to ponder what he was doing and give it second and third thoughts. But he never deviated, and spoke neither to God nor to Isaac.

Once they have arrived at the mountain, "Abraham said to his young men, 'Stay here with the donkey; the boy and I will go over there; we will worship, and then we will come back to you'" (22:5). "Worship" meant sacrifice, but they had nothing to sacrifice. "We will come back. . . ." Is this a hint that Abraham has divined the true significance and outcome of what he is doing, or is it merely a ruse to get the boy to accompany him without difficulty?

Abraham could have given Isaac the knife to carry, caused him to fall and thereby, having blemished him, eliminated him as an acceptable

sacrificial object. Abraham—full of horror? numb? resolute? hopeful?—
carries the knife instead. It is clear that he means to carry the act out,
even more clear when he responds to his son's inquiry about what they
will sacrifice.[104] He says, "God will see-to-himself for the lamb to sacrifice my son" (Gen 22:8; *ʾĕlōhîm yirʾeh-lô haśśeh lĕʿōlâ bĕnî*). Hebrew has no
punctuation, so "my son" may simply be words of address or may be an
identification of the intended lamb. After this, the sole dialogue between
Abraham and Isaac in the Bible, Isaac does not speak again. Silence re-
sumes and the reader is left behind as they continue their walk.

> The boy knows however. His eyes have clouded, crouched backward
> darkly. *The sheep is me.* He had finally hoped it might be a slave, till they
> left the slaves.
>
> The man knows the boy knows, thinks he'll surrender. He has not even
> posted slaves as guards.
>
> The boy is going to run. About-face and run. The way is just behind him,
> a quick trail down. He will, and will escape. He is seeing, this instant,
> that his father offers it—his only chance—that his father is too old to
> hold even him; that his father has worn too many clothes . . . that the
> slaves, if they see him at all, will not care.[105]

Pace—which passed over a three-day journey in silence and a
phrase—slackens in 22:9 as Abraham meticulously builds an altar.
Then an angel calls from heaven, to save this son just as the other son
had been saved. And the turning point is achieved. For the third time—
once to God, once to Isaac, and once to the angel—Abraham says that
he is ready. But the angel's call only raises more questions. Would not
God have always known that Abraham feared God? But perhaps he
did not really fear God until this moment. Abraham offers the ram and
names the place "On the mountain of Yʜᴡʜ there is vision." With
blessing renewed, he then returns, but Isaac is not mentioned. Where
did he go?

In the tradition. One modern commentator can see no other way to
understand the passage than to think Abraham was, for a time, mad.

> No, there can be no question that the normal, honest and rational reaction
> of the audience to Abraham's obedience is the judgment that, in the forty-
> eight to seventy-two hours from call to slay to call to desist, he was a
> madman. And it follows therefore that this was precisely the reaction that

---

[104] Note that Isaac mentions the wood and the fire but passes over in silence
what would be the most frightening object, the knife.
[105] Price, *Things,* 264.

the author is inviting. . . . The lesson, the kerygma, of the Binding of Isaac is that if you will not make the ultimate sacrifice except at the call of Scripture's god, you will never hear that call. For he is the God of life and blessing. But if you think that to respond to such a call from God—were it to come—would be madness, you will find that the call will come indeed. But it will come from the domain of the less than ultimate. And it will come with an importunacy that you will not withstand.[106]

But this is not an understanding that the tradition is comfortable with. If he was not mad and the test was real and sent from God, why did God test him? Surely God would have known what he would do. Rabbenu Nissim said:

> The nature of this trial calls for explanation, since there is no doubt that the Almighty does not try a person in order to prove to himself whether he is capable of withstanding the trial since God is allknowing and is in no doubt about anything.[107]

For Maimonides, the answer is clear. Abraham obeyed immediately, without question and without hesitation, because God commanded him, and it is the duty of humanity to obey God's commands.

> For Abraham did not hasten to kill Isaac out of fear that God might slay him or make him poor, but solely because it is man's duty to love and to fear God, even without hope of reward or fear of punishment.[108]

Abraham's perfect obedience was to be an exemplar to all people.

> The trial was not a test evolved by God to find out what He did not know, but God made a demonstration, the root of the word being from *ness* meaning wonder or sign which Abraham performed at the word of God, as an example and banner to all the peoples for them to follow.[109]

Another approach is to say that Abraham's utter obedience was, until this test, more potential than actual. Witness Ramban:

> This is my idea of what the term *nisayon* implies. Since man is complete master of his own actions, possessing the free will to act or to refrain from acting, the term *nisayon* or trial expresses the situation from the

---

[106] Brichto, *Names of God*, 289, 290.
[107] In Leibowitz, *Bereshit*, 188.
[108] Maimonides, *Guide to the Perplexed*, in Leibowitz, *Bereshit*, 189.
[109] Abravanel, in Leibowitz, *Bereshit*, 190.

point of view of the person himself. On the other hand, God, who confronts him with the trial commands him in order to translate into action the potentialities of his character, and give him the reward of a good deed, in addition to the reward of a good heart.

Know also that the Lord tries the righteous. When he knows that the righteous man will do His will and wishes to show his righteousness, He confronts him with a trial. But He does not try the wicked who will not hearken. All the trials described in the Torah were directed to benefit the recipient.[110]

The Akedah is read daily in the Jewish liturgy. It appears far less frequently in the liturgy of the Catholic Church, but it is given especial prominence because it was read typologically, i.e., the ordeal of Isaac foreshadowed that of Christ.

> [Jesus was the fulfillment of] that which was foreshadowed in Isaac, who was offered upon the altar.[111]

> Since indeed Abraham, having followed, in keeping with his faith, the commandment of God's word, did with a ready mind give up his only begotten and well beloved son, for a sacrifice unto God, that God again might be well pleased to offer unto Abraham's whole seed His only begotten and dearly beloved son to be a sacrifice for our redemption.[112]

Saint Augustine also took this line.

> And on this account Isaac carried the wood on which he was to be offered up to the place of sacrifice, just as the Lord Himself carried His own cross. Finally, since Isaac himself was not killed—for his father had been forbidden to kill him—who was that ram which was offered instead, and by whose foreshadowing blood the sacrifice was accomplished? For when Abraham had caught sight of him, he was caught by the horns in a thicket. Who then did he represent but Jesus, who, before He was offered up, had been crowned with thorns?[113]

The modern writer Thomas Mann offers a very different reading of the scene, one that helps us to understand the subsequent silence between God and Abraham.

> ". . . And when I saw the mountain of the Lord from afar and the peak of the mountain, I sent the ass back with the young men and took the fire

---

[110] Ramban, in Leibowitz, *Bereshit*, 191.

[111] *Letter of Barnabas* 7:3, in Kugel, *Traditions*, 306.

[112] Irenaeus, *Against the Heresies* 4:5, 4, in Kugel, *Traditions*, 306.

[113] *City of God* 16, 32.

and a knife in my hand, and we went alone. And when thou spakest to me and said: 'My father,' then I could not say 'Here I am, my son,' but instead moaned in my throat. And when thou in thy voice saidest: 'Behold the fire and the wood, but where is the lamb for a burnt offering?' then could I not answer as I should that the Lord would provide himself a lamb, for I was sick within me, so that I could have spat out my soul with tears, and moaned again so that thou lookest at me as thou wentest beside me. And when we came to the place I builded an altar of stone and laid the wood in order and bound the child and laid him upon it. And took the knife with my left hand and covered thy two eyes. And when I drew the knife and the edge of the knife across thy throat, lo, then did I deny the Lord, and my arm fell from thy shoulder, and the knife fell down, and I fell upon my face upon the ground and bit the earth and the grass of the earth and struck at it with my feet and my fists and cried: 'Slay him, Thou, O Lord and Destroyer, for he is my one and only, and I am not Abraham and my soul fails before Thee.' And as I thrust about me and shrieked, lo, thunder rolled from the place along the heaven far and wide. And I had the child and had the Lord no more, for I could not do it for Him, no, no, no, I could not," he groaned and shook his head against the hand on the staff.[114]

22:20–25:10: The Substance of Life Afterwards

Although Abraham was to live for many more years, they are passed over in near silence. It is as though he goes on living after he has finished living. After the Akedah, God and he never speak again; he has no visions or, indeed, any encounters with the divine at all. His life passes back into the mundane where, in fact, he had spent most of the preceding years, despite its punctuation with extraordinary events. This whole section thus stands outside of the great structure that describes his life, just as the period before his call also stood outside.

This is not to say that nothing happens during these years. If God is absent as an active character, important events nonetheless do occur. So the whole section serves as a sort of overlapping hinge that covers the end of the first generation and the beginning of the second. Sarah dies; Abraham buys a field in which to bury her and so begins to possess the Promised Land; a wife is found for Isaac; Abraham remarries and raises a second family; and, finally, he dies and is buried by his sons Isaac and Ishmael. So the first generation comes to an end and the second takes the stage.

---

[114] Thomas Mann, *Joseph and His Brothers*, trans. H. T. Lowe-Porter (London: Vintage, 1999) 65–6.

Perhaps most surprising to the reader is the change in tone from what has gone before. These stories are long and leisurely, full of detail that is not strictly necessary to their narrative purpose. Isaac, the subject of so much concern, is absent from the scene of his mother's death, although his mourning for her is later said to be assuaged by his relationship with his wife Rebekah. The very lengthy Genesis 24 is also unusual in comparison to earlier parts of the book. The protagonist of that story is a nameless servant who is never mentioned before and who disappears immediately after.

Structure. The section does hang together as a unity despite containing a number of subsections, and it will be treated here as a unity. Its structure, if for no other reason than its length and the length of the various subsections, is complex and has been variously described.[115]

Transitional genealogical note (22:20-24)

A. The death and burial of Sarah at Machpelah (23:1-20)

   a. Narrative introduction (23:1-2)

   b. First Dialogue (23:3-6)

   b'. Second dialogue (23:7-11)

   b". Third dialogue (23:12-15)

   + Land contract (23:16-18)

   a'. Narrative conclusion (23:19-20)

B. A wife for Isaac (24:1-67)

   Scene 1—24:1-9

   Scene 2—24:10-14

      Narrator's voice (24:10-11)

      Servant's voice (24:12-14)

   Scene 3—24:15-21

   Scene 4—24:22-27

      A. The servant acts (24:22)

      B^1. The servant asks (24:23a)

      B^2. The servant asks (24:23b)

      $B^{1'}$. Rebekah answers (24:24)

      $B^{2'}$. Rebekah answers (24:25-27)

      A'. The servant acts (24:26)

   Scene 5—24:28-29

---

[115] The structure to be followed and commented upon here is adapted from Walsh, *Style and Structure*, 135–8, 167, 187–8. For an alternative see Coats, *Genesis*, especially 166–7.

Scene 6—24:30-51
  Subscene 1—24:30-33
  Subscene 2a—24:34-49
  Subscene 2b—24:50-51
Scene 7—24:52-61
Scene 8—24:62-67
  Introduction—24:62
  Subscene 1—24:63
  Subscene 2—24:64-65
  Transition—24:66
  Subscene 3—24:67
B'. A wife and another family for Abraham (25:1-6)
A'. The death and burial of Abraham (25:7-10)

The brief genealogical note at the end of Genesis 22 serves an important narratological point. Some nameless agent tells Abraham that his brother has been very fruitful, in stark contrast to Abraham's difficulties in having children. In fact, by his wife and concubine Nahor has had twelve sons. Of these there is further information only about one, Bethuel, because he became the father of Rebekah. Thus in a way reminiscent of Abraham himself, Rebekah is introduced and things start to turn toward the second generation. Although Abraham has years to live and another family to raise, the truly active part of Abraham's life, during which he and God spoke so familiarly, is now over.

Genesis 23 is wholly concerned with the death of Sarah. That she is old is well known to the reader of the book, but one is nonetheless surprised at her death. After Abraham rises early and takes Isaac and his slaves with him to Mount Moriah, there is no record of Sarah and Isaac meeting again. Isaac, as the reader will recall, is absent on the return trip. One is tempted to fill this enormous gap in the narrative. How did Sarah discover their absence? One can hardly imagine that she, who had waited so terribly long for the pleasure and laughter that a son would bring her and was so jealous for her son's welfare vis-à-vis Ishmael, would have readily acquiesced in Abraham's decision to sacrifice him. Surely, one thinks, Abraham sneaked away without his wife's knowledge. Did she wait with mounting fear as she discovered not only that they were gone but also that they had taken with them the implements for a sacrifice without any animal to be sacrificed? Was she enraged? Grief-stricken? Simply confused? Did she die from grief and trauma resulting from Abraham's obedience? Was she perhaps the real victim of the Akedah?

No one confronting the tale of Sarah's death should be left unaware of Rashi's comment on Genesis 23:3: "And the death of Sarah was placed next to the Binding of Isaac, for through the announcement of the Binding, that her son had been prepared for slaughter and had almost been slaughtered, her soul fled from her and she died."[116]

This brief comment on the part of the great thirteenth-century commentator has itself a long history and reflects a number of previous midrashim, each of which sheds a different light on this tragic text. Consider this version from *Pirkei de Rabbi Eliezer*:

> When Abraham came from Mount Moriah, Samael (Satan) was furious that he had failed to realize his lust to abort Abraham's sacrifice. What did he do? He went off and told Sarah, "Ah, Sarah, have you not heard what's been happening in the world?" She replied, "No." He said, "Your old husband has taken the boy Isaac and sacrificed him as a burnt offering, while the boy cried and wailed in his helplessness [lit., for he could not be saved]." Immediately she began to cry and wail. She cried three sobs, corresponding to the three *Tekʾiah* notes of the Shofar, and she wailed (Yelalot) three times, corresponding to the *Yevava*, staccato notes of the Shofar. Then she gave up the ghost and died. Abraham came and found her dead, as it is said, "And Abraham came [literal translation] to mourn for Sarah and to bewail her."[117]

Zornberg comments on this passage that the cry of the Shofar, the ram's horn trumpet used in Jewish liturgy, announces the possibility of redemption, of symbolic substitution. The ram has taken the place of Isaac, and the substitutionary sacrifice was accepted by God. Yet, at the same time, it announces that in Sarah's mind Isaac was not saved so the cries of despair at her loss are forever commingled with the announcement of redemption. Redemption and loss are somehow inextricably intertwined.[118] Another midrash works toward a different but not unrelated point. Abraham's joy at the salvation of his son is tempered by the loss of his wife. True, unequivocal joy is not for this world but is reserved for the future.[119] Here one knows the vertigo "which comes from the possibility there was of being different, of not having been at all."[120]

---

[116] Rashi, *Pentateuch*, 209. What follows is in large part dependent on the chapter "ḤAYYEI SARAH: Vertigo—The Residue of the Akedah," in Zornberg, *Genesis*, 123–43, an essential work.

[117] In Zornberg, *Genesis*, 124.

[118] Ibid.

[119] Ibid., 126.

[120] Ibid., 127, quoting Paul Ricoeur, *History and Truth* (Chicago: Northwestern University Press, 1965) 290.

If Sarah dies from the dizziness caused by the pain of realization that the world she thought so firm has no firmness in it at all, it also leads to the possibility of blessing becoming realized. In her death Abraham has an opportunity at least to begin to possess a bit of the land so long promised to him, in which he has so long sojourned, but always on sufferance, since until now he has owned none of it despite his other wealth.

Of course, all of this is the sort of speculation raised less by the biblical text that stands before us today than by the gaps in that text. As we continue through these chapters at the end of Abraham's life, we will continue to see that gaps abound.

The NRSV smooths out the report of Sarah's death with which the chapter begins. This use of repetition, to be seen again in the death notices of Abraham and Ishmael, serves to heighten and emphasize Sarah's importance. Also, she is the only woman in the Bible whose life span is recorded, further emphasizing her singular importance in the history of this chosen people. A literal translation of the Hebrew would read:

> And Sarah's life was a hundred years and twenty years and seven years: the years of Sarah (23:1, AT; *wayyihyû ḥayyê śārâ mēʾâ šānâ wěʿeśrîm šānâ wěšebaʿ šānîm šěnê ḥayyê śārâ*).

The backdrop of the chapter is Abraham's sojourner status. This theme is introduced right at the beginning when we are told that Sarah died in Kiriath Arba,[121] (an alternate name for Hebron) in the land of Canaan. Thus, after all this time and despite the repeated promises of God, Abraham remains an outsider in a land where he possesses nothing. The death of Sarah is provocative because it is noted that Abraham "came" to mourn her.[122] Why was he in Beer Sheba and she in Hebron? How might this gap be filled? One cannot say since the Bible is silent on this surprising separation.

The dialogues that follow are replete with ancient Near Eastern legal terminology and practice. This begins right away when Abraham identifies himself in 23:4 as *gēr-wětôšāb ʾānōkî ʿimmākem* ("I am an alien and sojourner with you"[123]). He lives in their midst but is not one of

---

[121] The name means "City of Four," possibly referring to a group of federated towns (like the later Decapolis), four hills, or, according to Alter (*Genesis*, 108) it might simply be the Hebrew version of a non-Hebrew name.

[122] Speiser remarks that these formal rites have no bearing, "one way or another, on the survivor's personal feelings." *Genesis*, 169.

[123] The phrase is a hendiadys referring to one who lacks the normal rights of a citizen, notably the right to own land. Cf. Speiser, *Genesis*, 170.

the Hittites,[124] and since he owns no property, he has no legal rights (see also 12:10; 19:9). Out of politeness, and skilled at a rhetoric of indirection wherein one does not speak too immediately or directly about what one wants, he does not ask to buy property but asks instead for a "grant of property for a grave" *(ʾăḥuzzat-qeber)*, which implies permanent legal possession.

The Hittites respond[125] as a group with a sort of ultra-polite rhetoric. They flatter Abraham, telling him that he is one of the big men in their community. They offer to let him use any tomb he desires out of the respect they have for him. Politely left aside is his request to *buy* some land for the purpose. They do not deny what he did not in fact ask. One imagines smiles all around as the conversation proceeds on two levels. On the surface all is respect and courtesy, but underneath the Hittites do not, yet at least, entertain Abraham's desire to buy.

Not to be outdone nor deflected from his aim, Abraham prostrates himself before these notables (literally, "the people of the land," *ʿam-hāʾāreṣ*) and describes precisely the property that he has in mind, a cave that is at the end of a field belonging to a man named Ephron. He has clearly studied the local real estate to find the area that best serves his needs and will least inflame local suspicion of the outsider. The way he describes it makes it clear that in reaching the cave he will not have to cross his neighbor's property or otherwise encroach on his holding.[126] He still avoids using the verb "to sell," contenting himself with the less specific "grant," but he makes his intentions clear when he offers to pay full price *(běkesep mālēʾ)*. There is no attempt to find the best price; he simply wants to buy and will pay whatever is asked. In the sentence which describes Ephron's response to Abraham's request the word "Hittites" appears three times, along with a more precise description of the scene as a meeting of the town council.[127] While the latter shows us that this is no mere chat among acquaintances but a formal negotiation, the former also underlines for the reader Abraham's status as an outsider. Ephron's threefold repetition of "I grant . . ." is, at least on the surface, a formal donation of the property to Abraham. But that is the last thing Abraham, and apparently Ephron as well, really wants. Note

[124] It is not clear who these "Hittites" were since Hittites lived in what would now be central Turkey. It might be a catchall term for non-Semites.

[125] Speiser's suggestion (*Genesis*, 170) that the final word of 23:5 *lô* ("to him") be repointed as *lû* and moved to the beginning of 23:6 is generally accepted in contemporary translations like the NRSV. This precative particle means "Would that . . ." or "But please . . . ," a sort of exaggerated politeness.

[126] See Alter, *Genesis*, 110.

[127] Speiser, *Genesis*, 170.

that Ephron offers more than Abraham has asked, the entire field instead of just the cave at the bottom of the field. But Abraham wants to
buy it, and Ephron—underneath his formal courtesy—wants to hear
what sort of offer he is willing to make. In the third dialogue, Abraham
declines to specify a price, simply saying that he will pay what is asked.
The price asked seems to have been exorbitant, but Abraham pays it immediately, further enhancing the impression we have of his wealth.[128]

As one might expect, verses 16-18 read like a contract for the con-
veyance of land and carefully describe precisely what Abraham buys.
That he buys this land, and does not merely lease it, is made clear by
the appearance here of the word *miqnâ* "possession," which is based on
the verbal root *qnh*, "to buy." Thus the language of purchase and buying, which has been so studiously avoided throughout the negotiations, appears here at the end. So Abraham, at long last, begins actually
to possess what has been so long promised. It is remarkable, however,
that he possesses it not on the basis of any divine intervention.[129] Unlike the encounters with Pharaoh and Abimelech, God does not influ-
ence any of this, not does Abraham pray or seek a vision. Keeping
with the distance between God and Abraham that entered Genesis at
the Akedah, Abraham acts on his own without waiting for a voice
from God. Dealing as one man of affairs with some especially sharp
competitors, Abraham buys one small bit of what God has promised to
give to him. Earlier (Genesis 16), when Abraham felt that the promises
were threatened, he listened to the voice of his wife. That time things
went wrong. This time, having lifted up his voice in mourning for the
wife whose death he missed, he bows, not to God, but to these Hittites
and acts to make the promise begin to come true. God, for reasons of
his own—another of the vexing gaps in the text—remains silent. Abraham is learning to act in accord with his destiny but without recourse

---

[128] A shekel is not currency, for we are still before the introduction of coinage,
but a weight of precious metal that varied according to time and place. So it is not
possible to compute an accurate estimate for this sum. Speiser notes that sales of
entire villages from this era range from 100–1000 shekels. By way of comparison—
although from a much later time, so the weight may well have changed—Omri
paid 6000 shekels for the entire site of the city of Samaria (1 Kgs 16:24), and Jeremiah
(Jer 32:9) paid only seventeen shekels (at what were probably depressed prices since
the Assyrian army was camped on it!) for a similar field.

[129] The chapter begins and ends with the note that this all takes place at Hebron.
When preparing to return to the Promised Land after their sojourn as slaves in
Egypt, Israel's spies first go to Hebron (Num 13:22). Thus—whatever the historical
realities of the Exodus and the origins of Israel's presence in the land—Hebron was
remembered as the bit they owned and to which they felt entitled to return.

to God, simply trusting his own understanding of God's will. This is another legacy of the Binding of Isaac.

Genesis 24 does not ordinarily excite much comment or interest in those commenting on the book. Indeed, in comparison with other chapters in the book it appears to have little of real importance to add to the developing saga. However, it does contain some interesting examples of narrative technique (such as the so-called "type scene" where the future betrothed is encountered at a well) and provides interesting insight into the characters of the barely known Isaac and his wife Rebekah. It also gives us an introduction to the character of Laban, uncle of the yet unborn Jacob, with whom the latter will contend in due time.

Like the other important moments in Abraham's life, this one is marked by a journey. Abraham is elderly, near to death, and it is time to find a wife for his successor, Isaac. The wife must come from his own family; apparently they are endogamous and only marry within the kinship group in order to keep the family line clear of intrusions. Isaac may not return to Mesopotamia because God's promises are tied to the land in which he is now living. From the very beginning it is clear that Isaac's role in the ongoing history of this family is to be largely passive.

The story unfolds in a series of complex scenes. I will comment here on some of the more important and interesting details of the narrative.

The ordinary word order of the first sentence is inverted and gives rise to a certain tension as the reader wonders what use is going to be made of Abraham's age. It turns out that he intends to provide a wife for his son Isaac and asks his servant, the nameless protagonist of the piece, to swear an oath "under his thigh"—apparently meaning either to touch the master's genitals or to rest his hand near the genitals. This way of taking an oath appears again only in Genesis 47:29, and its meaning is not clear, but it is certainly connected with procreation. It might be a reminder to the servant of the nature of his task and his goal, or it might remind him that he is under a curse (and that his own procreation is at risk) unless his task is successful. The conditions are set out: the betrothed is to be from the same family, and Isaac may not go there. (Indeed Isaac never leaves the promised land.) The instructions are reminiscent of Genesis 12, a reiteration of the language of covenant and promise that binds Abraham and his line to this land (and binds the land to them). It appears here but is not repeated to the family. So the servant, with a caravan of ten camels, sets out for what would have been a month-long journey. The camels that appear here require some comment, for historically they were not yet domesticated. If this is some sort of an error, it would be a surprise, since the other details of the story are rather scrupulously correct: there are no horses (also not yet domesticated), there is no coinage, but silver is used by weight.

The details of betrothal negotiation, with the brother acting as principal agent for the family, the bestowal of a dowry on the bride and betrothal gifts for the family, are equally accurate for the middle of the second millennium B.C.E.[130]

With so much else that is correct, why the camels? Alter goes on to suggest that camels may have simply become so synonymous with desert travel by the time this story was composed that its author could not tell the tale without them. It may also be that they were available in limited numbers for a man of such great wealth as Abraham (sort of a Bronze Age luxury car?). At any rate, they play an important role in the latter part of the story, so perhaps they were a stock part of the well-betrothal scene.

The nameless servant sets out laden with wealth to serve as dowry and betrothal gifts. The journey begins and ends without any description, and the servant is immediately at his goal. When he arrives there he prays. As I noted in the Introduction, prayer is rather unusual in these narrative books of the Hebrew Bible, and when it does occur it has an important narratological point. First, God does not intrude on the action of the story, although he is invoked by name and reminded of his covenant responsibility (steadfast love) to Abraham, whose God he is. Clearly he can work his will outside of the land of promise. But the story is gradually becoming less supernaturally charged in that human beings work out God's designs for humanity without his immediate intervention. In his prayer, the servant sets up a test whereby the woman who gives him water and waters his camels will be the one chosen. This may seem to be a small task, but to water ten camels after a month in the desert would have required both heroic strength and generosity.

The type-scene begins to unfold immediately. Alter points out the sequence of events in this sort of episode:

a. travel to foreign land;
b. an encounter with the future bride (the "young girl," *na⁼ărâ*) at a well;
c. drawing of water;
d. "hurrying" or "running" to bring the news of the stranger's arrival;
e. a feast at which a betrothal agreement is concluded.[131]

---

[130] Alter, *Genesis*, 114.
[131] Ibid., 115.

This is the most complete version of the scene,[132] full of leisurely repetition. It is the only version where the bridegroom is not present and in which the young woman, not the man, draws the water. But since characters are made known to us by what they do, this indicates the nature of Rebekah's personality both now and in her future marriage with Isaac. She has the energy and power. He is content to be in the background, kept, eventually quite literally, in the dark. After the servant politely asks for a sip of water (when he probably wanted huge draughts), he stands gawping at her until it becomes clear that he has found the one intended by God as a bride for Isaac. He would be gawping because of her beauty, and because he found her so readily, but also because of the sheer prodigious physicality of what she was doing.

The next scene (Scene 4 in the scheme adopted here) is bordered by the servant's actions. He first produces jewelry (and apparently also puts it on her although the text omits this detail) and lastly prays again. In between, a dialogue of question and answer takes place that establishes Rebekah's identity and secures for the servant an invitation to her home. His prayer thanks God for the "steadfast love and faithfulness" (*ḥasdô waʾămittô*)[133] that he has shown to Abraham.

A brief scene shows Rebekah running home to tell the news of the stranger's arrival. While this is part of the stock scene, it serves here to characterize Rebekah further by demonstrating her energy, vitality, and excitement, even after such a hard task. Her brother Laban returns, also running.

The plot now slows down to a leisurely pace and is divided into a series of scenes and subscenes that describe the marriage negotiations. Laban is succinctly characterized in his very first actions; he sees the rich jewelry, has repeated to him what the servant had to say, and is out the door. A more telling exposition, or showing, of greed would be hard to imagine.

The servant is shown exemplary hospitality but puts it aside until his errand is laid out. His speech recapitulates his task, with some judicious and diplomatic inclusions and exclusions. Conscious that everyone knows a proposal is coming, he describes in detail the ways in which YHWH has blessed his master. Conscious as well of his need

---

[132] See chapter 3, "Biblical Type-Scenes and the Uses of Convention," in Robert Alter's *The Art of Biblical Narrative* (New York: Basic Books, 1981) 47–62.

[133] This hendiadys is frequently used to describe the relationship between God and the chosen family. According to Speiser, the first element means "kindness, grace, loyalty" and the second "firmness, permanence, truth." Taken together they refer to God's attitude of unflagging loyalty to these people.

not to offend his hosts, he omits that Isaac is forbidden to leave the land and come to them. So Rebekah's family must judge the proposal sight (of the bridegroom) unseen. He also omits language that would sound as though Abraham has rejected the family's traditional gods. True, his God is YHWH, but the exclusivity that this God expects is omitted from the servant's briefing.

The family readily agrees to the proposed marriage (24:50-51).[134] The servant gives rich gifts and expresses a desire to set out immediately. At this the family demurs, but Rebekah, when asked if she acquiesces to the arrangement and the speedy departure, agrees by saying, "I will go" (AT; *ʾēlēk*). The family sends her (and her maid) off with a poetic blessing.

The subsequent scene (after once again skipping over the journey entirely) begins from Isaac's point of view. He was last seen at the Akedah, from which he did not return with his father. We are here told that he has been living at the well where Hagar had seen God and is now in the Negeb. First we see him from a distance, engaged in some activity,[135] but *hinnēh* marks a nice shift in point of view. Now we are with Isaac and with him we see, approaching from the distance, the line of camels. Suddenly, by the use of the same word *(hinnēh)* once again, we are with Rebekah as she sees her betrothed for the first time. As a betrothed woman in the presence of her future husband, she veils her face. It seems that Abraham has died by now, and Isaac takes Rebekah—as the new matriarch of the clan—to the tent that will be her home. He is comforted by her and loves her.[136]

The section ends with nice symmetry. Genesis 25 begins with a reference to Abraham's second family. Since it is likely that he has already died, this note appears here to balance the marriage of Isaac, just as the notice of his death will balance the death of Sarah. In this way the first generation and their doings are neatly finished but overlap the beginnings of the second generation. This gives a strong sense of continuity to the whole. The name of this last wife of Abraham is linked etymologically with the word for incense, and her children are linked with tribes along the incense trading routes. Thus he is already becoming father of a host of nations. Keturah is the mother of Midian. Jethro, priest

---

[134] Since Laban is the spokesman and the house is referred to as Rebekah's mother's house, the reference to Bethuel in 24:50 is probably an addition. He seems to be dead already.

[135] *lāśûaḥ* appears only here and its meaning is frankly unknown. It might mean "strolled," "walked," or even "pondered."

[136] This is the first reference to marital love in the Bible and only the second use of the word "love" (*ʾhb*) in the Bible.

of Midian, will be the father-in-law of Moses. In this way the priest-hood that derives from Moses will also derive from Abraham.

Before his death Abraham provides for his sons by Keturah, but they do not participate in the promise. He dies at the age of 175 and is buried in the cave in the field he possessed, at Hebron. Isaac and Ishmael, his two sons and both to be fathers of nations, bury him together. So we pass to the second generation.

Excursus

GOD AS A DEVELOPING CHARACTER
IN GENESIS 12–25

In Chapter 2 of his book *God: A Biography*,[1] Jack Miles describes what he calls the domestication of God in Genesis. He focuses principally on the relationship between God and Abraham, arguing that as God and Abraham interact there is a shift in power such that Abraham, who had initially belonged to God, becomes himself the proprietor of the eventually tamed deity. The principal issues involved in these stories are power and control, especially the power to control reproduction.

I agree that there is development in the character of God in Genesis 12–25, especially in the relationship between God and Abraham. That is to say, the God of Genesis 22 and the latter chapters of the Abraham cycle has changed—one might equally well say grown or matured—in some identifiable ways from the way in which that character first appears in Genesis 12. But while there is an element of change, I am not entirely persuaded by Miles's attempt to connect the change with the power to control fertility. Other issues may usefully be read as dominating the section.

My agreement that there is development in the character of God is only partial. When one looks at the stories about women that are also part of this section, e.g., Sarai in Genesis 12–13 and Hagar in Genesis 16, one must conclude that the character of God does not change and that God appears over and over to be the same, behaving in the same way and with the same motivation.

In Part One of this excursus, I show that God acts always to create the best possible future for the women of Abraham's world, given the constraints and restraints of the social realities of that time and place. In

[1] *God: A Biography* (New York: A. A. Knopf, 1995).

Part Two, I show a relationship that, on Abraham's part, begins with silent acquiescence and partial obedience, moves through dialogue, to arrive finally at a silence unlike that with which it began, a silence that allows trust even in mystery. God moves from command coupled with promises of future glory, through self-disclosure in dialogue, to a silence that allows trust in the mystery of Abraham's heart. The way in which God and Abraham relate shows a growing intimacy between the two that is less about a shift in power than it is the complexity of a relationship tested by both, in which both achieve the security of long familiarity and, what is more, love. Indeed, in both Parts One and Two, love, not power and control, is the motivation for God and the foundation of both God's stability and change, for love is unchanging and ever new.

Having mentioned Miles and the thesis he develops in the second chapter of his book, I will not attempt to do any kind of point-by-point refutation of his work to show somehow that he is wrong and I am right. I think that, with perhaps some rare exceptions, claims of absolute rightness and certain wrongness about matters of biblical interpretation are misguided. These texts continue to be read precisely because their meaning eludes readers. There is room for many readings, some more convincing to a particular time than others but not necessarily more true in any absolute sense. Miles chooses to view these texts from a particular perspective, which throws some things into highlight even as it necessarily ignores others. I offer a different reading but not one that is essentially more correct. I hope that my perspective provides a fruitful view.

In the last couple of decades there has been a shift in the world of biblical scholarship toward reading the texts that are the focus of our concern as works of literature. Since we confront here literature as subtle and highly crafted as any other our world has produced, I am less than sure that my knowing some few things about ancient Near Eastern history, culture, languages, and archaeology—all areas of specialization that are much needed and highly to be applauded—has made me an especially sensitive reader of literature. Perhaps, in order to read poetry, one needs a poet's skills and sensibilities.

Allow me then to bring to my reading of Genesis 12–25 three ideas from the modern German poet Rainer Maria Rilke.

The first idea: In speaking about his conception of God and his relationship to God, Rilke wrote, "The comprehensible slips away, is transformed; instead of possession one learns relationship *(statt des Besitzes lernt man den Bezug)*."[2]

---

[2] To Ilse Jahr, February 22, 1923 (Rainer Maria Rilke, *Ahead of All Parting: The Selected Poetry and Prose of Rainer Maria Rilke*, trans. Stephen Mitchell [New York: Modern Library, 1995] 216).

The second idea: In speaking of love, Rilke wrote,

> Love does not mean principally merging, surrendering, and uniting with
> another person. . . . Rather, it is a high inducement for the individual to
> ripen, to become something in himself, to become world, to become
> world in himself for another's sake. . . . Love consists in this—that two
> solitudes protect and border and greet each other.[3]

The third idea: The third idea is in fact a story[4] about a woman
Rilke greatly admired, Leonora Christina Ulfeldt, daughter of King
Christian IV of Denmark, who was imprisoned in Copenhagen from
1663–1685 because her husband had been accused of treason. Rilke
told this story about her:

> It seems to me that you could predict her conduct in prison if you knew of a
> certain little scene that was enacted just before her arrest in England. At this
> critical juncture it happened that a young officer who was sent to her mis-
> understood his orders and demanded that she take off all the jewelry she
> was wearing and hand it over to him. Although this ought to have startled
> her (since she was not yet aware that she was in any danger) and thrown
> her into the utmost alarm, nevertheless, after a moment's consideration,
> she takes off all her jewelry—the earrings, the necklaces, the brooches, the
> bracelets, the rings—and puts them into the officer's hands. The young man
> brings these treasures to his superior, who, at first terrified, then enraged, at
> this imprudence which threatens to upset the whole undertaking, orders
> him, curtly, and in the coarsest language, to return and give everything back
> to the Countess, and to beg her forgiveness, in any way he can think of, for
> his unauthorized blunder. What happened now is unforgettable. After con-
> sidering for a moment, not longer than that first moment was, Countess
> Ulfeldt gestures for the bewildered officer to follow her, walks over to the
> mirror, and there takes the magnificent necklaces and brooches and rings
> from his hands, as if from the hands of a servant, and puts them on, with the
> greatest attentiveness and serenity, one after another.
>
> Tell me, dear friend, do you know any other story in which it is so sub-
> limely evident how we ought to behave toward the vicissitudes of life? This
> went through and through me: this same repose vis-à-vis giving up and
> keeping, this repose that is so filled with power . . . [t]his silent, composed
> keeping and letting go . . . is full of moderation, is still earthly through and
> through, and yet it is already so great as to be incomprehensible.[5]

---

[3] To Franz Xaver Kappus, May 14, 1904 (Rilke, *Ahead of All Parting*, 227).

[4] As ever, the words story, narrative, and the like will be used interchangeably,
despite the different ways in which they are often defined by scholars.

[5] To Sidonie Nádherný von Borutin, February 4, 1912 (Rilke, *Ahead of All Parting*,
229).

These are the three ideas that I hope to bring to bear on Genesis 12–25. With God one can speak only of relationship and never of possession, because this latter is inimical to the meaning of relationship. The purpose of love is creative, to make the other a world, a completeness or totality. The solitude that each is, and that cannot be overcome, can protect the other, but can never own the other. Giving up and keeping is part of the very stuff of life. Repose and acceptance of the continual possibility of loss is definitive of human maturity.

Part One: Unchanging Love

One of the truisms of the study of narrative is that characters reveal themselves by what they say and do. To that is often added the idea that characters in ancient literatures are static, i.e., that they are presented the first time as they will always be. So Achilles is always angry and Nestor is always the wise counselor. One never expects anything else of them. This is, I think, true to some extent in the narratives of the Hebrew Bible as well. For instance, Jonathan is the ever-faithful, self-sacrificing friend of David. It is true in part with the character of God in Genesis as well. If God's character grows and develops in the context of the relationship with Abraham, if we see different aspects of God and Abraham come into play as their years together multiply, I do not think that is the case with the relationship between God and the other characters who appear in this section of Genesis. With them God remains the same.

Let me demonstrate this by a comparison of several stories in which the same motifs appear. In Genesis 12, almost immediately after Abram arrives in the Promised Land, he leaves it in order to escape a famine. There follows the unlovely tale of Abram's use of his wife to better his own prospects, albeit it at her very considerable expense. Taken by Pharaoh, she is trapped inside his house, seemingly powerless to effect her escape. God intervenes (Gen 12:17), so plaguing Pharaoh that Sarai is set free. God acts to free the powerless, to give her back to life.

In Genesis 16, Sarai, previously the beneficiary of God's action, becomes herself the oppressor of her too uppity slave, Hagar. Hagar, enslaved, impregnated, utterly powerless, is driven out into the desert by the violence she endures at Sarai's hands. There she encounters God's angel who promises her powerful new life (Gen 16:11ff). She is told to return to Sarai, and there is no further mention of the physical abuse that has driven her to the desert. This might seem like a gruesome choice for Hagar, but pregnant, resourceless, lacking any connections in a world defined by family connections, there may be no better choice at the moment. Once again, God intervenes to save the life of the powerless.

Sarah is once again subjected to the practice of being given away by a husband desirous of protecting himself more than his wife, when, in Genesis 20, Abraham gives her to Abimelech. Once again God brings Sarah out of this house and restores her to her own home.

As if to underline this theme, we encounter it once again in Genesis 21. This time Hagar and Ishmael have been driven into the desert after the birth of Isaac, an attempt by Sarah to remove potential rivals from the scene. Thirsty and awaiting death in the desert, Hagar calls upon God, who hears the voice of the boy, saves their lives, and remains with them (Gen 21:15-21). Once again, God acts in the same way, to save the lives of the powerless and to give those persons a future.

This creates an interesting pattern: Sarah, Hagar, Sarah, Hagar. In each instance, the wife, whether primary or secondary, is, after her salvation from a sort of death, allowed to return to life. Granted, they are caused to return to what is to us a less than ideal life in which they are not astonishingly free either, but a life that is better than a harem or starvation in the desert.

The story of Hagar in Genesis 21 is important in the development of our principle, that the character of God is unchanging in respect to the women characters in Genesis 12–25, because there seems at first to be a contrast, and so a development, between the character of God here and in the similar story about Hagar found in Genesis 16. God is conspicuously silent with Abram and Sarai in Genesis 16. The idea seems to be that to attend to the voice of God, as Abraham does in both Genesis 15 and 17, is to behave correctly. To attend to some other voice is to make a grave error, as Abram does in Genesis 16, when he listens to the voice of his wife and goes in to Hagar who, having conceived, is driven away to be found by God in the desert.

The story found in Genesis 21 seems to be a replay, a doublet, of Genesis 16, perhaps included only because it existed and some tradent was reluctant to lose it, but inspection shows that there are some significant differences between the two stories. In Genesis 21 Sarah, once again moved by jealousy, demands that Hagar and Ishmael be driven away. Abraham is distressed both by the loss of the boy and the loss of Hagar. One would expect God to be silent, as God had been previously when the similar scheme was tried, or to disapprove. Rather we find a God who has apparently changed and who falls in with the suggestion that Hagar leave and not remain with or return to the one abusing her. Why? Is this a change? Does God no longer act on behalf of the powerless? The desert scene seems also to be a replay, but again there are subtle differences. In Genesis 16, God hears the voice of Hagar.

Here, although Hagar prays, God hears the voice of the boy. Might it be that the boy, older now, can care for his mother? Before Hagar really had nowhere to go, whereas now she can live. So there seems not really to be a change in God's character, but a remarkable consistency. Once again God frees the powerless and gives her a future, even if not ideal and even if its goodness is not immediately apparent.

But what of Rilke's three ideas? These are clearly seen in the person of Hagar and her relationship with God. As a slave, Hagar has been fundamentally alone, quite literally owned and used by others for their own ends, yet she is freed by the God with whom she speaks, to whom she relates, and she becomes the mother of a people marked by assertive freedom. Her solitude is fruitful and she creates and becomes a world. Her repose and acceptance of the vicissitudes of her life are remarkable. Relationship, fruitful solitude and repose in the face of life are all hallmarks of the unchanging love that binds God and Hagar.

In line with the general principle that character is revealed in what one says and does, we find that the character of God in Genesis acts repeatedly, without either real change or development, to help the unfree and powerless. Parallel to this apparent lack of development is the relationship between God and Abraham, where there is change and development.

Part Two: Changing Love

The story of Abraham and his relationship with God begins in Genesis 12, reaches its high point in the dialogue between God and Abraham in Genesis 18, and ends in Genesis 22. The parts of Abraham's life that precede and follow those points do not affect this central relationship. I have already taken note of the pattern of four stories about Sarah and Hagar, where God's character is revealed as unchanging. Two of these precede the central moment of Abraham's life in Genesis 18 and two follow. Change is centered in the midst of lack of change so as to be highlighted by it.

God speaks to Abram for the first time in Genesis 12:1. There is a threefold command to leave land, kindred, and the paternal household. Abram only partly obeys, since be brings Lot, his nephew, along with him. Might one understand Genesis 12:4 to mean, "So Abram did go as YHWH had commanded him, *but* Lot went with him"? Why does Abraham bring his nephew? Might it be because he cannot yet bring himself to obey in a more absolute way, leaving behind all of those whom he loves, all of his kindred?

God, or more precisely the angel of God, speaks to Abraham for the final time in Genesis 22:16, saying, "because you have done this and not withheld your son, your only son. . . ." This is a near repetition of Genesis 22:12, where the angel of God says, "Do not lay your hand on the boy or do anything to him; for now I know that you fear God, since you have not withheld your son, your only one, from me." This is itself a near repetition of the sentence with which the chapter begins, "Take your son, your only son Isaac, whom you love . . ." (Gen 22:2). It is, however, only a *near* repetition, which throws into relief the word "love," used here for the first time in the Hebrew Bible. This is a story about what it means to love. This threefold repetition of a threefold command certainly draws our attention and invites comment.

Many indeed have commented, showing the various similarities and echoes between Genesis 12 and 22, such that they form an envelope around the Abraham stories. That is true as far as it goes, but I am not aware that anyone has noticed the only near-obedience of Genesis 12 and its contrast with the absolute obedience of Genesis 22. If that shows a change and development on the part of Abraham, I think there is also evidence here of change and development on the part of God, who says in the latter instance, "now I know that you fear God." There has evidently come to God some new awareness about Abraham. It cannot simply be that Abraham fears God and obeys. This has been reiterated time after time. Can it be that God has learned that, even though Abraham obeys, Abraham also loves? That Abraham will obey, even at great cost? Is this something that even Abraham is only learning in the events of Genesis 21 and 22? The second and third ideas drawn from Rilke throw light on this. He says:

> Love does not mean at first merging, surrendering, and uniting with another person. . . . Rather, it is a high inducement for the individual to ripen, to become something in himself, to become world, to become world in himself for another's sake. . . . Love consists in this—that two solitudes protect and border and greet each other.[6]

The goal of love is the inducement of the other to become world in himself for another's sake. Abraham has, throughout his career with God, thrown away the other in an astonishingly casual way. Four times he disposed of an inconvenient wife and twice of a less-favored son, even while the latter was still in the womb. This makes his eloquent pleading for the lives of the ten just people of Sodom appear somewhat disingenuous. God needs to test Abraham precisely in this area, to see

---

[6] See note 3 above.

whether he loves, and in so doing, God discovers a changed individual. The chatty Abraham of Genesis 15, 17 and 18 is replaced by one who obeys in silence. Abraham obeys, but he does so without opening his mind to God. Perhaps he no longer needs to, realizing he is complete in himself, a world. Perhaps he has learned the repose and self-possession of the Countess Ulfeldt that Rilke described, so that when his son is returned to him, he silently receives him back "as . . . from the hands of a servant . . . with the greatest attentiveness and serenity." God and Abraham do not speak after this point. It is hard to say why, except insofar as the comprehensible has slipped away and the mutual possessiveness that marked their earlier years has been replaced by relationship, a non-needy, solitary relationship best expressed by silence. God no longer demands that Abraham send those he loves away, rather he gives back the object of love. Has God too changed, to the point where he will accept that Abraham can love another alongside God, that even divine love means relationship and not possession?

The center of the stories about Abraham is the great drama of Genesis 18–19. Its importance is marked by the appearance here of the only dialogue between God and Abraham. Abraham is presented in Genesis 18–19 as the ideal of the human, utterly oriented to the other, to whom he gives hospitality. The foil is Lot, the nephew he brought with him from their homeland. Lot serves here as the opposite of Abraham, the one who does not care for the other, who does not protect the other from violence. One of the mysteries of this story is why Abraham, who must be aware of Lot's presence in Sodom, does not plead for him and his family. God saves them for Abraham's sake (Gen 19:29) but does so without Abraham's having asked for them. Is this a failure on Abraham's part, one that God must rectify for him? Is the request of Genesis 21, that the life of Hagar and Ishmael be saved, a growth beyond this moment for Abraham?

This central event in the relationship of God and Abraham seems also to contain a moment of decisive change and development on the part of God. In Genesis 18:17-19 there is a moment of interior monologue, a rarity in Hebrew narrative, which draws our attention. That this interior monologue, itself unusual, takes place inside the mind of God is even more striking. God wonders whether or not to disclose the plans for Sodom and Gomorrah to Abraham. Reasons are weighed and a decision made on the basis of Abraham's future destiny. God decides to change because the ongoing relationship between God and Abraham requires a new turning at this point. A moment of decisive test has arrived. God must become more intimately open to Abraham, allowing Abraham to see within God's mind, if God hopes to know who Abraham is and whether he is worthy of the future for which he is destined. In line with what Rilke says, love ripens when it recognizes that the other is a world, that God's solitude must be breached and he must reach out to Abraham in an intimate fashion.

I am left with many more questions about God and the relationship between God and Abraham than I had when I began to think about these matters. I have focused more than I had expected on the beginning, middle, and end of this relationship and spent more time than I had expected on the stories of Sarah and Hagar. How do the two covenants fit in? Are they also about possession? Does God, in Genesis 15, allow himself to be possessed by Abram, seeking to become the kindred that Abram has had to leave behind? Is the covenant of circumcision a reflection of God's desire to possess Abraham in some fundamental way, such that even his body must be marked by the experience? Is Genesis 22 then a sign that God is willing to respect the separateness of Abraham's world, willing to accept that Abraham can love another and leave him for that other?

Conclusion

One can reasonably argue that the character of God changes and does not change in these chapters in a way differently from that perceived by Miles and perhaps in ways that are well pointed out by Rilke. We may view the characters in these chapters not from the perspective of control but from the perspective of love, as defined in three ideas drawn from Rilke. God chooses to relate to Abraham, Sarah, and Hagar because God loves them. For Sarah and Hagar, God's constant desire is to create for them a future better, more free, and more life-affirming than their world would have provided for them.

God and Abraham have learned that instead of possession, one must learn relationship. And relationship, as we all know whether from reading the Bible or simply living our own lives, is full of paradox. One can be drawn to the other but cannot possess the other. The task of a lover is to protect the beloved, but they greet each other from a nearly unbridgeable solitude. Just as Abraham must learn to give away the ones he loves, so too God learns that Abraham loves another. Abraham will obey God, but does so in silence. God, accepting that silence, honoring that love, greeting that other solitude across the border between them, leaves Abraham in peace. No more commands will come from God, God has moved beyond commanding Abraham. Perhaps God loves him too much.

Chapter 6

IN THE TIME OF THE SECOND GENERATION

Genesis 25–28

How Is the Story Structured?

The various commentaries on Genesis all seem to refer to Isaac with similar words: he is a dim and transitional figure. True enough. Isaac, who never has his name changed, who never leaves the promised land, is a figure whose main task in life is to effect the transition from the second to the third generation of the chosen family. He plays a central and active role in only one narrative, Genesis 26. But even that story, the by now hoary ruse of passing off the wife as the sister, is borrowed from his father. Isaac is a passive figure, more acted upon than acting.

How, then, is one to structure the parts of Genesis which follow the death of Abraham? Scholars take various approaches. David Dorsey, for instance, sees a great concentric structure stretching from 21:8 to 28:4, centered on the choice of Rebekah as matriarch in succession to Sarah.

A. Yahweh's choice of the younger son Isaac (21:8-19)
    B. Marriage of non-chosen elder son (21:20-21)
        C. Strife with King Abimelech of Gerar over Abraham's wells (21:22-34)
            D. Risking everything for the covenant (22:1-19)
                E. Non-chosen genealogy (22:20-24)
                    F. Death of Sarah (23:1-20)
                        G. Yahweh selects Rebekah (24:1-67)

F'. Death of Abraham (25:1-10)
E'. Non-chosen genealogy (25:11-18)
D'. Scorning the covenant (25:19-34)
C'. Strife with King Abimelech of Gerar over Abraham's
    wells (26:1-33)
B'. Marriage of non-chosen elder son (26:34-35)
A'. Yahweh's choice of the younger son (27:1–28:4)[1]

This is an interesting attempt, and helps us better to understand why Genesis 24 should be by far the longest chapter in the book, highlighting, as it does, the strife between older and younger brother. This was introduced as a theme as early as Genesis 4 in the story of Cain and Abel, continued in the stories of Isaac and Ishmael, but will not fully develop until the latter part of the book in the conflicts between Jacob and Esau and between Judah and Joseph. Also, especially in view of the arrangement suggested here that the stories about the first generation center on Hagar, there is something attractive in a structure that centers on Rebekah. There is a real difficulty in its apparent asymmetry, with D and D' not really offering a contrast as one would expect. Other arrangements deserve serious consideration. Consider Walsh, who offers two versions of possible structures that include the material in this section, one simpler and one more elaborate.[2]

A. Jacob cheats Esau of his birthright and flees from him
   (25:19–28:9)
   B. Jacob encounters God at Bethel (28:10-22)
      C. Jacob works for Laban at Paddan-Aram (29:1–31:55)
   B'. Jacob encounters God at the Jabbok (32:1-32)
A'. Jacob returns and is reconciled with Esau (33:1–35:29)

Walsh's more elaborate structure:

---

[1] David Dorsey, *The Literary Structure of the Old Testament* (Grand Rapids, Mich.: Baker, 1999) 27. Dorsey notes that there is no strong link between D and D'.

[2] Jerome T. Walsh, *Style and Structure in Biblical Hebrew Narrative* (Collegeville: The Liturgical Press, 2001) 31. He says that the simpler symmetry is evident "even to the casual reader." In the second version, symmetry is achieved by leaving 26:34-35 out of consideration. This is based on the work of Michael Fishbane, "Composition and Structure in the Jacob Cycle (Gen. 25:19–35:22)," *Journal of Jewish Studies* 26 (1975) 15–38, and idem, *Text and Texture: Close Readings of Selected Biblical Texts* (New York: Schocken, 1979) 40–62. It was taken up by Gary Rendsburg, *The Redaction of Genesis* (Winona Lake, Ind.: Eisenbrauns, 1986) 53–69.

    A. The descendants of Ishmael (25:12-18)
      B. Rebekah struggles in childbirth; Jacob and Esau born (25:19-26)
        C. Jacob obtains Esau's birthright (*bkrh*) (25:27-34)
          D. Rebekah in a foreign palace; foreign pact (26:1-33)
            E. Blessing (*brkh*) taken from Esau (27:1-46)
              F. Jacob flees Esau, encounters God on his journey (28:1-22)
                G. Jacob arrives at Haran (deception, wages) (29:1-30)
                H. Jacob's wives are fertile (29:31–30:24)
                H'. Jacob's flocks are fertile (30:25-43)
              G'. Jacob leaves Haran (deception, wages) (31:1-55)
              F'. Jacob returns to Esau, encounters God on his journey (32:1-32)
            E'. Blessing-gift (*brkh*, 33:11) returned to Esau (33:1-20)
          D'. Dinah in a foreign palace; foreign pact thwarted (34:1-31)
        C'. Jacob receives God's blessing (*brkh*) (35:1-15)
      B'. Rachel struggles in childbirth, Benjamin born (35:16-22)
    A'. The descendants of Jacob (35:23-26)

Of course, it goes without saying that these arrangements are, in some sense, perfectly correct and that the contrasts they describe are truly present in the text. Again, however, one must be troubled by a symmetrical arrangement that is arrived at only by leaving out a section of the text and that seems to equate the fertility of Jacob's wives and his livestock.

These arrangements ignore an aspect of these stories that is also apparent even to the casual reader and leads us to the much simpler arrangement adopted here. The genealogical note that ends at 25:18 is quite different in kind from the narratives that follow and serves as a conclusion to the narratives about the first generation. From 25:34 to 28:9 the focus of the text is on the admittedly troubled family of Isaac. It is important that we consider these stories well, because they describe the family in which Jacob was formed, where he learned— sometimes for good and sometimes for ill—how to be in the world. His passive and withdrawn father, with whom he apparently had a problematic relationship (we are told after all that Isaac loved *Esau*), taught him to pursue an active path through life. No one would accuse Jacob of being a pale copy of his father, as Isaac was of his, and of simply letting life happen to him, as Isaac did. Too, he learned from his mother (we are told after all that Rebekah loved *Jacob*) to seek a partner who, like him, was vigorous and active. Beginning at 28:10, Jacob leaves the family fold to strike out on his own, marking the beginning of a new narrative bloc. These two then form a nice frame around the family of Isaac. It can be sketched simply.

> Fraternal strife (25:19-34)
>   Isaac and his wife (26:1-33)
> Fraternal strife (26:34–28:9)

As soon as Rebekah becomes pregnant the brothers Esau and Jacob fight. They fight before birth, they fight as young men, and they fight in adulthood. These two portraits of brothers and a family in strife bracket the one incident in which Isaac acts. The second generation of the chosen family is riven with strife and anger and collapses early on, but for these three chapters, the focus is on them. Immediately thereafter, when Jacob flees, the focus shifts to the third generation of the chosen family. It is almost as though the storyteller cannot get away from Isaac, Rebekah, and their sons fast enough. Chosen and blessed these people were. Ideal models as human beings they were not. The Bible is remarkable in letting us see their frailty and failure.

Commentary

25:19-34: FRATERNAL STRIFE

The latter part of Genesis 25 consists of two very brief narratives, both of which focus on the same theme, the strife between the two sons of Isaac and Rebekah. Jan P. Fokkelman has done extensive work on these chapters, and it is interesting to see how two different approaches reach very similar conclusions. Fokkelman's concentric arrangement appears on the left of the following table.[3] Using the traditional lan-

---

[3] Jan P. Fokkelman, *Narrative Art in Genesis: Specimens of Stylistic and Structural Analysis* (Assen/Amsterdam: Van Gorcum, 1975) 93. He says of this arrangement:

> The pattern comprises all the moments of the scene, but the concentric structure is not everywhere compelling. It can hardly be, for B' is not a striking counterpart to B, and the division between B and C and between B' and C' is not clear-cut.

guage of plot analysis, the elements of the plot may be described as in the column on the right:

A	Isaac was forty years old when he took to wife Rebekah		20	Exposition
B	Rebekah was barren; prayer for children answered		20-21	Development
C	His wife Rebekah conceived		21	
	The children struggled within her		22a	
D	Rebekah asks for	An ORACLE	22b	Turning point
D'	Yahweh grants her		23	
C'	Her days to be delivered were fulfilled		24a	Resolution
	And behold, there were twins in her womb		24b	
B'	Birth and appearance of Jacob and Esau		25-26a	
A'	Isaac was sixty years old when she bore them		26b	Conclusion

As was the case with Sarah—and will be the case with Jacob's wives —Rebekah is unable to conceive. This information sets the stage for what follows, her attempt to become pregnant with the help of God. She conceives but—a unique case in the Bible— has a difficult pregnancy, with the unborn children wrestling within her. The story hinges on the oracle she receives from God, which allows insight into her, and their, futures. The latter part of the story describes the reversal of her inability to conceive, because she gives birth to twins—a rare event in the Bible—and the unusual manner of their birth shows that God's oracle is beginning to come true.

Nevertheless the structure of this passage betrays what is at the heart of the matter in Gen. 26:19-26, that which is the center of the symmetrical composition, D+D'. The oracle is central. . . .

Once again, we see at least a hint of the outsider motif so important in Genesis. It is when Rebekah goes to inquire of YHWH, i.e., goes outside of the place where she normally dwelt, that she receives revelation.

However, if there is substantial agreement on the organization of the first of these two brief narratives, that is not the case with the second. Here Fokkelman presents a neat concentric structure but arrives at it by eliminating Genesis 25:27-28 from consideration. These verses are essential for understanding later developments in this family and serve nicely in a more traditional analysis of the plot as the exposition, the setting of the stage that allows the rest of the story to unroll. Before looking in a more detailed way at the content of the tales, let us compare these two structures.

Fokkelman describes a structure centered on Esau and his rejection of his birthright.[4] While that is intriguing, some other parts of the structure do not really show much correspondence. For example, A and A' seem less to reflect a reversal than simply the beginning and end of the piece. Were Esau to speak again in C', rather than remain silent, it would create a better contrast. However, as the detailed analysis of the passage below will show, many of Fokkelman's insights about the constituent parts are sharp and perceptive.

A. Jacob was boiling pottage (25:29a)
   B. Esau came in from the field, he was tired (25:29b)
      C. *wayyōmer ʿEsaw*: Let me eat some of that red red pottage . . . I am so tired (25:30)
         D. *wayyōmer Yaʿqob*: first sell me your *bkrh* (25:31)
            X. *wayyōmer ʿEsaw*: I depart, I die; of what use is a *bkrh* to me? (25:32)
         D'. *wayyōmer Yaʿqob*: swear to me first.—So he swore to him and sold his *bkrh* to Jacob (25:33)
      C'. Jacob gave Esau bread and pottage of lentils; he ate and he drank (25:34a?)
   B'. He rose and went his way (25:34a?)
A'. Thus Esau despised his *bkrh* (25:34b)

A more traditional plot analysis of the passage would look like this:

Exposition: 25:27-28
Development: 25:29-32
Turning point: 25:33-34a
Conclusion: 25:34b

[4] Ibid., 95

The second brief tale is divided from the first by the passage of time; the boys, then youthful, are now grown. The exposition sets the stage nicely by giving us information that allows us to characterize the two protagonists and their parents. Esau is an outdoorsy sort of man—or does his being a hunter mean more than simply that? Jacob is a stay-at-home—or does the composer of the tale intend us to read more into his quiet, homebody ways than that? However, there is no difficulty in understanding the division in the family. Love appears again, but this time to mark division, not intimacy. Jacob's craftiness and Esau's apparent dullness drive the rest of the story, as the former is enriched and the latter despises what was once his. One wonders whether Esau has only gotten what he deserves. Or, once again, is the story a good deal subtler than at first appears?

When Isaac marries, some decades have passed since the Binding, when he was last heard of. Where has he been, and why has he waited so long to marry? We are told where he has been living, but not why he has so long delayed. A clue might lie in the blindness that afflicts him: having seen his father raise a knife against him, he can no longer see his way in the world but is somehow stifled by the inertia of grief and shock. Somehow, given the connection of his marriage with Sarah's death but not Abraham's, he is able to seek the comfort and love he needed only after the death of his mother. Again, Paul Ricoeur:

> By means of the horror-stricken feeling which comes upon me from the silence of those who are absent and who will no longer respond, the death of another pierces me as an injury to our communal existence; death "touches me"; and insofar as I am also another for others and ultimately for myself, I anticipate my future death as my eventual lack of response to all the words of all men.[5]

Isaac was touched by Sarah's death to confront his own eventual death and so decided to take up what life he had and to build a family. For it is only when we confront the fact of our own mortality, accept that we are no longer the young but must cede that place to another, and embrace the fact that we will die, that we can engender another generation behind us. To bear children is, in a very real sense, to accept the reality of our own eventual death.

As the story begins to develop, we encounter the second occurrence of another type-scene, the "barren wife." In this instance, Isaac prays for

---

[5] Avivah Gottlieb Zornberg, *Genesis: The Beginning of Desire* (Philadelphia: Jewish Publication Society, 1995) 134, quoting Paul Ricoeur, *History and Truth* (Chicago: Northwestern University Press, 1965) 289.

his wife, who readily conceives. But there is no indication that Isaac heard anything back from God as a result of his prayer. Rather, it is Rebekah who seeks and receives an oracle from God. Why? The pregnancy is clearly difficult, so difficult that her cry of anguish *ʾim-kēn lāmmâ zeh ʾānōkî* is almost unintelligible, according to Alter, a sort of broken-off sentence.[6] Twins are wrestling, crushing, contending within her. This is more than a variation on a narrative convention. In all of the stories about the second generation of this family, it is Rebekah who is vigorous and cunning and who sees to it that God's plan for this family is carried out. So it is to her, and not to the passive Isaac, that God speaks.

In speaking to her, God explains her situation in these words, which seem familiar but are in fact ambiguous and difficult: "Two nations are in your womb, and two peoples born of you shall be divided; the one shall be stronger than the other, the elder shall serve the younger" (25:23, NRSV; *šĕnê gōyîm bĕbiṭnēk ûšĕnê lĕʾummîm mimmēʿayik yippārēdû ûlĕʾōm milʾōm yeʾĕmāṣ wĕrab yaʿăbōd ṣāʿîr*).

The NRSV adopts the typical reading that the elder, Esau, is destined by God to be a servant to the younger, Jacob. According to this reading, Rebekah's later deception of Isaac, which enables Jacob to steal his father's blessing, is no real fault at all since she is simply bringing about the express will of God. But Richard Friedman points out that the language here is not so clear:

> The text does not in fact say that the elder son will serve the younger son. In biblical Hebrew, the subject may either precede or follow the verb, and the object likewise may either precede or follow the verb. That means that it is sometimes impossible to tell which word in a biblical verse is the subject and which is the object, especially if the verse is in poetry. That is the case in this oracle to Rebekah, which is in poetry. It can mean:
>   "the elder will serve the younger"
> But it can equally well mean:
>   "the elder, the younger will serve"

---

[6] Note how various translations, basing their renderings on another ancient translation that is less enigmatic, differ in trying to capture what she means. The NRSV says, "If it is to be this way, why do I live?" E. A. Speiser's version is "If this is how it is to be, why do I go on living?" (*Genesis*, AB 1 [New York: Doubleday, 1962], 193). Richard Elliott Friedman: "If it's like this, why do I exist?" (*Commentary on the Torah* [San Francisco: HarperSanFrancisco, 2001] 87). Robert Alter: "Then why me?" or "Then why am I . . ." (*Genesis: Translation and Commentary* [New York: Norton, 1996] 127). Everett Fox: "If this be so, why do I exist?" (*The Five Books of Moses* [New York: Schocken, 1995] 115). A literal rendering of the Hebrew would be: "If so, why is this, me?"

Like the Delphic oracles in Greece, this prediction contains two opposite meanings and thus the person who receives it—Rebekah—can
hear whatever she wants (consciously or subconsciously) to hear. It can
be understood to mean that Jacob will serve Esau or that Esau will serve
Jacob.[7]

This ambiguity about who is intended by God to serve whom brings
to the fore the theme of the displacement of the older brother by the
younger, which was first seen in the conflict between Isaac and Ishmael
and which will become a staple of biblical narrative. It introduces a
real tension into the text as the reader wonders how, or even whether,
this displacement will come about, and it renders profoundly ambiguous the acts of Rebekah and Jacob as they bring it about. More than
that, much of Jacob's life will be lived out under this heading of moral
ambiguity—whether lying to his father, making a deal with God, or
manipulating his father-in-law's livestock, so the ambivalence of this
introduction is appropriate.

In due time the twins are born and given names that evoke their per-
sonalities and the manner of their birth. The first was reddish (*ʾadmônî*)
and covered with hair (*śēʿār*) so was named Esau. These two words
sound enough like "Edom" and "Seir" (a synonym for Edom) for the
original audience to perceive a connection between Esau and this traditional regional rival of historical Israel. The name and description mean,
rather loosely, something like Red Hairy. His younger brother was born
grasping the elder's heel, which caused him to be given the name Jacob
(*yaʿăqōb*),[8] based on the word for heel (*ʿāqēb*) . Thus the two boys are
known as Hairy and the Heel. While the former evokes uncouthness, the
latter evokes trickery and supplanting. How they live up to these names
will be the subject of the stories which follow.

No sooner are the boys born than they are at least young adults—
the voyage through time passing as rapidly and free of comment in the
Bible as does a voyage from one place to another. In one of the most
provocative sentences in the Bible, the situation is introduced in this
way:

> When the boys grew up, Esau was a skillful hunter, a man of the field,
> while Jacob was a quiet man, living in tents. Isaac loved Esau, because
> he was fond of game; but Rebekah loved Jacob. (Gen 25:27-28)

---

[7] Friedman, *Torah*, 88.

[8] The suggestion is generally made that Jacob's name would really have been
yʿqb-ʾl, or "God protects," a much more normal sort of name for a Hebrew man, but
that this name was replaced by the more evocative Jacob, "the Heel."

It is apparent from this that Esau is an outdoorsman, but what about Jacob? He is called *tām*, a word that connotes integrity or innocence (other translations use "quiet" or "plain" or "simple" or "retiring," opting for a less morally charged word). But as Alter points out, there may be more here than that, since the antonym of this innocence is "crookedness" (*ʿoqbâ*), a word formed from the same root as Jacob/Heel.[9] What he does next in the story is hardly innocent.

Traditional commentary makes much of Esau's description here to vilify him and so to soften the blow of Jacob's deceit—saying in effect that Esau had it coming. One example, easily multiplied from both Jewish and Christian sources, will show the tendency.

> Scripture thus shows that Esau did not sell his birthright because of hunger, since it says that after he ate, "Esau got up and left and [still] despised his birthright." He did not sell it because of hunger, therefore, but because he indeed considered it to be worthless and sold it for nothing.[10]

Jacob, on the contrary, is regarded not only as a quiet man, but also as morally perfect. Again, one example out of many:

> And the two boys grew up, and Esau became a man knowledgeable in hunting, a man [who was] lord of the field, and Jacob was a man perfect in good work, dwelling in schoolhouses.[11]

The chosen family is shown to be deeply divided. The word "love" appears here for only the third time in the book (cf. 22:2; 24:67). The first time it showed the intense bond between Abraham and his son. In the second instance it showed Isaac's intense bond with his wife. Now it shows not only an intense bond but also division. Love, which should unite in intimacy, is here a sign of division, a division that will bear awful fruit in the lie with which Esau's blessing is stolen.

In order to understand the force of the following tale, one must be aware of Deuteronomy 21:15-17.

---

[9] Alter, *Genesis*, 128.

[10] Ephraem, *Commentary on Genesis* 23:2, quoted in James L. Kugel, *Traditions of the Bible* (Cambridge, Mass.: Harvard University Press, 1998) 359. It should be noted that Esau is spoken of with a similar lack of sympathy in the New Testament.

> See to it that no one becomes like Esau, an immoral and godless person, who sold his birthright for a single meal. You know that later, when he wanted to inherit the blessing, he was rejected, for he found no chance to repent, even though he sought the blessing with tears. (Heb 12:16-17)

[11] *Targum Neophyti* Gen 25:27, in Kugel, *Traditions*, 353.

If a man has two wives, one of them loved and the other disliked, and if both the loved and the disliked have borne him sons, the firstborn being the son of the one who is disliked, then on the day when he wills his possessions to his sons, he is not permitted to treat the son of the loved as the firstborn in preference to the son of the disliked, who is the firstborn. He must acknowledge as firstborn the son of the one who is disliked, giving him a double portion of all that he has; since he is the first issue of his virility, the right of the firstborn is his.

In short, the firstborn son is to receive a double share of his father's inheritance. What Jacob desires is to exchange birthplaces with Esau and so enrich himself at his brother's expense. If nothing else the story shows us that Jacob can wait, postpone gratification and think for the future, while Esau is more given to impulsive activity and does not regard the future.

Jacob is cooking a stew when Esau bursts on the scene. He is famished and blurts out, according to the NRSV, "Let me eat some of that red stuff, for I am famished!" Sadly, this is rather more poetic than the original would warrant. The verb he uses for "eat" appears nowhere else in biblical Hebrew but is used in later Hebrew for animals eating—the distinction is rather like that of German between *essen*, reserved for humans, and *fressen*, reserved for animals—and very rude when applied to humans. Nor does he actually say "stuff" or anything like it. He just asks for that "red red," and so appears to the reader as an uncouth boor. The red soup—there is a pun here the second time the food is referred to, given the similarity in sound between the Hebrew word for blood (*dām*) and Edom (*ʾĕdôm*)—was perhaps thought by Esau to be a restorative blood stew.

Jacob is quite willing to exploit his brother's misery but wants an oath. This given, and the birthright thereby transferred, the identity of the soup is revealed—simply red lentil soup. Despite Esau's uncouth language, one is still sympathetic to him. Sympathy lessens in the conclusion of the piece when, with four quick verbs of action, Esau's lack of concern and his nature as a creature of fleshly appetite is underlined: "Then Jacob gave Esau bread and lentil stew, and he (1) ate and (2) drank, and (3) rose and (4) went his way" (Gen 25:34a).

The story ends, somewhat surprisingly, with a focus on Esau rather than Jacob.

26:1-33: ISAAC, HIS WIFE, AND HIS FATHER'S WELLS

This chapter, the only one in which Isaac is protagonist, has collected quite an extensive literature. The scenario of the sister/wife deception and the possible transfer of the wife to a king's harem appears here for the third time. Many scholars have tried to discern how it relates to the similar occurrences in Abraham's life recounted in Genesis 12 and 20. Opinion differs widely, with this chapter being assigned to one or another, or none, of the putative documentary sources. Commentaries with a historical-critical bent should be studied if a reader is interested in these questions. Our interest here is different, so we focus rather on the final form of the text to see how it furthers the developing story of the chosen family. Since neither Jacob nor Esau appears here, the temptation is to think that there is no particular connection and that this chapter is placed here for some reason that can no longer be recovered. However, the connection between this chapter and the subsequent one seems clear. In this chapter Isaac lies about his wife—who loves Jacob—for his own advantage. In the next chapter Jacob does much the same thing and lies to his father—who loves Esau—for his own advantage. Where did Jacob learn to lie? From his father. What did he learn makes a lie acceptable? When it can be used to create an advantage for oneself. Why did he feel no compunction in lying to his father? "Isaac loved Esau, because he was fond of game; but Rebekah loved Jacob" (Gen 25:28).

The chapter consists of two brief narratives, both of which are tightly connected to events in the life of Abraham. We read ahead and are reminded of the past. Recall the words with which I began the Introduction to the book:

> The tectonic layers of our lives rest so tightly one on top of the other that we always come up against earlier events in the later ones, not as a matter that has been fully formed and pushed aside, but absolutely present and alive. I understand this. Nevertheless, I sometimes find it hard to bear. Maybe I did write our story to be free of it, even if I never can be.[12]

This is in itself a large part of the chapter's purpose.

> Thus the perceived repetitions begin to create a sense of design to what otherwise might be considered random, indeed rambling, stories. Each generation, at least to some extent, relives the plot of its predecessor. The larger story of the family is not simply linear, but frequently coils around to pick up bits of the past—failures as well as successes. Every generation essentially provides the same kind of "stuff" from which God is to build a "great nation." Yet there is always variation—as the "wife-sister" story makes clear—and always possibilities for change and movement into a new story. And with each new story and each new generation we

---

[12] Bernhard Schlink, *The Reader* (New York: Pantheon Books, 1997) 217–8.

look for the character and the event that will fulfill God's desire for relationship and blessing for the world.[13]

The first narrative, which describes Isaac's use of his father's never very successful ruse about his wife being his sister, is easily described:

Exposition: 26:1a
Development: 26:1b-6
Turning point: 26:7
Resolution: 26:8
Conclusion: 26:9.

The first of our two brief narratives begins with two explicit references to earlier events in the life of Abraham. Once again there is a famine and, lest one miss the point, the narrator helpfully reminds the reader of the former famine in the time of Abraham (cf. 12:10). Isaac journeys to Gerar (which lay on one of the possible routes to Egypt) in the realm of the same King Abimelech with whom his father had dealings. That the Philistines were not yet resident in the land does not bother the narrator, who moves rapidly on to Isaac's reception of YHWH's promises. Just as he received his name from God, not from his parents, he also receives the promises from God; however, he must remain in the Promised Land and not proceed to Egypt. Even here Isaac's transitional status is made evident. The promises and blessings will come to pass not because of Isaac but "because Abraham obeyed my voice and kept my charge, my commandments, my statutes, and my laws" (26:5; compare 12:1-3 with 26:2-4).

However, it is useful to spend some time looking at exactly what these blessings consist of, since in the very next chapter the two sons of Isaac will fight vigorously to get them. Consider the following:

- God assures him, "I am with you," when Isaac enters an unknown, perhaps even dangerous territory (vv. 3, 24, and 26), so that Isaac is under protection.
- Isaac will inherit the land of Canaan (vv. 3b, 4b).
- He will have numerous descendants (vv. 4a, 24b), the fertility and meaning of which will pass into a proverb (v. 4b).
- God's blessing surrounds Isaac as an iron defense so that Abimelech cannot hit him with a punishment (v. 10f).
- Isaac enjoys hundredfold crops (*mēʾâ šĕʿārîm*) by Yahweh's blessing (v. 12) and becomes so rich (v. 13) that he is envied (v. 14).

[13] David M. Gunn and Danna Nolan Fewell, *Narrative in the Hebrew Bible* (New York: Oxford University Press, 1993) 109.

- In spite of the Philistines' sabotage Isaac finds new wells again and again, and eventually he finds access to "living water" (the phrase refers to a free-flowing spring; vv. 19-22, 32).
- From the mouths of the Philistines themselves we hear the acknowledgment that nothing can be detracted from the accomplished fact of Isaac's blessedness; their speech (v. 28f) is perfectly framed by "YHWH is with you . . . you are the blessed of YHWH."
- The blessing is so desirable and so secure a source of prosperity that the lord-servant relationship of Gerar and Isaac becomes reversed; humbly, the Philistines come to ask Isaac for a share in his blessing. The Philistines' claim that they have "done nothing but good" for Isaac and "sent him away in peace" is hypocrisy (v. 29); it is the patriarch who has the power to "send *them* away in peace" (v. 31).[14]

This is a set of blessings worthy of contention indeed. The sons of Isaac would have seen all of this and known all of this. Esau, the first-born, would have regarded it as his right to inherit all of these blessings. Jacob, the Heel, the Supplanter, would have regarded acquiring them in some manner, fair or foul, as a deed he needed to accomplish in order to make God's oracle about the elder serving the younger come about.

The turning point is reached when Isaac follows the example of his father (cf. 12:11-14; 20:11-13) and lies about his relationship with his wife. The story is not a mere copy of what has preceded, however, because Rebekah is not taken into the king's house. She remains with Isaac but is known in the community as his sister.

With the passage of time—another note that is absent in the earlier versions of the story—Isaac apparently lets his guard down and is seen in a compromising position with his wife. Here the verb used (*mĕṣaḥēq*) variously rendered as "fondling" or "playing with" creates a pun that cannot be translated because it implies play, laughter, and sexual activity. Too, it is based on the same verb "to laugh" that is embedded in Isaac's name. This rather reckless behavior is seen by the king—another difference with the other versions and one that makes it seem more natural—who upbraids Isaac for his lie (cf. 12:18-19; 20:9-10). The lie did not endanger the king, but Isaac excuses it because it served his own self-interest. The king does not banish Isaac (perhaps out of respect for Abraham's memory) but does ban anyone having contact with his wife under pain of death.

---

[14] See Fokkelman, *Genesis*, 114.

The second brief story also recapitulates an event in the life of Abraham, when he made the covenant with Abimelech that gained him the right of access to a well at Beer Sheba. This version makes evident the scarcity of resources in this not especially hospitable land and the tension between farmers and pastoralists and between Isaac and the indigenous population; it also explains some local place names. The scarcity of resources should be kept in mind for the next chapter, when Isaac—a very wealthy man indeed—is not able to replicate the blessing he gave to Jacob for his son Esau. Even for him there is not enough to spread it around twice.

The plot is readily described:

> Exposition: 26:12a
> Development: 26:12b-18
> Turning point: 26:19-23
> Resolution: 26:24-33a
> Conclusion: 26:33b

Isaac undertakes agriculture, in contrast to Abraham, and becomes extremely wealthy. His wealth arouses envy, and the competition is such that Abimelech requires him to move away. In the meantime, in a nice frame break, we learn that the wells Abraham used are now filled in. This gives the story what dramatic tension it has because Isaac needs access to water, and one wonders how that will be achieved.

The extended turning point of the story tells us that contention focused on three wells: one called Esek,[15] another called Sitnah,[16] and a third called Rehoboth.[17] The turning point is quite literally marked by Isaac's turning aside to Beer Sheba.

There is a parallel here between Isaac and Lot, which seems not to have been noticed. In Genesis 12, Lot became so wealthy that he and Abraham had to part. Lot took the wrong direction, headed into the valley where Sodom was found. In Genesis 26 Isaac heads into a valley and finds danger there, but unlike Lot—who after the destruction of Sodom went away from Abraham—Isaac goes in the right direction, toward Beer Sheba.

There, having flirted—whether consciously or not—with a way that strayed from the one laid out for him by his father Abraham, Isaac recapitulates the covenant with Abimelech that gives him access to the water at the well to be found there (21:34; 26:26-31). The end of the story reminds the audience of the etymology of the well's name. In

---

[15] "Bickering" (Fox, *Moses*, 120); "Contention" (Alter, *Genesis*, 134).

[16] "Animosity" (Fox, *Moses*, 121); "Accusation" or "Hostility" (Alter, *Genesis*, 134).

[17] "Space" (Fox, *Moses*, 121); "Open Spaces" (Alter, *Genesis*, 135).

Genesis 21, the name refers either to the oath made there or the seven lambs exchanged in recognition of the agreement. This is repeated here, and so the chapter comes to an end.

26:34–28:9: FRATERNAL STRIFE

Genesis 26 serves, as we have seen, a number of important functions in the ongoing characterization of Jacob, despite the fact that he is, along with his brother Esau, absent from—or at least unmentioned in—the events described there. He would have known about the danger his beloved mother faced and perhaps stored up some resentment on her behalf, and he would also have learned that it is acceptable to lie in order to create a situation advantageous to oneself. The next narrative bloc, Genesis 26:34–28:9, returns to the theme of fraternal strife and shows the reader how Jacob's reaction to his father's deception leads to his own. The tale, one of the most powerfully crafted in the whole book, works a paradoxical effect on its reader. One's sympathies are with Esau as his brother, with the connivance of his mother, steals what is precious and vital to him. His murderous anger (the turning point of the sequence, Gen 27:41) is almost understandable, especially give the previous extortion of his birthright. However, the frame—the references to his marriages with outsiders in 26:34-35 and 28:6-9—makes one wonder whether Esau would be capable of bearing the promises were they to devolve upon him. So what one encounters here is a story in which one's natural sympathies are skillfully confused so that one is not entirely sure which character is deserving of sympathy.

The commentator must decide first of all how to delimit the next bloc; I have tipped my hand by suggesting that it begins and ends with the frame described above. The tale is about blessing—the root appears some twenty-five times and the nominal form appears seven times—and who should bear it, Esau or his younger brother Jacob the Heel/Trickster. Everett Fox draws our attention to a number of other motifs: "game" is mentioned seven times, "delicacy" or "tasty dish" six times, Isaac "feels" Jacob three times, and Jacob "comes close" four times. All five of the senses appear in the story, but sight alone is defective (and that defect drives the rest of the story). Sight is also related in the Hebrew Bible to prophetic ability; to see can be to see what God wills. The paradox here is that the dim-sighted one does in fact see correctly and chooses the son best suited to bear the promises. Other motifs appear here only to recur importantly later. The exclusive love that divides a family here will also divide Jacob's family when, in turn, he marries. Recognition and non-recognition also recur later in the story about Joseph.[18]

---

[18] Fox, *Moses*, 122.

The tale has a different structure from others we have studied thus far and unrolls in a sequence of seven scenes, surrounded by an envelope. In each scene, two of the characters appear, orchestrated in such a way as to give the reader a masterful portrait of a family in very deep distress. Rebekah and Esau never appear together, nor do Jacob and Esau. The scene changes when the characters change. As is usual in biblical Hebrew narrative, there are always two characters per scene, never more or less. In the one scene where husband and wife appear together there is no dialogue between them; Rebekah says one sentence to her husband who apparently acts on her words but does not respond to them. In the first scene, Isaac and Esau are together whereas in the last Isaac and Jacob are together, and Esau's displacement is complete.[19] Throughout the whole, Rebekah orchestrates the entire affair, even when absent from a scene. The section of the story that falls within the frame is neatly concentric, showing the same sort of reversal—Jacob supplanting Esau—that is evident from the scenic plot structure.[20]

Frame A: Esau's Hittite wives (26:34-35)	
Scene 1: Isaac and Esau (27:1-5)	A. Isaac + son of the *brkh/bkrh* (=Esau) (27:1-5)
Scene 2: Rebekah and Jacob (27:5-17)	B. Rebekah sends Jacob on the stage (27:6-17)
Scene 3: Isaac and Jacob (27:18-30)	C. Jacob appears before Isaac, receives blessing (27:18-29)
Scene 4: Isaac and Esau (27:30-41)	C'. Esau appears before Isaac, receives anti-blessing (27:30-40)
Scene 5: Rebekah and Jacob (27:42-45)	B'. Rebekah sends Jacob from the stage (27:41-45)
Scene 6: Rebekah and Isaac (27:46)	A'. Isaac + son of the *brkh/bkrh* (=Jacob!) (27:46 + 28:1-5)
Scene 7: Isaac and Jacob: (28:1-5)	
Frame A': Esau's Ishmaelite wife (28:6-9)	

[19] By far the most insightful treatment of this passage is that of Fokkelman in *Genesis*, 97–112. Although the conclusions reached here differ in some respects from his, his work is seminal for all who investigate Genesis, and any serious reader should study it in detail.

[20] The right hand column is the scheme devised by Fokkelman, *Genesis*, 98. The left hand column is my own arrangement.

As in any story there is a rising and falling arc of tension. It moves from its low point, Esau's marriage to the foreign women (26:34-35), through the deception (27:1-40), to its high point at Esau's hatred (27:41), through its descent as Jacob flees (27:42–28:5), and returns to its original state as Esau, attempting to curry favor with his parents, marries yet another foreign woman (28:6-9).

Although we will examine the various scenes in detail below, a number of details that will be important for the developing characterization of the four actors are immediately apparent. The family is already deeply divided when the story starts. In phrasing reminiscent of 25:28 it is said of Esau that he is Isaac's son (27:1) and of Jacob that he is Rebekah's son (27:6). Of Rebekah, we know that she is an active partisan of "her son" Jacob. She listens in freely to what one might expect to be private conversations, is kept informed of developments in the family that take place out of her hearing, and is completely willing to manipulate situations—whether facilitating Jacob's lie or manipulating Isaac's feeling about Esau's foreign wives—so that her ends are achieved.

Of Isaac we know that he is equally a partisan of his son Esau, but on the whole he remains a dim figure. However, the ways in which he is dim are manifold. He sees poorly and, although he will live on for decades, is apparently in ill health and living in retirement. He is also dim enough neither to recognize Jacob's voice nor the fact that he is covered with the gore of freshly killed goats' skins.

Esau is depicted as one who is trying desperately to please his parents and win his father's blessing. But he does it in such an inept fashion, marrying yet another foreign woman, that it is clear that he, too, is somewhat dim and lacks any sort of keen insight into what the family needs and wants.

The entire section is dominated by interest point of view. Everyone, from Isaac's initial desire for a spicy meal to Esau's marriage to a daughter of Ishmael, is acting out of self-interest. But at the same time, the narrative pace speeds up and slackens repeatedly to serve the larger purpose of the tale. As the plotters create their deceit in v. 14ff, the pace slackens noticeably to allow us to savor the plotters' misdeed. Similarly the pace becomes agonizingly slow in v. 18 as Jacob tries desperately to speak as little and as indistinctly as possible; is he trying to disguise his voice or to lie as little as possible? Verse 30 neatly overlaps the two brothers' activities, increasing tension by demonstrating that one is barely gone when the other arrives. In verse 33 the reader is reminded that Jacob had done none of the things his father had asked— thus reminding the reader of Jacob's deceit—as Esau realizes that something evil has been done to him.

Esau's marriages to Hittite women—and later to the Ishmaelite woman—are passed over in blazing speed, although we have previously known nothing at all of Esau's domestic arrangements. But the reader needs to know this material in order to make sense of Rebekah's complaint in 27:42-46.

Fokkelman summarizes the whole succinctly:

> Rebekah and Jacob carry out her plan and win; Isaac and Esau are beaten. But again the winning party is the moral loser. What price is paid here for this guile! The family is torn apart, the latent contrasts come to light completely. It is characteristic that after Rebekah and Jacob's energetic actions nothing is left for Esau to do but comment. Jacob acts, Esau is left empty-handed. Esau may cry, gnash his teeth, whimper for one more blessing, brood on revenge—the blessing has been given away once and for all.[21]

Forewarned now about the complexity of the passage, we will look in detail at each of its constituent scenes.

Frame A: Esau's Hittite wives (26:34-35). Esau marries Hittite women. What, after all, is wrong with marrying women from the locality? The chosen family practices endogamy, as is evident both from Abraham's marrying Sarah and the necessity felt on Abraham's part for Isaac to marry someone to whom he is related. Esau's exogamous marriage is thus a transgression of an important cultural norm. In order to do so he would have had to marry without his parent's permission. He would also have violated his family's honor by marrying a local person. Of course, it does set up Rebekah's reason for sending Jacob away. According to the NRSV and most other translations, these foreign wives "made life bitter for Isaac and Rebekah." This assumes that the first element of the phrase *mōrat rûaḥ* stems from the verb *mrr*, "to be bitter." Alter argues that it is better understood as deriving from the root *mrh*, "to rebel" or "to defy," and translates the pertinent phrase "And they were a provocation to Isaac and to Rebekah."[22] This is an extremely fine insight and helps us to understand even better Rebekah's determination that Esau not inherit. He married at forty, the same age as his father, and would have intentionally—and provocatively—married inappropriately. His mother might well have thought he was trying to copy his father, step into the father's place, so stealing a march on his twin brother and making his claim on the family inheritance unquestionable. The reaction of his already estranged mother becomes clearer in its motivation, if no less morally appalling.

[21] Ibid., 100.
[22] Alter, *Genesis*, 136.

Scene 1: Isaac and Esau (27:1-5). Isaac is not really that old yet and will live on for another twenty years. This is the second reference to his senses; in Genesis 26 he fondled his wife, creating a stir in Abimelech's household. Yet in this story the sense that would help him most, sight, is denied him. Isaac's blindness fascinated the sages of Jewish tradition. Consider the Midrash:

> "Isaac's eyes became dimmed *from seeing*" [literal translation of *mērĕ[>]ōt*]: from the impact of that vision. For when Abraham bound his son on the altar, the ministering angels cried, as it is written, "Hark the Arielites cry aloud" [Isaiah 33:7]. And tears dropped from their eyes into his eyes, and were imprinted into his eyes. And when he became old, his eyes became dimmed, from seeing.[23]

Zornberg explains that the Midrash understands Isaac's blindness to be a delayed reaction to the Akedah. Successful in life, he is nonetheless the bearer of an unbearable memory. In his advancing years, as a result of that fundamental moment in his life, all else falls into darkness. "Death haunts his imagination, the *angst* of one who saw nothing else in an eternal moment in his youth . . . Isaac lives indeed, a kind of death-in-life, passionless."[24] It is as though having seen what he was forced to see, he can see nothing else, is blind to all other experience. His wife and second son quite consciously take advantage of his weakness and exploit it to their advantage.

Isaac calls Esau to him. The narrator refers to Esau as "his son" while in direct discourse Isaac calls him "my son." Of course, this may be nothing more than the proclamation of the obvious, for Esau is in fact Isaac's son. But in this most dysfunctional of families one hears other echoes of favoritism on Isaac's part for this elder son of his. He complains in a somewhat whining fashion of his age and infirmity and asks Esau to being him "savory things which I love" (AT, *maṭ^cammîm ka[>]ăšer [>]āhabtî*). The phrase will recur two other times in the chapter (vv. 9, 14) to show how the enthusiasm that unites Isaac and Esau is used to their disadvantage. The purpose of their meal together will be to provide an opportunity after which Isaac will pass his blessings to Esau.

Scene 2: Rebekah and Jacob (27:5-17). The second scene begins in v. 5, with Rebekah calmly and without compunction listening as her husband and son converse in what they thought was privacy. Of special note here at the beginning of the scene is the way the sons are identified. Isaac is speaking to "his son," and Rebekah calls "her son" (v. 6).

---

²³ *Bereshit Rabbah* 65:5, quoted in Zornberg, *Genesis*, 156.
²⁴ Zornberg, *Genesis*, 158.

Rebekah understands the need for haste—Isaac has spoken of his impending death—and she prepares to wrest the blessings from "his son" so that "her son" might enjoy them.

One is astonished when Jacob raises no word of protest or objection. He seems to have no moral qualms about the proposed ruse—but then it is a family well used to ruses, and his mother was one of those who has suffered as a result. His only qualm is that he and his brother differ so much in appearance that his father will not be fooled. Being cursed by his father is not in his action plan. Rebekah cooks the food Jacob brings to her and dresses him in what must have been the still warm skins of the freshly killed goats. Of course, kid goats and their blood will loom large later in Jacob's life, something our author surely expects us to know already. Deceitfully, his sons will bring him a tunic soaked in goat's blood after they sell his beloved son Joseph into Egyptian slavery. In Genesis 38 he will promise to pay kid goats to the veiled woman with whom he has intercourse—unaware that she is actually his daughter-in-law, deceiving him to gain what is hers by right but which he has denied her. So the goatskins foreshadow the deceiver being deceived. Armed with the food his father loves, Jacob prepares to deceive the father he should love.

Before we leave this section, a word or two should be said about the contrast Jacob draws between himself and his brother. His brother, he says, is hairy, whereas he is "smooth" (ḥālāq). Why did Jacob hit on that particular aspect of their difference, for surely there were others? Esau was a skillful hunter and Jacob was not, for instance. Once again it is the traditional commentators who are most interested in this seemingly insignificant detail.

> One dimension of the contrast is registered in the passage we have quoted from Bereshit Rabbah; to be hairy is to become entangled with the world, to find it impossible simply to wipe oneself free of sin. In a real sense, the symbolism of hair suggests impurity, complication, a lodging place for dirt, as Mary Douglas defines it: matter out of place. Impurity and danger inhere in this modality. Simple, clear categories—the me and the not-me—are confused. Hair represents the anomalous; it obscures the pattern. As soon as he reaches the age of self-construction, Jacob defines himself as a "simple man"—a word that evokes purity and order.
>
> To be smooth, however, also suggests the lack of a densely evolved sense of self. Surely there is a certain fascination for Jacob in the imagining of his brother.[25]

[25] Zornberg, Genesis, 166, citing Mary Douglas, Purity and Danger (Penguin, 1970) ch. 2.

Could it be that Jacob, at least in some part of his unready being, recognizes the truth about himself—that he is as yet unready to take up the burden of these blessings, that he is too immature to know how to act and what to do with them? One is tempted to read into this a sense of moral unease about what he is going to undertake, but the next words make clear what Jacob's fear is—that instead of the blessings he will get a curse.

Scene 3: Isaac and Jacob (27:18-30). So, armed with food, dripping with bloody gore, but free of moral qualms, Jacob goes to his father. On entering the tent he seems eager to avoid speaking, knowing that his voice should give him away. Whereas the hearty and bluff Esau might well have announced his return and success Jacob says simply *ʾābî* ("my father") the two syllables offering Isaac little chance to hear that the voice is wrong. But Isaac's hearing is apparently better than his sight and he suspects right away that something is awry. He asks Jacob, "Who are you, my son?"

The trouble with Jacob may well be that he does not have a good answer to that question, that he does not really know who he is in his smooth immaturity masquerading as another. In his response, Jacob simply lies to his father and claims to be his brother Esau. This is deeply troubling to a modern reader but was more so to the traditional reader for whom Jacob, as the patriarch of the people of Israel, had to be a paragon throughout his life. How then to explain away a bald-faced lie? In the Book of Jubilees the tale unfolds in a subtly different fashion:

> He [Jacob] went in to his father and said, "**I am your son.** I have done as you told me; come and sit down and eat of what I have caught, father, so that you may bless me." . . . And Jacob went close to his father Isaac, and he [Isaac] felt him and said, "The voice is Jacob's but the hands are the hands of Esau," and he did not recognize him, because there was an ordering from heaven to turn his mind astray . . . And he said, "Are you my son Esau?" and he said, "**I am your son.**" (Jubilees 26:13-19)

James Kugel comments:

> Here Jacob tells no lie: he twice asserts what is only the truth, that he is indeed Isaac's son. But how could such a distortion square with what the Bible itself says?
>
> It should be remembered that the biblical text was originally transmitted without punctuation or capital letters, so that where a sentence begins and ends was often a matter of opinion. Exploiting this situation (along with the frequent omission of the verb "to be" in biblical Hebrew), an interpreter might maintain that the opening exchange between Jacob and his father—namely, "Who are you, my son?" "I am Esau your

firstborn"—could just as easily be read as follows: "Who are you? My son?" "I am. [But] Esau is your firstborn." It seems that the author of *Jubilees* had something like this in mind.[26]

That Jacob is innocent because of his fine parsing of the potential ambiguities of biblical Hebrew is too much for most readers. Rather, we are yet more taken aback when Jacob adds near-blasphemy to his lie by invoking God's name. He adds to his lie by using the loaded term "firstborn," not merely "elder son"; he claims to be the one to whom the blessing is owed. A final attempt by Isaac to test Jacob's identity with his sense of smell—the voice is still unconvincing, so he thinks to smell his son—has Isaac outwitted by his wife's foresight in dressing Jacob in Esau's clothing. Convinced at last, he blesses Jacob. In the blessing, Jacob is addressed seven times, seven times told that he will be the center of people's attention and service. This is a harbinger of Jacob's sevenfold bow to his brother Esau in Genesis 33:3.[27]

The blessing is unlike those that precede it in the book, omitting any mention of progeny and the possession of the land in which they sojourn. A number of its elements are noteworthy. His brother's subservience is made explicit, and a play is made on the word *min*, which means "from" or "of." For Jacob in v. 28 it is used partitively, to say that he will benefit "from" the world's riches. For Esau, in v. 39, it will be used spatially, to show that he will be kept away "from" the riches of the earth.[28] There is also, in v. 29, an ironic foreshadowing of Joseph's dream later in the book (37:9), when he sees his father Jacob bowing down to him.

Scene 4: Isaac and Esau (27:30-41). The first verse of the following scene—a scene which is the same length as the preceding and of which it is a sort of antitype—recalls the twins' birth and shows that the natural order which prevailed there has at last been reversed and Jacob has supplanted Esau: "And just as Jacob went out . . . there came in Esau his brother" (AT, *ʾak yāṣōʾ yāṣāʾ yaʿăqōb . . . wĕʿāśāw ʾāḥîw bāʾ*). One gets the impression that they barely miss each other and marvels at the speed with which Rebekah and Jacob have pulled off the trickery. As he enters his father's tent, Esau's volubility in inviting his father to taste some of what he has caught and cooked makes a stark contrast with Jacob's earlier two-syllable mumble. As recognition of the culprit and his deed dawns on both—can Isaac really not know who stole the

---

[26] Kugel, *Traditions*, 360.
[27] Fokkelman, *Genesis*, 109.
[28] Friedman, *Torah*, 94.

blessing or is he simply unable to believe it?—father and son cry out with great anguish. The remainder of the scene unfolds in a sort of parallel structure.[29]

> A. He cried out with an exceedingly great and bitter cry (27:34a)
>   B. and said to his father: bless me, even me also, my father? (27:34b)
> (Isaac's explanation//Esau's explanation; 27:35, 36a)
>   C. He said: have you not reserved a blessing for me? (27:36b)
> blessing summarized by Isaac (27:37)
>   C'. Esau said to his father: have you but one blessing, my father? (27:38a)
>   B'. Bless me, even me also, my father! (27:38a)
> A'. Esau lifted his voice and wept (27:38b)
> anti-blessing given by Isaac (27:39)

One notes the significant repetitions here: blessing, father, son, weeping, and cries. These make the situation of the actors so transparent that they nearly obviate the need for further interpretation. Father and son are crushed, but there is nothing they can do. The anti-blessing that is given to Esau may have some connection to the historical situation of the Edomites, who lived by raiding Israel. It is also worth noting that in v. 36 Esau continues the ongoing pun on Jacob's name when he says that his brother is rightly called Jacob. He uses the verbal root of Jacob's name in the next sentence when he says that Jacob has supplanted him. To paraphrase broadly, Esau says something like: "They were right to name him Jacob/Supplanter for he has supplanted me twice!"

The scene ends with one of the Bible's rare instances of interior monologue, "And Esau said [literally] in his heart . . ." (*wayyōʾmer ʿēśāw bĕlibbô*). No longer is there any mention of love, of foodstuffs, of blessing or anything else. Now as we reach the climax, the emotional high point of the tale, there is only hate as Esau resolves to kill the brother who has done him such harm.

Scene 5: Rebekah and Jacob (27:42-45). This scene marks a shift in the story's rhetoric, one that might indicate a movement in Rebekah's heart. Previously there had been a very strictly marked division of the family such that Jacob was Rebekah's son and Esau was Isaac's son. Here for the first time that changes. Rebekah is told what her elder son

---

[29] Fokkelman, *Genesis*, 104.

is planning, so she calls her younger son to her. While this adds to the ongoing characterization of Rebekah, it adds a nuance to our understanding of Esau as well. Bluff, hearty, and, most especially, impetuous, Esau has apparently been unable to keep his plan for revenge against his brother a secret and has told someone. By some route this frightening information has now made its way to Rebekah, who realizes that things are getting very much out of hand and that she must act. If Esau were to kill Jacob he would in turn be executed (cf. Gen 9:5-6), and she would lose both of her sons.

Rebekah identifies herself for the first time as the mother of both sons, and she acts in such a way as to preserve both of their lives. Esau remains impetuous and unable to plan coolly for his future. Jacob is still blithely unaware of the impact of his actions upon others and has to be told by his mother that his life is in danger. He seems unable to read other people and understand their inner lives, perhaps because he is still smooth and immature.

Scene 6: Rebekah and Isaac (27:46). This is by far the shortest scene in the story, consisting of one brief speech by Rebekah to her husband —a speech to which he does not even reply—and so seems to provide a telling insight into their marriage. Once again quick off the mark, she dashes to her husband to tell him, somewhat out of the blue it would seem, that her life is not worth living because of her daughters-in-law. Her words—themselves an echo of her complaint while pregnant—are a subtle rebuke to Isaac for having favored Esau (. . . who has made her life a misery!). Esau married local women, but such must not be allowed to happen to her precious Jacob.

Scene 7: Isaac and Jacob (28:1-5). In the seventh and final scene, Isaac instructs Jacob to travel to his uncle Laban's family and seek a wife there. In so doing he tells him to undertake a journey that was forbidden to Isaac himself. However, it provides Jacob with another reason for his flight, one less morally problematic than fleeing for his life from his murderously angry and betrayed brother. Isaac also blesses Jacob again, this time with the "blessing of Abraham" that includes numerous progeny and possession of the land.

This second, or supplementary, blessing seems to many to be a needless repetition of what has gone before, so it is assigned to another source (P, the Priestly source) and thought to have been added here because the final editor had it and wanted to use it somewhere. Given that the rest of this tale is told with such consummate artistry it seems unlikely that our author would simply insert something here because he had no better idea what to do with it. It is placed here to indicate a formal acceptance, after the fact, by Isaac of Jacob's senior status in the family, and the blessing given here is not the rather generic one given earlier but a formal recapitulation of the blessing that connects Abraham to Isaac and now Isaac to Jacob.

Frame A': Esau's Ishmaelite wife (28:6-9). This frame scene is almost heartbreakingly sad as poor Esau tries desperately to win the affection and approval of his family. Thinking that his difficulties have stemmed from his marriages with Hittite women, he marries an Ishmaelite cousin. Apparently he had never noticed the dismay of which the narrator had told us earlier (26:35) and about which Rebekah had complained (27:46). Alter points out that there is no record of Isaac's response to this move on Esau's part but that what Esau does is an echo of his cry of the heart when "Esau said to his father, 'Have you only one blessing, father? Bless me, me also, father!' And Esau lifted up his voice and wept" (27:38).[30]

One reaches the end of this chapter wondering where God is and how God reacts to the machinations effected in this tale. As in Genesis 16, God is silent in this chapter although voluble in the preceding and following chapters. Here the members of this chosen family have neither time nor inclination to listen to voices other than their own, nor is there any seeking of oracles or divine intervention. God will not be involved with actions such as these but will, in the next chapter, show that he is willing to work with the material he is given.[31] In subsequent chapters, God will mold Jacob into Israel and turn him from the lying sneak-thief into the man who prays to God and bows down to his brother in repentance, though we will not find the awe-inspiring transformation so often touted of him. But first, the man who would act with guile so that he might lord it over others must learn to be the object of guile and be lorded over. The smooth and immature man must learn to love wife and family, God and brother.

---

[30] Alter, *Genesis*, 143.

[31] Thomas Mann helps us to understand the emotional complexity, both for the reader of this section and for the characters themselves in the story world, when he writes:

> Such is the intemperance of the feelingful; and Jacob was encouraged in his by the tradition handed down in his tribe, of God's own intemperateness and majestic caprice in matters of sympathy and preference. El Elyon's way of preferring this and that one, without, or at least over and above, merit on their part, was very highhanded, hard to understand and humanly speaking often unjust; it was a fixed and lofty state of feeling which was not to be interpreted but simply to be honoured with fear and ecstasy. . . . (*Joseph and His Brothers*, trans. H. T. Lowe-Porter [London: Vintage, 1999] 51)

Chapter 7

IN THE TIME OF THE THIRD GENERATION

Genesis 28–36

How Is the Story Structured?

With the unusual division of the text adopted here, I argue that a new section begins with Jacob's departure from his family at the beginning of Genesis 28. From his birth in Genesis 25 through the deception and flight in Genesis 28 he had lived in the midst of Isaac and Rebekah's home and been formed, for good or ill, as a result of their influences and the tensions and dynamics found there. It was, as we have seen, a home lacking in discernment, where God, even in Genesis 26, seems only perfunctorily present. In order to grow, to become someone other than the slick deceiver he has been heretofore, Jacob must leave. And once he leaves his family he never returns nor, apparently, does he ever have any further contact with his mother. He encounters his father the next time only on his deathbed (Gen 35:29).

How best to organize the material in these chapters? Where shall we choose to stand? There is a general feeling among commentators that these chapters are somehow arranged concentrically. Even before we look at the section in detail, there is in the reader a certain perception that a reversal takes place. Jacob goes away a deceitful unmarried thief and later returns a transformed man, married, and willing to put others before himself.

One very fine description of this concentric arrangement—that leaves aside Jacob's encounter with God at Bethel—is offered by Walter Brueggemann.[1]

---

[1] *Genesis* (Atlanta: John Knox, 1982) 249. See page 259 of the same work for another interesting arrangement that centers not on the birth of Jacob's children but on God's remembering.

A. Friendly preliminary meeting (29:1-14)
  B. Meeting with Laban and a contract (29:15-20)
    C. Deception by Laban (29:21-30)
      X. Jacob's children (29:31–30:24)
    C'. Deception by Jacob (30:25-43)
  B'. Meeting with Laban and a dispute (31:17-42)
A'. Friendly departure and covenant (31:43-55)

While this arrangement does not include all elements of the material in these central chapters it does give the reader a feel for the general movement in the text. It makes great sense that this sequence of tales, in which Jacob—who becomes Israel and father of the eponymous ancestors of the twelve tribes—is a principal character, is centered on the birth of the twelve sons. Consider another version, which draws other aspects of these chapters to our attention:[2]

	d
1. Encapsulation	o
A. Arrival: Jacob meets Rachel (29:1-14)	w
B. *bd/skr* (marriage), Jacob vs. Laban (29:15-30)	n
	w
2. Oppression and Service	a
A. Wives and children (29:31–30:24)	r
	d
---	---
B. *bd/skr* (flocks), Jacob vs. Laban (30:25-43)	u
3. Flight from Service	p
A. Jacob to the wives: plan to escape (31:1-21)	w
B. *bd/skr* (departure with family and flocks),	a
Jacob vs. Laban (31:22-54)	r
	d

Fokkelman explains this diagram by saying that it describes three rounds of fighting between Jacob and Laban.

> In the first round Jacob is totally knocked off his feet by the deceiver Laban and bound to a fourteen year tenure of hard work. In the second round, precisely in the middle of this period, after Joseph's birth, the reversal takes place: Jacob makes proposals which introduce Laban's fall. . . . In the third round it seems for a while that Laban is going to gain ground (his *terafim* had been stolen), but failing to produce evidence and checked by the God of Abraham and Isaac, he becomes the loser. Jacob leaves, untouched, a blessed man.[3]

---

[2] Jan P. Fokkelman, *Narrative Art in Genesis: Specimens of Stylistic and Structural Analysis* (Assen/Amsterdam: Van Gorcum, 1975) 193.

[3] Ibid.

Again, this extremely insightful arrangement—to which we will return in due time—teaches us a great deal about Jacob in Haran but does not include the incidents that precede or follow. As a result the reader might see those incidents as not really belonging to the whole, as not being organically part of the section of the book which deals with the third generation of the chosen family, and might take them less seriously or accord them less attention. I would like to suggest a simple parallel arrangement that, while lacking total precision and failing to include all elements of these chapters, does show the general movement of the text.

> A. Jacob, alone and nowhere, encounters YHWH in a dream (28:10-22).
> B. Jacob leaves home, encounters Laban, and lives with wives and families in Haran (29:1–31:54).
> A'. Jacob, not alone and somewhere, encounters God face to face (32:1-32).
> B'. Jacob returns home, encounters Esau, and lives with wives and families in Canaan (33:1–35:29).

Although the pregnant phrase *lek-lĕkā* ("Go for yourself") does not occur here as it does in Genesis 12:1 and 22:2, it would not be out of place if it did, for Jacob is truly undertaking a journey that he needs to make for his own sake. To save his life he needs to be out of his brother Esau's reach. To find his wife, an appropriately endogamous wife, he must leave the land promised to him in his father's blessing and return to the land from which his family came. In a very real sense, Jacob must leave his country, his kindred, and his father's house and go to another land in what seems to be very much a reversal of his grandfather Abraham's journey. But the purpose for his journey is also the reverse of his grandfather's. For just as Abraham could only become truly himself in Canaan, confronting there the questions of paternity and obedience to God that so plagued him, so Jacob can only become himself in Haran, confronting there the patterns of deceit and the lack of other-relatedness that so plague him.

The Bible almost never recounts details of journeys. But the story of Jacob is a powerful exception to this rule, for the first thing recounted is an event that takes place as he travels—he encounters God at Bethel. Apparently entirely alone, with neither friend nor family nor servant to accompany him, Jacob spends the night at Bethel. In Fokkelman's trenchant phrase, "His sun has set."[4] The winner of his brother's

---

[4] Fokkelman, *Genesis*, 121.

birthright emerges victorious but bereft of all that gives life meaning. Here, a virtual no man in a virtual no where, he encounters God. But Jacob remains Jacob, and he makes deals with God.

Jacob travels to Haran, where he meets his match in his uncle Laban, who deceives him out of decades of his life. Here in Haran he loves, as in the past he has been loved. In three rounds of further strife he bests Laban but does so for the family he loves. Then he is free to undertake the same journey Abraham did and return to Canaan.

Before he can enter Canaan, again bereft of family and entirely alone in the middle of nowhere, he encounters God a second time. This time he does not emerge with a deal but with a limp and a new name. Most commentaries see these as signs of Jacob's partial transformation; I will try to show that the limp is rather a sign of *un*transformation. This man, no longer smooth and no longer content to dwell in tents, will then be as ready as he is ever likely to become to return home, put himself in danger, reconcile with his brother, and meet his father. Then, as was also the case with his grandfather Abraham, Jacob will begin to cede his place to his sons, even as he lives on for many years.

This scheme does not include all of the details present in the text, but it does show us that the latter part of Jacob's life parallels the first and that in those latter years he undoes what he had done earlier because he has undone the person he was earlier. Then he steps aside and lets the next generation take up their adult lives, making terrible mistakes of their own, but eventually transforming themselves from the family chosen for blessing into the people chosen for blessing.

Commentary

A. 28:10-22: JACOB, ALONE AND NOWHERE, ENCOUNTERS YHWH IN A DREAM

The relatively self-contained nature of this section is apparent since it begins and ends with notices of Jacob's previous and subsequent travels, which serve as brackets for the Bethel passage. The tale can be well described using the traditional language of plot structure, but in general it falls into three sections: Jacob's itinerary (28:10-11), the theophany itself (28:12-15), and Jacob's response to the theophany (28:16-22). This last element is itself divided into two parts, the first of which is an etiology for the name Bethel (28:16-19), and the second is Jacob's vow (28:20-22). The whole can be schematized:

Itinerary (28:10-11)
   Bridge (28:10)
   Exposition (28:11a)
   Inciting moment (28:11b)
Theophany (28:12-15)
   Development (28:12)
   Turning point (28:13-15)
Jacob's response: Resolution (28:16-22)
   Etiology (28:16-19)
   Vow (28:20-22)

Jacob travels eastward in the direction of Haran and, because night has fallen, finds a place to spend the night. The place (*māqôm*; the word appears six times in this brief story) is not identified, at least not yet, but—especially since Jacob is recapitulating Abraham's journey in reverse—it calls to mind Abraham's stopping for the first time in Canaan at a "place" at Shechem (Gen 12:6) where God appeared to him just before he moved near Bethel itself and built an altar there. In fact Abraham also worships YHWH at Bethel twice (Gen 12:8; 13:3f) although no mention of that is made here. Nor is any mention made of the centuries-old Canaanite use of Bethel as a place of worship.[5] All of that recedes and in this story the place is just a nowhere that serves as a backdrop for Jacob's encounter with God. Using a stone as a sort of pillow—Rashi[6] suggests that the stone(s) served to protect his head—he is, doubtless unwittingly, prepared for divine encounter. This is the first of three times that stones appear in significant places in Jacob's tales. He will roll a stone away from the well where he meets Rachel, and he will set up stones to mark his treaty with Laban.

Jacob has not previously shown any particular religious inclination; certainly no fear of divine sanction kept him from his deceitful behavior in the past. Nor is there any hint here that Jacob sought this experience as an oracle about his future as his mother had once done

---

[5] "As a matter of fact, all the evidence points in the direction of a Canaanite origin for 'Bethel' and the sanctuary situated at the place bearing that name. The second component of the name, El, betrays its pre-Israelite connections. It can refer to none other than El, a well-known Semitic deity and the name of the head of the Canaanite pantheon. Bethel derived its name from being the cultic center of this god" (Nahum M. Sarna, *Understanding Genesis: The Heritage of Biblical Israel* [New York: Schocken, 1966] 193).

[6] Rashi, *The Pentateuch and Rashi's Commentary: A Linear Translation into English*, trans. Abraham ben Isaiah and Benjamin Sharfman (Brooklyn: S. S. & R. Publishing, 1949) vol. 1: *Genesis*, 275.

(Gen 25:22). Indeed, it is only when he is asleep that God comes to him. Might this be because it is only when Jacob is asleep that he is un-guarded enough to be open to a divine encounter? This is in contrast to his grandfather and father, who experienced theophanies—both vi-sions and auditions—while awake. Commentators note that the mir-acle of a theophany is less remarkable here than is the fact that it is Jacob, treacherous, lying fugitive that he is, who receives it.

It is Jacob's sleep that allows the rest of the tale to unfold, for in his sleep he dreams and the dream changes his life. The text seems to imply that, unlike his father and grandfather, Jacob would not be amenable to such a revelation while awake, that he would not want to lose the time from his other activities. Consider what Walter Benjamin said about Kafka.

> "'But when do you sleep?' asked Karl, looking at the student in surprise. 'Oh, sleep!' said the student. 'I'll get some sleep when I'm finished with my studies.'" This reminds one of the reluctance with which children go to bed; after all, while they are asleep, something might happen that con-cerns them. . . . While they study, the students are awake, and perhaps their being kept awake is the best thing about these studies. The hungry artist fasts, the doorkeeper is silent, and the students are awake.[7]

Jacob would not have gotten to the place where he now finds him-self had he been less vigilant, had he not studied and prepared himself for the opportunities that came his way. But surely one must see that this is an ironic sort of success. Jacob, the student of advantage for self, has succeeded beyond his imagining, but what has it got him? He's lost. The sun is set. God arranges sleep so that, less than vigilant for once in his life, he can dream as God would have him dream.

Verse 12 is a good, if somewhat difficult to understand, shift of point of view. The word *hinnēh* (literally, "behold"), as we have seen a number of times, shows that the perceptual point of view moves to within the sub-ject's head, so that the reader is seeing out of the subject's eyes. What is re-markable here is that the subject is dreaming, so we as readers are given an especially privileged position, watching Jacob's dream just as he does.

The ramp (a more likely translation of this unique word—*sullām*—than the traditional "ladder" still used by the NRSV and many other translations because of the general Mesopotamian feel[8] of the whole

---

[7] Walter Benjamin, *Illuminations*, 136, quoted in Avivah Gottlieb Zornberg, *Gene-sis: The Beginning of Desire* (Philadelphia: Jewish Publication Society, 1995) 190.

[8] According to Sarna, the stairway "recalls at once the picture of the ziggurat with its external ramp linking each stage of the tower to the other" and the "note

piece) provides Jacob with a sort of gate into the realm of God. However, neither Jacob nor God use the ramp since the traffic on it seems to be restricted to angels. The nature of angels, and their relationship to God, has been discussed already (see the commentary on Genesis 16), but it will be useful to point out here that traditional commentaries have been curious both about their presence and the direction of their travels. Once again the word "behold" appears in the text (Gen 28: 12) to remind us readers that we are watching this alongside Jacob. Since angels are heavenly creatures, one might have expected them to descend and then ascend, rather than the reverse, as is the case in the biblical text (which reflects perfectly ordinary Hebrew idiom). According to one source:

> And he [Jacob] dreamt that there was a ladder set upon the earth and whose top reached to heaven, and the angels who had accompanied him from his father's house went up to announce to the angels on high. . . .
> (*Targum Neophyti, Fragment Targum* [MS. P] Gen 28:12)

Hence, these angels were already on earth—for some reason that the text does not explain—and traveled from there up to heaven. This explains the direction of their movement. Some commentators go on to explain that what is being referred to here is continuous movement back and forth, as angels keep going up and down. For what purpose? The final word of Genesis 28:12 in Hebrew is *bô*, which simply means "on it." But it can also be understood to mean "for him" or "because of him." So the angels kept going up and down to see the one of whom so much was expected.

This verse plays an important role in the New Testament as well, showing, if nothing else, how intrigued the entire tradition was with the details of this event in the life of Jacob. At the beginning of the Gospel of John, Jesus converses with Nathanael, who will become one of the Twelve. Nathanael wonders how Jesus came to know him and, in reply to Jesus' answer that he saw Nathanael under a fig tree, he replies:

---

that 'its top reached the sky' (28:12) and the identification of the site of the dream as 'the gateway to heaven' (28:17) is reminiscent of the stereotyped phraseology used in connection with Babylonian temple-towers." He goes on to show how much Jacob's experience of this shrine differs from any Mesopotamian model, since nothing was there before Jacob's visit (i.e., the place does not memorialize any event in the lives of the gods), and the stone was erected by Jacob simply as a memorial of his experience (not erected by the gods as a reminder of what occurred there). See Sarna, *Understanding Genesis*, 193–4.

"Rabbi, you are the Son of God! You are the King of Israel!" Jesus answered, "Do you believe because I told you that I saw you under the fig tree? You will see greater things than these." And he said to him, "Very truly, I tell you, you will see heaven opened and the angels of God ascending and descending upon the Son of Man." (John 1:49-51)

At first glance, this way of Jesus identifying himself with Israel's hopes and dreams seems far removed from the text we are now considering. However, it is evident that he is making the same interpretative move that the Jewish sages did. The final *bô*, which they read as "for him," Jesus understands to mean "on him," i.e., "upon the Son of Man." Thus Jesus becomes the place where revelation can be found, for the Christ is the place where the gate of heaven is rooted among us.[9]

Jacob does not travel up this ladder, as one might perhaps expect, for a glimpse of the heavenly realities. God does not call him upwards to interview him or instruct him in any way. Rather, while Jacob is still asleep and receptive to YHWH's word, YHWH is "beside him."

> . . . as God stands over him to protect him, a new synthesis is experienced, a still point in the turning world. The words describing God's "posture" suggest stability, unconditional attention and support.[10]

This marks the tale's turning point, quite literally. YHWH—and it is not without reason that God is always identified in the sequence with the proper name and not the generic word because the commitment made here is profoundly personal—takes decisive action to be at the side of Jacob, and all else in his life will flow from that stance on the part of God. God's first words to Jacob—the NRSV has "I am the LORD, the God of Abraham your father and the God of Isaac"— are better translated as "I, YHWH, am the God of Abraham your father and the God of Isaac." The change may seem unnecessarily subtle, but according to Speiser "the description applies not to the name but to the deeds."[11] In Exodus 20:2, YHWH speaks in a similar fashion to link his name with his saving action for Israel. Here, God links his name with what he has done for Jacob's forebears and what he will do for him in turn. For the third time the word "behold" appears (Gen 28:13) to remind us that we are in the midst of Jacob's experience. The three oc-

[9] Francis J. Moloney, *The Gospel of John* (Collegeville: The Liturgical Press, 1998) 57.

[10] Zornberg, *Genesis*, 192. Rashi simply says that YHWH stood beside him "to guard him" (Rashi, *Pentateuch*, 276).

[11] E. A. Speiser, *Genesis*, AB 1 (New York: Doubleday, 1962) 218.

currences of "behold"—sadly omitted from the NRSV—enable us as readers not only to identify with Jacob's point of view but also to identify with his experience. Over and over and over we see the ladder, see the angels ascend and descend, and see God stand by both of us, Jacob and reader, and so we too know protection and stillness in a turning world. The darkness that held revelation for him enlightens our darkness.

There follow the standard promises that we have seen so often already: Jacob is promised the land, extraordinarily numerous progeny and that he will be a blessing. What is unique to Jacob's experience follows in 28:15:

Behold, I am with you,	*wĕhinnēh ʾānōkî ʿimmāk*
and I will keep you wherever you go	*ûšĕmartîkā bĕkōl ʾăšer-tēlēk*
and I will bring you back to this land;	*wahăšibōtîkā ʾel-hāʾădāmâ hazzōʾt*
for I will not leave you	*kî lōʾ ʾeʿĕzābĕkā*
until I have done	*ʿad ʾăšer ʾim-ʿāśîtî*
that which I have spoken to you. (AT)	*ʾēt ʾăšer-dibbartî lāk*

Given the nature of the Hebrew inflectional system, pronouns are ordinarily expressed as suffixes appended to a verbal root, as is the case, for example, in modern Italian or Spanish as well. What one might call a freestanding pronoun can also be used for emphasis. This is the first thing the reader notices about Genesis 28:15. The first word *wĕhinnēh*, already used to such powerful effect in the Bethel story, appears once again here. This time it does not mark a shift in point of view but functions to summon Jacob's attention; God says something to him like, "Look," "Pay attention," "See here." This attention-getting device is followed immediately by the personal pronoun "I." Although it cannot be evident in any English translation, this is the only time the pronoun appears in the sentence; all the subsequent occurrences of "I" in English are simply pronominal suffixes in Hebrew. The effect of this freestanding pronoun is to give prominence to the personal involvement of the speaker. In the most emphatic way possible, God declares his personal involvement in what follows. Whatever the angels were doing in their continual ascent and descent, this is no angel speaking to Jacob but none other than YHWH. YHWH commits himself to be with Jacob ("I am with you"), to protect him ("I will keep you"), and to bring him back ("I will bring you back"). But what is reiterated twice is that YHWH will not leave Jacob alone. The one who is no one and no where, who has no one with him and does not know what his future holds, is assured that the profound existential loneliness that is the lot of all humans will not be his any longer, for God is irrevocably with him. This is why Jacob was brought to this place where heaven and earth meet.

This theme of "God with us" pervades the Bible, both Old and New Testaments. Witness these few texts, which speak to the common human desire, articulated here in Jacob, to know that we are not alone, that we are cared for by one who can see that we are safe and bring us home:

> But Moses said to God, "Who am I that I should go to Pharaoh, and bring the Israelites out of Egypt?" He said, "I will be with you; and this shall be the sign for you that it is I who sent you: when you have brought the people out of Egypt, you shall worship God on this mountain." (Exod 3:11-12)

> "Do not be afraid of them, for I am with you to deliver you, says the LORD." (Jer 1:8)

> Therefore the Lord himself will give you a sign. Look, the young woman is with child and shall bear a son, and shall name him Immanuel. (Isa 7:14)

> But now thus says the LORD, he who created you, O Jacob, he who formed you, O Israel: Do not fear, for I have redeemed you; I have called you by name, you are mine. When you pass through the waters, I will be with you; and through the rivers, they shall not overwhelm you; when you walk through fire you shall not be burned, and the flame shall not consume you. (Isa 43:1-2)

> Because you have made the LORD your refuge, the Most High your dwelling place, no evil shall befall you, no scourge come near your tent. For he will command his angels concerning you to guard you in all your ways. On their hands they will bear you up, so that you will not dash your foot against a stone. You will tread on the lion and the adder, the young lion and the serpent you will trample under foot. Those who love me, I will deliver; I will protect those who know my name. When they call to me, I will answer them; I will be with them in trouble, I will rescue them and honor them. (Ps 91:9-15)

> "Look, the virgin shall conceive and bear a son, and they shall name him Emmanuel," which means, "God is with us." (Matt 1:23)

> Go therefore and make disciples of all nations, baptizing them in the name of the Father and of the Son and of the Holy Spirit, and teaching them to obey everything that I have commanded you. And remember, I am with you always, to the end of the age. (Matt 28:20)

Fully awake now, Jacob recognizes the presence of YHWH in what had seemed like an anonymous piece of ground. But why fear when, having experienced such a powerful theophany, joy would make more emotional sense?

Did you know, then, that joy is, in reality, a terror whose outcome we don't fear? We go through terror from beginning to end, and that precisely is joy. A terror about which you know more than the beginning. A terror in which you have confidence.[12]

Jacob knows a kind of fear that is indistinguishable from joy. He marks the place with a memorial pillar, which he anoints with oil. In his exultation he renames the place Bethel, the House of God.

Paradox follows, however. He goes on to respond to God's commitment to him. And in so doing the author shows us that whatever transformations await us in Jacob's future, Jacob is still the Trickster. For the most prominent word in his response is the qualification "if." If God is with him, if he is guarded by God, if he is given food to eat, and if he comes home to his father's house in peace. If all of this happens, then—and one assumes this means *only* then—will Jacob serve the God who revealed himself at Bethel. As we have seen, Jacob's "way" is the way of Abraham, but in reverse. God will be with Jacob, to be sure, but as we will see, his way will lead him in directions he will never have imagined. For Jacob the Trickster is about to meet his match in his uncle Laban.

B. 29:1–31:54: Jacob Leaves Home, Encounters Laban, and Lives with Wives and Families in Haran

Of the many attempts in the literature to describe the structure of these chapters, I am most convinced by the suggestion of Fokkelman already described above because of the way in which it draws our attention as readers to the recurrence of the themes of Jacob's serving, based on the Hebrew root *'bd*, and wages, based on the Hebrew root *skr*. At the same time it allows us to regard the birth of Jacob's sons (the eponymous ancestors of Israel's tribes) in general and that of Joseph in particular as central to the purpose of these stories. The birth of the sons is represented in his diagram by the horizontal line at the far right that also serves to mark the point, the axis, at which Jacob's fortunes begin to ascend once more. I repeat it here for convenience as we look at these chapters in more detail.[13] My own commentary on this section will fall into three sections corresponding to Fokkelman's. Each of the large sections described here can itself be broken down into constituent

---

[12] Zornberg, *Genesis*, 198, quoting Rainer Maria Rilke, *Selected Works I: Prose*, trans. G. Craig Houston (New Directions, 1967) 24.

[13] Fokkelman, *Genesis*, 193.

parts, several stories that are brought together to form the larger whole.

4. Encapsulation A. Arrival: Jacob meets Rachel (29:1-14) B. *ʿbd/skr* (marriage), Jacob vs. Laban (29:15-30) 5. Oppression and Service A. Wives and children (29:31–30:24)	d o w n w a r d
B. *ʿbd/skr* (flocks), Jacob vs. Laban (30:25-43) 6. Flight from Service A. Jacob to the wives: plan to escape (31:1-21) B. *ʿbd/skr* (departure with family and flocks), Jacob vs. Laban (31:22-54)	u p w a r d

1. Encapsulation (29:1-30). This first part of the chapter, in the course of which Jacob meets the love of his life, his future wife Rachel, and the rival (and future father-in-law) who does his utmost to best him, Laban, consists of three stories linked together to form the whole. It forms a whole as it follows Jacob's downward travel; the son of the wealthy Jacob, who had previously lived in comfort and ease, is, by the end of this section, little more than a hired servant.

Betrothal, part 1: the meeting at the well.
Exposition: 29:1
Inciting moment: 29:2-3
Development: 29:4-8
Turning point: 29:9
Resolution: 29:10-11
Conclusion: 29:12

The integrity of this first story is marked by movement at its beginning (29:1) and end (29:12); the story begins with Jacob's arrival and ends with Rachel's departure. The phrase that marks the beginning of this brief story—literally "and he lifted up his feet and went"—is unique in the Hebrew Bible, where the normal idiom would simply be "he went." In this particular story it creates a nice echo with another phrase that occurs later in the chapter although, once again, this is not evident from the NRSV translation. In 29:11, after Jacob kisses his cousin Rachel, the Hebrew says, literally, "he lifted up his voice and wept" [AT]. His journey began as he lifted up his feet and ended when he lifted up his voice in tears of relief. Immediately thereafter, in 29:12, it is

Rachel who runs to her father, taking over from Jacob and indicating in a very nice narrative fashion the way in which their two lives will be inextricably joined henceforth.

The bulk of the story, as we might expect, is a variation on the type-scene of the encounter of the future spouses at a well already seen in Genesis 24. Once again stones appear as a significant element in the life of Jacob, although this stone is so large that it requires the strength of more than one man to roll it from its place blocking the mouth of the well and to return it when they are finished watering their flocks, but this seems not to be immediately apparent to Jacob. This information is given to us readers in an aside from the narrator in 29:2b-3. Jacob discovers that he is near enough to the end of his journey that his kinsman Laban is a well-known person in the vicinity and that his establishment is so near that this is the well also used by his herders, one of whom is his daughter Rachel, even then approaching. In this way Rachel enters the story for the first time.

Jacob, whose quiet life in tents seems not to have prepared him terribly well to survey and understand subtleties of the pastoral scene in front of him, takes the shepherds to task for shirking their duty. He is apparently so unfamiliar with the burden of stones that he cannot estimate that the well cover is too heavy for one man. Clearly, he has much to learn as he begins to move from the authoritative order-giver to the hired hand.

This first story reaches its turning point when Rachel appears on the scene. Somehow Jacob will have to confront her, and the way in which he does so and the way in which she responds will fix their characters for the rest of their relationship. Genesis 29:10, which marks Jacob's first sight of Rachel, also stresses the family relationship between the two; she is the daughter of his mother's brother, his cousin. A further phrase seems at first glance to be entirely unnecessary, since we already know that Laban is Jacob's uncle and that Rachel tends his flocks. But the information is repeated here—and once again before the end of the same verse for a total of three repetitions in the course of a very brief sentence—for stress; Jacob has entered thoroughly into a world of sheep owned by Laban. The next part of the scene, in which the flocks are watered, shows that Jacob is in some ways his father's opposite since he, not a servant, raises the stone and he, not the future betrothed, waters the sheep. However, while this shows Jacob's hitherto unmentioned and in fact somewhat surprising physical prowess it also reminds us, in a nicely ironic fashion, that Jacob is now in the position of the servant, one from which he will not emerge for twenty years. He is forced to do what they do because he ran servantless from his home after terrible deceit and will be forced to continue in that posture for twenty years because his deceitfulness will meet its match in the already oft-mentioned uncle Laban.

Jacob kisses his cousin and breaks into tears; his journey is at an end. And indeed the story concludes with him identifying himself to Rachel as a kinsman and her running to tell her father of his arrival. Without any indication of her own reaction, without any offer of a place to stay, and without any return of his kiss—a hint of Rachel's seeming emotional ambivalence to Jacob throughout their lives together—she runs off to her father.

This brief story does a number of important things in the ongoing saga of the third generation of God's chosen family. Jacob is now firmly outside of the land of promise—how and when, we wonder, will he return? He has encountered at least one member of the related family he is seeking and attempted to impress her with his physical prowess, although in a nicely ironic touch he, only moments before, had indicated little awareness of the weight of the stone in question. We do not know how she reacts, although from the form of the type-scene we know that she is his future wife. She leaves immediately, without inviting him to follow. So at the end of this first brief scene Jacob is somewhere, but still alone and still without any way to make progress in the world. In this way, the author has neatly set us up to wonder what happens next. And we are just as neatly set up to expect something confusing because Jacob is now taking the place of a servant, although very much within the realm of his apparently wealthy sheep-owning uncle Laban, where the immediate reaction of his cousin is to run away from him without a word.[14]

---

[14] This reading is very much in contrast with those of other commentators. Fokkelman, for example, says, "The balance and harmony of this arrival and recognition have been achieved by virtue of the blessing. God is indeed with him, leads him to the circle of relatives and inside it he meets the woman who is to be his bride" (*Genesis*, 124). It seems to me that the scene is much more fraught with uncertainty than Fokkelman recognizes. God is not anywhere to be seen or heard. Unlike in the parallel scene in Genesis 24, no prayer is answered by the expected behavior. Rather, Jacob misunderstands the scene into which he walks and is left alone at the end while the intended spouse runs away. Rather than entering a haven of security, Jacob's already tenuous security is soon to be further eroded. If, as Alter interestingly suggests, the stone is to be read as a symbol of female infertility (*Genesis: Translation and Commentary* [New York: Norton, 1996] 152), it will be a very long time indeed before that stone is lifted away from this relationship by God's intervention. Its symbolic nature is further heightened by Jacob's inability to understand its true import. While he, pumped up with adrenalin and testosterone, might just barely manage to heave the stone aside, he will be powerless to do so with the burden that weighs down his marriages, his inability to love Leah and the inability of Rachel to bear a child.

Betrothal, part 2: the deal.
Exposition: 29:13-14
Inciting moment: 29:15
Development: 29:16-17
Turning point: 29:18a
Resolution: 29:18b-19
Conclusion: 29:20

The exposition of the next brief story, or scene, overlaps with what precedes. Laban runs to meet Jacob just as, so many years earlier, he had run to meet the servant of Abraham. The most insightful reading, still a masterly example of intertextuality, is that of Rashi. Comparing the behavior of Laban in this instance with his behavior in Genesis 24:29ff, Rashi suggests that Laban ran because, remembering the wealth a servant of this family possessed, he could hardly imagine the wealth brought by a son of the household. Seeing no laden camels, he embraced him (thinking to feel money secreted on his person) and failing that, kissed him (thinking to find pearls held in his mouth).[15] This explains Laban's somewhat less than enthusiastic response to Jacob's news, which might be paraphrased something like "Well, we are relatives." The final element of the setting of the scene is Jacob's month-long stay. The earlier eagerness to push aside boulders and water flocks seems to have dissipated as there is no hint that Jacob did anything to contribute to the household during his month's rest. Indeed, he seems once again to have comfortably taken up the quiet tent life he had so long enjoyed in the household of his indulgent parents. Laban, however, is no indulgent parent. He knows what has brought Jacob to him (Gen 29:13b) and knows, therefore, that he can expect no shower of wealth from this discredited son of his sister. Nonetheless, his indulgence does last an entire month.

At the end of this month, Laban asks Jacob a question that advances his characterization and shows us readers how clever an adversary he will prove to be for Jacob. A month has passed during which nothing seems to have happened. We readers are tempted to fill in this narrative gap with what we already know of Jacob and these other characters. Laban, we suspect, will be quietly on the boil, disappointed in the poverty of the newly arrived nephew, who seems to be turning into just another non-contributing mouth to feed. Laban, the man interested in money, will not be content simply to support Jacob. Jacob, whose entire life so far has consisted in turning a situation to his advantage, seems to have done the same here. He has a roof over his head,

---

[15] Rashi, *Pentateuch*, 285.

meals on his table, and needs to do nothing in return. There is no hint that he has been working. He is after all a smooth man who likes to live quietly. And of Rachel, so interestingly introduced into the story as the future spouse, we hear nothing. We also wonder whether anyone else forms a part of this household. At any rate, there is tension enough and expectation enough to start a story rolling with even a small spark. Laban does the honors with his question, which might be paraphrased, "Look, just because we're related doesn't mean that I won't pay you for your work. Name me a price!" (AT).

Jacob, the man long practiced in clever schemes, has apparently foreseen this foray on the part of his uncle. This explains the apparent diversion in the story's development. All of a sudden we are redirected back to Laban's family and learn that, in addition to Rachel, there is an elder sister named Leah. The name Rachel means "ewe lamb," a nice enough appellative, which seems to indicate the tremendous fresh beauty we are now told she possesses (Gen 29:17). Leah, on the other hand, means "wild cow."[16] So we now know that there are two young women in Laban's household, that the younger is beautiful, but the appearance of the elder is ambiguous. We read in Genesis 29:17 that her eyes were *rak*, which is translated in a great many ways. The NRSV reads it as "lovely," thinking that Leah's one fine attribute is mentioned here by way of contrast with Rachel's overall beauty. Others read it as "weak," understanding it to be part of a negative overall assessment. Old, and still unmarried, "Cow" even had unattractive eyes in comparison to the younger, stunningly beautiful, and also still available "Lamb."[17] Might it be the biblical equivalent of being said to have "a nice personality"? However the word, so crucial and yet so difficult to understand, is translated, we still know that Leah suffers by comparison with her sister. No one is said to love her. No one works years on end for her sake. No one is desperate to have a family with her. So God will care for her and provide for her in a superabundance of fertility. Leah is both insider and outsider. She is tied up in a family where she is un-

---

[16] Everett Fox, *The Five Books of Moses* (New York: Schocken, 1995) 137.

[17] Robert Alter argues,

The precise meaning in this context of the adjective is uncertain. Generally, the word *rakh* is an antonym of "hard" and means "soft," "gentle," "tender," or in a few instances "weak." The claim that here it refers to dullness, or a lusterless quality, is pure translation by immediate context because *rakh* nowhere else has that meaning. Still, there is no way of confidently deciding whether the word indicates some sort of impairment ("weak" eyes or perhaps odd-looking eyes) or rather suggests that Leah has sweet eyes that are her one asset of appearance, in contrast to her beautiful sister. (*Genesis*, 153)

wanted and unloved yet always the outsider in this family insofar as she is outside of the bonds of affection that bind it together. The one for whom no one else cares will be freed by God from her affliction and given sons who will love her.

Jacob loved Rachel (Gen 29:18). Yet there is no indication here or later that his ardent feelings for her were returned. Jacob offers seven years of work as a bride-price for Rachel, the younger daughter. Laban's response is a study in evasion, seeming to say and mean one thing while leaving a reader uncertain as to what was meant after all. Laban does not promise anything or anyone to Jacob. He simply says that Rachel's marriage to him would be appropriate since they are related and that Jacob should stay. Jacob must clearly have heard this as a promise for he serves the seven years.

The story's boundaries are marked by references to time, beginning with a month that passes in silence and ending with seven years that also pass in silence. The month seems to pass in indolence, but then narrative time speeds up enormously because the next seven years are fueled by anticipation and love.

The scene is marked as well by service, which appears repeatedly, and love, which appears twice. By its end all of the characters are known to us and the complications of their interrelationships have been hinted at. Jacob serves for love, but is he loved? Both Leah and Rachel are silent bystanders, although we feel an innate empathy for the former and wonder about the latter. Laban is firmly in control and has transformed the deceitful schemer into a schemed upon servant. Once again, this brief interlude sets us readers up for what follows by raising more questions than it answers. And so we are on to the third brief story in what is becoming an extremely complex chapter.

Marriage: Laban's deception and the question of justice.
Inciting moment: 29:21
Development: 29:22-23
Frame break: 29:24
Turning point: 29:25
Resolution: 29:26-27
Conclusion: 29:28-30
Frame break: 29:28

The first brief story in Genesis 29 was afforded its unity by the movement that marked its boundaries. The second was unified by the mention of time. The third and final one of these short tales is given its unity by Jacob's demand for his wife so that he could go in to her (Gen

29:21) and the note that he went in to Rachel (Gen 29:30). While this envelope device gives an apparently straightforward unity to the end of the chapter, in fact it encloses an extremely complicated passage, whether regarded as a piece of narrative structuring or a study in psychology and manipulation. At its center will be Leah, the unloved one cared for by God, just as at the center of Abraham's stories was found Hagar, the unloved one cared for by God.

Right at the beginning one notices the abrupt tone with which Jacob demands that his wife be given to him. His language is even a bit coarse, indicating that the seven years have perhaps been less easy for Jacob than the narrator has let on. The story has, most unusually for the Hebrew Bible, no real exposition as it begins without any mention of where or precisely when the encounter between Jacob and Laban takes place. This is in stark contrast to the remainder of the tale, which slows down considerably so that we can follow the events of the wedding night(s) carefully.

Just as there is no mention of time or place at the story's beginning, there is no mention of Laban's reply to Jacob. This should cause us readers to be wary because we recall Laban's less than straightforward reply to Jacob's initial request to be allowed to marry Rachel. A wedding feast follows, and we discover that our suspicion of Laban's trustworthiness has been repaid because, instead of Rachel, Jacob has been married to Leah. The notice that Jacob went in to Leah is followed by a frame break that slows down the pace of the narrative—the giving of Zilpah as a maid to Leah—and gives us something to wonder about in the future. How will Zilpah figure, and what role will she play, for surely she is introduced for some reason?

All commentators understand this as a comeuppance for Jacob. The deceiver has been deceived, and that by the use of darkness, just as Jacob used the darkness of his father's blindness to deceive his father. But the standard commentaries take little notice of Leah and how it might have felt for her to be made the wife of someone who was panting not for her but for her sister. Nor is there any indication of Rachel's feelings about the events that are unfolding.

Rather, the point of view in 29:25 is very much Jacob's. A literal translation reads, "And it was morning and, behold, it was Leah" (AT). Commentators since ancient days have wondered how the night could have passed without Jacob discerning that it was not Rachel with whom he was spending the night. Genesis Rabbah imagines the following conversation taking place at this moment.

He said, "How could you have deceived me, you daughter of a deceiver?" She said to him, "And is there a book without faithful readers? Did not your father call you 'Esau,' and you answered him accordingly? So you called me by a name other than my own, and I answered you accordingly."[18]

Leah, in this version, is represented as having studied Jacob's life and works, learned from them, and faithfully copied them. What he has done to others has come back upon him. This, however a persuasive reading it might appear to be, remains an imaginative construction; according to the biblical text there is no discussion between the two. Jacob runs off to Laban and, using the same verb used of his own actions in 27:35, accuses Laban of deceit. But if both midrash and modern commentators tend to ignore Leah, let us for just a moment turn our attention to her.

Leah is at the center of the story and is being seen. But by whom? Our first inclination must be to think that it is Jacob who is seeing her. But it might be less simple than that. Genesis 29:31 says that YHWH sees Leah and sees that she is unloved. This must call to mind the experience of Hagar, also undesired, but also at the center of a narrative structure and seen by God. Might one imagine that the shift in point of view that takes place in 29:25 does not take us into Jacob to see through his eyes but that it takes us within the mind of God? That is, it is not Jacob seeing the undesired Leah but God, once again, seeing the unloved one and giving her the support her world does not otherwise provide her. In this way God is in the story where he does not otherwise seem to appear and is there in the way he has been before—looking upon the undesired, the one trapped where she is unfree, and giving her the sort of freedom, albeit limited, that is better than none.

Laban's response is incisive and must cut Jacob deeply. He begins reminding Jacob that he is—through his own actions—not at home, that he is a visitor in a place with different customs. He also reminds Jacob that, at least in his home, the younger does not precede the firstborn—alluding to Jacob's extortion of the rights of the firstborn from his brother Esau. But the remainder of his speech, in which the two women concerned are merely grammatical particles, unnamed and unquestioned as to their own wishes, lets Jacob know that he can have Rachel in return for another seven-year period of unpaid service.

Jacob completes the bridal week with Leah and is then married to Rachel. The narrator breaks frame once again to tell the reader about Bilhah being given to Rachel as a maid. The story then concludes with Jacob going in to Rachel, loving her more than Leah, and serving another

---

[18] Jacob Neusner, *Confronting Creation: How Judaism Reads Genesis: An Anthology of Genesis Rabbah* (Columbia, S.C.: University of South Carolina Press, 1991) 263.

seven years. As Fokkelman rightly notes, Jacob is now thoroughly en-
capsulated in this family. Although married, he has no freedom and is
even more firmly entangled in a web of relationships that are complicated at best. He loves where he may well not be loved in return and,
once again, he is reduced to servitude. This time there is no indication
that time passed swiftly, for the next years will be fraught with tension
and distress for all of the people we have met so far.

   2. Oppression and service (29:31–30:43). According to Fokkelman's
scheme, the next major section of the story about the third generation
of the chosen family plays out under the rubric of oppression and service. At first glance this may seem an inadequate title because it seems
to ignore the birth of Jacob's sons, the eponymous ancestors of Israel's
tribes. Jacob does indeed labor under the oppression of Laban, but the
emotional oppression of dueling pregnancies and, at least on Leah's
part, competition for her husband's affections, and the oppression on
Jacob's part of being torn hither and yon by the demands of his families are also real oppressions.

   This section falls into two subsections. The first, Genesis 29:31–30:24,
will be called Dueling Pregnancies here. The second, Genesis 30:25-43,
will be called similarly: Dueling Flocks. As a whole, this passage causes
problems for the narrative analyst. There is certainly tension aplenty, a
sense of grim necessity as the two sisters attempt to have children and,
at least on Leah's part, attract thereby the attention of Jacob and YHWH
(as we will see, there seems little distinction between the two for her).
Equally, one learns a great deal about the characters involved, through
what the two wives say to each other and to their husband Jacob and
what they name their sons. But what makes the section difficult is that
there seems to be no turning point, no lessening of tension. Perhaps that
is because the section has been put at the service of the naming of the ancestors of Israel's tribes; that process has pushed narrative development
aside for the time being. Perhaps I have wrongly discerned the boundaries of the narrative in question and, as a result, am trying to make a
story out of what is only a scene in a longer and more developed tale. Or
it may be that I am trying to force this brief passage into a sort of theoretical straitjacket, forcing it to submit to a narrative framework that is
foreign to it and not helpful in our understanding of it. Be all of this as it
may, at least two things happen here; sons are born and characters are
revealed. Both are important in the ongoing story of this chosen family.

   There is as well a complex tangle of points of view being used here,
and one is tempted to say that this is the dominant narrative device
used. The story is told under the gaze of God ("When the LORD saw
. . . ," 29:31), but what God is seeing is not only the characters and
their actions but a concept, hatred of one's wife (29:31) and the interest

of that wife in having children. So all three sorts of point of view, perceptual (God watching what is taking place), conceptual (God disapproving of hatred and so creating new life to circumvent it), and interest (Leah and Rachel both act out of their self-interest, the former looking for love and the latter looking to even the score) come into play here. Jacob here is more acted upon than acting, although ultimately all of these sons are in his self-interest. Dinah, the sole daughter, is less a character in her own right than an agent who is acted upon in the gruesome story of Genesis 34—but more of her in due time.

YHWH sees that Leah is unloved. The root involved might be better translated as hated, although it refers, at least in this instance, less to an emotional reality than to a legal one. Consider, for instance, the legal text from Deuteronomy 21:15-16 that speaks to this situation.

> If a man has two wives, one of them loved and the other disliked, and if both the loved and the disliked have borne him sons, the firstborn being the son of the one who is disliked, then on the day when he wills his possessions to his sons, he is not permitted to treat the son of the loved as the firstborn in preference to the son of the disliked, who is the firstborn.

This law might be read as a paradoxical commentary on much that has happened so far in the book. The firstborn son of the despised wife (Ishmael) was set aside for Isaac's sake. So, in reading the story of Leah and her sons we are reminded, once again, of Hagar and her son. We are wary, knowing Jacob, that he will attempt to supplant the firstborn son of the despised wife by the firstborn son of the favored wife, as indeed he will. While this will unfold later, right now the text is important for us as it indicates at least one of the senses in which Leah is hated. In a polygamous household equality of treatment and affection must be difficult to maintain. In this household there is not even a pretense; Leah is hated. That, both according to this story and the Word of God, is wrong; so God intervenes.

God intervenes by allowing Leah to conceive, while Rachel remains unable to conceive. Leah bears a son and names him in a way that tells us about God and about Leah. God has seen her affliction, that she is unloved, and given her a son. In typical biblical fashion, the name has a meaning that evokes the meaning of the person. The name Reuben means something like "Look, a son." She hopes that it is Jacob who will finally see her, but she remains invisible to him and seen only by God.[19] This is the third time that love has entered the story. The narrator

---

[19] Friedman offers a very useful insight into the naming pattern (Richard Elliott Friedman, *Commentary on the Torah* [San Francisco: HarperSanFrancisco, 2001] 100).

has informed us twice that Jacob loved Rachel (29:20, 30), and now we hear from Leah that she desires to be loved. The period between the birth of the first and second sons is passed over in silence, but one can assume that Leah's hopes are disappointed and that Jacob still fails to love her, given the tragic name she gives her second son.

This second son is named Simeon[20] because she says that he is a gift from God, since he has heard that her husband hates her. What was obvious previously to the narrator and God (29:32) is now obvious to Leah as well, and she will not use the word love again, although she continues to long for her husband. God's seeing and God's hearing affect the names of the first two sons. These, of course, are the two senses that Jacob used to deceive his father.[21]

The pattern of the mother naming the son is altered with the birth of the next son, Levi. The name still bespeaks Leah's desire, even if she avoids the use of the word love, but she does not name this child. The NRSV switches to the passive voice ("he was named"), but the Hebrew simply says, "he named him" (AT).

Perhaps there was indeed some upturn in their relationship, because Leah immediately conceives again and names the son who is born Judah because she desires to praise YHWH. At this point, having borne four sons and many disappointed hopes, she ceases to bear. During this period Rachel has been invisible. Leah acts, apparently, not to spite her sister but to win the love of her husband.

Who names children? Jacob's wives name their children and those of the maids. Is there a convention? The person who does the naming is the person on whom that story is principally focused. Since the rivalry between Leah and Rachel is the focus of the story it makes sense that they name the children. Friedman suggests that one of the occasions when this pattern does not hold is in Genesis 38, where Tamar names her sons Perez and Zerah. I will argue, when we get to that part of the book, that Tamar is very much the focus of that story, so the pattern will be seen to hold even there.

[20] Fox (*Moses*, 138–42) gives us a good list of the names and their purported meanings. It should be said that the meanings of the names do not stand up to rigorous linguistic scrutiny, but in each case there is enough similarity of sound between name and meaning for the identification to be sensible to a hearer or reader of Hebrew. Fox's list reads:

> *Leah's sons:* Reuben = See, a son (29:32); Simeon = Hearing (29:33); Levi = Joining 29:34); Judah = Giving thanks (29:35); *Bilhah's sons:* Dan = He has done justice (30:6); Naphtali = My struggle (30:8); *Zilpah's sons:* Gad = Fortune (30:11); Asher = Happiness (30:13); *Leah's sons:* Issachar = There is hire (30:18); Zebulon = Prince (30:20); Dinah (no explanation is given; 30:21); *Rachel's son:* Joseph = Add (30:24).

[21] Alter, *Genesis*, 156.

Genesis 30:1 marks not only a change in chapter but also a shift in point of view. Whereas God saw that Leah was unloved and caused her to bear as a result, God does not see Rachel, and Rachel does not act for love. Rather, Rachel sees that she is behind in the number of births and desires to catch up. God does not see her nor does she invoke God; rather she angrily confronts Jacob and demands that he give her sons.[22] This is the first time that Jacob's beloved has spoken and thus we expect her to speak and act in a way that will set her character for us. She speaks not of love but of jealousy. There is no hint that she returns Jacob's feelings, although there are many indications that Leah might well have had she been allowed to do so. The commentaries criticize Rachel at this point for impetuosity but that charge seems ill placed. She has, after all, been married for at least four years to a man who was hotly desirous of her. It is hardly impetuous to think that after years of marriage a pregnancy should have resulted.

Jacob responds in a similarly angry tone, saying that he does not stand in the place of God (perhaps an implicit criticism of her lack of divine invocation in comparison to Leah). Rachel chooses not to pray, but takes the route of Sarah in giving a maidservant (now we know why they were mentioned earlier) to her husband as yet another wife of secondary rank. Rachel names the resulting son Dan—thus adopting him—and invokes God as having judged her. That she is perhaps less concerned with God than with Leah becomes evident after the birth of the second son, whom she names Naphtali because she has prevailed in wrestling with her sister.

Leah reenters the fray and offers her own maidservant Zilpah as another secondary wife, and a son is born to her, whom Leah names Gad. The next son, also born to Zilpah and named by Leah, is named Asher. One wonders at this point why she is happy. Is she saying that her sons give her joy, or that she has definitely beaten her rival? At any rate, as Leah still strives to win the love of one who seems fundamentally unaware of her, one thinks of the words of Richard Russo:

> After all, what was the whole wide world but a place for people to yearn for their hearts' impossible desires, for those desires to become entrenched in the defiance of logic, plausibility, and even the passage of time, as eternal as polished marble.[23]

---

[22] The NRSV opts for a more inclusive and generous "children" for the Hebrew *bānîm*. While it is perfectly true that the word can refer to both genders, the lack of interest shown in the birth of the one daughter Dinah allows the reader to surmise that the mothers were not disinterestedly desirous of children in general but of sons in particular. It was in this currency that they traded in the internal economy of this family.

[23] Richard Russo, *Empire Falls* (New York: A. A. Knopf, 2001) 295.

There follows a strange scene, the only conversation between women in Genesis, which centers on mandrakes. These fruits are said to be aphrodisiacs, and their appearance here is somewhat mysterious. Apparently Jacob has been avoiding Leah; at least that is the obvious sense of 30:15-16. But can it be that he has also been experiencing sexual difficulty with Rachel? She does not seem to be uneager for him, so is it Jacob that needs to have his vigor for her rekindled? Is he taking a sort of sexual time out from the emotional maelstrom of this family? That seems the most likely way to read this passage.

Jacob, oddly passive throughout these events, meekly acquiesces, goes in to Leah, and she conceives yet again. The name Issachar shows us once again how thoroughly Jacob has become a servant who works for wages. He works, God pays. Leah bears a sixth son. Although still avoiding the word love, she hopes for honor from her husband. Perhaps she gained some, for, without having to resort to the device of the mandrakes, she conceives and bears again, this time a daughter.

Then, in the climax to the entire passage, God remembers Rachel (as he had remembered Noah and Abraham), and she bears Joseph. Now, all of a sudden, Jacob is ready to leave. Fokkelman, as ever, gives us solid insight into the meaning of this section:

> The meaning of the entire story 29.31–30.24 is, as we see now, that the real issue of the sisters' fret and fray is the same as that of the brothers Esau and Jacob's struggle: who will take the lead, who will be the first and who will be he who must serve?
>
> Rachel gives up the only thing that shows her precedence, the access to Jacob, and after that God shows mercy. Now we understand that it is because of this he shows mercy. Post hoc propter hoc. As soon as the younger one gives up the high-handedness of Jacob's policy and is prepared to bend, God grants her children. Her barrenness was at the same time a symbol, envy and oppression towards Leah having condemned Rachel to sterility.[24]

Transformation within herself brings a change from God. Rachel's transformation, the new life that it affords her, will be the catalyst for further change in Jacob, and he will begin his upward journey and his homeward journey. After all, "All of us are better when we're loved,"[25] and to love is what Jacob seems to have learned. This love will lead him to reconciliation. But first Jacob must manage to get home. In order to do that he must create wealth for himself and his family that is separate from Laban's. In short, he must enrich himself and disentangle

---

[24] Fokkelman, *Genesis*, 141.
[25] Alistair MacLeod, *No Great Mischief* (New York: Norton, 1999) 283.

himself from his service to Laban. And he must do this without raising undue suspicion on Laban's part. He will do this not by deceit, for deceit is now in his past, but by clever manipulation of the opportunities that come his way. Laban however will try his old tricks.

Motivated by the birth of Joseph from his favored wife, Jacob is ready to return home and so approaches his father-in-law with a speech that barely conceals his bitterness at his years of servitude. In a brief speech Jacob asks to be sent home with wives and children. Three times in these few words he uses the verb "to serve,"[26] as though he were saying "I have served you, and served you, and served you, and now I want to take what is mine and go home."

Laban is now the smooth one and asks Jacob once again to name his wages. He claims that divination has told him that YHWH has blessed him through Jacob. The NRSV omits the words "and he said" at the beginning of 30:28, but they should be retained since they serve a real purpose. There seems to be a pause between v. 27 and v. 28, when Laban hesitates for a moment to let tension build. Jacob must have expected him to say something like, "Thanks for all you've done for me. All the best on your journey home and take care of my daughters and grandchildren." Rather, Laban shows that his character is unchanging. Once again, he asks Jacob to name wages. Laban does not propose to let him leave, but offers him a deal-sweetening raise instead.

Jacob's anger in response is palpable. He reminds Laban that his present success is all due to Jacob and that his presence and hard work are the reasons YHWH has so blessed Laban. But now, Jacob says, he must think about his own family and provide for them.

Laban remains unmoved and simply reiterates his offer. Jacob makes an offer of his own, one that seems to Laban to be folly and to which he, of course, immediately agrees. It was a goat that got Jacob into this mess (Gen 27:9), so it is appropriate that goats will get him out. Jacob offers to take as his wages only those sheep and goats that have unusual markings or colors. Laban figures that he cannot lose, since most sheep and goats can be relied on to bear normally colored offspring. After he makes the deal, he removes all unusually marked sheep and goats from his flocks, to further lessen Jacob's chances of success.

What happens next confuses nearly all commentators. Jacob sets up peeled rods in front of which the animals breed. It seems that they produce offspring alike in appearance to the rods in front of which they bred. This would be a sort of folkloristic explanation, a kind of superstition. But

---

[26] Only two are evident in the NRSV. However, where the NRSV reads "for you know very well the service I have given you," a more literal, although not idiomatic, translation would read "for you know the service I have served you" (AT).

Robert Alter, quoting Yehuda Feliks, offers an explanation that is more convincing. Feliks says that the rods are a ruse, set up only to fool the unsophisticated and distract onlookers from what Jacob was really about.

> Using a Mendelian table, Feliks argues that the recessive traits would have shown up in 25 percent of the animals born in the first breeding season, 12.5 percent in the second season, 6.25 percent in the third season. Jacob is, moreover, careful to encourage the breeding of only the more vigorous animals, which, according to Feliks, would be more likely to be heterozygotes, bearing the recessive genes. It is noteworthy that Jacob makes no mention of the peeled rods when in the next chapter he tells his wives how he acquired his flocks.[27]

However Jacob managed his feat, whether through the sympathetic magic of the peeled rods, careful breeding of the flocks, or miraculous divine intervention, the conclusion of this section shares with us the narrator's unambiguous judgment: "Thus the man grew exceedingly rich, and had large flocks, and male and female slaves, and camels and donkeys" (30:43). Having reached absolute bottom as Laban's hired hand, Jacob moves strongly up again. Wealthy, surrounded by a large (if somewhat contentious) family, he is ready to leave. He is given the impetus to do so in 31:1, and so we come to the next, and final, part of this section of the story of the third generation.

3. Flight from service (31:1-54). This final section of the stories about Jacob's stay in the home of Laban consists of two brief scenes; as we will see, they can both be understood as short stories on their own, albeit tightly interconnected. The first, using Fokkelman's convenient names, is "Wives and children," and runs from 31:1-21, and the second, "Departure with family and flocks," extends from 31:22-54. In both cases they may be described with the traditional language of plot analysis and studied on their own in detail.

Wives and children (31:1-21).[28]
Exposition: 31:1-2
Inciting moment: 31:3
Development: 31:4-13
Turning point: 31:14-16
Resolution: 31:17-20
Conclusion: 31:21

---

[27] Alter, *Genesis*, 165, quoting Yehuda Feliks in *The World of the Bible Encyclopedia: Genesis* [Hebrew] (Tel Aviv: Revivim, 1982).

[28] Fokkelman (*Genesis*, 151) uses different terminology but comes up with more or less the same division: Introduction, vv. 1-3; Jacob's speech to his wives, vv. 4-13;

The chapter division serves to mark the beginning of a new section in the story of the third generation. The point of view remains firmly fixed on Jacob, at least for the moment, as a new situation arises. He has already decided to return home and is well on the way to making himself a person of impressively independent means. That he is doing so is not lost on Laban's family, and their reaction sets the scene for the next moment in Jacob's story. The "sons" of Laban see that Jacob is getting richer, and they disapprove. These sons had not been mentioned previously and some commentators, quite rightly, suggest that they were not sons at all but simply other male members of Laban's extended family. On the contrary, their invisibility before this point and their appearance now serve as a tacit criticism of Laban and of the implied indolence of his brood. Not being visibly hardworking themselves, they criticize Jacob for doing what they would rather not do. Verse 2 is a touch obscure. The NRSV opts for "And Jacob saw that Laban did not regard him as favorably as he did before" although a more literal translation would be "And Jacob looked at Laban's face and, behold, he was not with him as yesterday and the day before" (AT). The sense is clear, and the use of "behold" to shift the point of view underlines it, for when Jacob looked at Laban he saw something new and apparently deeply off-putting there. Whatever Laban looked like, things were getting too tense for Jacob to remain, although what action he might take is not at all apparent, and the story has, as yet, no particular direction.

At this point, YHWH reenters the story, or perhaps it is more precise to say that the narrator allows us to see that YHWH is still part of the story. As we readers know, YHWH was very much in charge of the birth process, and, as we learn in 31:11, Jacob has been the recipient of divine experiences for some time, although he had not divulged them to anyone. YHWH tells Jacob to return home, but his words to Jacob are subtler than they seem at first glance. Abraham had been told to leave the land of his forebears and family (12:1) to journey to land that would belong to his family. When Jacob is told to return to the land of his

---

Their answer, vv. 14-16; Flight, vv. 17-21. While the two schemes may seem so similar as to be identical, there are important differences. YHWH appears here for the first time since Jacob's encounter at Bethel. It seems apt to describe that as an inciting moment, as the spark of dramatic tension that causes the story to move in a particular direction. Too, in my description, the speech of the wives is regarded as the turning point. This speech is so unusual, both in the context of this story and in the Hebrew Bible as a whole, as I explain in the commentary, that it seems useful to allow it to stand on its own.

forebears and family (31:3), it reminds us that Haran is no longer the family home and that Canaan has already become, at least for Jacob and his family, the place from which his ancestors and family stem. So the promise of Genesis 12 has started to come true. YHWH's words "I will be with you" also hark back to Jacob's experience at Bethel (ch. 28) and Jacob's promise to God there (28:22). God, it seems, is now calling in his debt while at the same time promising support. There are many links between this present story and the Exodus. One of them appears here in vs. 3. The words "I will be with you" are an allusion to the revelation of God's name and the promise to accompany Moses made at Exodus 3:14.

The following scene, during which the tension develops as we wonder what Jacob will do, is unusual in that three persons are present at the same time; ordinarily Hebrew narrative allows only two principal characters in the same scene. So at the outset the scene is marked as important. In a somewhat lengthy speech made to both wives, Jacob rehearses his grievances, Laban's repeated cheating and changes of the arrangements already agreed upon for wages. But the presence of his father's God with him has prevented Laban from harming him. Jacob then sets out a different version of the breeding program from what we have seen before, which makes it seem as though his success is not due to breeding after all but is a miraculous intervention. It is God who is increasing the numbers of unusually colored animals because he has seen how unjustly Laban has acted. Verse 13 is difficult although, once again, the sense is plain enough and is made clearer by the ancient versions.[29] Although Jacob does not tell his wives about his more recent divine visitation (31:3), this earlier vision contains the same message. God is calling in the debt incurred by the vow made at Bethel. But how his wives will react to this demand that they leave family and homeland is not at all clear, so tension—which one might expect to be dissipated by a divine command twice received—continues to rise.

Jacob's wives reply in vv. 14-16. Their brief speech is extraordinary in a number of respects. We learn that they too have long been nursing grievances against their father because of his behavior toward them, but they express their feelings in a way that is, I believe, unique in Scripture: they speak in unison. Both what they say and the way they say it marks this as the turning point. According to the sisters, they have been deprived of their rightful share in the family's wealth. The

---

[29] The LXX reads *egō eimi ho theos ho ophtheis soi en topō theou*, i.e., "I am the God who appeared to you in the Place of God." Most modern translations are based on this reading.

bride-price—we are reminded that Jacob worked fourteen years to provide a bride-price with which to acquire the right to marry the women—has never been given to them as it should have been according to the law and custom of that time and place.[30] Since the "heir's portion,"[31] which they should rightfully expect, will never come to them, whatever wealth has accrued to Jacob is the legitimate property of Laban's defrauded daughters. The upshot is that they forcefully tell Jacob to do whatever God has told him to.

Here, right at the turning point of the story, the outsider motif appears again, and the importance of women in the sight of God is marked once more. When these women are trapped inside their father's family, they are unfree and treated unjustly. God desires that they be taken outside of this suffocating structure, for only there will they be free. They and their concerns are central to this brief story, but central for God as well. The story turns, it must be noted, not on Jacob's concerns but on those of his wives.

Before their departure Rachel takes their father's *teraphim*. These would have been small images of the deities who were the special protectors of Laban's household. It is not entirely clear why Rachel takes them. It may be as simple as an act of spite against her father; it may be an act whereby she derogates Laban's gods as powerless to help him; she may also be laying claim to her share in Laban's wealth. Jacob too steals something, Laban's heart. Here the NRSV uses the rather colorless "And Jacob deceived Laban the Aramean, in that he did not tell him that he intended to flee" (31:20), whereas the Hebrew is a great deal more forceful: "And Jacob stole[32] the heart of Laban the Aramean by not telling him that he was leaving" (AT). Having acted together with his beloved wife Rachel to take from Laban the things he held most dear, Jacob gathers together everything that he has come to possess and everyone for whom he is responsible and prepares to leave and return to Canaan. He is able to do this because of Laban's absence; he is away shearing his flock. The latter are at some remove from the homestead, and the occasion of shearing also brought with it a period of post-shearing relaxation. Jacob has chosen his time well.

---

[30] Speiser, *Genesis*, 244–5.

[31] Ibid. The Hebrew of 31:14b reads "portion and inheritance." This is an example of hendiadys, a figure of speech according to which two words are linked and mean one concept.

[32] "Theft" and "robbery" are prominent words throughout the story. Jacob denies that he has "stolen" anything from Laban but accuses Laban of having "robbed" him, i.e., taken by force what did not belong to him.

Departure with family and flocks (31:22-54).
Exposition: 31:22-23
Inciting moment: 31:24
Development: 31:25-35
Turning point: 31:36-42
Resolution: 31:43-54
Conclusion: 31:55[33]

The language with which this final section begins is reminiscent of that used for the departure of the people of Israel from their slavery in Egypt.

Genesis 31:22-23, 25	Exodus 14:5-9
On the third day Laban was told that Jacob had fled. So he took his kinsfolk with him and pursued him for seven days until he caught up with him in the hill country of Gilead. . . . Laban overtook Jacob. Now Jacob had pitched his tent in the hill country, and Laban with his kinsfolk camped in the hill country of Gilead.	When the king of Egypt was told that the people had fled, the minds of Pharaoh and his officials were changed toward the people, and they said, "What have we done, letting Israel leave our service?" So he had his chariot made ready, and took his army with him; he took six hundred picked chariots and all the other chariots of Egypt with officers over all of them. The LORD hardened the heart of Pharaoh king of Egypt and he pursued the Israelites, who were going out boldly. The Egyptians pursued them, all Pharaoh's horses and chariots, his chariot drivers and his army; they overtook them camped by the sea, by Pi-hahiroth, in front of Baal-zephon.

[33] A word of warning to readers. Gen 31:55, as it appears in most translations, is Gen 32:1 in the traditional Hebrew text, so the verse numbering differs by one throughout ch. 32 between the Hebrew text and the translations. Since I assume that most readers of this commentary will be reading it along with a translation I use that system here. For readers who are using the Hebrew text, I suggest that they simply add one to get the correct verse in Hebrew, so 32:1 here is 32:2 in Hebrew.

Just as the people would later be freed from their slavery in Egypt, so Jacob and his family are saved from their servitude to Laban. This exodus from Haran prefigures the later Exodus from Egypt. In both cases, it is YHWH who acts to free the chosen people.

The scene for this particular story is set when some nameless agent tells Laban of Jacob's flight. For three days he pursues his son-in-law. But here there is something a bit odd in the text. We read both in v. 23 and v. 25 that he caught up with him. But in v. 24 we read of a dream that affects the way in which Laban treats Jacob. It is as though God stopped the action with a sort of freeze-frame in order to give an important message to Laban. God—the particular name by which the family of Abraham knows God, YHWH, is not used in this instance—tells Laban: "Take heed, lest you say [or "do"; the Hebrew can mean this as well] anything to Jacob, good or bad" (AT, 31:24).[34] Actually, this inciting moment may be even subtler than this. The word "god" is plural in form. It may well be that it is not God (i.e., YHWH) who speaks to Laban in his dream; after all, Laban has shown neither knowledge of nor interest in the God of Jacob's family heretofore. It may be that "the gods" speak to Laban and tell him not to do anything to Jacob. This would help us to make sense of Genesis 31:30, where Jacob is accused by Laban of having stolen his gods. Not only did Rachel take the *teraphim*, but also Jacob now has Laban's "gods" working for him.[35] This dream functions here as the inciting moment, since it causes Laban to take a particular sort of action against Jacob. It must be admitted, however, that even in the most generous reading Laban seems to largely ignore this command, since he says quite a bit to Jacob before the story ends!

Jacob has pitched his tents in Gilead, right on the border of what would be Israel, so the ensuing scene takes place on the boundary between Laban's realm and Jacob's. Acting, it seems, on the basis of the dictum that the best defense is a strong offense, Laban goes on the (verbal) attack. He accuses Jacob of having absconded deceitfully, depriving

---

[34] It would be better to read the verb here as "do" rather than "say," since Laban does speak to Jacob in a way anyone would describe as bad, but he refrains from physical harm.

[35] As attractive as this reading is, one must admit that it is most unlikely to have been intended by the text's author. The Hebrew Bible is, if not precisely always monotheistic, certain that if other gods exist they are powerless—virtual nonentities in comparison to the God of Israel. For "the gods" to be given a voice and a role in Israel's story, even such a subsidiary one as that suggested here, would be unique and improbable. Still, one may wonder whether Laban, who neither knew nor worshiped YHWH, might have heard the voice of Jacob's God and thought, albeit mistakenly, that it was the voice of his, now stolen, god(s).

Laban of his beloved daughters and grandchildren, and acting foolishly. This speech appears more than a little disingenuous, since Laban has hitherto shown no particular interest in his daughters' welfare or his grandchildren's existence. We learn that it was not "the gods" who spoke to Laban in a dream but the God of Isaac before Laban ends with his most serious complaint: why has Jacob stolen Laban's gods?[36] Although we readers are aware of this act on Rachel's part, Jacob knows nothing of it and in his ignorance inadvertently curses Rachel (31:32) and thereby predicts her early death. At the same time, he tells Laban to "point out" anything that is his and take it back. The verb used (*hakker-lĕkā*) is the imperative of the verb "to recognize" and was used, as we readers remember, to powerful effect in the story of Jacob's deception of his father. Here, the deceiver (now honest) is telling another deceiver (disingenuous at best) to recognize that he is no longer deceitful. But tension rises for readers, for we know that real deceit has been practiced, and we wonder whether Laban will "recognize" it and "point it out." The effects of deceit still plague Jacob's life.

Laban searches carefully but does not find the *teraphim* since they are concealed under Rachel and she excuses herself from rising to greet her father on the (apparently deceitful) basis that she is experiencing her monthly period. This statement also functions as ironic humor. One presumes that Laban wants his gods returned since they are real and powerful. But how powerful can they be if they allow themselves to be sat upon by a ritually unclean woman?

The story reaches a turning point in Jacob's explosion of speech in 31:36-42. Jacob rehearses the grievances of twenty years and steadfastly (and, as far as we readers can tell, quite honestly) protests his innocence. He has even gone beyond what was required of him in making good any losses to Laban's flocks. If there was theft he was not the cause of it. Jacob's emotionally fraught state is evident in the way that his complaints seem to come running out of him. He also seems, in 31:40, to stumble verbally, beginning a sentence that he does not end. The rough grammar is smoothed over in English translations. That he has emerged from Laban's den of deceit at all is due not to Laban generously deciding that he can leave but to the intervention of the God of Abraham and the Fear of Isaac. This latter divine title might mean something like "the One who inspired fear in Isaac."[37] If some of the grammar in Jacob's speech is rough many commentators also point

---

[36] Here, Laban does not use the word *teraphim*, i.e., images of gods, but the word "gods."

[37] Fox, *Moses*, 149.

out that it takes the form of a formal oath of innocence. Jacob swears in formal, legal fashion that Laban has no justifiable complaint to make against him.

In his response Laban does not yield an inch. He continues to claim possession of Jacob's entire household. But the bluster seems no more than that, since he moves immediately to the suggestion that the two reach some agreement and make a covenant to ratify it. A mound of stones serves as a witness of their agreement and is called "Mound of Witness." Laban the Aramean names it in Aramaic while Jacob names it in Hebrew. Laban demands, calling God to witness his act, good treatment of his daughters and that Jacob not marry again, both reasonable demands and ones found in ancient marriage contracts.

They set up a boundary between them and both promise not to cross it into the territory of the other. There is clearly no affection or trust between the two. They swear by their gods, but note that Jacob avoids using the word "god" since it might seem to equate the gods of Laban with the God his family worships. So once again he swears by the Fear of Isaac. A formal sacrificial meal follows to seal the deal, after which Laban, having taken leave of his daughters and their children, departs. Jacob is now free to reenter, as a different man in many ways, the land he fled twenty years earlier. God, present so much in this story even if mostly working behind the scenes, is still savior; Jacob was saved not only from Laban, he was also saved from himself.

A'. 32:1-32: JACOB, NOT ALONE AND SOMEWHERE, ENCOUNTERS GOD FACE TO FACE

In the structuring suggestion I made above for the stories in Genesis 28–35, which focus on the third generation of the chosen family, the passage we are about to consider is labeled A' in parallel to A (28:10-22: "Jacob, alone and nowhere, encounters YHWH in a dream"). In both cases Jacob is on the threshold between one world and another and the particular situation in which he finds himself at that moment exemplifies his overall situation. In Genesis 28, he is alone and nowhere, the man who has betrayed his family. As a result of his lies and deceptions he is alone, without friend or supporter, without any way to live in the world, and he finds himself in the middle of nowhere making a deal with the God who inserts himself into his life. Compare that to the situation in which he finds himself now: greeted by angels (who previously had passed him by without notice), surrounded by family (where before he had been alone), praying (where before he had been dealing). In prayer he raises himself and his family up to God; his prayer is answered with a nightlong wrestling match. Why? To finally test him? Or to make him recognize in himself what is known already to God?

Waiting and praying (32:1-21).
Exposition: 32:1-2
Inciting moment: 32:3-5
Development: 32:6-8
Turning point: 32:9-12
Resolution: 32:13-20
Conclusion: 32:21

Before we get to the wrestling match, however, another important story intervenes. What is most important about this story is that Jacob is shown thinking of his family and their welfare before his own, and he is also shown praying. If we know characters primarily by what they say and do, it is obvious that this story plays an important part in the ongoing characterization of Jacob.

It begins when Jacob is met by angels. This calls to mind Genesis 28, Jacob's previous liminal experience, when he saw angels in his dream, but they seemed to ignore him, or, if that seems to impute too active an aversion on their part, at least one can say that they took no apparent notice of him. Here, as he crosses the threshold back into the land promised to him, he is met by angels. The spot seems to have been nameless beforehand, so Jacob gives it the name Mahanaim,[38] "[God's] Two Camps," another allusion to Genesis 28 where the non-place was named Bethel, House of God. Since the words "go" and "way" do not occur together except in the Bethel narrative,[39] that is yet another allusion to the

---

[38] Grammatically this name Mahanaim is a dual ("Two Camps"). Unlike English or other modern European languages, Hebrew has a dual form in addition to the familiar singular and plural. It is normally used for things which come in pairs, eyes for example. Some commentaries, traditional and modern, speculate about why the dual form is used here. Is there one camp for God's followers and another for Jacob's? However, place names are occasionally dual in form as well, Jerusalem being the prime example. In this instance, while it is possible that Mahanaim is simply another example of this geographical use of the dual, Jacob does divide his household into two camps (so that if one is attacked the other might survive), and there are two sets of actors (divine and human). It is perhaps to this sort of duality that the name alludes. Robert Alter points out that a binary division runs throughout the Jacob story: "twin brothers struggling over a blessing that cannot be halved, two sisters struggling over a husband's love, flocks divided into unicolored and parti-colored animals, Jacob's material blessings now divided into two camps" (Alter, *Genesis*, 178).

[39] Fokkelman, *Genesis*, 197.

earlier incident. In all of these ways, the two stories are tied together and the latter needs to be read in light of the former.

The scene is thus nicely set, and the story is ready to begin. Jacob is now free to take any number of actions. He might return to Bethel to fulfill his vow. He might return to his parents whom he has not seen for twenty years. He is quite free to act and to go where he wills. However, his first action is to seek reconciliation with his brother Esau. In the interim we learn from the narrator that Esau, whose name called to mind words for hairy and red (25:25), has found a place in the world where he is at home, as is indicated by its names, Seir (an allusion to "hairy," *śēʿār*) and Edom (an allusion to "red," *ʾadmônî*). Thus, before we even meet him again we have the idea that he has a place to be in the world and has rooted himself there, so much so that it bears his name. This is a hint at the strength with which he will come to confront Jacob and an indication of the person he is; having had everything stolen from him in his youth he has, in the intervening twenty years, made himself a nation. This is very much in contrast to Jacob who has been a servant for twenty years.

The contrast between the two forms the basis of his message to Esau. Just as God has sent messengers to meet him (32:1), now Jacob sends messengers (32:3)[40] to his brother. One may read this in a somewhat cynical light, that Jacob wants to buy off his brother to forestall any further difficulty with him as Jacob reestablishes himself in the land, or more charitably, that Jacob desires reconciliation with the person whom he has most damaged before he does anything else. There is nothing in the text to favor one reading over the other.

The message is consciously shaped by Jacob to undo his previous attitude towards his brother. He addresses Esau as "lord" and describes himself as "your servant." One might be tempted to think that this is nothing other than the typical pattern of address seen in letters of the time,[41] but even though using the form of address customary at the time, Jacob intends more. He is voluntarily undoing the interpretation of God's ambiguous prenatal prediction (Gen 25:23) on which he and his mother had based their deception, namely, that "the elder should serve the younger." In the rest of his message he makes other contrasts between himself and his brother. Whereas Esau has become a nation, Jacob has been an alien, a person without even a home. His alien status explains

[40] The same Hebrew word is translated "angels" in 32:1 [NRSV] and "messengers" in 32:3 [NRSV].

[41] As indeed it was, quite like the contemporary usage of "Dear. . . ." And so it might mean nothing in particular about the social relationship of the two, just as the use of "Dear" does not imply any particular intimacy between the one addressing and the one being addressed. See Speiser, *Genesis*, 254.

his long absence and serves as a reason for this reconciliation being so very tardy. However, he has latterly become wealthy and sends to tell "his lord"—the second time in the brief message and one not required by convention, so indicating that Jacob really does mean to undo the effects of Genesis 25:23—that he desires to find favor in Esau's sight.

In line with the conventions of Hebrew narrative we have no idea what Jacob is thinking or what he expects Esau to do, but tension leaps dramatically when his messengers return with the news that Esau is on his way, accompanied by four hundred men. Nor is there any indication of the messengers' comportment. Are they frightened? At ease? Did they even deliver the message, or did they turn tail and run at the sight of Esau's company?[42] Do they feel lucky to have escaped with their lives? Were they feted as bearers of good news? Jacob might wonder why they were allowed to return. Does their safe return mean that Esau will come in peace? Does their safe return mean only that Esau desires to lull Jacob into quiet so that Esau might attack with greater hope of success? After all, would Esau be coming with four hundred retainers if he intended peace? We cannot know what Esau intends; we can only watch what Jacob does and listen to what he says. He acts by dividing his household into two camps, thinking that one might survive if the other is attacked. His first thought is not for himself but for the safety of others. He is already acting like a man transformed, when one recalls the self-absorbed dealer of Bethel.

His second action is to pray. Again, the contrast is with the deal he cut for himself in Genesis 28. There he dealt, without any hint of religious feeling, dependence, or awe. Here he prays. Prayer is unusual in the Hebrew Bible and serves as an extremely important method of characterization, since a character can be assumed to be honest before God. So in his prayer, Jacob gives us a glimpse into his interior life.

His prayer begins with a threefold address. Not claiming YHWH as his own, Jacob reminds God of his relationship first to his grandfather Abraham and then to his father Isaac. Only then does he name YHWH and remind him (quoting 31:3) of the command given to Jacob to return to his home and family and the assurance that God would act on his behalf. In humility, he confesses his unworthiness for the steadfast love and fidelity shown him (*mikkōl haḥăsādîm ûmikkol-hāʾĕmet*). But he expresses his humility in a way that is especially appropriate for this man who has always tried to subvert the order of elder before younger. Where the NRSV reads "I am not worthy . . ." (32:10) the Hebrew reads "I am too small. . . ." This is the first time that Jacob recognizes his own status.

---

[42] Thanks to Jerome T. Walsh for this suggestion.

His prayer continues with the focus not on his own survival but on the survival of his family. Given what he has done to Esau in the past, he cannot conceive that his brother is coming in anything other than murderous rage, so he asks for protection for his family, since it is through them that the promise of numerous progeny will be fulfilled. In a sense, the entire prayer is summed up in two expressions, both of which are uncharacteristic of the Jacob we have come to know as readers: "Deliver me," he says, "for I am afraid." For the first time in his life, Jacob asks for help, asks God to be a savior for him. Also for the first time he calls himself a servant of God. So the one who loathed being the servant of Laban learns that he can nonetheless honestly take the term for himself as he stands before God and as he attempts to reconcile with his brother. These two, God and Esau, he will willingly serve.

God does not answer Jacob's prayer; at least there is no record of an answer, so Jacob begins to act on his own. He sends an enormous tribute[43] to his brother. Those leading the flocks and herds are told to say— if they encounter Esau—that the tribute precedes Jacob and that he can be found in back. This seems to be an attempt to curry favor with his long aggrieved and probably still angry brother. Jacob is attempting to make up with this gift for what he had taken from Esau so long before.

The climax to Jacob's attempt is in vs. 20. The NRSV opts for idiomatic English in translating, "For he thought, 'I may appease him with the present that goes ahead of me, and afterwards I shall see his face; perhaps he will accept me.'" However, this loses the force of the Hebrew, which more literally reads, "For he said to himself: 'Let me cover up his face with the present before my face; afterwards I shall see his face: perhaps he will lift up my face.' The present passed on before his face."[44] Friedman comments most perceptively concerning the repetition of the word "face":

> The repetition conveys the force of this juncture in Jacob's life. He must face his past. He must face his brother, whom he has wronged. And in the middle of the account of his facing his brother will come the account of his most immediate contact with God in his life, his struggle after which he will say, "I've seen God face-to-face." And the two encounters, first with his God and then with his brother, will be brought together as he says to Esau, "I've seen your face—like seeing God's face!" (33:10)

[43] The word is *minḥâ* and can mean, depending on context, "gift," "sacrifice," or "tribute." Here, given the sheer amount of what Jacob sends and given the repeated use of "lord" and "servant" language, it seems clear that Jacob is presenting himself to his brother as a faithful vassal sending tribute to his overlord.

[44] Fokkelman, *Genesis*, 206.

This is also ironic because Jacob left twenty years earlier in the wake of his deception, which worked because his weak-eyed father could not see his face![45]

He thinks, at this point, that he has done what he could by way of preparation, and he settles down with his family for the night. He does not suspect that the night in front of him does not hold peaceful rest, but the most difficult struggle of his life.

The Heel is made to limp (32:22-32).
Exposition: 32:22-23
Development: 32:24-27
Turning point: 32:28-29
Resolution: 32:30-31
Etiological frame break: 32:32

The point of the story is contained in a threefold play on the sounds of words, which is lost on the reader of a translation. Jacob (*ya'ăqōb*) the man, who even in the womb contended with others, now must wrestle (*yē'ābēq*) someone—God or man, river demon or dream, the Jacob part of himself or his brother—on the banks of the Jabbok (*yabbōq*), and so attempt to undo the life he has lived until now. In other words, Jacob's life has been defined by adversarial relationships, first with his brother and then with Laban. Somehow this encounter with a final adversary—who I will argue must be God—at last roots out of Jacob's being the need for conflict. At least that is its intent; whether or not it is successful has yet to be seen. As a result of this experience he will no longer be Jacob, the Con Artist, but Israel, the one who has fought with all comers and emerged, not unscathed, but stronger because of his weakness.

In his book *The Epic of the Patriarch: The Jacob Cycle and the Narrative Traditions of Canaan and Israel*, Ronald S. Hendel quotes the French philosopher Alain:

> The object that belongs to the hero and shapes the hero is the enemy; that is to say, the equal, the much-praised equal, the rival, a rival whom he judges worthy of himself. Therefore there can be no complete hero without a solemn war, without some provocation, without the long anticipation of another hero, subject of fame and legend.[46]

---

[45] Friedman, *Torah*, 111.
[46] Harvard Semitic Monographs 42 (Atlanta: Scholars Press, 1987) 101–2, quoting Alain, *The Gods*, trans. R. Pevear (New York: New Directions, 1974 [1934]) 113.

One is defined by one's adversary, so Jacob, the greatest of Israel's heroes, the one who gives his name to the entire nation, must have a most formidable adversary. Jacob has always found in The Other—whoever it might be—an adversary. Since in religious terms The Other is ultimately God, Jacob must eventually enter into conflict with God. This he does here.

The beginning of the story is a bit difficult to understand. Why, we wonder, did Jacob arise and set out with his family in the middle of the night? Was he moving toward some protected spot? Was he attempting to flee? Was he looking for solitude? Unfortunately the text gives us no firm idea why he acted in such a fashion. But in bringing himself closer to his brother while sending his family farther away, it seems that Jacob has decided to go and meet Esau himself. So he is neither seeking solitude nor attempting to flee. He encounters someone who, to the eternal frustration of readers, is described only as "a man" (*îš*). This throws us back on what we have learned thus far about characterization in the Hebrew Bible. We know characters by what they say and do. As far as Jacob can tell, the one with whom he wrestles throughout the night is a man, so that is what he is called here. After a night of inconclusive struggle, the mysterious man touches[47] Jacob on the hip and dislocates it. Nonetheless, Jacob does not let go and when the man pleads to be allowed to go before daybreak, Jacob refuses unless he receives a blessing first. Who is this that needs to leave before dawn but can still be the source of blessing? Some commentators suggest that the night adversary is a river demon of some sort. Whatever the origin of the tale, it seems obvious that Jacob, who has already met YHWH once at Bethel, could tell the difference between the God of his ancestors and a local river demon. The sages of the Midrash suggest that it was the spirit of Esau. This was a wise insight, that Jacob had to come to terms with his brother before he could be reconciled with him. As ever, Robert Alter has wisdom to offer.

> [H]e is the embodiment of portentous antagonism in Jacob's dark night of the soul. He is obviously in some sense a doubling of Esau as adversary, but he is also a doubling of all with whom Jacob has had to contend, and he may equally well be an externalization of all that Jacob has to wrestle with within himself. A powerful physical metaphor is intimated

---

[47] The NRSV, in line with other modern translations uses "struck" here. Alter rightly points out that the verb in question (*ngʿ*) in the Qal conjugation means "to touch" (Alter, *Genesis*, 181). Jacob is maimed not by a mighty blow—after all the night has passed without mighty blows having any real effect on either side—but by a touch of the divine.

by the story of wrestling: Jacob, whose name can be construed as "he who acts crookedly," is bent, permanently lamed, by his nameless adversary in order to be made straight before his reunion with Esau.[48]

As perceptive as this comment is, we will delay yet awhile before identifying the man. We must know all that he says and does, and what Jacob says of him, before we can firmly identify him. The stranger needs to know how Jacob thinks of himself, what name he bears, for the name evokes the person's nature. Jacob must confess who he is, and the nameless man changes Jacob's name. The sneak, con artist, trickster he has always been cannot receive a blessing, so he is given a new name, Israel. Sadly, there is no agreement about the name's meaning. An explanation is given along with the name: "you have striven with God and with humans" (32:28). It seems to mean that Jacob has taken on anyone who desired to contend with him and has survived. Other commentators suggest other possibilities. Speiser: "May El persevere"; Fox: "God-Fighter"; Friedman: "He struggles with God"; Fokkelman: "God fights with you, because he is forced to by your stubbornness and pride. And also: henceforth God will fight for you, for he appreciates your absolutely sincere and undivided commitment."[49] Details of etymology aside, the change in name indicates a change in person, but only partly so in Jacob's case. Jacob is not consistently called Israel after this event, in contrast to Abram/Abraham, for instance. This might mean that Jacob, however transformed, never entirely leaves his old self behind. He really never entirely reconciles with Esau. His relationships with his sons are contentious. Jacob is, throughout the rest of his long life, both "before" and "after," and the lack of consistency in the use of his name indicates that.

But Jacob is not satisfied with this change in name. He also wants to know the name of his adversary. The commentaries speculate a great deal on why Jacob seeks this information, but it seems clear enough. Like Moses (Exodus 3) he desires to know with which divine being he has been contending so that he may adopt him as his own personal deity; he needs to know if this God is the same as the God of his forebears. The blessing he receives, given in place of the name, which is never revealed, somehow leads Jacob to conclude that this was indeed the God of his forebears, so he names the place "Face of God" and goes his way limping. He has acquired a new name, a new limp, and a new way of being in the world.

---

[48] Alter, *Genesis*, 181.
[49] Speiser, *Genesis*, 255; Fox, *Moses*, 155; Friedman, *Torah*, 113; Fokkelman, *Genesis*, 217.

Israel will always strive with God, proudly and obstinately as His high-handed first-born, and God will admit defeat and recognize and accept Israel. God will continue fighting for Israel and be the only one to bring about deeds of deliverance for them.[50]

The earliest comment on this story is found in the book of the prophet Hosea, who wrote:

> In the womb he tried to supplant his brother, and in his manhood he strove with God. He strove with the angel and prevailed, he wept and sought his favor; he met him at Bethel, and there he spoke with him. (Hos 12:3-4 [MT 12:4-5])

The easiest way to read this interpretation is, in accord with the canons of Hebrew poetry, to understand the two lines in parallel; so "God" in v. 3 is paralleled by "angels" in v. 4. In other words, the angel with whom Jacob wrestled on the banks of the river was a physical manifestation of God, as was the case in Hagar's experience in Genesis 16. Early commentators were not entirely comfortable with this, however, and had Jacob fighting against some being other than God. The early Christian biblical commentator Origen is a good example.

> Now we understand the passage in this way, that to wrestle *with* Jacob does not mean to wrestle *against* Jacob, but that the angel, who was present in order to save him, and who after learning of the progress he had made gave him the additional name of Israel, **wrestled together with him**, that is, was on his side in the contest and helped him in the struggle. For undoubtedly it was some other against whom Jacob was fighting and against whom his struggle was being waged.[51]

It is understandable that early post-biblical commentators were trying to preserve the transcendence and immutability of God, but it is easier to take the story on its own terms. Jacob said that he saw God, and the name he receives indicates that he fought with God. God certainly does not need us to protect his being, so I will take the story as it stands. Jacob saw God, fought with him, and survived as a (mostly) transformed person. In Israel, then, all can find a home because the task that Jacob undertook is common to all humanity.

---

[50] Fokkelman, *Genesis*, 221–2.

[51] Origen, *On First Principles*, 3.2.5, in James L. Kugel, *Traditions of the Bible* (Cambridge, Mass.: Harvard University Press, 1998) 387.

Or maybe not. I am not aware that anyone has proposed this view, but let me try it here because it may give us better perspective on the character of Jacob in the subsequent chapters and on the character of God in this chapter. All commentaries, including this one, wax rhapsodic—using the cliche is the only way to get the flavor of commentary about this passage—about the transformation that Jacob undergoes before and during his wrestling bout with God. But the Jacob who remains a character in the following chapters does not seem notably transformed; he is still contentious, still very much the one who favors one over the other, who loves unequally and suffers—and causes to suffer—as a result. Maybe the point of the story of Jacob's wrestling is precisely that Jacob was not transformed, that he was a lame human being. He survived, to be sure, as he had survived so many adversities. And he is better than he was, also to be sure. But he never fully became Israel and always remained Jacob. And as Jacob, he was lame.

God then, in this test of Jacob, which parallels the test of Abraham in Genesis 22, needed to teach something to Jacob and to learn something about Jacob, just as previously he had taught something to Abraham—about obedience—and learned something from him—about the cost of obedience. God needed to learn whether Jacob knew how lame he was, but Jacob did not. Jacob still thought that he was in charge, that he was in a position to make demands. So God made him visibly lame so that Jacob could never ignore that reality again. And God blessed him, because God—as hard as it may be for onlookers, wives, and children to understand—had chosen him for love. Read in this way, Jacob/Israel is more readily a model for us, his descendants in the biblical tradition, visibly lame as he was, only partially transformed (at best) as he was, but still blessed because chosen out of love—as he was. God remains a savior in this story but cannot make someone into a person he does not want to be.

This tale also brings to a close this section of the story of the third generation of the chosen family. Jacob is no longer alone and is no longer nowhere. In fact, he is no longer Jacob. This utterly (or more accurately, nearly or partly) transformed man can now undertake the next stage in his life and meet his brother.

B'. 33:1–35:29: Jacob Returns Home, Encounters Esau,
and Lives with Wives and Families in Canaan

Genesis 35 ends (at verse 29) with the death of Isaac and is followed in Genesis 36 by a lengthy genealogy of Esau. At that point, although Jacob is still alive and will remain so for many more years, the focus shifts from the third generation of the chosen family to the fourth. So Genesis 33:1 serves as the beginning of the next bloc of narrative and 35:29 serves as its end. Within those outer borders there is little cohesion. In Genesis 33 we find the tale of Jacob and Esau's at best very hesitant and tentative reconciliation; perhaps it would be better to term it simply a meeting. Genesis 34 tells the horrific tale of the rape of Jacob's daughter Dinah and the revenge her brothers and half-brothers exact. While these two chapters present more or less integral wholes, the case is different for Genesis 35. It consists of a series of odds and ends, as though our author were somehow anxious to tie up stories that had been left unfinished but does so without any real resolution. One is left at the end of Genesis 35 with the feeling that Jacob's life, because of the way in which he has lived it and the effects his choices have made upon other members of his family, will not achieve any resolution. The family that appeared so terribly dysfunctional even at his conception remains so—and indeed will become more so in the fourth generation.

A meeting, if not precisely a reconciliation (33:1-17).
Exposition: 33:1a
Development: 33:1b-3
Turning point: 33:4
Resolution: 33:5-15
Conclusion: 33:16-17

There is an odd emotional texture to this story that recounts the first meeting of the estranged brothers, who have not seen each other for some twenty years. Although told from Jacob's point of view (marked by the *hinnēh* in v. 1a, which, as is so often the case, allows us readers to share what the character is seeing), it remains oddly detached. As we will see, Esau cries, but Jacob does not. Esau desires further contact, but Jacob does not. Jacob gives a gift, but Esau does not. Jacob is effusive in his gestures of self-deprecation, but Esau does not gainsay him. Esau calls Jacob "my brother," whereas Jacob calls Esau "my lord." Esau does not correct him.

The story begins when, all of a sudden, hardly recovered from his nightlong ordeal, Jacob sees Esau appear with the aforementioned four hundred retainers. Since the scene has become so crowded all of sudden, Jacob must take some action, so he divides his family in order of importance—emotional importance—to him. The maids and their children go first and are followed by Leah and her children, who in turn are followed by Rachel and Joseph. Jacob takes the position of greatest danger himself, preceding the entire party. He approaches Esau with the utmost deference and courtesy, bowing to the ground seven times as contemporary court ritual prescribed. And rightly so, for in the interim Esau has become a prince, and a nation carries his name. Throughout this brief scene, tension rises as one wonders how Esau will act. Are the retainers simply an indication of his status, the retinue of an important lord, or are they an offensive force? After all, when Jacob's grandfather—and surely both of his grandsons knew the story—went out against the four kings to rescue Lot he was able to muster only 318 men.

Esau is shown to be as changed and unchanged as his brother for, and this is the turning point of the tale which points it in a particular direction, he rushes forward to embrace him. In Genesis 25:34 five verbs follow in quick succession and characterize him as impulsive. Here, in Genesis 33:4 five (or six, as we shall see) verbs ("ran . . . , embraced . . . , fell on . . . , kissed . . . , wept") serve the same purpose. The text is frustratingly ambiguous about who wept. The standard Hebrew text (MT) has both weeping, but some suggest that the suffix on the verb "wept" that shows that both wept is a scribal error, a duplication of the first letter of the next word, and that Esau alone wept.[52] This reading is to be preferred because it fits better with the emotional tone of the entire chapter. Jacob is, and remains, detached and wants to be on his way as soon as possible. This also fits well with the view suggested in the preceding chapter that Jacob is not really entirely transformed. He had always treated his brother with ill-disguised contempt and continues to hold him at arm's length—even while embracing him—here. Esau remains impulsive and is still the same character, trying somehow to win the affection of a family that does not want to know him.

But the meaning of the kiss goes beyond mere high spirits on Esau's part. It calls to mind the kiss (27:27) that stole the blessing that was his by birth, and the addition of the detail that Esau fell upon Jacob's neck recalls that twenty years earlier Jacob had covered that same neck with goatskins to deceive his father. Kissing and necks are by no means chance details in this tale.

Tension can now begin to be resolved with the turning point past. Esau does not intend to slaughter his brother, but seems to have come

---

[52] The last words of 33:4 and the first words of 33:5 read . . . *wayyiššāqēhû wayyibkû wayyiśśāʾ ʾet-ʿēnāyw wayyarʾ*. . . . The underlined letters are the same in Hebrew. This is a common scribal error called dittography, the accidental writing of the same letter twice. See Alter, *Genesis*, 185 and Speiser, *Genesis*, 259.

in open welcome. Having been asked by Esau to identify those with him, Jacob introduces his family. The readers should notice that in their conversational exchange Esau calls Jacob "my brother" but that Jacob does not reciprocate. Rather, he calls Esau "my lord" and refers to himself as Esau's servant. Nor does Esau correct him. Perhaps it feels good, and seems just, for Esau to hear Jacob humble himself in Esau's presence.

Having met his family—none of Esau's seems to have accompanied him, perhaps raising Jacob's suspicions a bit—Esau asks what Jacob meant by "the camp" that he had met on the way. Jacob explains that this was a gift. Esau demurs, at least once, but when pressed accepts it without offering a gift of his own. In his demurral he tells Jacob, pointedly, that he has "much" or "enough," but clearly it is not all that he might once have had. Jacob replies that to have seen Esau is like having seen the face of God. This, of course, is just what Jacob has done the previous night. If he can wrestle with God all night without having been bested, he can certainly wriggle out of an extended meeting with Esau. Esau can only have heard the end of his reply with incredulity, however. In response to Esau's assertion that he has much, Jacob says that Esau should take the offered gift—literally "blessing"—because Jacob has "all." However much Esau may have, including the "blessing" that Jacob offers him, he will never have "all" because Jacob has taken that which Esau most desired, the blessing of their father. One can, as a reader, almost hear Esau's intake of breath, so astounded must he have been at Jacob's sheer nerve.

After this exchange the brothers part. Jacob sets aside Esau's offer of accompaniment; he wants to get away from Esau as quickly as possible. Also, he says he will come to Esau later but actually heads in the opposite direction. This long anticipated meeting was extremely brief; there was no meal, no lengthy exchange of courtesies. Indeed, the whole could have encompassed only a few minutes. The brothers part to meet again only at their father's burial. As a character God is absent from this story; that detail alone might indicate to us that what transpired here he did not approve. It was a meeting, but it was certainly not a reconciliation.

There follows a brief notice that serves as a bridge to the story of the rape of Dinah. Having pastured his cattle at Succoth, Jacob "came in peace" (33:18, AT; NRSV, "came safely") to Shechem where he bought some property. He departed (28:10), and now he has returned (33:18). Like his grandfather Abraham, Jacob too was now starting to possess the land promised to him. But like his uncle Lot he was rather too near a city for safety, and his bargain with God (28:21) entailed returning safely. This bridges us to the next tale, the rape of Dinah.

The rape of Dinah and its aftermath (34:1-31).
Exposition: 34:1
Inciting moment: 34:2
Development: 34:3-12
Turning point: 34:13-17
Resolution: 34:18-29
Conclusion: 34:30-31

In each generation of this family thus far there is a nightmare for a woman. In the first generation, Abraham gave away his wife not once, but twice, in order to obtain safety for himself (Genesis 14, 20); Isaac gave his wife away once (Genesis 26). In these cases (as well as in the tales of Hagar in Genesis 16 and 21) we saw a repeated motif that we have called the Outsider. God desires that woman be outside of relationships and structures that shut her in, and he will free a woman who finds herself in such a situation. Jacob, unlike his father and grandfather, never gives one of his wives away in order to win an advantage for himself, but Leah's years of being hated must have been a nightmare for her. There is a nightmare story of which a woman is the subject in this generation as well.

Jacob's daughter Dinah was first mentioned in 30:21 as the daughter of Leah. She seems to disappear as soon as she is born; Leah names her, although the meaning of the name is not given, in contrast to the sons born to Jacob, and then she disappears. No further notice is taken of her until Genesis 34:1, when she seems to be reintroduced to the reader who might well have forgotten that she had been born.

Her nightmare begins with a seemingly innocuous sentence: "Now Dinah the daughter of Leah, whom she had borne to Jacob, went out to visit the women of the region" (Gen 34:1). Why did she go out? It might seem a simple enough thing for a young woman to do, to meet local women with whom she might form friendships since she lives in such a male household. But ancient commentators were nonetheless curious, and two reasons emerged in their interpretations. One line of reasoning held that she wanted to go to a local festival, either for its own sake or to see what local fashions were like.[53] Other interpreters, however, were

---

[53] "And Dinah, still a virgin, came into Shechem when there was a festival, since she wished to see the city" (Theodotus, Fragment 4, cited from Alexander Polyhistor in Eusebius, *Praeparatio Evangelica* 9.22.4-6); also, "Since the people of Shechem were holding a festival, Dinah, Jacob's only daughter, went into the city to see the adornments of the women of the place" (Josephus, *Jewish Antiquities* 1:337)—both quoted in Kugel, *Traditions*, 415. One interested in this chapter and its early interpretations should read his entire chapter on Dinah, pp. 404–35.

less charitable to a person who must have lived in most lonely circumstances. They saw her "going out" as a sign of immodest behavior—in which Dinah was merely following the example of her mother, who is also said to have "gone out" (Gen 30:16). In the latter instance, Leah clearly went out for purposes of cohabitation; so, these exegetes reasoned, perhaps Dinah's "going out" was similarly motivated.[54]

However, these early sources are not univocal in placing the blame on Dinah. Even *Midrash Rabbah* presents a more complex picture than might at first appear. In *Midrash Rabbah* 80:4.1-3 the blame for this catastrophe is assigned unambiguously to Jacob, who failed to care for Dinah and provide for her future in a way that a father of that time and place ought to have done, and whose pride caused him to be unaware of Dinah and her needs.[55] But these speculations are expected in readers who are all intrigued by Dinah's motivation. Why, after all, did Dinah "go out" and who is responsible for what happened to her?

This exposition, which after all merely provides the setting in which the remainder of the story is played out, is yet more complex and invites more reflection. Dinah is presented as Jacob's daughter, more precisely the daughter Leah bore to Jacob. Since this is information we already possess, why should it be repeated here? Over and over, we have seen in these stories how the characters are heavily weighed down with terms denoting family affiliation. In the stories of the Given-Away Wives, readers are reminded time and again that the women are already married to men who dispose of them when they so desire. The early stories of Jacob and Esau, the selling of the birthright and the deceitful theft of the blessing, are also fraught with such words, which indicated the degree of dysfunction that particular family suffers from. In this story, violence is done to Dinah because she is trapped from the beginning, trapped inside a web of relationships with a family that nonetheless fails to care for her, trapped by Shechem, trapped inside the city as her family tries to extricate her. And all of this, including her desire to see other women in her new neighborhood, flows from the fact that she is the unnoticed daughter of the unfavored wife. Lack of love traps her over and over, and it is her brothers, not her father, who will act to free her despite the long-term consequences for themselves.

If she is marked as already trapped, what is it that she wanted to do? The NRSV, in a way that is typical of contemporary translations, says that she "went out to visit the women of the region" (34:1). A more literal

---

[54] See *Genesis Rabba* 80:1, *Midrash Tanḥuma, Vayyišlaḥ* 7, and similar works mentioned in Kugel, *Traditions*, 415.

[55] Neusner, *Creation*, 285–6.

reading would be that "Dinah went out to see the daughters of the land" (AT). This more literal reading reinforces our awareness of two words that will be most important in the development of story, "to see" and "daughter." We have already seen how "daughter" shows Dinah to be enclosed within complicated family relationships. It also makes us aware of other family relationship language, of Shechem's sonship to Hamor his father, and of the way Dinah's brothers relate to her and to their father. This same phrase makes us aware, right at the beginning of the story, that Dinah is in a very real sense exposed and vulnerable as she goes out to see the daughters of the land. They belong here; she does not. They can expect a certain amount of respect because they are part of the local community; she is a stranger without any obvious resources.

Dinah goes out "to see," and she is seen by Shechem in return. In this way, what is seen and not seen enters the story as important. Perhaps more than any other exposition in the book, this one verse is pregnant with meaning and causes real foreboding in us readers.

Dinah went out to see the local women. There is absolutely no hint in the text that she went out to see the men of the region. But in v. 2 the brutal action commences as she is seen by Shechem. Three verbs show the rapidity of Shechem's behavior and its violence, but in a way that is not well captured by the NRSV's translation: "[Shechem] saw her, he seized her and lay with her by force." (34:2) Better would be—after marking Shechem as the son of the local ruler and therefore a man of power, whereas Dinah is a vulnerable newcomer: ". . . saw her, he took her, lay [with] her and humiliated [or: degraded, or debased] her" (AT).[56]

What follows this act of violence? Quite literally (if not idiomatically): "And his very self clung to Dinah, daughter of Jacob, and he loved the young woman and spoke to the heart of the young woman" (34:3, AT). This is quite a development indeed.[57] Shechem apparently tries to persuade the young woman—this is the meaning of the phrase "spoke to the heart of"—to marry him since he has experienced such a powerful emotional response to her. She, once again, is marked as Jacob's daughter, and it is that relationship that will move the story to

---

[56] Ordinarily the verb translated here as "lay" would be followed by a preposition meaning "with." That preposition is absent here, so "her" follows the verb immediately. The result is a sort of coarse and vulgar Hebrew used for instances of improper or brutal sexual encounter. This coarseness is, of course, further heightened by the use of the verb "to humiliate, degrade, debase." To call this something other than rape, as some commentaries do, seems incomprehensible to me.

[57] And pointedly the opposite of the emotion Amnon experiences when he rapes his half-sister Tamar in 2 Samuel 13, where the emotions he experienced in her regard prior to his act of violence are immediately transformed into loathing.

its grisly conclusion. Without any indication of a response—Dinah is voiceless throughout—Shechem approaches his father and asks that he acquire the girl for him as a wife (literally, "as a woman" since the same word is used for both in Hebrew).

Jacob, having heard what has happened to his daughter, waits until his sons return from seeing to the family's livestock. Hamor, Shechem's father, visits Jacob, but what the text notices is not Jacob's response—there is none—but the angry response of his sons. There is no record of any emotional reaction on Jacob's part to this act of violence either in v. 5 or in v. 7. He seems strangely flat, especially considering the life-changing transformation that he supposedly underwent in the previous chapter. It is the sons who react with anger at what they call a *něbālâ*, an act of disgraceful folly that takes no regard of moral norms or proper behavior. That it is committed "in Israel" means at this point, of course, that it was an unbearable offense committed against Jacob and his family.

Hamor's speech ignores an important fact, one that the reader too might have lost track of; Dinah is still inside the city, trapped there with Shechem. While the Shechemites offer unrestricted grazing rights, the possibility of buying property, and the right to intermarry with the local populace, they offer no apology for the outrage done against Dinah (and her family). Hamor seems to say that they can either take the proffered deal and be quiet and have their daughter legitimately marry Shechem or not, in which case she will remain inside the city without any legitimizing of her status. At any rate, Shechem still possesses her, and implicitly at least, intends to continue to possess her; no offer is made to give her back. Hamor's offer to Jacob and his sons also hints at their unprotected alien status. They need grazing rights and they need to buy property. Since we already know the attitude of the family toward exogamy, we can guess that part, at least, of Hamor's offer will go down poorly. At the same time, but still without apology, Shechem pleads to be allowed to marry Dinah. Is this merely a crass offer to buy silence? Or is it an attempt, perhaps the best to be expected, of a haughty local ruler to make recompense to a stranger? In other words, is this as close as Hamor can get to apology, or is he condescendingly dismissive of Jacob and his family?

The sons of Jacob show themselves to have learned carefully from their father, because they set out to deceive their opponent. Once again, one is tempted to imagine the scene; awash in apparent courtesy, Jacob's sons reply that money is no concern of theirs, but it would be disgraceful to offer their sister to one who is uncircumcised. Shechem will have to pay by inflicting on himself and all the men of his town pain in their offending organ. But since circumcision is also connected with cleanliness, they are implicitly accusing Hamor, Shechem, and all the community of being too unclean for Jacob's family to mingle with. Underneath the apparent politeness is really breathtaking rudeness. They are unconcerned about the money, what really galls them is the locals' uncleanness. Either they can clean themselves up, or Jacob's sons will take their sister and depart.

So we have reached the turning point of this tale. An offer was made and rejected. A counteroffer was then laid on the table, and which way the story continues will depend on Hamor and Shechem's reaction. They take the proffered—and unbeknownst to them deceitful—deal and head back to town to try to sell it to their fellow townsmen. Shechem, the duped rapist, is the most honored man in his family, because he is immediately and unhesitatingly circumcised, an example of damning with faint praise if there ever was one! His inability to control his sexuality wins him praise and honor.

Omitting any reference to the original offense, or to his offer of property rights, Hamor sells the deal to the locals by presenting it as a way to get their hands on the property, and women, of Jacob's family. They agree, and all the men are circumcised. On the third day, when the men would be most uncomfortable, Simeon and Levi (Dinah's full brothers) lead a raid and kill Hamor, Shechem, and all the other men of the city. They depart at that point, having been motivated more by revenge than by greed. The other brothers descend and take all the wealth and all the survivors of the town as plunder.

It is only at this point, in the conclusion to the story, that Jacob finds speech. He upbraids his sons Simeon and Levi for having made him vulnerable in the face of the regional hostility they will now inevitably face. His sons disdain to answer his objection but respond with what seems to be real contempt: "Should our sister be treated like a whore?" (Gen 34:31).

And what of Dinah? She who has never had a voice lacks one still. She made a timid attempt—although doubtless the best she could—to go outside of her family, for no purpose other than to see other women. Immediately she was trapped inside another man's house and although freed by her brothers is once more, still voiceless, returned to the family. One is hard put to know what sort of character she is. She is certainly not full or rounded—we know little of her, and she has no chance to develop as a character. Is she a type? Not the Given-Away Wife, like Sarah and Rebekah, but the Discardable Daughter—at least discardable by her father.[58] Perhaps she is the opposite of the agent, the one

---

[58] Dinah is by no means the only "discarded daughter" in the biblical text. See, for instance, Lot's daughters (Gen 19:8), Jephthah's daughter (Judges 11), the daughter

who carries out some action necessary for the advancement of the plot. Since she is allowed to do nothing on her own, not even see, we will call her the Acted Upon and mourn her.

God is conspicuously absent here, as he was during Sarah's machinations in Genesis 16. Just as God was conspicuously present in the chapters surrounding that one, Genesis 15 and 17, so God is very present in Genesis 33 and 35. What does God's absence mean here? Perhaps that Jacob is still just Jacob and not yet Israel. Perhaps that love gone wrong will always have terrible effects, as it has in the lives of Jacob, Leah, and now Dinah. Perhaps that humans are still free to know what paradise is, and then to sully it in such a way that no one can live there. Perhaps just this: that we are as free to destroy as God is free to choose.

A Vow Finally Kept, Endings and Passing to the Next Generation (35:1-29). The casting away of Hagar and her vision of the God Who Sees Her (Genesis 16) is bracketed by Abraham's two covenants, the Covenant between the Pieces (Genesis 15)—a terrifying incident that takes place at night—and the Covenant of Circumcision (Genesis 17)—which incorporates a name change. I am struck that the Rape of Dinah is placed between Jacob's terrifying night experience in Genesis 32 and his revisiting Bethel in Genesis 35—in both of which Jacob receives a new name. There are some interesting parallels between the experiences of Abraham and Jacob: encountering God at night in the guise of some symbol, whether a burning firepot or a wrestling assailant, that never appears again in the context of their stories, and the giving of a new name, which—at least as I have argued above—does not signal the transformation of the person. After Abram's name is changed to Abraham he continues to doubt that God's promises to him will be fulfilled, and his obedience still needs to be tested, just as after Jacob's name is changed he still doubts Esau's intentions, and the fulfillment of his vow at Bethel comes about only after he is told to do so by God. And, as I have noted above, God's silence to Abram and Sarai in Genesis 16 is similar to God's silence in Genesis 34. God will not be involved in the evil that people choose to do.

One reaches this point of the book, which has focused for such a lengthy period on the third generation of the chosen family, wondering whether any advance has been made. Are these people, despite their decades-long relationship of intense intimacy with YHWH, any closer to being a blessing? Has God succeeded in forming them for blessing any more than he was able to instill in Adam and Eve a love

---

of the Levite's host (Judg 19:24), and David's refusal to punish his daughter Tamar's rapist (2 Sam 13:21).

for Paradise and a desire to remain there? Has the story of the entire relationship between God and Humanity been one more redolent of failure than success? The Flood failed to eradicate the human tendency toward violence. Abraham finally obeyed utterly but never spoke to God thereafter. Isaac and Rebekah's family was torn with strife. Jacob's family is distrustful of each other and dismissive of its patriarchal figure. But still God endures. I think that the story is less one about human transformation than it is about divine perseverance. God is savior. God is always savior. So God will attempt, once again, to save a relationship with the one who fights with him.

This chapter consists of several brief notices, all of which have some obvious narrative content and help us to get a clearer picture of the state of this family as the time of the third generation comes to an end. However, none of these brief notices, albeit useful for characterization, are really stories as such. The result is that the chapter feels like a conglomeration of odds and ends, pieces of narrative that are included in order to finish off earlier stories but that are not really self-contained or are repetitive of earlier material.

If the chapter reads like something of a jumble, it does have a clear enough structure based on journeying. However, even the journeys leave the reader feeling as though things are a bit aimless at this point in Jacob's life. He goes from here to there without having a clear goal or coming to a place where he can finally live.

In 35:1-15 Jacob and his household journey from Shechem to Bethel, there to fulfill the as yet unfulfilled vow made in Genesis 28. In the midst of this scene there is a frame break (35:8), an intrusion on the part of the narrator, which announces the death of Rebekah's nurse to the reader.

In 35:16 another journey ensues, but it does not reach its goal before Rachel gives birth to Jacob's twelfth son, the one she names Ben Oni and Jacob renames Benjamin. The birth was difficult, and Rachel dies. Another frame break (35:20b) relates her memory to a monument still extant in the reader's day.

Once again they travel and dwell near the tower of Eder, where Reuben sleeps with Bilhah (35:21-22a). This is followed by yet another frame break that helps the reader to place Reuben in the list of Jacob's sons.

Finally, they travel to Kiriath Arba, or Hebron, where Isaac dies and is buried by Jacob and Esau. It is at Hebron that we leave this moment of the family's evolution, since Genesis 36 is given over to a lengthy genealogical entry about Esau and his descendants in Edom.

From Paddan-aram to Bethel (35:1-15). Without any preparation, any exposition or setting of a scene, God suddenly speaks to Jacob and tells him to travel to Bethel and there build an altar to the God who appeared to him as he fled from Esau's wrath. Furthermore, he is told by God to settle there. The reader will recall that Jacob made a vow to do just that and has yet to fulfill it. He requires all the members of his household to purify themselves, separating themselves from foreign gods (images of whom were sometimes made into earrings) and donning fresh clothes. They comply and Jacob makes a cache of these objects under a tree.[59] As they travel, dread of them fills all the people through whose land they pass. The NRSV describes this as a "terror from God"; however the word *ĕlōhîm*, literally "god" or "gods," can indicate a superlative. Since Jacob's sons have just wiped out an entire city it seems far more likely that people round about were simply terribly scared of them and of the violence of which they were capable than that a divine awe overwhelmed the local populace. In due course, they arrive at Luz/Bethel, and Jacob builds the altar he had been commanded to build.

After the intervening notice about the death of Deborah, Rebekah's nurse, and her burial at a place named Oak of Weeping, another version of the change of Jacob's name to "Israel" is given. This version has the change take place at Bethel and is associated with the promise of the land and with the divine name El Shaddai, God Almighty. No explanation of the new name is given, neither of its meaning nor of the reasons for the change. God leaves Jacob at this point; Jacob makes a sacred pillar, anoints it, and names the place Bethel. Just as Abraham's obedience in Genesis 22 marked the end of his active relationship with God, it may well be that Jacob's obedience in returning to Bethel marks the end of his active relationship with God.

Most historical critical commentaries assume that these brief notices are not from the same narrative source as the earlier versions of the same events that we have already read. That may well be the case, but our author must have had some reason for including them here, since we can safely assume that he was not a slavish redactor and that he selected and shaped the material he used. I would suggest that the purpose of this chapter is to bracket Genesis 34 just as Genesis 16 was bracketed. Also, it further underlines for us that Jacob was not transformed at the Jabbok, although he was lamed. He is still a lame human being—witness his inaction at Shechem and later in this chapter—but a lame human being with a new name.

---

[59] Alter aptly points out that the verb used in this instance (*tmn*) is used to refer to placing treasure in a hidden place, and is different from the verb used later in the chapter that denotes the burial of bodies (*Genesis*, 196).

From Bethel to (not quite) Ephrath (35:16-20). Jacob had been told by God to settle at Bethel, but he does not. Rather he continues to travel toward Ephrath. While they are on the journey, but still in the middle of nowhere, Rachel gives birth to another son. She names him Ben Oni, which might mean something like Son of My Vigor.[60] Jacob understands it to mean Son of My Woe, an inauspicious name, so he immediately changes it to the similar sounding Benjamin, Son of my Right Hand, i.e., Favored Son. Without any notice that he mourns for the wife for whose sake he labored twenty years and who has borne him two sons, Jacob buries her at Ephrath/Bethlehem, erects a pillar, and continues to travel on. This is surprising given the tenderness with which his earlier love for her was noted in the text. Yet even there we saw that there was never any notice of reciprocal feelings on her part. One wonders what woe she was referring to in the naming of her son, that she was dying in giving him birth? Or that the emotions of her family had been so painful throughout her life? At any rate, she dies and is buried without great ceremony, although Jacob does erect yet another pillar.

The journey beyond Eder (35:21-22). There follows a strange notice indeed. In what most commentators agree would have been an implicit grab for power within the clan, Reuben, Jacob's eldest son—lest we have forgotten the birth order, our author handily appends a list in 35:22b-26—lay with Bilhah. This seems to be a challenge to Jacob's strength and ability to continue leading the clan. Yet although Jacob hears of it, he does nothing. One wonders whether the household has split up at this point, as one can hardly imagine Reuben doing this under his father's nose or in the presence of Bilhah's sons. Jacob seems at this point merely to be wandering somewhat aimlessly, and one might well understand that his sons think that he has somehow lost his way, especially with the memory of Shechem still in their minds. Yet if Reuben made a bid for power it seems somehow to have failed because there is no hint anywhere that he led the family.

Arrival at Hebron (35:27-29). Jacob's wanderings finally end at Hebron, where he and his brother attend the death of their father, aged one hundred eighty years. What is most important in this brief notice is that Esau, the firstborn—although displaced—son is mentioned first. Esau was Isaac's favorite, and it is right that he come first here, since he was first in his father's love and the intended object of his blessing.

---

[60] Alter, *Genesis*, 199.

A Note on Genesis 36:1-43
ESAU AND HIS STRENGTHS

Just as Ishmael's genealogy appears in Genesis 25, so too Esau's appears here. In both cases the intention seems to be to sum up the life and inheritance of the non-chosen son before moving on to an extended treatment of what happened to the favored son. These genealogies also mark the end of long narrative units, and, as is obvious from Genesis 37, the story now shifts from the third generation of the chosen family to the fourth.

Yet this list has another effect on the reader. It causes us to wonder whether the prediction in Genesis 25:23 has in fact come true, for the elder is not serving the younger. In fact, were one to say at this point in the narrative which of the two brothers is more successful, more "blessed," one might well say that it is Esau. He is surrounded by a large and prosperous family, so large, in fact, that it has become a prosperous nation. It seems not to know the terrible divisions and emotional stresses of Jacob's family. Jacob is still, despite God's instructions to settle at Bethel, wandering without a home, whereas Esau is settled.

A reader who is interested in the details of Esau's genealogy, insofar as anything can be said about who these people were and how they were related to Israel, should consult one of the many fine historical critical commentaries or biblical encyclopedias. Our intention here is simply to see how this list of names and brief narrative asides helps us to understand better the characters of Jacob and Esau.

Jacob is a lame man who contends with anyone, even God. While he prevails, he does so at a cost. All around him are formed by him and have become like him. Just as his birth family was torn by emotional divisions, so is his own. Just as he tried to supplant the natural order of the family of his birth, so too his son has tried to supplant him in the

261

family's natural order. Neither Jacob nor his family seems to be a blessing or to have any ability to communicate blessing.

Contrast that with Esau and his family, the unblessed one who has become a nation. Of the two sons he is the more attractive, the one to whom we as readers are more drawn. All of this serves as a reminder that Jacob and his family were chosen to be the source of blessing in the world, not for any immediately apparent emotional attractiveness on their part or suitability for the task but because they were childless. They stood in need of what later theological traditions might well have called grace and what their own world may have called God's steadfast love and faithfulness. On their own they could not accomplish what they needed in order to survive in the world. They needed a gift from God. In that sense Jacob, still wandering, still lame, is an apt choice to carry the promise because he needs the grace it conveys. To anticipate the Christian New Testament, one can say of Jacob that his strength lies in his weakness. Were he strong, like Esau perhaps, he would have been less in need of God.

Chapter 8

IN THE TIME OF THE FOURTH GENERATION

Genesis 37–50

How Is the Story Structured?

As we approach the final large section of the book of Genesis, those chapters that focus on the fourth generation of the chosen family, we must once again choose somewhere to stand from which we may profitably view the whole. As part of that process, the name we assign to this section remains important, as it has been throughout the book. In every commentary of which I am aware this section is given a title which focuses on Joseph, e.g., the Joseph Story, the Joseph Novella, or the like. Nor could one deny that, like Abraham, Isaac and Jacob in turn, Joseph plays a powerful role in this final section of the book. However, and for the same reasons spelled out so frequently already in the preceding sections of the commentary, I would like to argue that this section not be named after him because in so doing we are tempted to see him and no one else; we are then tempted to ignore Genesis 38, for instance.

In the Excursus on the Outsider motif found elsewhere in this commentary, I cite the great commentators E. A. Speiser and Rashi on this particular subject. The former asserts that Genesis 38 is a "completely independent unit. It has no connection with the drama of the Joseph story which it interrupts at the conclusion of Act I"[1]—in other words, it is just a filler that provides some information about the origin of two

---

[1] E. A. Speiser, *Genesis*, AB 1 (New York: Doubleday, 1962) 299.

Judahite clans, which has been rather clumsily inserted in its current location because there was no better place for it. And Rashi, as I say in that Excursus, teaches that the Joseph story is interrupted at this point in order for Judah's character development to be given narrative space.

Robert Alter showed that Genesis 38 is tightly woven into the whole of Genesis 37–50,[2] that there is a tight web of connection involving theme, motif, and language between Genesis 38 and its frame that shows the development of Judah.

Genesis 37, then, appears at the beginning of this section and shows the development of Joseph, and the subsequent chapter, tightly connected to the whole, shows the development of Judah. The final chapters of the book, Genesis 48–50, are a foretelling of the fate of all the various tribes who descend from Jacob, yet, rather like Genesis 38, they are often eliminated in structural analyses of this final section.[3] The result can seem to a reader as though, in order to keep the focus firmly on Joseph—this is after all "The Joseph Story"—others are eliminated. One prominent example will show how this works.

George Coats describes the overall structure of what he calls the Joseph Story.

I.   Exposition: introduction of principals (37:1-4)

II. Complication: Joseph's power is challenged, the family is broken (37:5-36)

III. Digression: Joseph rises to new power (39:1–41:57)

IV. Complication: Joseph challenges the power of his brothers (42:1-38)

V.   Denouement: by Joseph's power, reconciliation of the family (43:1–45:28)

VI. Conclusion: from Canaan to Egypt (46:1–47:27)[4]

Of course, this is fine as far as it goes; however, Coats not only leaves out important parts of the final section—otherwise shown to be tightly connected to the whole—but he must also admit that his scheme also lacks a certain tight integrity. Consider what he has to say about Genesis 39–41.

---

[2] Robert Alter, *The Art of Biblical Narrative* (New York: Basic Books, 1981) 3–12.

[3] See, for instance, George W. Coats, *Genesis: With an Introduction to Narrative Literature*, FOTL 1 (Grand Rapids, Mich.: Eerdmans, 1983) 263–4.

[4] Ibid. In this earlier work, Coats referred to the whole as a novella (Ibid., 265), but later, in the *ABD*, although he uses the same description of the plot structure, he refers to this part of Genesis as a saga. See *ABD*, s.v. "Joseph, son of Jacob."

In the middle of the rather tight structure for the Joseph story, Genesis 39–41 represents a discrete, perhaps originally independent story about Joseph. The story has been used by the editor of the larger narrative about Joseph. But in the present position as digression in the movement of narrative about Joseph and his brothers, this unit reveals its character as a story within a story, a story with its own independent structure, genre and intention.[5]

Two interesting, if perhaps unintentional, points emerge from this quotation. The first is that it is possible to see Genesis 37–50 as a collection of stories, rather than as an integral whole, and the second is that one can see Genesis 37–50 as about Joseph and his brothers, rather than simply about Joseph.

The most complete study of Genesis 37–50 of which I am aware is *Joseph and His Family: A Literary Study* by W. Lee Humphreys.[6] As one would expect from Humphreys, the book is full of perceptive insights into the literary nature of these chapters. However, he does adopt a position similar to Coats in his description of the section's plot structure, as the following makes clear.[7]

Exposition: 37:1-4
Complication: 37:5-36
(Interludes: 38–41)
Further complications: 42–44
Resolution: 45:1-15
Denouement: 45:16–50:21
Conclusion: 50:22-26

Coats and Humphreys agree on their understanding of Genesis 37, but from there on they diverge. In a sense both are, of course, correct, so that if one chooses to regard, say, Genesis 42–44 as Further Complications the rest of the section begins to fall into place around it, and the end result is a plot analysis that is coherent and makes good sense. My trouble, however, remains the same as it did when I considered Coats. Genesis 38 is regarded as not integral to the plot but as an interlude, as are the following chapters (39–41). It is hard for me, at any rate, to understand how four such powerful chapters, stories that offer great

---

[5] Coats, *ABD*, s.v. "Joseph, son of Jacob."
[6] Columbia, S.C.: University of South Carolina Press, 1988.
[7] Ibid., 32. Of course, I am doing an injustice to Humphrey's great work by citing from it so briefly and not engaging it in a detailed analysis. I recommend that all readers turn to his complete treatment in *Joseph*, 32–67.

insight into the development of the main characters in this part of the book, and that are tightly connected to the remainder by way of continuing themes and motifs (pairs of dreams and changes in clothing, for instance, in the case of 39–41), can be relegated to being "Interludes."

Hence, since even commentators so very committed to the integral unity of the Joseph Saga as Coats and Humphreys see that there are other ways to address this section of the book, we will, in line with the pattern established earlier, choose not to view this final section of the book as about Joseph but as about the fourth generation of the chosen family. Genesis 37–50 tells us readers what happened in the time of the fourth generation, so we will apply that name to the whole. If Joseph appears in a prominent position in his generation, this was also the case with Abraham, Isaac, and Jacob. One might also argue that the greater coherence of Genesis 37–50 indicates something about its origin, that it emerged as a unit from an author's mind. Coats shows that it is not so unified, but there is more to be said on this score. In the series of stories told about each succeeding generation throughout the book, there has been greater coherence. Stories about Abraham and the first generation were mostly brief episodes, while those about Isaac were longer and more unified. This tendency was even more marked in the stories about the third generation, such that some sections stretch over chapters—Genesis 29–31 for instance—and are readily understood as long narrative blocs. This tendency, which has been developing right along, is even more pronounced in this final section of the book, so much so that—as Coats very properly notes—stories seem to extend not only over a chapter or two but over several chapters. However I do not believe that we should derive from this only, or even mostly, a conclusion about origin. Rather, the author (or editor) is showing us—rather than telling us—an important thematic point. As the family becomes more accustomed to their chosenness, the promises need to be repeated less often, and the lives of the family become more coherent. The gradual disappearance of God as an active character in the story—commentators often remark upon the "secular" nature of this part of the book, the relative paucity of visions, auditions, and other divine manifestations—makes a similar point, although other theological intentions can be read into it as well. As the family becomes more self-sufficient there is simply less need of God to intrude. However, if visions and such are no longer part of the narrative vocabulary of this section, God is not absent nor is the atmosphere secular. God is guiding what seems to be random—Joseph finds a man in the middle of the countryside who gives him the correct directions, the caravan is going to Egypt, and Yʜᴡʜ is with Joseph in Potiphar's house—and is frequently called upon by Joseph, when confronted by Potiphar's wife, when he interprets dreams, and when he tests his brothers. The manner in which YHWH is present has evolved, but God is still a very important actor in the story; indeed, he is guiding it in the direction it needs to go for the people to survive.

But not everything changes; on the contrary, some things remain distressingly unchanged. Family strife continues to threaten the family. The younger continues to try to supplant his elder. And in each generation, a woman's experience is central and formative for the family. Hagar was central to the first generation. In the second, Rebekah comforted Isaac. In her turn, Leah was hated by Jacob and so was lovingly gifted with fertility and children by an attentive God. Rachel was remembered by God, although neither before nor after that event did she show any awareness of YHWH. In the time of the fourth generation, Tamar shows us how to be just, by breaking out of strictures that are not life giving. What remains the same then? Strife remains the same, but women—heirs of Mother Eve—show how to be free and to give life.

What structure, then, can we apply to the whole of the stories told about the fourth generation? In other words, where can we stand to view the whole of Genesis 37–50? Of course, Coats is not the only commentator to struggle with the issue. Although he regards this section as "The Joseph Story," David Dorsey respects the integrity of Genesis 37–50 and is much nearer the mark with his parallel pattern, reproduced here in an abridged fashion.[8]

a. Trouble between Joseph and his brothers (37:2-11)
    a'. More trouble between Joseph and his brothers (37:12-36)
b. Sexual temptation involving Judah (38:1-30)
    b'. Sexual temptation involving Joseph (39:1-23)
c. Joseph interprets two dreams of prison mates (40:1-23)
    c'. Joseph interprets two dreams of Pharaoh (41:1-57)
d. Brothers come to Egypt for food (42:1-38)
    d'. Brothers again come to Egypt for food (43:1–44:3)
e. Joseph has some of his family brought to him (44:4–45:15)
    e'. Joseph has all of his family brought to him (45:16–47:12)
f. Prospering in Egypt: Joseph in ascendancy (47:13-26)
    f'. Prospering in Egypt: Blessings on Jacob's sons (47:27–49:32)
g. Death of patriarch: Jacob (49:33–50:14)
    g'. Death of patriarch: Joseph (50:15-26)

---

[8] David Dorsey, *The Literary Structure of the Old Testament* (Grand Rapids, Mich.: Baker, 1999) 59.

Dorsey's intuition that there is a parallel movement in these chapters is sound, the tip-off being the focus on Joseph in Genesis 37 and the focus on Judah in Genesis 38.[9] Rather than being mere filler, the story about the injustice done to Tamar by Judah and the family strife that ensues serves to introduce the counterweight to Joseph. What happens to Joseph is paralleled by what happens to Judah (and the rest of the brothers); Joseph goes where the others will later go, undergoes trials like those the others will later undergo. Why not simply adopt Dorsey's various descriptions of the structure of this section, then? It may seem trivial, but it just seems too complex, too perfect, and a bit foreign to the organic way in which writers work. I prefer to note a general parallel tendency while not necessarily insisting that every piece be tightly fit into several additional structural schemes. So I present the rather simpler arrangement described below.

a. Joseph and the family strife he incites (37:1-36)

a'. Judah and the family strife he incites (38:1-30)

b. The descent and ascent of Joseph (39:1–41:57)

b'. The descent and ascent of the brothers (42:1–47:27)

c. Blessings: Joseph (47:28–48:22)

c'. Blessings: all the brothers (49:1-28)

d. The end for Jacob (49:29–50:14)

d'. The end for Joseph (50:15-26)

Joseph becomes the source of (nearly) murderous family rage and strife, such that he is expelled from the family and finds himself in Egypt. After (it seems) his departure, Judah is also the source of tremendous strife in his part of the chosen family, failing to support his daughter-in-law Tamar, forcing her to break out for freedom, unwittingly impregnating her, and, having accused her of promiscuity, being forced to acknowledge her righteousness and his paternity of her children. Strife parallels strife. Joseph ascends and descends a number of times while in Egypt. Having gone down as a slave to Egypt, he reaches a position of prominence in the house of Potiphar, but descends into jail when falsely accused of attempted rape. He ascends again into the serv-

---

[9] One should really read Dorsey's entire treatment of the Joseph story. In addition to the parallel structure excerpted here, he also offers a number of other ways of reading the whole section and its constituent parts. This is too detailed to be repeated here, so suffice it to say that his perceptions of parallel and concentric structures are most instructive and thought provoking. See Dorsey, *Literary Structure*, 60–3.

ice of the pharaoh when he correctly interprets the latter's dreams. His goings down and comings up are later mirrored in the travels of his brothers back and forth to Egypt.

Near the end of Jacob's life he blesses Joseph and, in a subsequent parallel, blesses the rest of the brothers as well. Finally, as the book ends Jacob's life ends. This has repercussions for Joseph and the rest of the family. Their strife seems (but only seems) to end, and Joseph, who brought them all down to Egypt so that they might later reascend to the Promised Land, dies.

Commentary

A. 37:1-36: Joseph and the Family Strife He Incites

This chapter introduces both the major figure of his generation, Jacob's second youngest son Joseph, and the major themes of this final part of the book. These themes are hardly new; family strife and the elder being supplanted by the younger, the intemperate love of a father for a particular son, and the use of pairs (two sets of two dreams, two ascents and descents by the brothers, etc.) remain unchanged. However, the motif of dreams is new and marks an important change in the religious atmosphere of this part of the book. God does not intrude into the lives of the characters in the fourth generation. Rather God influences people's actions either by means of significant dreams or simply by guiding the actions they take. The most famous theological proposition of these final chapters is found in Genesis 50:20: "Even though you intended to do harm to me, God intended it for good, in order to preserve a numerous people, as he is doing today." Joseph's brothers meant to harm him, but despite appearances to the contrary, God was able to use their ill-intended actions for a good end. The members of the family he had chosen would need to go to Egypt to escape famine, so God used the actions of Joseph's brothers to create a safe haven for them upon their arrival. God's plans for humanity are carried forward despite human obstreperousness. God saves humanity despite itself and can even use evilly intended acts to create a good effect.

In Joseph, unlike Jacob, we see an example of real human transformation; the self-absorbed teenager of Genesis 37 becomes the generous and forgiving man of Genesis 50. No spectacular divine manifestations were required in order to create the effect. Human life, the apparently secular life we all lead, is itself enough to transform us, if lived well.

All of this is still far in the future, however. The story opens with Joseph, the self-absorbed and self-important being doted upon by his father, lording it over his brothers and being roundly hated as a result. There have been few initially less attractive heroes ever presented.

Various commentators treat the chapter rather differently. Some attach 37:1 ("Jacob settled in the land where his father had lived as an alien, the land of Canaan") to the previous chapter, regarding it as the conclusion to the previous section, rather than as the introduction to this final part of the book. The latter, they feel, is more properly introduced by the so-called *tōlĕdôt* formula in 37:2a ("This is the story of the family [*tōlĕdôt*] of Jacob"). One might well dismiss this as a problem created by commentators, since the text flows continuously from one story to the next, from one generation to the next. But it is worth a word. Genesis 37:1 forms a nice bridge between the two generations and creates a contrast between the chosen—if not terribly likable and still untransformed son—Jacob and his more likable—but not chosen—brother, Esau. The latter dwells in the hill country whereas Jacob dwells (*yēšeb*, 37:1; i.e., is a legal, property-owning inhabitant) in the land promised to his family but in which his father had been no more than a resident alien, one who "sojourned" (*mĕgûrê*, 37:1). That Jacob dwells there in the land promised to his family sets up the tension in the stories that follow, wherein they are required to give up even the minimal stake they possess in order to survive. So the days of sojourning—the state the family has lived in since the days of Abraham—are done. They are now dwellers in the land, but their grip on it is still minimal and even that is tenuous.

Some commentators divide the chapter in two, distinguishing between the section in which Joseph dreams and describes his dreams (37:1-11) and the section in which the brothers plot concerning Joseph and Jacob mourns him (37:12-36). However, the latter flows from the former, and in any case the chapter is given clear boundaries on either side by Esau's genealogy and the story of Tamar. As a result, it is good to treat this chapter as a self-contained story.

Exposition: 37:1-2b
Inciting moment: 37:2c-3
Development: 37:4-17
Turning point: 37:18
Resolution: 37:19-33
Conclusion: 37:34-36

In this introductory chapter, the characters of those actors who will be important in the history of the fourth generation are fixed, although we will see that two of them—Joseph and Judah—are truly transformed by their lives. Our author uses a number of narrative techniques to introduce their characters to us, especially repetition and changes in point of view. Dreams are repeated, as are mentions of Joseph's coat and the leading roles of Reuben, the eldest brother, and Judah, who will figure prominently in the next chapter. Similarly, the meal taken while Joseph languishes in the cistern, himself possibly a meal for passing "bad" animals, and the detailed list of caravan goods, of which Joseph will himself shortly be a part, are also important in setting up tensions to be resolved later.

However, of the various narrative techniques available, it is manipulation of point of view that is most striking in this chapter. The brothers' collective point of view is invoked three times, 37:4, 18 and 25. In the first they see, i.e., understand, that Joseph is loved more than they are by their father. This interest point of view fuels their hatred for their younger brother since as far as they are concerned it means that their standing in their father's eyes is lessened thereby. He does not have eyes to see them, but sees only the insufferable prat Joseph. In 37:18 they see the object of their hatred approach and decide to rid themselves of him. When they see traders pass by, 37:25, they are relieved of the responsibility of killing him themselves; they will let Egyptian slavery do it for them. Finally, in 37:32b, they invite readers—and their father—to shift from a focus on them to a focus on their brother's blood-spattered coat. As they invite him to see the coat, the metonymic symbol of the object of their hatred, one can only be impressed by their cold anger.

But Joseph is not much better. He dreams twice and twice invites his family to share his point of view, to come inside his own mind and view his dreams with him. In 37:7 and 9 Joseph uses the word *hinnēh* in recounting his dream. Readers are now familiar with the technique whereby this word, which means "behold," effects a shift in point of view. We are no longer looking at the character who is the subject of the utterance, rather we are sharing that character's own point of view, seeing what he or she is seeing. In this case we see Joseph's dreams of lordly domination over his family twice. Not content merely to tell us what he has dreamed, he invites us to enter his mind and so to share his dreams.

Of course, not all points of view are so literally marked. By the end of the chapter one may indeed say that from the brothers' point of view they are well rid of the dreamer. But from Jacob's point of view, his heart is utterly bereft of consolation. One wonders what Reuben and Judah make of it, since they made at least a half-hearted attempt to save Joseph.

The exposition, as expected, tells us readers where we are and who is on stage. We are with Jacob's family, dwelling in Canaan. The narrator, having tempted us with all the details of Esau and his progeny and successes, now reorients us away from them, toward the main, chosen, line of the family. No time is wasted in showing us that the dysfunction and internal strife of this family are as bitter as ever. Joseph, foisted on his brothers as their helper, makes himself unpalatable to them by carrying tales and gossip about them to their father. The narrator tells us that Joseph is fully seventeen years old, underlining for us the dichotomy between Joseph's childish behavior and his age.[10] However, we do not know yet how his brothers feel toward him; perhaps they regard him with a certain benign indifference, perhaps they are even fond of him despite his immaturity. The internal emotional lives of families are, after all, mysteries to outsiders.

This bad report, though, introduces tension into the story. Rather than head for a quick resolution the tension is heightened by the note taken of Jacob's preferential love for Joseph, a love that is given physical reality with the gift of a coat—the famous, and unfortunately untranslatable, *kĕtōnet passîm*. No one knows what this garment was, so, although the NRSV chooses to call it a "long robe with sleeves"[11] one might equally well stick with the traditional coat of many colors.

What is important about the garment, however, is not its appearance but what it means in the overall dynamics of the family. It was the symbol of the father's preference for Joseph and a symbol that was easily read by Jacob's other sons. Since they see by it they are loved less than their brother, and since their brother behaves in a fashion that is most unpleasant for them, they react by feeling increasingly angry toward Joseph. Indeed, they hate him and are unable even to speak to him in a civil fashion. So the coat, intended by its donor probably simply as a gift, serves to poison yet further the atmosphere in this already

---

[10] This is a note not only of his immaturity. The attentive reader will note symmetry here. Joseph lived with his father for the first seventeen years of his own life and will live with him again for the last seventeen years of his father's life. See Everett Fox, *The Five Books of Moses* (New York: Schocken, 1995) 175.

[11] The garment appears only one other time in the Bible, 2 Samuel 13, where it is worn by Tamar and said to be the customary garment of royal virgin daughters. Friedman shows that these two stories are closely connected. In both the wearer of this coat is a victim of fraternal violence, and as a result both coats are torn. He regards it as a symbol of injustice done by a brother, so its appearance is less important than its symbolic value (Richard Elliott Friedman, *Commentary on the Torah* [San Francisco: HarperSanFrancisco, 2001] 123–4). Speiser finds an Akkadian parallel in elaborate ornamented garments either worn by the wealthy or draped over statues of gods. He argues that it is the appliquéd ornamentation that is remarkable about it (*Genesis*, 289–90).

emotionally fraught family. What incites further action? Is it the coat? Is it the favoritism? Is it the hatred? Whichever one decides, the brothers are nearly at the end of their patience and will soon be prepared to take some action.

His first dream is easily understood; Joseph will lord it over the rest of the family. His inability to read the emotional reality of others is implicit in his blithe assumption that his brothers will be fascinated by his dreams. He is apparently simply unaware of their dislike for him, so he not only tells his dream, he even invites his brothers to share his point of view. Sharing his point of view is something they are singularly unwilling to do, so hatred—mentioned here in vs. 8 for the third time already[12]—increases.

The first dream had not involved his parents, so Joseph had not shared it with them. His second dream seems to include his father and mother,[13] so Jacob hears it as well after Joseph tells it to his brothers. They are silent at both tellings, which should have made Joseph suspicious, but he still seems unaware of their feelings. Jacob reacts with what seems to be incredulous surprise and ponders the meaning of what Joseph dreamed and what he should do about the dream. The brothers' emotional reality is made more complex as we learn that they are jealous.[14]

---

[12] See Gen 37:4, 5 for the two previous instances. Fox points out that hatred has, once before in the case of Leah in 29:31, led to the fulfillment of God's plan (*Moses*, 175).

[13] Some think that this means that Rachel is still alive at this point. This is, quite rightly, taken by historical critics as evidence that these stories about Jacob, Joseph, and the rest of their family stem from a different source than stories about the same characters that are found earlier in the book. The Jacob found here is still the strong patriarch, unlike the weak figure in the story of Dinah. Rachel seems to be still alive, although the earlier part of the book asserts that she died years before. The complexity of sources in this chapter will become even more evident later in the chapter when the identity of Joseph's captors shifts repeatedly. That the chapter derives from various sources is clear. Those interested in the latest state of such questions of origin would do well to study Jean-Louis Ska, *Introduction à la lecture du Pentateuque: Clés pour l'interprétation des cinq premiers livres de la Bible*, Le livre et le rouleau 5 (Brussels: Éditions Lessius, 2000) 98–101.

[14] BDB, s.v. קנא, connects jealousy with the facial color aroused by the emotion. One can picture the brothers red in the face with anger and frustration. Thus they might be feeling not precisely what we most commonly mean by jealousy, i.e., envy of what another possesses, but rather resentment, suspicion or distrust. In other words, this is not an emotion that they feel in addition to their underlying anger but a different way of describing their anger.

The scene shifts as the brothers move off toward Shechem to pasture their father's livestock. Since Shechem has already figured ominously in the stories about the third generation (cf. Genesis 34), a reader views its reappearance here in the fourth generation with a certain foreboding. Lest a reader fail to catch the nuance, the word is repeated three times for emphasis.

Since we readers have been let into the emotional reality of the brothers' feelings about Joseph, we are more than a little surprised when Jacob decides to send Joseph to them. They have either disguised their feelings well or Jacob, never especially adept at understanding what others were feeling, has simply not noticed them. So taken up is he with his feelings for Joseph that he barely sees his other children.

If Joseph is not terribly attractive to us readers, we must recognize that he is nonetheless persistent. The journey to Shechem was about fifty miles, some five days on foot. If Joseph was a tattletale, he was not a weakling. He is helped on his way by a man who rather mysteriously appears in the middle of the countryside and, even more mysteriously, knows precisely where his brothers have gone. There is no particular sense that the man is really an angel (although see 32:25), but it is clear that Joseph's life is being directed. Whether toward disaster or not we have yet to see.

We reach the turning point of the story in 37:18: "They saw him from a distance, and before he came near to them, they conspired to kill him." The story takes quite a literal turn here as we move from Joseph's point of view to that of the brothers. Along with them, we now watch him approach. We also understand that, since Joseph is now and perhaps only now without the protective presence of their father, it is in their interest to act here and now by killing him (the narrator uses the verb *mwt* [Hiphil]). They decide to kill him, using—in vv. 20 and 26—the verb *hrg*, which connotes greater violence than the one used by the narrator; *hrg* was first used in Genesis to describe Cain's killing of Abel (Gen 4:8). The brothers decide to kill Joseph, throw the unburied body into a cistern—thus denying him burial and thereby humiliating him still further—and tell their father that a wild beast has devoured him.

Reuben, the eldest brother, steps in at this point and says, using an imperative verb, not to shed Joseph's blood. In so doing, he avoids both the verb used by the narrator and that used by the brothers and introduces yet a third verb into their conversation (*špk*), one that has been previously used only in Genesis 9:6 and so calls to mind the prohibition of one human being shedding the blood of another. In other words, Reuben reminds his brothers that what they plan to do is among those actions that are most forbidden. Readers will recall that he did not take part in the slaughter at Shechem; nonetheless, by repeating the brothers' language about throwing Joseph into a pit, he seems to buy into their anger—they can allow wild beasts to kill their brother, doing for them what they are forbidden to do—while he actually intends to return and rescue him. The brothers apparently acquiesce and throw Joseph into an empty pit. But, still sharing their point of view, we understand all of a sudden what it is that has so piqued their anger. Joseph has, for whatever reason, chosen to wear his ornamented tunic for his desert journey. This shows, once again, how poorly he understands his brothers, and they have reacted to it with rage. Thomas Mann captures the scene better than any commentator.

> They fell upon him as the pack of hungry wolves falls upon the prey; their blood-blinded lust knew no pause or consideration, it was as though they would tear him into fourteen pieces at least. Rending, tearing apart, tearing off—upon that they were bent, to their very marrow. "Down, down, down!" they panted with one voice; it was the *ketonet* they meant, the picture-robe, the veil. It must come off, and that was not so easy, for it was wound about him and fastened at head and shoulder; and they were too many for the deed. They got in each other's way; one thrust another away from the victim as he flew and fell and bounded among them.[15]

Why was it that the coat aroused such rage? In the minds of his brothers, and perhaps in Joseph's mind as well, it had become identified with Joseph's very person. So when it was torn off him, Reuben could well say "The boy is not" (37:30, AT). Without his coat, Joseph really is not there any more. The pit is empty, so perhaps they have decided not to shed his blood personally but rather to let wild animals or thirst do the deed for them. Their coldness is clear from their ability to have a meal next to the pit in which their brother is intended to die. Equally remarkable is Joseph's silence throughout the scene.

A caravan passes by bearing expensive trade goods, led by Ishmaelites. These and the Midianites who follow are both related peoples. By Hagar Abraham gave rise to the Ishmaelites, and by Keturah, whom he married after Sarah's death, he gave rise to the Midianites. Judah now takes the leading role, persuading his brothers that they have nothing to gain by simply killing Joseph, better to sell him into slavery and make a profit at the same time. Thus, sold into slavery by his own brothers—for the standard price of twenty shekels—Abraham's family will bring Joseph down to Egypt.

---

[15] Thomas Mann, *Joseph and His Brothers*, trans. H. T. Lowe-Porter (London: Vintage, 1999) 373.

Genesis 37:28 is regarded by most commentators as a somewhat awkward stitching together of two sources, two originally separate versions of these events. No Midianites have been mentioned yet, but elsewhere "Midianites" and "Ishmaelites" seem to refer to the same group (cf. Judg 8:22 and 24); two different versions of these events, each using one of the two interchangeable names, have been combined here. The combination is awkward because in one version the brothers had decided to pull Joseph out of the pit themselves and sell him to the Ishmaelites, while in the final version the Midianites did so without the brothers' intervention. The absent Reuben is given the role of finding the empty pit and thereby showing why the plan to sell Joseph went awry. There is no way to smooth out the awkwardness of the result, which remains strong evidence of this story having come down in Israel's pre-biblical traditions in two different versions.[16]

Reuben, who seems to have been absent for this interchange, returns, searches the pit, and fails to find Joseph. In despair he wonders what action to take, and sees no way to escape his father's grief. They take Joseph's special garment and dip it in goat's blood to deceive their father, intending to tell him that Joseph was killed by a wild beast. Thus Jacob, who used a change of garments and a dead goat to deceive his father, is similarly deceived in turn. Note the switch in point of view as they show the tunic to their father. They invite him to examine, not their brother's tunic, but "your son's tunic" (Gen 37:32). Unlike his father, who did not recognize him in his disguise, Jacob does recognize his son's clothing. In fact, they are saved from having to lie to their father— in contrast to Jacob's lie to Isaac—because Jacob jumps to the conclusion that the robe is bloodied because a wild beast has torn it from his son. While he grieves, in what seems to us to be a somewhat overwrought fashion, the narrator reminds the readers that Joseph is alive and sold into the house of Potiphar in Egypt. So the story of Joseph and the strife he incites comes to its conclusion. What becomes of Joseph in Egypt will not be made known to us for a while. However, we can begin to intuit what shape the future might take for this family. Both Joseph and the rest of the brothers will have to undo in some fashion what they have done here, so as to resolve the tensions that have begun here. Joseph, having been stripped of his identity, will have to reclothe himself somehow, have to weave a new persona. The brothers, having taken upon themselves the identity of brother slayers, will have to atone for that and for the grief that they have caused to their father. New identity and atonement must somehow lie in their futures.

---

[16] See Robert Alter, *Genesis: Translation and Commentary* (New York: Norton, 1996) 214 and Speiser, *Genesis*, 291 for a fuller argument.

A'. 38:1-30: JUDAH AND THE FAMILY STRIFE HE INCITES

I have written elsewhere in this commentary on the principal motif found in this chapter, which I have called the Outsider motif. A woman finds herself trapped inside a network of life- and soul-destroying relationships. This is often paralleled by her being moved ever more deeply into a building or structure of some sort to symbolize her trappedness. God desires that she be freed from whatever stifles her and in some manner moves her outside both structure and relationship to a position of freedom. This is in keeping with God's fundamental characteristic in these stories, that of savior.

Readers can turn to the appropriate excursus in order to study this motif in greater detail; I do not intend to repeat the entire argument here. In fact, in this part of the commentary, I would like to expand our perspective a bit to focus not only on Tamar but also on Judah, so better to understand what this chapter tells us about him and his development as a character in the stories told about the fourth generation in Genesis 37–50.

First, let us tackle the most difficult question: how does Genesis 38 relate to its surroundings? Is it just filler inserted here to raise tension because of the way in which it interrupts the larger Joseph story? Or was it placed here because Judah is, after all, important in the history of Israel and this story about him was worth preserving but did not fit better anywhere else? Or is it an integral part of the developing story? I argue for the last, as do an increasing number of commentators. Everett Fox lines up the evidence in a most compelling fashion.[17]

> 1. It demonstrates his growth of character. Judah, although not the eldest of the sons of Jacob, had already demonstrated leadership among the brothers when he argued for the preservation of Joseph's life in Genesis 37. He has already saved Joseph's life and will, in time, be the one to save (at least as far as he knew at the time) his younger brother Benjamin's life as well in Genesis 43–44. Genesis 38 helps us to understand why he acts in such a fashion. He has known grief and has lost sons and would save his elderly father from the same pain. Just as he wants to protect his youngest son from an untimely death, so too he desires to protect Jacob's youngest son and acts to prevent it.
>
> 2. He accepts blame and can develop as a character. Judah, once Tamar reveals what she has done, is willing to accept the blame for his misdeeds. He confesses in public to having been in the wrong in his behavior toward Tamar, although since he was a powerful man and she was a mere widow

---

[17] Fox, *Moses*, 178–80.

he might easily enough have tried to bluster his way through the difficulty and deny her accusations. He learns to do what is right because it is the right thing to do. He will apply this learning and the ability to accept responsibility before Joseph, before the latter's true identity is revealed and while he still thinks of him as simply the vizier of Egypt.

3. The chronology works well. Some twenty years elapse (cf. 41:46, 53-54) between the sale of Joseph and his encounters with his brothers. If Joseph was seventeen in Genesis 37, Judah would have been some years older and probably already a father. Thus, Fox argues, the events in Genesis 38 would have ended just before the events described in Genesis 43. Judah "reaches full maturity just in time."[18]

4. This chapter carries forward the major theme in Genesis of continuity and discontinuity. David will be a descendant of the Perez mentioned in 38:29. Thus it is not only important that the brothers and the rest of the family survive but that this particular grandson of Jacob be born so that the future line of David will be able to come into the world.

5. There is continuity of narrative motifs from Genesis 37. Once again someone has to recognize objects to establish the identity of an important character. Once again a young goat plays an important role. And finally, a brother is betrayed.

6. The principal source of connection between the two chapters, however, is something other than these, viz., a garment that defines who a person is. In Genesis 37 Joseph is completely identified with his ornamented tunic, and when it is taken from him he becomes a speechless prop. In Genesis 38 Judah attempts to do to Tamar what has been done to Joseph, except in a fashion that brutalizes her socially rather than physically. He imposes on her the widow's garment, which implies that she should remain a speechless prop for the remainder of her life. Unlike Joseph, she voluntarily takes it off and replaces it with another. Like Joseph's *kĕtōnet*, the description of which no one can satisfactorily define, the veil with which she covers herself by the wayside is not well understood. But it is a persona that she chooses for herself and puts on and takes off at will. Unlike Joseph she is in charge of her own destiny, to the consternation of those who would be her keepers, and she requires no further transformational adventures.

With all of these connections, about which more will be said in the course of the commentary on this chapter, it is highly unlikely that this chapter was simply inserted here because it fit no better anywhere else and because some filler was needed before the so-called Joseph Story could be taken up again. Rather, it introduces the other key character in the fourth generation, Judah, and shows us how he grows enough to

---

[18] Ibid., 178.

take on the challenges that his generation will face and to lead it successfully through them.

The plot structure of Genesis 38 is concentric. It is centered on Tamar's free act, and the events that follow her act are a reversal of those that precede it.

A. Judah's marriage and the birth of his sons (38:1-5)
    B. Evil is punished
        a. The marriage of Er to Tamar, his evil, and his death (38:6-7)
        b. The marriage of Onan to Tamar, his evil, and his death (38:8-10)
        C. The banishment of Tamar (38:11)
            D. Judah's wife dies; he is comforted and travels (38:12)
                X. Tamar acts (38:13-14)
            D'. Judah goes in to Tamar (38:15-18)
        C'. Tamar retires (38:19)
    B'. Restitution is made; justice is done
        a. Judah's attempt to repay the pledge fails (38:20-23)
        b. Judah confesses his sin and Tamar's innocence (38:24-26)
A'. Tamar gives birth (38:27-30)

A. Judah's marriage and the birth of his sons (38:1-5). The story begins with a somewhat vague reference to time, which does not allow us to place it very definitely in relation to the story that precedes. However, as we have seen, given Judah's age in relation to Joseph, these events could well overlap, at least in part, with the events described in Genesis 37. Of more significance is the phrase "went down, away from his brothers." This invites comparison with the beginning of Genesis 39:1, "Now Joseph was taken down to Egypt. . . ." The same verb (*yrd*, "to descend" or "go down") is used in both cases. This is the normal verb used for journeying to Egypt, but its twofold use here links and contrasts the beginnings of both stories. Both are separated from their brothers, but Judah is free to act on his own whereas Joseph is involuntarily separated and involuntarily taken to Egypt. But what does Judah do with his freedom? He turns aside—a literal translation to be preferred to the NRSV's "settled near"[19]— to a man named Hirah.

[19] Fox points out that the name Adullam sounds like the Arabic word for "to turn aside" (*Moses*, 181).

While with Hirah he sees and marries a woman who remains nameless throughout the remainder of the story. In each generation of the family's history women have been poorly treated by their spouses and/or other male relations, whether given away to potentially threatening foreigners to win protection for their menfolk in the case of Sarah and Rebekah, hated because another was preferred in the case of Leah, or allowed to be taken away and mistreated in the case of Dinah. But each of these at least had her own name and so a semblance of an identity. The daughter of Shua is denied even that dignity. Judah took her—again the literal translation is to be preferred to the NRSV's more decorous "married"[20]—and went in to her.

All of this calls to mind the behavior of Esau who married outside of the kinship group to the great annoyance of his parents (Gen 26:34-35), and it causes us to ponder what our narrator intends by inserting this material. Are we to understand that Judah was behaving in a socially unacceptable manner? That conclusion seems inescapable from his behavior at the births of his sons, when he is absent and does not name them. Judah has left the family and "taken" a woman from a forbidden social group without the permission of his parents. It would seem that his behavior so far is more to be decried than was that of Esau, but worse is yet to come. Our author is making Judah increasingly distasteful to us so that his eventual transformation will be more striking.

She bears three sons to Judah. According to the traditional Hebrew text, he names the first[21] in proper fashion. However, this birth is quickly followed by two others after which she, the nameless mother, names the sons. Judah seems to be shirking his responsibility in not naming them and, in the third case, he is not even present when the nameless "she" bears his son. His absence is made all the more mysterious by his being in a place named Chezib.[22]

We are by now long accustomed to the way biblical figures reveal their characters by what they say and do. Judah has yet to say any-

---

[20] The typical Hebrew idiom translated into English as "married" would be "took as a wife." The Hebrew of 38:2 simply says "took." Since we have seen that the family of Abraham was rigorous in its practice of endogamy, i.e., marrying only with the kinship group and not marrying foreigners at all, the implication might be that Judah did not marry the Canaanite woman, but simply took her as an unofficial wife.

[21] Speiser (*Genesis*, 295) adopts the neutral "was named" here. As noted, the Hebrew says, "he named"; however, other important manuscript traditions (Sam, TJ) have "she," just as in vv. 4 and 5. Speiser feels that this feminine version is correct. Normally fathers named their sons (cf. Gen 16:15 where Abraham names Ishmael and in so doing acknowledges his paternity).

[22] The root behind this name means "to be a liar."

thing, but he has done a great deal: left his family, taken a woman apparently in an informal marriage although she was not within the kinship group, done so without permission, bothered to be present only for the birth of his first son, and not bothered to name the second two. For the birth of his third son, he is in a place called "Falsehood." A more suggestive portrait of inappropriate behavior is hard to imagine.

B. Evil is punished (38:6-10). The second section of the story of Tamar shows that God punishes those who do evil. But here, too, the negative characterization of Judah continues. In contrast to his own taking a woman without the involvement of his parents, Judah takes a wife for his eldest son Er, a woman named Tamar.[23] The narrator heightens the contrast with Judah's own behavior by using the proper Hebrew idiom in this instance (*wayyiqqaḥ yĕhûdâ ʾiššâ lĕʿēr bĕkôrô*; literally, "And Judah took a wife for his eldest son Er" [AT]) and telling us her name.

Er was guilty of some unnamed moral evil[24] and is killed by God as a result, the only instance in the Bible, as far as I am aware, of God being said to kill someone. As ever Robert Alter offers a wise comment:

> The nature of his moral failing remains unspecified, but given the insistent pattern of reversal of primogeniture in all these stories, it seems almost sufficient merely to be first-born in order to incur God's displeasure: though the firstborn is not necessarily evil, he usually turns out to be obtuse, rash, wild, or otherwise disqualified from carrying on the heritage. It is noteworthy that Judah, who invented the lie that triggered his own father's mourning for a dead son, is bereaved of two sons in rapid sequence. In contrast to Jacob's extravagant grief, nothing is said about Judah's emotional response to the losses.[25]

So yet another element is added to our knowledge of Judah. Choosing for his son—the only one he bothered to name and so acknowledge—

---

[23] The name "Tamar" means "Date Palm." Hebrew names for men tend to have a theophoric element or reference. "Judah" means something like "Praise"; and readers will recall that the interpretations of the names of his brothers as they were being born to Leah, Rachel, Bilhah, and Zilpah, all made reference to God's action. Women's names however tend to refer to some element of nature. This too has been seen already in both Leah and Rachel. This earth-connectedness of women continues in the name of Tamar and can be seen in many others as well, e.g. Susannah (Lily) or Deborah (Honeybee).

[24] The word *raʿ*, "evil," is used to refer to failings of a moral nature as opposed to those of a ritual nature. The latter are referred to by the word *ḥaṭṭāʾ*, usually translated "sin." See commentaries on Ps 1:1, for instance, for more detail on the contrast.

[25] Alter, *Genesis*, 218.

where he refused to be chosen for, he does not even seem to grieve his loss. Nor does he grieve the loss of the next son, Onan.

Onan's moral failing is made explicit. He had been ordered by his father to undertake a so-called "levirate" marriage.[26] Rather than act as the law prescribed or accept the public humiliation that the law foresaw for such an offender, he acts on his own[27] to make it impossible for Tamar to become pregnant. For this moral failing, he too is put to death by God.

C. The banishment of Tamar (38:11). Since Tamar is silent throughout it is possible that Judah thought her somehow at fault[28] and there-

---

[26] The word *levir* means "brother-in-law." A levirate marriage was one in which the brother of a man who died childless was required to marry his deceased brother's wife. The firstborn son of the resulting union would legally be that of his late brother. This situation is described in Deut 25:5-10, as is what would happen should he be unwilling to do so.

> When brothers reside together, and one of them dies and has no son, the wife of the deceased shall not be married outside the family to a stranger. Her husband's brother shall go in to her, taking her in marriage, and performing the duty of a husband's brother to her, and the firstborn whom she bears shall succeed to the name of the deceased brother, so that his name may not be blotted out of Israel. But if the man has no desire to marry his brother's widow, then his brother's widow shall go up to the elders at the gate and say, "My husband's brother refuses to perpetuate his brother's name in Israel; he will not perform the duty of a husband's brother to me." Then the elders of his town shall summon him and speak to him. If he persists, saying, "I have no desire to marry her," then his brother's wife shall go up to him in the presence of the elders, pull his sandal off his foot, spit in his face, and declare, "This is what is done to the man who does not build up his brother's house." Throughout Israel his family shall be known as "the house of him whose sandal was pulled off."

While, of course, there is no way of knowing whether this law was ever really enforced, it holds force in the story world of Genesis 38, and Onan acts outside the law in refusing to impregnate Tamar.

[27] Rashi says, "He threshed within and winnowed without" (Rashi, *The Pentateuch and Rashi's Commentary: A Linear Translation into English*, trans. Abraham ben Isaiah and Benjamin Sharfman [Brooklyn: S. S. & R. Publishing, 1949] vol. 1: *Genesis*, 384).

[28] Readers may well be reminded of the situation faced in the deuterocanonical book of Tobit by Sarah, the daughter of Raguel, whose seven successive husbands died at the hand of a demon but who was thought by all to be guilty herself of their deaths.

> On the same day, at Ecbatana in Media, it also happened that Sarah, the daughter of Raguel, was reproached by one of her father's maids. For she had been married to seven husbands, and the wicked demon Asmodeus had killed each of them before they had been with her as is customary for wives. So the maid

fore banished her rather than marry her to his youngest son Shelah. This was, of course, a humiliation for her, and she would have been, in all likelihood, not welcomed back by her own family. Her situation was impossibly ambiguous; she was not free to marry, was still under the legal responsibility of her erstwhile father-in-law, and had no way to earn a living, but had to be supported by her family. To both her and her family she must have seemed almost buried alive. She is now utterly inside, trapped in structures real and cultural: inside her father's house (while still being legally part of her father-in-law's household), inside the clothing that marks her as a widow and a daughter-in-law (while denied the husband that would provide her income, status, and progeny). Utterly inside, she is utterly unfree.

D. Judah's wife dies; he is comforted and travels (38:12). Some number of years passes—enough apparently for Shelah to have reached marriageable age—but instead of reading about his upcoming marriage to Tamar, we read that Judah is now a free man. The NRSV, adopting the most charitable possible reading of the Hebrew, says, "In course of time the wife of Judah, Shua's daughter, died; when Judah's time of mourning was over . . ." (Gen 38:12a). However, this should be compared with the more ambiguous original: "*wayyirbû hayyāmîm wattāmot bat-šûaʿ ʾēšet-yĕhûdâ wayyinnāḥem yĕhûdâ . . .*" (Gen 38:12a). This latter might be more literally translated: "And the days were many, and Judah's woman[29] died. He was comforted. . . ." Judah, in all likelihood, had not formally married this nameless woman but simply "taken" her. He had not been with her when their latter two sons had been born, nor had he named them. One is tempted to think that at the time of her death he was less taken up with mourning rites for her than with being comforted, relieved, himself. Again, Judah's emotional reality is pointedly contrasted with that of his extravagantly mourning father, who had also observed proper mourning rites for Rachel, although there is no mention there of the extremes he underwent at the report of Joseph's death (cf. Gen 35:19-20).

At the beginning of the chapter Judah had "gone down" from his family. Here, in v. 12, he "goes up" to the sheep shearing of his friend

---

said to her, "You are the one who kills your husbands! See, you already have already been married to seven husbands and have not borne the name of a single one of them. Why do you beat us? Because your husbands are dead? Go with them! May we never see a son or daughter of yours!" (Tobit 3:7-9)

[29] Recalling that the English words "wife" and "woman" represent the same Hebrew word and that Judah's taking of her was not described with the idiom that refers to marriage.

Hirah. After the death of the daughter of Shua he is apparently in the mood for the sort of festivities that accompany the end of the exertions of sheep shearing.

X. Tamar acts (38:13-14). We now reach the center of story where, very much in contrast to Joseph, Tamar takes off the garment (and the identity) given to her and replaces it with one of her own choosing, one which, as we will see, no one knows how to interpret.

Tamar is told of Judah's traveling plans, knows that she will never be married to Shelah and acts in a free and unexpected fashion to create a future for herself. In so doing she must go outside of her father's house, her role as widow, and the expectations for behavior associated with that role, and behave in a manner that all would likely deem immoral. Covered in a garment that does not allow her status or intentions to be readily understood, she seats herself by the road to Enaim (literally, "at the entrance, or opening, of Enaim," *petaḥ ʿênayim*).

A certain amount of discussion has taken place in the literature on the meaning and significance of this place name. Alter[30] understands "Enaim" as a place name meaning "Twin Wells." Read in this way, the scene is a sort of parody of the typical betrothal by the well scene that we have encountered so many times already. Instead of betrothal, however, this scene is an abrupt exchange of interest and price. Friedman takes the phrase literally as "the opening of the eyes," and translates, "in a visible place."[31] Johanna Bos derives further insight from this meaning:

> Literally, however, the words are quite clear; they mean "opening of the eyes," words that certainly set up echoes on a deeper level of the story. It is here that the process begins by which Judah will receive his eyeopener as to righteousness.[32]

[30] *Genesis*, 220. Fox agrees (see *Moses*, 183). The word *ʿênayim* is the dual form of *ʿayin*, which can mean either "well" or "eye."

[31] Friedman, *Torah*, 128.

[32] Johanna W. H. Bos, "An Eyeopener at the Gate: George Coats and Genesis 38," *Lexington Theological Quarterly* 27 (1992) 121. I suspect that Bos understands something very true about the story but does not go far enough in her reading of the story as subversive of "the sin of patriarchy." She says of Tamar, "Within her context the most that can be said is that Tamar provides an eyeopener to the patriarch and sets at least a limit to patriarchal power. She does not, however, change the structure, nor the injustices inherent in the system." One suspects that Tamar was simply trying to create a future for herself and, like Hagar in Genesis 16, had to accept the limitations imposed by the reality of her world. One demeans her and her bravery by suggesting that somehow she did not do enough. She stepped outside of the bonds that her world placed on her and in so doing acted righteously. And, as we learned in Genesis 15, to act righteously is, at least in God's eyes, enough.

I suspect that both readings are correct. We have here a perversion of the betrothal scene because Judah had perverted marriage and needed as a result to have his eyes opened.

D'. Judah goes in to Tamar (38:15-18). The reversal of Tamar's situation begins in v. 15. She—who has been invisible to all eyes for years in her widow's seclusion—is now visible to the eyes (*ʿênayim*) of her father-in-law who has been ignoring her existence. In truth he does not know who she is and, assuming her availability for his satisfaction, says something like, "Hey, let me come in to you" (*hābâ-nāʾ ʾābôʾ ʾēlayik*, 38:16). This is remarkable both for its brusqueness and for the way in which Judah simply assumes that a woman dressed in an unfamiliar fashion must be a prostitute. Of course, there is also a contrast drawn between Judah's randy behavior here and Joseph's modesty in Genesis 39.

There are further contrasts as well. Judah used a garment to deceive his father, just as Tamar uses a garment to deceive him. Judah used a goat to deceive his father, and Tamar demands payment of a goat. Since Judah can only promise to send the goat later she demands as a pledge those things that establish his legal and personal identity. The signet ring was used as a signature and the staff would be recognizable as well as belonging to him. That he would part so readily with these important objects underlines his impetuosity, which reminds us of Esau.

Tamar conceives, exactly as she had wanted to, but the events that led to the conception are, as indicated by the abrupt nature of the verbs used, hardly fraught with romance: "he went in to her and she got pregnant" (38:18b).

C'. Tamar retires (38:19). Tamar is now about as outside as she can get. Not only is she outside of town, she is also outside of her expected uniform and outside of any role for which her society had a name; indeed, she is outside of any sort of legally understandable relationship. But she does not choose to stay there. Not for her is the role of the social outcast or of the social reformer. She simply wants to create a future for herself. Having done that, she reverses what she has done and goes back inside. She takes off the veil, dons once more the widow's garb, and takes up again the role assigned to her—at least as far as on-lookers can tell for the moment.

B'. Restitution is made; justice is done (38:20-26). The injustices done at the beginning of the story must now be reversed. The first step in doing so is to make payment to Tamar. But when Judah sends his ever-trusty friend Hirah back to eye-opening Twin Wells he is unable to find the woman. He asks where the cult prostitute[33] is who was there

---

[33] For whatever reason Hirah asks whether the cult prostitute (*qĕdēšâ*) is still in the area, rather than inquiring as to the whereabouts of the prostitute (*zônâ*). The

previously. Unable to find her, Hirah returns to Judah, who suggests that better than running around trying to find her he should simply let her keep his pledge. After all, he says, he tried to make good his debt to her. This is unwitting irony on Judah's part since he had not, in fact, tried at all to make good his pledge to Tamar in her persona as his daughter-in-law.

After enough time has passed for it to be evident that Tamar is pregnant, Judah learns of the fact and, without any hesitation, orders her to be burnt alive. She has, he is told, been whoring and become pregnant as a result of her whoring.[34] The compact nature of Hebrew syntax reduces his command to two words: *hôṣî*ʾ*ûhā wĕti*ʾ*śśārēp* ("Take-her-out, that-she-might-be-burned").

But Tamar remains in decorous seclusion. Just as she is to be taken out and executed, she, like Judah and his brothers, sends (cf. 37:32; NRSV, "had . . . taken") evidence—although hers is genuine—and even uses Judah's own word "Recognize . . ." (37:32; NRSV, "see"). Judah's response is to acknowledge them and say, "She is more in the right than I, since I did not give her to my son Shelah" (Gen 38:26). What does his use of the comparative mean? That she was right in some absolute sense? That given the wrongness of both of their choices, hers was better than his? Traditional commentary takes two different lines. One understanding is that Judah declares her completely innocent and places himself squarely in the wrong.

> And Judah recognized them and said, "She is in the right. She is pregnant from me, on account of the fact that I did not give her to my son Shelah."[35]

Another approach suggests how Tamar's behavior has been, in comparison with Judah's behavior, better. Judah had, in a way forbidden to

---

qĕdēšâ seems to have had a role in fertility cults. Thus sexual intercourse with a *qĕdēšâ* might be seen as more respectable, since it would fall into the realm of religious activity—albeit one forbidden to members of Abraham's family—while the latter undertook prostitution as a purely commercial activity. A very useful study of the institution of sacred prostitution in itself and in this particular text may be found in the paper by Joan Goodnick Westenholz, "Tamar, *QĒDĒŠĀ, QADIŠTU* and Sacred Prostitution in Mesopotamia," *Harvard Theological Review* 82 (1989) 245–65.

[34] The verb corresponding to the word *zônâ* is used twice in the same sentence. This reminds us that Judah was perfectly willing to visit a *zônâ* himself, even if he was unwilling to show his face when paying and his emissary was unwilling even to use the word.

[35] *Targum Onqelos* Gen. 38:26, in James L. Kugel, *Traditions of the Bible* (Cambridge, Mass.: Harvard University Press, 1998) 454.

this endogamous family, married outside the kinship group. Tamar could have done the same when she perceived that there were no available members of the kinship group for her to wed. However, rather than do that, she became pregnant by the only available descendant of Abraham, Judah himself. Thus her behavior, however unorthodox, was closer to the ideal of endogamy than Judah's had been.

> [Amram said to his compatriots:] "And so did our ancestress Tamar behave, for her intent had not been fornication, but, not wishing to withdraw from the sons of Israel, she thoughtfully declared: It is better for me to die in becoming pregnant by my father-in-law than to be mingled with the Gentiles . . ." And her intent saved her from all danger.[36]

A'. Tamar gives birth (38:27-30). The final reversal closes the chapter and the story. Judah took a nameless woman, made her pregnant, and was absent as her sons were born. Tamar is unmarried, so there is no one to abandon her. She is alone but not abandoned, because she has her midwife to assist her. She is delivered of twins, in a way that recalls the birth of Jacob and Esau. The first twin to emerge at all from the womb has his wrist marked with a red cord. The name given to him, Zerah, refers to the red of dawn[37] and recalls Esau, whose other name, Edom, means "Red." But, like Esau, he is pushed aside by his brother. His name, "Perez," means "Breach," and refers to the way in which Perez pushed aside his brother—much like Jacob—and made room for himself in the world.

We saw that Hagar was central to the experience of the first generation because in her and in what happened to her we learned something vital about the nature of God and humanity. In a very real sense Tamar is the Hagar of the fourth generation. Like Hagar, Tamar was cast aside. In this case that meant that she was simply put on hold in her father's house. Not content to have her future dictated for her and, in fact, simply turned into a blank, she went outside of any relationship, any constraint that denied her a future. And she was judged righteous by those who saw her. In an earlier day perhaps an angel would have pronounced that judgment. That is no longer the case in her day, but she was nonetheless publicly proclaimed to possess that quality that made Abraham stand in right relationship with God. True, Judah only admits it grudgingly and tries at the same time to salvage some scrap of righteousness for himself, but the fact remains that in

---

[36] Pseudo-Philo, *Biblical Antiquities* 9:5, in Kugel, *Traditions*, 454.
[37] Fox, *Moses*, 186.

the entire book of Genesis only two people are called "righteous," Abraham and Tamar.

And what of Judah? In him we have another picture of a partial transformation. His eyes are opened at Twin Wells because after that encounter he is able finally to see a woman with a name, and he understands what righteousness is. Before that encounter, he was self-absorbed and unfeeling. After it he was capricious and discounted Tamar so thoroughly that he was willing simply to consign her to the flames. It was only when she revealed himself to himself that he changed.[38]

In Genesis 37–38 we see images of strife. Beyond that, in Joseph, we see a need for maturity. In Judah, who will become the spokesman for the brothers, we see the possibility of transformation. With these two intimately connected parallel stories we can go on now to see what happens next in the time of the fourth generation.

B. 39:1–41:57: THE DESCENT AND ASCENT OF JOSEPH

Tamar disappears from the story at this point because there is nothing more for her to accomplish; she has become who she—and God—want her to be. She wanted to be a mother, and she is one. God desires righteousness, and she is righteous. For a while, as well, Judah disappears from the story. He will reappear later as a spokesman for the brothers and will bring his experience with Tamar to bear in his discussion with the Egyptian vizier who is, unbeknownst to him, his long-lost brother Joseph.

In the meantime, our attention is directed once more to the other major figure of the fourth generation, Joseph. Introduced to us in Genesis 37 as the vain favorite of his father, proud of the future that he (and possibly God) dreamed for him, obtuse in his relations with others, he was stripped of his identity when his coat was stripped off. This attack rendered him mute because, all of a sudden, he was nobody, and a nobody has no voice.

Genesis 39:1–41:57 tells the story of Joseph's ups and downs and follows the process of maturation and transformation that he undergoes as a result of his time as an Egyptian slave. This larger story is divided into three shorter scenes, which are brief stories in themselves. These

---

[38] Those interested in traditional Jewish exegesis of the story of Judah and Tamar should read the masterful study by Esther Menn, *Judah and Tamar in Ancient Jewish Exegesis: Studies in Literary Form and Hermeneutics*, Supplements to the Journal for the Study of Judaism 51 (Leiden: E. J. Brill, 1997).

scenes are separated by references to the passage of time as well as changes of locale and the introduction of new characters. The scenes are connected by the continuation of certain motifs and themes as well as by the continuing presence of the character Joseph. Pairs of dreams play an important role in the latter two, as they did in chapter 37. Joseph's appearance and changes in his clothing figure in all three. Fox also points out a parallel movement between these three scenes, which follow a pattern of success/authority → imprisonment → success/authority, and the larger process of the stories that focus on Joseph and his movement from favorite son → slavery → viceroy of Egypt.[39] In all three Joseph's development and maturation remain the focus.

A temporary garment (39:1-23). The first of these three brief tales might be called "A Temporary Garment." It is one of the best known, and best told, tales in Genesis, in which our author provides us with careful insight into the inner lives of the characters without ever deviating from the canons of Hebrew narrative art. As ever, characters are known by what they say and what they do, and, despite the fundamental opacity of their interior lives, they become well known to us. The plot might be described in this manner.

	Exposition: 39:1
Joseph in Potiphar's house	Development: 39:2-6a
	Complication: 39:6b
An attempted seduction	Turning point: 39:7
	Resolution: 37:8-19
Joseph in the king's prison-house	Conclusion: 39:20-23

As we encounter Joseph again, he has gone down to Egypt and gone down in status; once a favorite son, he is now a slave. But if Jacob is no longer with him, YHWH is (vv. 2, 3, 5, 21, and 23), and we will see that his downward trajectory is soon—if only momentarily—arrested. Hands, which already figured importantly in Genesis 38:19-20, 28-30, remain important here. Joseph's success is tied to his hands six times (39:3, 4, 6, 8, 22, 23). He is thrown into prison because he leaves his

---

[39] *Moses*, 184. Other key thematic words are "all," "house," "blessing" and "succeed" and the phrase "the LORD was with Joseph." See Alter, *Genesis*, 224.

garment in his mistress's hands (vv. 12, 13). Eyes are a symbol of authority in v. 4, then figure in the attempted seduction in v. 7 and reemerge as a symbol of authority in v. 12.

In typical fashion, Joseph's journey down to Egypt, and whatever travails he might have suffered along the way as he became used to the idea that his own brothers had sold him and that he was now a slave, are passed over in absolute silence. We meet him again just at the moment when he is sold to a high Egyptian official, a man named Potiphar.[40] We are told three times that he is sold into slavery, an allusion to Genesis 15:13, which we see beginning to come to pass.

With the scene set, development follows rapidly and the key thematic words mentioned above are introduced. Because YHWH is so evidently with him (we are told this four times), Joseph finds favor in his master's eyes—a hint of what is to come as the master's wife becomes obsessed with him. Joseph is blessed with success, and all his master's enterprises come under his direction. All readers are struck by the tremendous change that has already occurred in Joseph. The spoiled teenager who did not seem terribly given to hard work—given his choice of the expensive ornamented tunic as work clothes—is all of a sudden a strong and hardworking adult. Some explain this on the basis of difference in sources, Genesis 37 and 39 deriving from different narrative traditions about Joseph. However these source questions are answered, Joseph is changed here because of the LORD's unseen and, for all we know, unacknowledged presence with him.

Actually, one can discern four stages in Joseph's rise to success. In the first place he is not sent to work in the fields as a hand. Since he remains in the house he has an opportunity to be seen and to show his talents. In so doing he comes into close contact with his master's wife. Secondly, he wins favor in his master's eyes and as a result—the third

---

[40] The name appears only twice, here and in 37:36. He is referred to afterwards as the Egyptian or the master. This highlights one aspect of Joseph's plight, the difference in status between him, a non-Egyptian slave, and his owner, a powerful man well integrated into the power structures of Egypt. They occupy, as it were, opposite poles of social location, and Joseph could never forget the fragility of his position. Potiphar's wife is never named. There is some suggestion that his native Egyptian ethnicity is mentioned because there were non-Egyptians in service to the Egyptian court, as indeed Joseph will shortly be. Otherwise, as a character Potiphar is pure agent, simply a plot device needed to effect its movement. His nameless wife is by far the more striking character although she too is little more than an agent, at best the type of the sexually rapacious person. In the entire chapter, Joseph is the only rounded character, although YHWH is constantly in the background, and readers are never able to forget that it is YHWH who is directing Joseph's fate.

stage—he becomes the personal assistant of his master. Finally, the fourth stage, he is in charge of the whole household, which—considering all of the aspects of agriculture and housekeeping involved for a large group of people—would have made him not unlike the chief operating officer of a corporation of modest size.

Joseph is now at the pinnacle of his career. Having come down to Egypt as a slave, he has journeyed inexorably upwards in the estimation of his owner and now enjoys his absolute confidence. However, we must never forget that all of this is because of the presence and blessing of YHWH. Potiphar is now said to be concerned only with the food he ate (39:6a). If Genesis 39:6a is an allusion to sexual activity and appetites,[41] then the phrase that follows (39:6b) becomes even more meaningful: "Now Joseph was handsome and good-looking." Actually, the Hebrew is a bit more striking and poetic than the NRSV indicates: *wayhî yôsēp yĕpēh-tō'ar wîpēh mar'eh* ("And Joseph was fair of feature and fair to look upon" [AT]). The shift in point of view ("Behold" seems to be understood, especially in the context of the next verse) adds an important complication to the ongoing development of the story and brings tension to the point where something has to be done about it. This sort of language in reference to male beauty is unusual in the Bible and draws our attention for that reason if no other. But in addition it teaches us something about Jacob's reasons for feeling so close to this particular son. The same words, making allowance for difference in gender, are used of Rachel, Joseph's mother, in Genesis 29:17, although it is not immediately apparent to those dependent on translation: "Rachel was graceful and beautiful" (*wĕrāḥēl hāyĕtâ yĕpat-tō'ar wîpat mar'eh*). Joseph resembled his mother and so was a constant reminder of her for the bereaved Jacob. Likewise he would have been a constant source of irritation for his brothers, who would have been reminded thereby of their own mothers' lower status.

The effect of his looks on the wife of Potiphar creates the turning point of the story: "And after a time his master's wife raised her eyes to Joseph and said, 'Lie with me'" (Gen 39:7, AT). To call this a seduction is somewhat imprecise, since that word calls to mind a process of wooing whereby the defenses of the object of one's appetites might be weakened. Such is not the case here, as the original (*šikbâ 'immî*) is a two-word command, the peremptory tone of which is difficult to capture in English.

---

[41] Some see here a euphemistic allusion to sexual activity and make a connection with Prov 30:20, "This is the way of an adulteress: she eats, and wipes her mouth, and says, 'I have done no wrong.'" Thus Potiphar is able to enjoy leisure with his wife, but she is looking elsewhere for something (or someone) to slake her appetite.

Throughout the passage the nameless woman is always called "his master's wife." This helps us to understand the complex moral quandary in which Joseph finds himself. In one sense, he has become the master of his mistress since she is so utterly in thrall to him. As such, he is in a position to make a clever career move since, as his mistress's lover his position would be even more secure than it already is. At the same time, though, and for the same reasons, his position is frighteningly tenuous, for if he were to take up his mistress's offer and later fall out of favor he would likely end up in a much less comfortable position than he currently enjoys.

If the story turns here, in what direction does it go? Joseph the slave is now in charge, so how will he respond to the importuning of his master's wife? The reader gets the impression that she has boiled over after a long time of growing obsession. If so, it is likely that Joseph has long been preparing a response. To her two-word command, he replies with a lengthy speech in which he calmly outlines his three reasons for refusing her: 1. his master has entrusted everything he possesses to him; 2. except his wife (who seems to be considered a possession, albeit a highly prized one); and 3. Joseph has religious objections since, for him, this would be a sin. His response is calm, not condemnatory or angry, and he does not preach to her. In an almost impossible situation he seems to have hit exactly the right note. Clearly the prat of Genesis 37 has matured almost beyond recognition and has grown into a new identity.

Although the woman's reply is not recorded, she does not give up. She continues to try to wear him down despite his repeated refusals and general avoidance of her. He tries not to be alone with her, perhaps foreseeing what she, in the totality of her obsession with him, does next. Finding herself alone with him, she grabs him and repeats her desire. He wriggles out of her grasp, at the same time leaving behind his outer garment. Although he does not yet know it, he is leaving behind the identity that this garment, for a time, gave him. In short order he will no longer be the valued household retainer but will continue his downward journey into an Egyptian prison.

But that has not yet occurred. His master's wife is hot for revenge and moves first to get the remainder of the household staff on her side. She plays on their xenophobia by reminding them that her husband brought a Hebrew man—she avoids the word slave in talking to other slaves—into the house, and tries to get them to identify with her by speaking of "us." She claims, "He came in to me, to lie with me."[42] Al-

---

[42] *bāʾ ʾēlay liškab ʿimmî wāʾeqrāʾ bĕqôl gādôl.* Robert Alter points out that she shrewdly uses an ambiguous expression that can mean either that he came to the

though we readers know that she cried out only after he had left, she rearranges events to claim that she cried out when he appeared, thus establishing that she had fought off his attempt at rape. As evidence, she produces the garment he left "by her side"—not "in her hand," since saying that it was by her side implies that he had removed it prior to lying down with her.

Having established a set of "facts" with the first witnesses available, she waits for her husband to come home. While waiting she keeps the garment with her. This is another clever bit of characterization. One imagines her fondling this possession of Joseph, the only bit of him that she will ever get to touch, all the while torn between desire and rage. She repeats essentially the same tale to her husband but makes a couple of significant changes. In the second version, Joseph is a Hebrew slave (not a "man") who came to her to insult her (not "to lie with" her). Why the change? Would her husband not believe her? Does she still have some hopes of getting together with a chastened Joseph after some punishment has softened him up?

Potiphar becomes enraged, but we are not told the object of his anger. Is he angry with Joseph for the attempted insult or might he be angry at his wife for corrupting what has been a useful relationship with a trusted retainer? Be that as it may, Joseph is not executed but imprisoned. He leaves behind this part of his life never to revisit it again. Being a majordomo to a highly placed Egyptian, though merely a temporary identity for him, was one that left him transformed.

With Joseph in prison, at a moment when his life seems to have taken a tremendous turn for the worse, YHWH's presence returns. Just as YHWH was absent in Genesis 16 when Abraham and Sarah attempted to use Hagar to their own advantage, so too is YHWH absent when Potiphar's wife attempts to use Joseph to her own advantage. Hagar found herself for a while back in Abraham's household, in what must have been a prison for her. So too, in a seeming paradox, after being freed from the ongoing threat of attack by his master's wife, Joseph finds himself in prison. But since YHWH is with him, prison is transformed into another place of triumph and blessing.[43]

---

part of the house where she was at the time or that he violently attempted intercourse with her (*Genesis*, 226).

[43] Anyone interested in the interpretation of Genesis 39 should turn to James Kugel's masterful *In Potiphar's House* (San Francisco: HarperCollins, 1990; 2nd ed., Cambridge, Mass.: Harvard University Press, 1994) as well as the same author's *Traditions*, 442–51. Any attempt to summarize that material here would fail to do justice to Kugel's wisdom, erudition, and humor.

Having had his temporary identity taken from him, Joseph must now construct yet another, his third so far. No longer the spoiled adolescent who wore the ornamented tunic, nor even the trusted steward whose garment was torn from him, Joseph—because YHWH is with him—becomes the trusty who reads dreams.

The trusty who reads dreams (39:20–40:23). Genesis 40 serves several purposes. It increases tension in the larger story of which this serves as a small part because, since Joseph here reaches his lowest point, we wonder how he can get out and contribute to the fourth generation of his family. Dreams recur, and we are reminded of Genesis 37. If he interprets them correctly here, will he not have done so earlier? But how will the future foretold in the dreams of Genesis 37 come to pass with Joseph in prison? However, it is prison that sets him up for his rise, for here he meets important officials who can help him.

Genesis 40 also has theological import. God is with Joseph and saves him, although there is nothing miraculous or even supernatural in the chapter. God saves Joseph by helping him turn into the sort of person whose resourcefulness finds a way through difficulty. If this story seems to lack the transcendent, one is nevertheless reminded that Joseph transcends his dismal circumstances. In Joseph's day that is how transcendence manifests itself. Further, Joseph is forgotten in this chapter. This is the reverse of the experience of Noah and Rachel, both of whom were remembered and so brought out of seeming death to life. But just because the royal official forgot Joseph does not mean that God had. Behind the natural, in the stories of this generation, God is always working toward the fulfillment of his plan.

The beginning of this story neatly overlaps with the end of the one that precedes and has a plot that can be described in this manner. It has a tripartite structure, similar to the preceding scene.

	Exposition: 39:20-23
Joseph in the king's jailhouse	Inciting moment: 40:1
	Development: 40:2-8a
The interpretation	Turning point: 40:8b
	Resolution: 40:9-22
Joseph (still) in the king's jailhouse	Conclusion: 40:23

In Genesis 41:46, when Joseph enters the service of the pharaoh, he is said to be thirty years old. Since that happens two years after the events described in this chapter we know that he is twenty-eight years old at this point and has been a slave for eleven years; we do not know how long he has been in prison. During that time he has risen in the esteem of those in charge of the prison's administration for the same reason that enabled him to shine in Potiphar's household: YHWH is still with him.

Joseph, who has become something like a trusty in modern prison life, is eventually given special charge of two important prisoners, the pharaoh's chief cupbearer and chief baker, who have fallen seriously out of favor. One should not think of these men as menial workers; rather they were highly placed officials responsible for feeding the king's large household. As such they had ready access to him, were responsible for nothing untoward coming to him in his food, and were people whose favor would have been eagerly curried by those desiring a word to be placed in the king's ear. When they arrived in prison—perhaps to emerge once again in favor, given the vagaries of royal temperaments—the prison authorities wanted them to receive prime treatment. Joseph, capable in all things, seemed the man for the job.

In prison they each have dreams that seem to them inexplicable but at the same time portentous, since they are so similar and they occur at the same time. Lacking the means to interpret them, they fret and worry. In a nice bit of shifting the reader's point of view, in 40:6 we see—by means of the Hebrew word *hinnām*, which shifts us into seeing what Joseph sees—that their faces are troubled. They explain their situation. Joseph replies that the decoding of dreams belongs to God. One might think that this is a rhetorical shrug on Joseph's part, as though he wants to disclaim any involvement with dangerous people and their dangerous dreams, and is saying, more or less, "Sorry that I can't help, but dreams are understood only by God." After all, in Genesis 37 his family interpreted his dreams, not he; since they got him in such trouble then, one could well understand a certain hesitancy now. That is not the case, though. As soon as he says that the interpretation of dreams is a divine capacity, he asks his fellow prisoners to recount their dreams to him. So the story takes a particular direction, and its turning point is reached. Somehow what happens from now on will flow from Joseph's offer. Readers should note that this is yet another in the series of real transformations on Joseph's part. The selfish and immature adolescent has become a sober young man. At the same time, the one who did not understand dreams now understands them. No supernatural intervention has occurred to effect these changes nor would one expect such an event in the time of the fourth generation.

Rather, it is life itself—always purposefully guided and directed by YHWH—that is changing Joseph.

The dreams are straightforward, aside from the notion that the number three refers to the passage of three days. Joseph plays on a common Hebrew idiom—"to lift up the head"—in his interpretation. Alter explains clearly:

> To lift up someone's head, in administrative and royal contexts, means to single out (as in a census), to invite, to grant favor or extend reconciliation (as when a monarch lifts up with a gesture the downcast head of a contrite subject).[44]

At least that is what it means for the cupbearer. In three days he will be restored to his old position and will once again be pouring wine for the king. The other meaning of the idiom comes to the fore in Joseph's reading of the next dream. The baker's head too will be lifted up, from off his shoulders and impaled.[45] So we, as readers, appreciate Joseph's skill and wonder which of these meanings will be applied to him, for as yet his own fate is entirely unclear as he languishes in prison.

Joseph is clearly worried, too, and attempts to do a bit of networking with the cupbearer. Recalling the cistern into which his brothers threw him, he explains that he is innocent of any wrongdoing but has once again been cast into the pit. He asks, by way of recompense for his prophecy of restoration, only that the cupbearer remember him and bring him "out of this house" (Gen 40:14; cf. Exod 20:2).

Both dreams come true; the cupbearer's head is lifted up and the baker's head is lifted off. We expect that gratitude will cause the cupbearer to remember the one who foretold the future with such accuracy and possessed the divine gift of interpretation. Yet memory fails the cupbearer, at least for a time, and Joseph continues to molder forgotten by all—or so it would seem—in the jailhouse. More dreams will be needed before Joseph can don yet another identity.

Reclothed in a new identity (40:23–41:57). As he did in the previous scene, the narrator uses the conclusion of the preceding scene as the exposition of the new one. Forgotten by the cupbearer, Joseph is still languishing in jail two years later, when the story picks up again. During those two years, we may surmise, Joseph was still en-

---

[44] Alter, *Genesis*, 231.
[45] Ibid.

joying the trust of his jailers, still being effective, but still—however favored by YHWH—a nonentity in the consciousness of the wider Egyptian society.

The end of the passage—and the end of this section of the story of the fourth generation that focuses on the growth and maturation of Joseph—is clearly marked in Genesis 42:1 when the point of view shifts back to Jacob in Canaan and we rejoin the rest of the family there. Given its length, one might well expect that the remainder of this chapter is similarly complicated, and it is. It will be noted right away that the development is divided into two parts. The first phase is the dreams of Pharaoh and his attempts to decipher them prior to the involvement of Joseph. The second phase is that period during which Joseph is involved and offers a reading. He is brought into the story by the memory of the cupbearer in the inciting moment, and the story moves on from there. The purely narrative section ends at v. 45, to be followed by what I call a concluding report. This fills us in on what happened after Joseph's elevation, although it does so without resort to narrative devices.

> Development [first phase]: 41:1-8
> Inciting moment: 41:9-13
> Development [second phase]: 41:14-36
> Turning point: 41:37
> Resolution: 41:38-45
> Concluding report: 41:46-57
> > Joseph went out to Egypt: 41:46-49
> > Joseph's sons: 41:50-52
> > All the world came to Joseph: 41:53-57

The dull passage of tedious time is hinted at in the opening words of the chapter: *wayhî miqqēṣ šĕnātayim yāmîm*; literally, "and at the end of two years of days" (AT). This is translated in the NRSV as "After two whole years . . . ," a perfectly reasonable way to render the Hebrew into English, but the addition in Hebrew of the unnecessary "of days" seems to hint at the long dragging out of years of tedious days. At the end of this period, and after Joseph's dull sojourn is hinted at, we are suddenly moved to an entirely different scene. Not only are we at court, we are immediately moved—by the repeated use of *hinnēh*—into Pharaoh's very mind to experience his dreams with him. Compare the NRSV and the older RSV translations of this—at least for Joseph—crucial passage.

RSV [altered]	NRSV
[41:1]After two whole years, Pharaoh dreamed, and **behold**,[46] he was standing by the Nile,	[41:1]After two whole years, Pharaoh dreamed that he was standing by the Nile,
[2]and **behold**, there came up out of the Nile seven cows sleek and fat, and they fed in the reed grass.	[2]and there came up out of the Nile seven sleek and fat cows, and they grazed in the reed grass.
[3]And **behold**, seven other cows, gaunt and thin, came up out of the Nile after them, and stood by the other cows on the bank of the Nile.	[3]Then seven other cows, ugly and thin, came up out of the Nile after them, and stood by the other cows on the bank of the Nile.
[4]And the gaunt and thin cows ate up the seven sleek and fat cows. And Pharaoh awoke.	[4]The ugly and thin cows ate up the seven sleek and fat cows. And Pharaoh awoke.
[5]And he fell asleep and dreamed a second time; and **behold**, seven ears of grain, plump and good, were growing on one stalk.	[5]Then he fell asleep and dreamed a second time; seven ears of grain, plump and good, were growing on one stalk.
[6]And **behold**, after them sprouted seven ears, thin and blighted by the east wind.	[6]Then seven ears, thin and blighted by the east wind, sprouted after them.
[7]And the thin ears swallowed up the seven plump and full ears. And Pharaoh awoke, and **behold**, it was a dream.	[7]The thin ears swallowed up the seven plump and full ears. Pharaoh awoke, and it was a dream.

The two are nearly identical, differing only in some minor choices of vocabulary (e.g., "fed" instead of "grazed" in v. 2), except for the six-fold repetition of "behold" (vv. 1, 2, 3, 5, 6, 7) in the RSV. The effect of the multiple repetitions of "behold" is important, especially if we can imagine ourselves in the mind of Pharaoh, seeing what he sees and sharing his horror at the unfolding scene. To imagine the sequence as it might appear in film is useful. He dreams and suddenly sees himself

---

[46] Even the RSV omits this first use of "behold," which is present in the original, so I have restored it.

standing on the banks of the Nile.[47] Since it is the Nile that gives life to Egypt, it is no surprise that a dream about a future threat to the life of Egypt should take place there. In his dream he—and we as well—sees seven fine, fat cows come out of the Nile and graze. Then his attention is captured—as is ours—by the appearance of seven skeletally thin cows. The second set of cows does not graze but simply stands there for a time. Tension rises in the dream, and in the dreamer, and in the reader, until all of a sudden the second seven fall upon and devour the first. We can almost feel the king's pulse racing as he starts in horror, suddenly awakened from his nightmare. Even if he does not understand it, he can sense that it bodes ill for Egypt.

He falls asleep again and dreams. Once more we watch with him as seven ears of wheat sprout only to be followed—we look on in horror too—by seven heat-blasted ears that devour the first. Again Pharaoh wakes—and again we share his reaction—as he looks around, finds himself in a familiar setting and realizes that it was "only" a dream. The repeated use of "behold" shifts the point of view and allows us entrée to Pharaoh's emotional and physical reactions to the nightmares he has seen but cannot comprehend. The typically laconic Hebrew says only that "his spirit was disturbed" (41:8), but we can imagine how confused and upset he was as he tried to figure out what, if anything, these strange dreams might mean for him and the land he ruled.

He calls upon his experts for advice, but none is forthcoming. This seems surprising since the dreams are, like the others in the story, fairly transparent. Rashi wisely reads between the lines and says:

> They (the magicians) did interpret them, but not (satisfactorily) for Pharaoh. For their voice did not enter his ears and he had no ease of mind by their interpretations. For they said "Seven daughters will you beget and seven daughters will you bury."[48]

In other words, they told him something that, while upsetting in itself, simply did not match the feeling of dread that the dreams had aroused in him. At this point the story seems to have reached an impasse,

---

[47] Robert Alter points out that the Egyptian flavor of the chapter is heightened by the inclusion of a series of words that the Hebrew language borrowed from Egyptian: the Nile (*yĕʾōr*), soothsayers (*ḥarṭummîm*), rushes (*ʾāḥû*; translated "reed grass" in the RSV and NRSV), ring (*ṭabbaʿt*), and fine linen (*šēš*). See Alter, *Genesis*, 234.

[48] Rashi, *Pentateuch*, 405. The words for both "cow" and "ear of grain" are feminine in gender in Hebrew. Rashi suggests that the soothsayers focused on the feminine gender and saw both cows and ears of grain as symbols for daughters. This led them to the idea that seven daughters would be born but would also die.

and there is nowhere for it to go unless some new element is added. This comes from the cupbearer, who suddenly recalls his own dream while in prison and the debt of gratitude he owes to the young man who interpreted it for him correctly. Joseph, who had been forgotten, is now remembered. Since this gives the rest of the story an impetus, we call this the inciting moment.

Pharaoh summons Joseph and, once again, he is brought out of a pit to face an unknown future. Once again he changes his appearance[49] to accord with a changed status and to appear presentable in Pharaoh's court.

The second phase of the story's development begins as Pharaoh recounts his dreams to Joseph. Once again Joseph disclaims the ability to interpret dreams, saying that is the task of God and Joseph is simply an intermediary. Nevertheless, Pharaoh tells his story once more. In recounting his first dream he uses the "behold"[50] to show that he can still see what so horrified him. But he does not merely repeat his dream, because he comments that in all the land of Egypt he has never seen anything as repulsive as the second set of cows, and he describes how they swallow the first set but remain as gaunt and disgusting as before. His comment is more vivid than the narrator's was, and we can well understand his horror.[51] Too, by using the phrase "in all the land of Egypt," he

---

[49] He was given the ornamented tunic and had it removed. He must have been dressed as a slave in Potiphar's house but that garment was lost as well. This then marks his third, but not final, change in appearance. When a garment is taken from him, his fate is heading downwards. When he is given a new garment his fate is ascending. One might well imagine that after years in prison Joseph might require more than a little scrubbing up before he is presentable to a king. However, he also had to shave because Egyptians were clean shaven; again in accord with Egyptian custom, he may for the same reason have shaven his head as well or at least cut his hair very short.

[50] Once again, the NRSV fails to translate the "beholds" that Pharaoh uses in recounting his dreams. In using them even in retelling, the text not only invites us to see and share again what we have already seen and shared but to realize that, for Pharaoh, the experience was so vivid that he can still see the dreams even as he tells them.

More literally, vv. 18ff reads: "And Pharaoh said to Joseph, 'In my dream, behold, I'm standing on the shore of the Nile and, behold, seven cows that are fat of flesh and fair of form are coming up out of the river and they graze in the rushes. And, behold, another seven cows are coming after them [AT] wretched and exceedingly ill of form and lank of flesh'" (Fox, *Moses*, 194).

[51] In part his description differs because of his use of the word *raqqôt*, which means something like gaunt or skeletal, whereas the narrator had used the word *daqqôt*, which means thin. Unless Pharaoh simply wanted to use a stronger word, the difference might stem from a scribal mistake since the former word begins with the letter "r" (ר) and the latter begins with the letter "d" (ד); the two are so similar that they can be easily confused.

hints at the measures Joseph will take, which will affect the whole land.[52] He retells the dream about the ears of grain in similar fashion and explains that no one has been able to interpret the dreams for him. Joseph's interpretation is immediate and is followed by a plan of action. The latter was not asked for, but Joseph doubtless figures that he should seize this unexpected opportunity, since there is no way of knowing whether another will ever present itself. Actually, he would have been helped in his understanding of the dreams insofar as they made use of a typical ancient Near Eastern motif, as Nahum Sarna points out.

A very common motif in ancient Near Eastern literature is the seven-year cycle during which nature is dormant and unproductive and famine stalks the land. In unraveling the symbolism of Pharaoh's dream Joseph finds a premonition of just such a seven-year famine. A late Egyptian text dealing with the reign of King Djoser (ca. twenty-eighth century B.C.E.) well illustrates the setting. It reads:

> I was in distress on the Great Throne, and those who are in the palace were in heart's affliction from a very great evil, since the Nile had not come in my time for a space of seven years. Grain was scant, fruits were dried up, and everything which they eat was short.[53]

In vv. 26ff the phrase "seven-year" and "seven years of famine" are repeated over and over, such that it appears to be the key Joseph uses to decipher the dreams. He recognizes that both dreams carry the same meaning and that its doubling means that the events foretold are certain and irrevocable and cannot be long in the future.

His suggestions follow, although unasked for. His first suggestion is that Pharaoh find a "discerning and wise man" (ʾîš nābôn wĕḥākām) and place him over the land of Egypt with special responsibility for famine preparation. Since we have seen that Joseph has proven to be just such a person twice—in Potiphar's house as well as in prison—his candidacy immediately suggests itself to us readers. However, that a recently imprisoned slave should be given such status might not seem entirely self-evident to the king of Egypt, no matter how discerning of dreams the slave might be. This person should ḥimmēš the land of Egypt. Sadly the meaning of this crucial verb is not clear. It might be related to the word for the number five in Hebrew (ḥāmēš). The NRSV adopts this suggestion and understands it to refer to a twenty-percent tax on produce

---

[52] Cf. Alter, *Genesis*, 237.

[53] Nahum Sarna, *Understanding Genesis: The Heritage of Biblical Israel* (New York: Schocken, 1966) 219.

in the years leading up to the crisis; hence its translation that overseers appointed by the crisis leader take "take one-fifth of the produce of the land of Egypt during the seven plenteous years." Others suggest that the land should be divided into five parts for administrative purposes in the build-up to the famine[54] or that the land be put on quasi-military footing to aid preparations.[55] All of this will be overseen under Pharaoh's authority, but one person should be given delegated authority to focus on this task so that it might be well carried out.

It is only now that we reach the turning point of the story. Pharaoh, or his jealous advisors, might react in any fashion to this speech. The magicians might dispute the interpretation of an interloper. Senior advisors of the king, intimately familiar with the administration of the vast enterprise that was Egypt at this time, might well have other ideas besides a twenty-percent tax and regional collection centers. Pharaoh might simply dismiss Joseph with thanks and send him back to prison. So what will happen? For on his decision rests not only Joseph's fate but also the fate of the entire chosen family.

Pharaoh is pleased not only with the interpretation but with the man, for God (or "the gods," for the same Hebrew word is used for both) is/are clearly active in him. So Joseph is selected for the position, and once again his career is in the ascendancy. Just as Potiphar trusted him with everything in his house, so Pharaoh will trust him with everything in the realm. Once again, to the speechless Joseph, Pharaoh says that he is placed over the whole land of Egypt. Signs of office and privilege follow, a ring, a gold collar, and fine linen garments. He is allowed a fine chariot, with a herald to cry out before him.[56] This is all promulgated with an official decree in which Joseph's authority is spelled out—"I am Pharaoh, and without your consent no one shall lift up hand or foot in all the land of Egypt" (41:44). Finally he is given an Egyptian name, Zaphenath-paneah,[57] and a wife from a prestigious Egyptian family. Thus Egyptianized, Joseph will be acceptable in his role as authority over the whole land of Egypt.

The story of Joseph's descent and ascent ends at this point. He is now a thoroughly transformed, Egyptianized adult. His brothers meant to kill him, even if indirectly, but he just would not die. Because God

---

[54] Fox, *Moses*, 195; Friedman, *Torah*, 136.

[55] Alter proposes the translation "mustered" (*Genesis*, 239).

[56] The NRSV's "Bow the knee!" (41:43) is as good a suggestion as any for the obscure Hebrew *ʾabrēk*. Although its meaning is unknown it seems to be related to the word for knee.

[57] Which apparently means "God speaks, he lives." See Alter, *Genesis*, 241.

was with him, the experiences he underwent served only to make him better than he was. The new name that Jacob received twice at the hand of God was a sign of non-transformation; he was the one who fought with God and man and was a lame human being as a result. Joseph's name, given at the hand of Pharaoh in this new world where God does not personally intervene but nonetheless directs events, is a sign of true transformation. God does speak, and God does live, even when the opposite seems to be the case and where no miracle can be seen. The proof is Joseph.

The chapter ends with a brief recapitulation of events. As seen above, these last verses, Genesis 41:46-57, fall into three sections (Joseph went out to Egypt, 41:46-49; Joseph's sons, 41:50-52; all the world came to Joseph, 41:53-57), which show in the first place that he carried out his plans, and his predictions came to pass.[58] All the world came to Egypt because in all of Egypt there was food to be had. Joseph is indeed the wise and discerning man who was needed. But in the middle of this successful career we learn one more piece of information, that he had two sons with his wife. That his history was not purged from his mind is evident in the name he gave them. In the name Manasseh we hear him say that he has forgotten everything, and in the name Ephraim we hear that he has been fruitful. While the latter is true enough we can justifiably doubt the former. So this dry report raises questions in our mind that the next story will answer. Since all the world is hungry, all the world will come to Egypt. Among them will be his brothers who must undergo their own descent and ascent. It is that stage of the family's development to which we now turn.

B'. 42:1–47:27: THE DESCENT AND ASCENT OF THE BROTHERS

In her recent novel *We Were the Mulvaneys*, Joyce Carol Oates writes, "What is a family, after all, except memories?—haphazard and precious as the contents of a catchall drawer in the kitchen. . . ."[59]

This is by far the longest and most complex single bloc of narrative that we encounter in the whole book. In it many of the principal themes and conflicts of the book reach their conclusion and resolution. In

---

[58] Although our treatment of this section is quite brief, Jerome T. Walsh demonstrates convincingly that they possess an extremely intricate structure. While it is too complex to reproduce here, those interested should study his treatment in *Style and Structure in Biblical Hebrew Narrative* (Collegeville: The Liturgical Press, 2001) 169–72.

[59] Joyce Carol Oates, *We Were the Mulvaneys* (London: Fourth Estate, 2001) 4.

many ways the entire book of Genesis is about family, most particularly the dysfunctions of the particular family chosen by God to be the bearers of blessing for the world, but in this family we see reflected the disorders and dysfunctions of all of our own families, whether those into which we were born or those we have chosen for ourselves as we moved through life. In this section, as the brothers of Joseph descend to Egypt and ascend back to Canaan over and over, this theme of family reaches a final resolution in the reconciliation that follows upon confession. What it means to be a brother is explored here, as is the nature of fatherhood. And this particular assemblage of men cannot move forward and live until they remember what they did to Joseph—and not at all incidentally to Tamar as well—and come to terms with it.

This coming to terms with the past will not be simple for them, and the structure of this section of the book is similarly complicated. I have divided the section into seven episodes, each of which corresponds to a journey down to Egypt or up to Canaan. The various episodes are themselves, with one exception, further subdivided into constituent scenes. The scenic division is based on movement of the characters from one place to another or on entry or departure of characters from the scene. The seventh episode is also interrupted by a genealogical note (46:8-27) that helps the reader understand more precisely who went down to Egypt. Finally, the entire section is brought to an end with three conclusions. The first and second shift point of view so that we readers can discover the overall condition of the family of Jacob and the people of the land during the time of famine. The third, which brings the section to its end, reiterates what we need to know about Jacob's family and in so doing firmly fixes our interest point of view on Jacob and his family.

> Episode one: the first journey down to Egypt: 42:1-26
> Scene A: 42:1-5
> Scene B: 42:6-17
> Scene C: 42:18-26
> Episode two: the first journey up to Canaan: 42:27-38
> Scene A: 42:27-28
> Scene B: 42:29-38
> Episode three: the second journey down to Egypt: 43:1–44:2
> Scene A: 43:1-15a
> Scene B: 43:15b-23
> Scene C: 43:24-29
> Scene D: 43:30
> Scene E: 43:31–44:2

Episode four: the second journey up to Canaan: 44:3-13a
    Scene A: 44:3-5
    Scene B: 44:6-13a
Episode five: the third journey down to Egypt: 44:13b–45:24
    Scene A: 44:13b–45:15
    Scene B: 45:16-21a
    Scene C: 45:21b-24
Episode six: the third journey up to Canaan: 45:25-28
Episode seven: the fourth journey down to Egypt: 46:1–47:27
    Scene A: 46:1-4
    Scene B: 46:5-7
    Genealogy: 46:8-27
    Scene C: 46:28-34
    Scene D: 47:1
    Scene E: 47:2-6
    Scene F: 47:7-10
    Concluding report A: the settlement of the family in Egypt: 47:11-12
    Concluding report B: the condition of the rest of the people and of the land of Egypt: 47:13-26
    Overall conclusion: Israel settled in Egypt: 47:27

The scene shifts back to Canaan at the beginning of Genesis 42, a place we have not seen for many years now, in the narrative world created in the latter part of Genesis. Caught up in the preparations for the oncoming famine Joseph may very well have forgotten those early years of his life; after all he is settled now, with a family and great responsibilities. If we never entirely forget the pains that we have suffered in our lives, we are able to put them aside much of the time and live as though the person to whom they happened is a person other than the one we are now. Perhaps that is what Zaphenath-paneah had done—after all he named one of his sons something like "God has allowed me to forget"—immersing himself in family and work. But "what is a family after all except memories?"—and Joseph, and all the rest, must remember before they can survive.

Episode one: the first journey down to Egypt (42:1-26). The words "brother" and "recognition" dominate the first episode, the tension being on who recognizes and who fails to recognize. The center of the twenty-six verse episode is 42:13, which, wittingly or unwittingly on the part of our author, sums up the entire piece. As the ten sons of Jacob are led before Joseph they—apparently all speaking with one voice—

say "We, your servants, are twelve brothers, the sons of a certain man in the land of Canaan; the youngest, however, is now with our father, and one is no more." They speak in the present tense, asserting that they are twelve, not that they were twelve. Little do they know that they are finally telling the truth—the last time they spoke as a group of brothers was in 37:32, when they lied—and that the missing twelfth brother is standing before them. They are also telling the truth in naming themselves his servants. In the remainder of the section they will come to the place where they can say the same things wittingly.

This episode falls neatly into three scenes. In the first Jacob addresses his sons with enigmatic words, asking them why they are simply sitting looking at each other. It is as though some sort of emotional inertia has caused them to freeze in position, unable to move because they do not know what the others might do in their absence. Since we are unaware of what they have been doing in the intervening years, with the exception of Judah, who will emerge as their spokesman and who will use what he has learned from his relationship to Tamar to their advantage, the reader almost gets the impression that they have not moved since the end of Genesis 37 and are frozen in time around the bloodied tunic of their brother.

They do not answer when Jacob speaks to them, so he speaks again. He, at any rate, is aware of his surroundings and tells his sons to go down to Egypt to get some grain. So they do, but the narrator carefully directs our point of view in calling them "the ten brothers of Joseph" (Gen 42:3). Benjamin, however, remains at home lest danger strike him. Does Jacob not trust the ten to take care of their youngest brother?

The scene shifts to Egypt and the brothers are brought before Joseph. They bow before him—so the childhood dream comes true—but do not recognize in the haughty (to say nothing of clean-shaven) Egyptian adult their long-missing little brother. Joseph recognizes them but does not make himself known to them.[60] Joseph is no longer at his brothers' mercy, but it is not yet clear whether he wants either to make himself known to them or, without their knowing it, somehow to punish them. Along with recognition comes memory (42:9), both of the dreams and

---

[60] Note that the verbs "recognized" (*wayyakkirēm*) and "treated them like strangers" (*wayyitnakkēr*) in 42:7 ("When Joseph saw his brothers, he recognized them, but he treated them like strangers . . .") both come from the same root in Hebrew (*nkr*). Thus the theme of recognition, seen in Genesis 37 when Jacob was asked to "recognize" Joseph's ornamented coat and in Genesis 38 when Judah was asked to "recognize" the evidence that proved he had been with Tamar, returns to the center of the story.

of their cruelty to him, so he decides to test them. But the tests he gives the brothers reveal as much about Joseph as they do about his siblings, for we will discover that he and they have both been scarred for decades by their anger of long ago.

Joseph accuses the brothers of being spies and they reply in the strangest manner. One cannot immediately see how their protestation that they are sons of a man in Canaan, formerly twelve in number but now eleven, has any bearing at all on the accusation they face. It seems that the guilt they bear lies so close to the surface of their conscious- ness that it has become the prism through which all of their experience is viewed, so a connection that seems incongruous to outsiders seems to them clear and cogent. "Spies? Not us, we are twelve brothers al- though one is missing." The first part seems to lead naturally to the second in their minds.[61] That this all lies close to the surface is also in- dicated by the three staccato sentences with which they stutter their in- nocence in 42:11: "We are all sons of one man; we are honest men; your servants have never been spies."

Joseph demands living proof of the truth of their story; their youngest brother must be brought to him. One can imagine that Joseph is torn between a desire to plan something carefully—he has, after all, been taken by surprise and is struggling to hold himself together, as will later become evident—and a desire for news about his beloved father Jacob and his full brother Benjamin.

We now arrive at the final scene of the first episode. Three days have passed, enough time for them to stew, for anger and divisions to arise— and the same amount of time Abraham had to ponder the implications of the test he was to undergo in Genesis 22. In this final scene the narra- tor gives us important information that we have not had before now, that Joseph is speaking to them through an interpreter (42:23) and that Joseph pleaded with them when they sold him into slavery (42:21).

Joseph presents the same challenge to them that he had posed three days earlier: they must bring their youngest brother to him. Until they do, one of their number will remain as a hostage. Reuben—the el- dest, the brother who lay with his father's concubine and the brother

---

[61] It should be said that Joseph's accusation that they were spies was not entirely absurd. The land bridge that connects Egypt to Canaan was Egypt's most vulner- able border. During a time of regional crisis, when many were seeking opportuni- ties for economic migration due to widespread famine, it was entirely reasonable to fear that foreigners like Joseph's brothers would look for weaknesses (what is called its "nakedness" in Gen 42:9) in Egypt's defenses so that they might steal into that more prosperous land and take advantage of the wealth they found there.

who had tried to save Joseph—accuses the others of reaping what they sowed so long before. Joseph nearly loses his composure but turns away lest his tears[62] be seen. Then he selects Simeon—the second eldest—as the hostage. Finally he gives them the grain they wanted, provisions for the journey and—unbeknownst to them—returns their money. So weighed down in many more ways than they know, they depart.

Episode two: the first journey up to Canaan (42:27-38). So we reach the second episode, which recounts what happened as they journeyed back up to Canaan. It consists of two scenes, which are distinguished by locale; the first takes place on the journey back and the second tells us what happened immediately upon their return.

In the first scene we are with the brothers during the course of the journey. This is striking because we know that the recounting of events that take place during a journey is extremely rare in Hebrew narrative. One of their number opens his sack and discovers that his money has been replaced. We will learn in 43:21 that all of the brothers follow suit, although they will play it out differently for their father in Scene B of this episode. The version of 43:21 makes more psychological sense, since we can imagine neither that their packs went unopened during a journal of several days nor that the panic they experienced when one brother found the money would not drive the others to see if they had been similarly treated. So this first scene allows us not to be surprised when they come before Jacob and give him a highly edited version of events and stage a surprise discovery for him. The brothers will fail this first stage of the test. They still lie and are willing to tear the family asunder to cover up their lies.

The scene also creates a real irony in that the brothers bewail what God has done to them. In fact it is Joseph who has done this, but the brothers have bowed down to him as before God, and he is playing the role of the divinely omniscient one and placer of tests in this tale. This will later fit into the theme of humanity's disposal of the divine will; in this time, when divine manifestations in the world seem to have ceased, what God wants to happen, people cause to come about.

The second scene places them back at home in Canaan and apparently takes place immediately upon their return. Given the urgency of their errand one can readily imagine that Jacob would be waiting impatiently for the delivery of the food they would bring. The food

---

[62] This is the first of three times that Joseph weeps, each instance becoming more intense and overwhelming for him.

delivery and the relief it means disappear however beneath the story they have to tell. We are surprised how heavily edited it is; there is no mention of their three-day stay in prison, nor of Simeon being led away in chains, nor that they—or at least one of them—discovered that the payment money had surreptitiously been returned. One suspects that they staged the discovery of the money to add further emotional tension to the situation and make their speedy return to Egypt all the more imperative. We are shifted to the brothers' point of view with the use in 42:35 of the particle *hinnēh* ("behold"), to which we have become accustomed. Here, however, it has the effect of emotionally distancing us readers from the brothers' plight because we sense, even if we do not yet know, that they are being dishonest about events. What else might we not know? In what other ways ought we to distrust them?

Verse 36 is a little masterpiece of characterization by speech, to which our attention is drawn by the unusual Hebrew syntax:[63]

> And their father Jacob said to them, "Me you have bereaved. Joseph is no more. And Simeon is no more. And you would now take Benjamin. To me has this all happened!"

What is remarkable about the speech is Jacob's self-absorption, with "me" at the beginning. He seems to assume the worst, that neither of the two missing sons is still alive. Reuben blurts out the most absurd of offers, that the lives of his two sons may be taken should Benjamin not be returned. It is so foolish that Jacob does not even bother to acknowledge it even to refuse it but bluntly says that Benjamin will not go. Still he tells us as much about himself as he does about the situation when he says that Benjamin is all he has left (42:38), apparently ignoring the existence of his numerous other offspring and putting them in their (non-)place as far as he is concerned emotionally. So the second episode ends with Jacob bewailing his fate and the possibility of Sheol for him should he lose another son. Jacob the untransformed is as narrowly focused upon his own benefit as he was when first he bought Esau's birthright. Jacob's lack of real awareness of the other highlights for us readers Joseph's intense consciousness of the other and his manipulation of events to create a desired end. What is for Jacob a haphazard world trying to hurt him is for Joseph a place

---

[63] An accusative pronoun precedes the verb instead of the more usual pattern of an accusative suffix appended to the verb. See Alter, *Genesis*, 250.

to carefully test his brothers and create a place for him and his family to thrive. Even in his pain Joseph sees the other, and Jacob feels only for himself.

Episode three: the second journey down to Egypt (43:1–44:2). This brings us to the third episode in this sequence. It is the longest and serves to raise tension even higher than it has been so far. It consists of five scenes, again separated from each other by location and/or change in time.

The intractable severity of the famine causes the forbidden subject of going down to Egypt to recur. Note that Jacob introduces the topic of once more going down to Egypt for food not because of his anxiety over the fate of Simeon, who is, we must remember although the narrator neglects to remind us, still in Egyptian custody. In this way the self-absorption of Jacob, with which the last episode concluded, is once again introduced to the story. This remains the dominant theme of this first scene of the episode. So, although time had evidently passed, we are still somehow in the same position. Judah replies bluntly to his father's query saying that they received strict orders from "the man"—a term that serves to underline that Joseph remains known to them only as an anonymous and probably worryingly haughty Egyptian official—not to return unless their youngest brother accompanied them. Jacob, as one might expect, turns the crisis into an attack on himself when he asks why Judah treated him so badly as to tell the Egyptians that Jacob had another son. Note once more the self-absorption that is most cripplingly characteristic of him. Judah does not rise to this but offers to be personally responsible for Benjamin's well being with a phrase that indicates that his words have the force of a legally binding oath. That he is nonetheless angry is evident from his final words in 43:10; they could have been there and back twice if Jacob had not so maddeningly dithered.

Jacob gives in. The brothers are to take a list of items that overlaps in part with the trade goods of the caravan that took Joseph to Egypt (cf. 37:25) but is still grander. Thus the brothers unwittingly make restitution. They take twice—or three times[64]—the money they took the first time and their brother. Jacob indicates that he is resigned to further bereavement if need be, perhaps moved by Judah's impli-

---

[64] It is not entirely clear whether they were to take twice the original sum plus the original money (thus three times the original amount) or the original sum plus an equal amount (thus twice the original amount). The increased outlay might have allowed them to buy more food or might have been an attempt to account for price rises during their absence.

cation that the youngsters of the clan would die unless food were found soon.

The second scene of the episode begins with the brothers already in Egypt. With the typical biblical disinterest in what happens on a journey, the brothers leave Canaan and arrive in Egypt in a single sentence. They are brought before Joseph, who seems not to speak directly to them at all, simply instructing his steward to bring "the men" to his house and to prepare a meal that he will share with "the men." The brothers, so carefully identified until this point either as Joseph's brothers or the sons of Israel, are now simply "the men." Their identity has been taken from them for the duration of the test just as Joseph's identity had been taken from him. Both he, "the man," and they, "the men," will have to work out now slowly and carefully whether they will once again be brothers. The men are understandably afraid, not seeing why they—perfectly anonymous grain buyers among a multitude of such—should be singled out for a dinner in a noble house unless it is a trap related to the money they found in their sacks. They confess their quandary to the steward, who simply dismisses it and brings Simeon out to them.

Once again the location of the action changes, and we find ourselves in the second scene of the episode. The brothers are now in Joseph's house, entirely under his control. They prepare for their encounter, washing themselves and feeding their pack animals. However, the center of the scene is found in 43:26b, when the brothers bow to the ground before Joseph for the second time. The dream continues to be true. Joseph inquires after the health of their father and suddenly sees his brother Benjamin. He maintains his demeanor for a moment at least, speaking to him in courtly fashion as "my son."

The location, and so the scene, changes swiftly again as Joseph hurries from the room lest he be seen to be overcome with weeping. This is the shortest scene of the episode, thus drawing our attention in a special way. For the second time Joseph weeps, but this time he is more seriously overcome by the rush of fraternal love[65] he feels when he sees Benjamin, who is pointedly identified as "his brother." The distance at which the narrator is trying to hold the brothers by calling them "the men" is already breaking down, just as Joseph is.

---

[65] The word used, *raḥămāyw* (literally, "his mercy"), refers to an especially tender emotion felt by one person for another. See Hosea 1 and 2, where the root occurs repeatedly. It is rendered variously in the NRSV, as "Lo-ruhamah" (literally, "Not Loved"; 1:6, 8; 2:23 [MT 2:25]); "have pity" (1:6-7; 2:4, 23 [MT 2:6, 25]); "Ruhamah" (2:1 [MT 2:3]); "mercy" (2:19 [MT 2:21]).

Again there is a change of scene as Joseph, having gotten himself under control and washed his face, reemerges. The two parties, the Egyptians and "the Hebrews,"[66] eat separately.[67] This they would have expected, but two other things happen during the meal that must have been deeply disconcerting; they were seated in order of their age from eldest to youngest—how could the Egyptian know this and why would he care?—and while tidbits were sent to all, those sent to Benjamin were five times the size of the others'—what could that mean? Was Joseph trying to see whether this favoritism would arouse envy? Was this part of the test? The NRSV says that the party grew "merry," but in rather plainer English it is clear that Joseph got the men drunk. Then he laid out the next stage of testing.

Repeating the ruse of the first test but upping the ante, Joseph tells the steward to put their money in their sacks and to put his favorite cup into the sack of the youngest. What will the brothers make of this? How will they react? Will they sacrifice the younger for their own bene-fit? Joseph's plan is not entirely clear, but he does seem to want to con-fuse the brothers, trapping them in a web of things they cannot explain and from which they cannot escape, try as they will. Note that the only two names that appear in the scene are Joseph and Benjamin. The scene is set in Joseph's house (43:34), and the steward obeys Joseph's orders (44:2). All is under Joseph's control, then, and our focus is especially on Benjamin. So the third episode draws to a close.

Episode four: the second journey up to Canaan (44:3-13a). The fourth episode, which recounts the brothers' second journey back up to Canaan, is quite brief, consisting of only two scenes. The first is a conversation between Joseph and his steward. The second recounts that official's confrontation with the brothers in mid-journey and his demand that they return to face the threatened repercussions.

Joseph tells his steward to chase after "the men"—their identity is still known only to him and us readers—and gives him a script to fol-low. What he says will make clear to the men not only that the object is

---

[66] The word "Hebrew" is of uncertain origin, although it seems to be related to Apiru/Habiru, a word used throughout the ancient Near East to refer to a social class of displaced people similar to our contemporary concept of economic refugee. In the Hebrew Bible, the term "Hebrew" is usually found only in contexts where a non-Israelite is speaking about, or with, an Israelite. It seems, then, to be a term that Israelites did not generally use of themselves.

[67] All of the commentaries remark that this dietary and social segregation was standard in Egyptian life, since both these semi-nomadic foreigners and the lamb, which was a staple of their diet, were somehow unclean to Egyptians.

precious and of special value to Joseph but also that he has sources of information that are closed to the brothers.

Armed with his task, the steward sets out and immediately overtakes the brothers. He confronts them with their supposed crime, but they react with bluff confidence. They have, they say, proven themselves trustworthy, and they still are. So confident are they that they pronounce a death sentence on the supposed culprit and commit the survivors to voluntary slavery. This and the following verse form the turning point of this entire section; tension can go no higher than this. Either the cup will be found or will not be. Either the consequences they have called down upon themselves will be acted upon or they will not. At any rate, something must happen and does. The sacks are opened, the cup is found, and they tear their clothes in frustration, anger, and mourning. Note however that the steward's words are not a precise restatement of the brothers'. They offered death and slavery. Although the steward seems to agree, he really has a very different sentence in mind, one that the brothers might even find more difficult to accept. The guilty party will be enslaved, but the rest will be free. This means that the brothers will have to return to Jacob and confess the loss of his "other" son, an event none of them can face with equanimity.

Episode five: the third journey down to Egypt (44:13b–45:24). So we arrive at the fifth episode, wherein the brothers—for they are now once again identified as brothers—return to Joseph's house. I have titled this the "Third Journey Down to Egypt," but that is a bit of a misnomer since their journey is forestalled, and they never really leave Egypt and return to Canaan. Nonetheless they were on the road home, so emotionally this would be a new journey down to the house of the now dreaded lord. Readers must be aware that the brothers are now really trapped. They are afraid to go home because Benjamin will be missing, but they are equally afraid to return to "the man" because he has made clear to them that he is master of a situation that has become nightmarish for them in its inscrutability. They simply no longer have any idea what is happening to them. The episode is divided into three scenes by changes in time and/or locale.

The first scene (44:13b–45:15) is both the longest scene of the entire section and the one that constitutes its central event. It is here that the brothers, through Judah, who has become their spokesman, pass their test, thus changing from the sort of people who could sell their brother into slavery into the sort of people who would sacrifice themselves for another. It is also here that the central theological assertion of the stories about the fourth generation (and indeed the entire book) is articulated: God is able to use human actions to achieve divinely intended ends even if the human actions seem thoroughly evil (Gen 45:5). God, who has seemed absent for so long, is shown still to be savior even if the agency by which that salvation is effected is no longer theophany but apparently ordinary human deeds and misdeeds.

The first of the episode's scenes begins with the brothers returning to the city. Once again they are named "brothers" and no longer anonymous "men," because they have decided to confess, face the way in which they have failed to be brothers, and try to make peace with their past. In addition to the word "brother," the scene is dominated by the word "father," which is mentioned some fourteen times, so placing family right at the heart of this important moment in the narrative.

Right at the very beginning Judah is identified as spokesman. Reuben, Simeon, and Levi have disqualified themselves, the first by his taking the concubine of his father and the second and third by their association with the destruction of Shechem. Why Judah, though? Why not one of the others? Does the text hold any hints for us? An unusual grammatical move, the subtle nuance of which is difficult to convey in idiomatic English, also highlights Judah. In 44:14 the NRSV reads, "Judah and his brothers came to Joseph's house while he was still there; and they fell to the ground before him." This reflects a Hebrew original that begins, *wayyābōʾ yĕhûdâ wĕʾeḥāyw*. In this phrase the verb *wayyābōʾ* is singular, not plural. This indicates that Judah, the first noun to follow the verb, is the principal subject.[68] One might translate, "Judah (and his brothers) came . . ." or "Judah, along with his brothers, came. . . ." In a sense, Judah is the spokesman simply because the text points to him and tells us that he is.

From the viewpoint of later history one might also say that Judah represents the tribe of which David was a member, the dominant one among the southern tribes. As the eponymous ancestor of the tribe of kings, it was natural that Judah would prefigure those later realities. In the same line, Joseph might be read as representing the northern tribes (cf. Psalm 81, especially verse 5 for one example). So Judah and Joseph stand for the totality of the nation and the reconciliation effected here stands for the desired reconciliation of the nation at some later point in history after which it had really been torn asunder.

However, there is a very different and, I feel, more satisfactory way of understanding his prominence and his fitness to speak of memory and the need for reconciliation. I said at the beginning of my treatment of this final section of the book that it would be better to conceive of it as about the whole fourth generation than simply about Joseph, that if we call it the Joseph Story or the like then it becomes about him alone

---

[68] Alter, *Genesis*, 262.

and the rest appear as mere appendages. As the story about the time of the fourth generation, it begins by focusing on Joseph (Genesis 37) and Judah (Genesis 38), the two main protagonists. Both learn from and are transformed by their times of suffering—Joseph by his years of being a slave and a prisoner, Judah from his misdeed against Tamar. From that experience Judah learned the need to speak truthfully and to recognize that the past has power over us until we admit what happened and make peace with it. Since, as far as we know, the other brothers had not learned this, it is appropriate that Judah speak for all. He knows what needs to be said as no one else would.

So Judah steps forward to say what all of them are thinking and feeling. Joseph speaks first making clear that they should have realized that a man such as he would both have the tools for divination (like the cup) and be able to divine where it was when it had been stolen. In response Judah says that they have indeed been found with the cup and they have no exculpatory evidence, but as Judah speaks it becomes clear that he is speaking not only about the cup but some deeper guilt for which he (and they) have never atoned. Overwhelmed by guilt he volunteers all of them for slavery; after all they have already been virtual slaves to their misdeed for years. Joseph hears what he has to say and seemingly dismisses it. Only the one with the cup—Benjamin—will be enslaved. The others can go home in peace to their father—as they so blithely did once before. Will they tolerate another enslavement, another brother sacrificed to their convenience?

Judah steps up to the still unidentified Joseph and tells the entire family secret, saying out loud what he has remembered and lived with for so long. The key verse here is 44:20:

> And we said to my lord, "We have a father, an old man, and a young brother, the child of his old age. His brother is dead; he alone is left of his mother's children, and his father loves him."

Twenty years have passed since Joseph was sold into slavery, and Judah cannot imagine that that rather precious young man will have survived. He acknowledges that he took one of his father's favorite sons away from him and cannot do it again. He has reconciled himself to his father's preference for the sons of Rachel. He is willing to stay as a slave rather than hurt the father he so evidently loves, despite the fact that his father loves him less than he might. This is real transformation, and it is effected not by any supernatural phenomenon but simply by a human being accepting the reality of his lot in life and responsibility for the choices he has made. Jacob's name was changed to indicate that he had not really changed. He was and always would be

Israel, the one who contended with God and other people. Judah's name is not changed, but he has really changed, from the one who orients the world toward himself—for selfishness is the primal sin—to the one who acts for the benefit of others. The speech of Genesis 44:18-34 is, in all likelihood, the longest single speech in the entire book and probably the most important. It does not have the pyrotechnics of Genesis 22 or 32, but it seems to touch something more universal than either of those, for here is a test with which we can all identify. Would we do what Judah did? Would we realize that the love we possess, however far short it might fall of the love we would desire, is nevertheless a love that deserves to be honored? Would we give ourselves for another for the sake of that imperfect love? Would we accept responsibility and the need to change?

Now it is Joseph's turn to react. Quickly he sends everyone out of the room and for the third time breaks down and weeps. This time, the final and climactic time, he does so in his brothers' presence but he is so loud it can be heard outside of his presence chamber—and one can imagine that there were ears pressed to those doors trying to hear more of this extraordinary event. His first words were, "I am Joseph. Is my father still alive?"[69] One can readily understand that his brothers would be stunned, dumbstruck even, so he calls them closer and repeats himself. His use of ʾābî is worth a brief mention. It literally means "my father" but in biblical Hebrew has the sense almost of "Dad" in contemporary idiom. All of a sudden the haughty official is speaking their own language like the mother tongue it is, breaks into tears, and inquires after "Dad's" health. He even knows the whole gruesome story about having been sold into slavery. No impostor he.

He dismisses the brothers' fears and explains how he has come to understand what fate has done with him. God intended to create a safe haven for the chosen family during the famine of which God was already aware.[70] He needed someone like Joseph, who had the organizational skills and would become like a very father—i.e., accepted source of authority—to Pharaoh, to arrange things beforehand.

He harbors no anger at all and has no will for vengeance. He sends an official message to his father to come to Egypt without delay for the famine has years to run. He begins and ends with the need to hurry. Then the scene breaks into mutual hugs and tears, for the joy at seeing

---

[69] Five compact words in Hebrew: ʾănî yôsēp haʿôd ʾăbî ḥāy.

[70] The land of Goshen is in the Nile Delta where pastures were rich and lay close to Canaan.

a long lost brother and the sheer relief of no longer bearing the guilt of twenty years. In a very real sense they are now all set free from slavery.

In the next scene, we shift to the court of Pharaoh who has heard what has occurred. He reaffirms Joseph's orders, giving them binding legal sanction. The sons of Israel—for we are reminded that this is not simply a family but the seed of the nation of Israel—act obediently. In the final scene, they are well provisioned for their return journey to Canaan, but Benjamin is singled out for extraordinary attention. The final line of the episode is, unfortunately, problematic. The NRSV has "Do not quarrel along the way" (45:24). The Hebrew is *ʾal-tirgĕzû baddārek* and the difficulty lies in the verb *ʾal-tirgĕzû*. Robert Alter translates: "Do not be perturbed on the journey" and explains that the verb

> is occasionally used in contexts that associate it with anger . . . but the primary meaning of the verb is to quake or shake, either physically (as a mountain in an earthquake) or emotionally (as a person trembling with fear), and it is the antonym of being tranquil or at peace.[71]

Thus, rather than fearing that his brothers would, once away from his presence, fall into arguments and reproaches for the past, Joseph is simply telling them, in what might be more contemporary idiom, not to worry about anything. But they must have worried about their elderly father's reactions to news of this order—not only that Joseph was alive but also that his brothers had sold him into slavery twenty years earlier. Transformed they may be, but there is a great deal of truth telling that must yet take place. Joseph's admonition not to worry about anything must have been rather difficult to put into practice.

Episode six: the third journey up to Canaan (45:25-28). The most intense episode, and the central one, is followed by the shortest, so short in fact that it consists of only one scene. Its brevity indicates the desire of Jacob to be on the road immediately, reclaiming the son lost to him. He simply cannot bear to wait, and the text speeds us along, too. The key phrase here, right at the center of the scene, is *wayyāpog libbô*, translated in the NRSV as "He was stunned . . ." (Gen 45:26). The verb here is the important element; it means "to be feeble, numb or cold,"[72] and indicates to us readers that Jacob is utterly, utterly taken aback, that his heart skips a beat, and he is reduced to a state of shock. It is the most unexpected news possible, and he reacts both physically and emotionally. After he recovers, he stops the brothers' equally

---

[71] Alter, *Genesis*, 271.
[72] Holladay, s.v. פוג

astonished ramblings about their brother's success and power and says that he has to go there. This brings us to the seventh and final episode. But notice that even here Jacob manages to be self-absorbed. "My son . . . I must go . . . before I die" (Gen 45:28). There is no hint here that Jacob is even aware of the other sons standing before him, no wonder about how they are making sense of all of this, nor any query as to how Joseph can still be alive when his death was so reliably reported. Nor is there any question of whether they might or might not want to go to Egypt. This man to whom such extraordinary things happened is still the same as he was when he took Esau's birthright; what he wants is of paramount importance. Unlike his sons, he remains untransformed and of an older day. That he is a remnant of a bygone time is indicated in the way the seventh episode begins, with a vision.

Episode seven: the fourth journey down to Egypt (46:1–47:27).

> ". . . because nothing between human beings isn't uncomplicated and there's no way to speak of human beings without simplifying and misrepresenting them."[73]

Of course it is an error to speak of any person as not having changed throughout the course of a life, and Jacob too has changed: he fell in love with Rachel, he acted to protect others while he himself was in danger. But there is something about him that is fundamentally crippled, unable to move forward. This aspect of Jacob, that he is part of an old world that has inexorably changed around him, is indicated to us readers in the first scene of this last episode. For here we have another vision in a time when vision has grown rare, a narrative hinge between the time of the fourth generation and the times that preceded it. It is also a sign that, just as Abraham's worship marked the entry of the chosen family into the land designated as theirs, so now they are leaving the land for a lengthy sojourn elsewhere. Jacob pulls up the stakes of his tents and sets off.

At Beer Sheba he has a vision, the sort of religious experience a man of his generation could understand, which reaffirms the old and so often repeated promises first made to Abraham. More than reaffirmation, this is also a promise of presence and accompaniment not unlike that first heard by Jacob at Bethel (Genesis 28). This is certainly a bittersweet moment in the story's development; just as Jacob was homeless and fleeing then, he is homeless and fleeing now. Then it was the wrath of Esau he fled whereas now it is the famine. Then it was merely for

---

[73] Oates, *Mulvaneys*, 377.

twenty years, but now it will be for centuries. Even if he dies in the presence of his son Joseph, he will not return to the land alive. So sobered, they journey on. God will be with him, and the journey will bring a meeting with much joy, but in doing so they will leave much else behind. As Anatole France said:

> All changes, even the most longed for, are melancholy. For what we leave behind us is a part of ourselves. We must die to one life before we can enter another.

Accepting that a death to the time in Canaan is necessary for a new life with a reconciled family, Jacob sets out for the future.

The scene changes with the notice that they set off from Beer Sheba and that they had a great deal to bring with them. The time in Canaan has not been without profit of many kinds, nor the least of which is that the family has grown to great size. Just as they leave Canaan, a genealogy is inserted. While it is not necessary here to go through all of the names, several things should be noted. Jacob had become the father of numerous children and grandchildren, far more than the thirteen with whom we are otherwise familiar. The total of seventy, while arithmetically accurate, indicates also that the family was complete, had achieved a necessary fullness, and that everyone was there, the entire family gathered in Egypt.

Judah is dispatched to bring Joseph to meet the family in the third scene of the episode. Joseph's Egyptian-ness is shown to us by his use of a chariot, such wheeled vehicles being unknown in Canaan before the time of the Exodus. And his urgency is shown to us by his harnessing—"made ready" (Gen 46:29, NRSV)—the vehicle himself, although that was hardly likely given his exalted position. His reunion with his father is somehow muted, for although Joseph's hearty embrace and lengthy sobbing are noted, there is no reciprocal show of emotion on Jacob's part. We recall that at the death of Rachel, his beloved wife, there was also no show of emotion (35:19-20). For whatever reason— he had cried all he could, he was simply overwhelmed, it was almost impossible to connect the Egyptian official in chariot and gold collar with the boy in the ornamented coat—Jacob did not weep but declared himself ready to die.

Joseph's reaction too is somewhat disconcerting. He and his father do not withdraw to speak and become reacquainted. Rather, immediately, as though he too were somewhat surprised by the laconic and unemotional manner of Jacob's greeting, Joseph is once again all business. When questioned, they are to say that they are shepherds, that they make their living raising livestock and thus pose no threat to the

Egyptian state at all. On the contrary they are content to live simply and quietly in Goshen, on the fringes of the Egyptian scene. This will sound pleasing and acceptable to an Egyptian monarch all too worried, in all likelihood, about a flood of what we would call refugees or economic migrants into Egypt at this time of regional crisis.

In the next very brief scene, Joseph reports that his family has in fact arrived and has stayed in Goshen and so prepares for the next scene in which some representative members of the family are presented to the monarch. In the next scene Joseph brings some of his siblings[74] who would make a favorable impression upon his Egyptian master. As instructed by Joseph—their metaphorical bowing down now takes the form of real obedience—they explain that they are herdsmen by occupation. Again in obedience to Joseph's instructions they explain that they have no political interests or ambitions; they have come to be resident aliens in Pharaoh's land only because the famine is so severe in their homeland that there is no pasturage for their livestock (*lāgûr bāʾāreṣ bāʾnû*). Also as instructed, they ask permission to settle (*yēšĕbû-nāʾ*) in Goshen.

Pharaoh's reply is subtle and the MT of Genesis 47:5 is not, I think, as problematic as some commentaries suggest. Although he was addressed by the brothers, Pharaoh responds only to Joseph. We have already seen that the Egyptians—at least in the story world of Genesis 37–50—practiced a rigid social separation from foreigners. Pharaoh declines to speak, even through an interpreter, to these men who are, after all, not only foreign but from a social class very far removed from the rarefied strata of Egyptian society where Pharaoh makes his home. Rather he addresses them indirectly, through the mediation of Joseph.[75] But he has a point to make to Joseph as well, telling him, in essence, that his family is his responsibility. It is as though he said to Joseph, "Your father and your brothers have come to you, not to us . . . they are in your charge." Although he generously lays before them the

---

[74] The Hebrew of 47:2 (*ûmiqṣēh ʾeḥāyw*) is a bit unclear. It seems to mean, on the basis of a parallel usage in Judg 18:2 that they are they most capable, the pick of the lot. Similarly one must regard the number five as simply meaning "some." Alter and many other commentators point out that certain numbers are used repeatedly in this section: twelve brothers become eleven and once again twelve at the end, three pairs of dreams. Five is one-half of the number guilty of selling Joseph, it is also the number of Joseph's changes of garments. Benjamin received five times what the others received at Joseph's banquet and the Egyptians paid one-fifth of the crop as tax (*Genesis*, 279).

[75] One is reminded perhaps of the parliamentary custom that forbids members to address each other directly. Rather all discourse is formally directed to the Speaker.

entire land from which they may choose the best portion, he more directly tells them that they are to dwell (*yēšĕbû*) in Goshen.

Finally, having placed them on the fringe, albeit it in a fine place for their way of life, he gives a small hint of the future. He finishes his directions to Joseph with the words "and if you know that there are capable men among them, put them in charge of my livestock" (Gen 47:6). Even during the lifetime of Joseph the family of Israel is not free from labor for the Egyptian monarch. Here it is posed as a request, although the sort of request posed by a sovereign that one could hardly decline. After the death of Joseph this seemingly casual arrangement will be codified, and the lot of the Hebrews will change dramatically. But that is still in the future and only hinted at here.

The scene shifts again as Jacob is brought before Pharaoh for his presentation. As a mark of respect for the aged patriarch of his clan and the father of his trusted advisor and official, Pharaoh speaks to Jacob more directly and asks how old he is. Jacob's response is typical of him.

Jacob said to Pharaoh, "The years of my earthly sojourn are one hundred thirty;	*wayyōʾmer yaʿăqōb ʾel-parʿōh yĕmê šĕnê mĕgûray šĕlōšîm ûmēʾat šānâ*
few and hard have been the years of my life.	*mĕʿaṭ wĕrāʿîm hāyû yĕmê šĕnê ḥayyay*
They do not compare with the years of the life of my ancestors during their long sojourn." (Gen 47:9)	*wĕlōʾ hiśśîgû ʾet-yĕmê šĕnê ḥayyê ʾăbōtay bîmê mĕgûrêhem* (Gen 47:9)

Jacob's life has indeed been hard but nearly always as a result of his own actions. He inveigled his brother's birthright away from him and later stole his blessing while acting in the most deceitful fashion, apparently without scruple. Having been bested at deceit by his father-in-law Laban, he repaid him in kind by enriching himself while impoverishing the father of his wives, one of whom, apparently, he frankly hated although he loved the other. He had eleven sons and, lest one forget, a daughter as well during the long and self-caused exile. Even God, after wrestling with him, recognized that he was fundamentally crippled. He allowed his daughter to be abducted and murderous discord to fester among his sons. He never visited the mother who had arranged for him to be preferred at the cost of her other son. He visited his father only on his deathbed and declined real reconciliation with his manifestly happier, however unblessed, brother. He mourned a son for more than twenty years, pining away at the expense of the many children who remained. All this in a man who met God repeatedly throughout the course of his long life. One can only marvel at the man's continuing self-absorption and God's continuing choice of him. Although he will live for seventeen more years, he complains of a life cut short. But then, he has been complaining for decades that he is soon to die. There is also a certain false humility at play here that may be meant to put the Egyptian in his place, since at 130 years old he has already far surpassed the ideal Egyptian lifespan of 110 years.[76] One should also note that Jacob, quite correctly, describes his life as a series of sojourns. He has never really settled down anywhere, always driven on by the exigencies of his life. Finally, he blesses Pharaoh, a gesture of respect from one head of family to another.

The section on the descent and ascent of the brothers (Gen 42:1–47:27) ends with a series of brief reports. The first (47:11-12) fills us in on the final status of the chosen family. This is followed (47:13-26) by a more lengthy description—which also serves as a contrast with the privileged position of Joseph's family—of the measures Joseph takes with the rest of the Egyptian populace. Finally, the point of view is shifted back to the family in a concluding sentence (47:27). Strictly speaking, these are reports and do not have much real narrative content, lacking plot or characterization for instance. Nonetheless, I will briefly describe what is going on in this final section so that we can have a good sense of where the story ends up.

The family settles, as instructed, in the land of Goshen. The designation "land of Rameses" is an anachronism, a frame-break by the narrator, hinting once again at the future of the chosen people in Egypt when they will build the city of Rameses as slaves (Exod 1:11). This is the second hint of that future in just a few verses, so it looms rather ominously behind this apparently happy ending. Joseph's family is preferentially treated and receives rations directly from Joseph (Gen 47:12). One assumes that this would be in addition to their own labors and livestock.

The privileged status of Joseph's family is in marked contrast to the treatment of the rest of the populace. This is made clear in verse 13—"Now there was no food in all the land"—and creates a pointed variation with verse 12. The remainder of this report shows how Joseph gradually reduced the people of Egypt to the position of state serfs. Having spent their money and sold their livestock, the Egyptians finally had nothing else to offer and so had to give up their freedom for food. Having become serfs, and having seen Pharaoh become owner of all the

---

[76] Alter, *Genesis*, 281.

land (except that which belonged to the various priesthoods), they were resettled as need be, still having to farm but having a tax of twenty percent imposed on their crop. This went immediately to Pharaoh, and the populace had to make do with the rest both for seed and for food. This seems to reflect the historical reality of Egyptian social organization.

The section ends with a most enigmatic statement in 47:27. Despite the reduction of the rest of the populace to a condition of slavery, where they were so impoverished as to describe themselves as nothing better than corpses (47:19) our attention is directed once again to the chosen family. Unlike those around them, they prosper. We have already seen that they receive special rations from Joseph. In Goshen they are also able to achieve wealth and grow in number. The family is well, reconciled amongst themselves and protected from the turmoil around them by the grace of God and of Joseph, but at this point in the story one knows that God acts through Joseph. Right now, then, all is as satisfactory as it could be.

The brothers have come down to Egypt, just as Joseph did. And just as Joseph did, they prosper. All this is God's doing, acting through the one he has chosen. But there is a hint of foreboding on a number of fronts. There are still unresolved tensions between father and sons, which must intensify as the former ages and death approaches. The famine shows no signs of abating so one wonders whether Joseph's treatment will be able to continue. And behind all of this, we know that they are still not in the promised land. So there is much tension still to be resolved before this book can end.

C. 47:28–48:22: Blessings: Joseph

We are now approaching the end, both of Jacob's life and of the book of Genesis. The major dramatic elements have already been played out, and there is little tension left in the story. Indeed, if the book is a story having a plot these final sections form the conclusion, that final part of a story that is a counterpart to the exposition. At the beginning the actors stand silently on the stage waiting for some spark of tension to put them into action. Here at the end, a different set of actors can be seen reaching their final marks, being placed here or there as the author decides is best. Tension is spent; the drama has come to an end and now we are able to see what we have been left with.

These final sections, then, are not brief stories but simply reports that serve to make clear to us readers what Israel (the family that is in the process of becoming a nation) looks like at this point. Each generation has been dominated by a particular figure—Abraham in the first, Isaac in the second, Jacob in the third, and Joseph in this fourth generation. The time has come (or will come shortly) for both of the last named to leave the scene, since they have accomplished their tasks, but there is some unfinished business yet to be done. Jacob still has some fears about the future, first his own—self-absorbed to the last but by now we should not be terribly surprised—and then that of his family. After the disposition of his own remains, the future status and role of Joseph's sons is the most immediate issue, so it is to those questions that we turn first.

The section is divided from what precedes it by a transitional verse (47:28) and from what follows by a change of scene and subject. Internally it may be divided into the following scenes.

> Transitional verse: 47:28
> A promise extracted: 47:29-31
> The appropriate status for Joseph's sons: 48:1-7
> A blessing for Joseph's sons: 48:8-22

A transitional verse orients us in time. Many years have passed and Jacob is now apparently dying. Before he dies he extracts from Joseph a promise that he will not be buried outside the land promised to his family by God. Joseph agrees to return his father's body to Canaan (47:29-31).

More important is the status of Joseph's two sons. They were born outside of the land and to a woman who was not part of their family, a foreigner. As we recall from Jacob's early life, Jacob's brother Esau committed the crime of marrying an outsider, and it caused him and his offspring to be separated from the family entirely. Although Joseph's offense is identical, Jacob does not want that to happen to Joseph's sons. Jacob, as patriarch of the clan, makes an important ruling that gives them standing in the family. They are, it seems, to have the places vacated by Reuben and Simeon. Their status, as we have seen, has long been shaky. The former slept with Jacob's concubine and made the mad suggestion that his sons be slain if he did not return from Egypt, and the latter initiated the slaughter at Shechem. Clearly they are not to be trusted with senior positions in the family, so Jacob adopts Joseph's sons in their place; together the words Jacob uses and the gesture of placing the boys on his knees have the effect of legal adoption. Note however the order in which the adoption occurs. Although Manasseh is the elder and Ephraim the younger, Jacob reverses their birth order. Ephraim comes first and Manasseh follows. Joseph's attempts to change that are not successful.

Jacob appears here as an old man for whom the past is more real than the present. The death of Rachel is still vivid for him, and he seems to grieve more for her now (47:7) than he did at the time of her death. His age is also apparent in 47:8 when he asks "Who are these?" although they are the grandsons who arrived with Joseph and Jacob has just finished his ruling on their future status. The old man is nearly blind, and his attention wanders back to Bethlehem and the death of Rachel. Joseph needs to recall him to the present, but when he is recalled, he is fully present. For reasons known only to him—but in line with the ongoing theme of the reversal of primogeniture—Jacob quite knowingly places his right hand on the head of Ephraim and his left on the head of Manasseh. He blesses them, extending to them the God-given fertility and vitality that God has given to this family. After Joseph tries to correct Jacob, Jacob reiterates what he has done in 49:20.

This brief section ends, unfortunately, with a famous crux, a Hebrew phrase the meaning of which is uncertain. The NRSV translates it as "I now give to you one portion more than to your brothers, the portion that I took from the hand of the Amorites with my sword and with my bow" (Gen 48:22). The problem is the meaning of the phrase *šĕkem ʾaḥad*. Commentators and translators are divided on the best way to render this in English. Solutions run the gamut from "Shechem" to "shoulder" to "intent" to "portion."[77] Speiser seems correct when he says, "For the present, at any rate, no plausible solution is in sight."[78] Indeed, despite the difficulty of the two words, nothing of great import hangs on them, whether from a theological or narrative viewpoint. What is really important in this chapter is the supplanting of Jacob's two eldest sons by his grandsons—thus reflecting both the reality of later Israelite history, when the tribe of Ephraim was large and dominant, and the effects of the misdeeds of the two eldest sons.

C'. 49:1-28: Blessings: All the Brothers

Having arranged the future status of Joseph's sons within the clan and then blessed them and their father, Jacob turns to blessings—of a sort—for the remainder of his sons. Once again, there is really no narrative here; we are still concluding things, drawing everything to a close. The poem is, at least in some of its parts, probably ancient and uses words the meaning of which is uncertain.[79] The tribe of Levi, to

---

[77] Speiser, *Genesis*, 358; Friedman, *Torah*, 158; Alter, *Genesis*, 291; Fox, *Moses*, 230.

[78] Speiser, *Genesis*, 358.

[79] Much time could be spent following the linguistic arguments for one translation or another. However, this is available in many places and given the nature of

take one example that hints at the age of the poem, has not yet been given its special position and privileges as the priestly tribe. As part of the ongoing narrative the poem serves to further characterize Jacob and offers some hints of characterization for the sons, most of whom have been simply names on a list throughout the ongoing course of the narrative.

Jacob takes some incident from the individual's past, or some aspect of the individual's character, and predicts the future both for him as an individual and for the tribe of which he is the eponymous ancestor.

> Reuben: He is the firstborn son of Jacob, his first fruit. Yet Reuben has shown himself to be untrustworthy of the status and respect accorded to the firstborn son. In Genesis 35:21-22 he slept with one of his father's wives in an attempt, it seems, to assert his own dominance in the place of his aging father. More recently he acted foolishly and intemperately when he offered the lives of his sons to Jacob if he failed to return Benjamin from Egypt. Such a man is not to be trusted and has the stability of water.
>
> Simeon and Levi: The next two sons are considered together. They are condemned for their intemperate anger at Shechem (34:25-26) and the slaughter they instigated there. Not content with slaughtering the inhabitants of Shechem, they went so far as to destroy even the livestock. For such behavior they are rejected and scattered.
>
> Judah: This fourth son has proved the most trustworthy. He attempted to save Joseph's life and acted to protect Benjamin. He was schooled in justice by Tamar, his daughter-in-law who bore twins to him, and he will become the ancestor of the royal house of Israel. David and all the kings descended from him were heirs of Judah. In his strength he is likened to a young lion, victorious in the hunt. Because of his trustworthiness the scepter of royal power will always remain in his grasp.
>
> Zebulon: He will occupy territory by the sea.
>
> Issachar: He will be a hard worker.
>
> Dan: He will be the northernmost tribe. Despite its position on the periphery it will still count as one of the tribes. Given its exposed position it will have to adapt to ongoing insecurity, opposing enemies with a sort of early guerilla warfare.
>
> Gad: The description of Gad's future is based on an elaborate Hebrew pun (*gād gĕdûd yĕgûdennû wĕhûʾ yāgud ʿāqēb*) on the tribe's name. To say that if attacked, Gad would respond to the goad gives some flavor of the original's meaning.
>
> Asher and Naphtali: These two are both quickly disposed of and the meaning of the predictions attached to them is hardly clear.

---

this commentary such argumentation might prove otiose; I will content myself with following the reasonable version offered by the NRSV.

Joseph: Much of what is said about Joseph is deeply obscure, for the meaning of the words cannot be established without doubt. Suffice it to say, for our purposes here, that Joseph is the only son who is really blessed. And the blessing given to him, the long-lost, best-beloved son of the still-mourned, best-beloved wife, is as extravagant as possible. Jacob calls down for him all the blessings of creation, heaven above and earth below. Even the breast and the womb will be blessed in his tribe. The blessings given to him will outlast the very mountains.

Benjamin: The youngest son's descendants will be renowned for their military prowess.

The section concludes with a few words of summary telling us that these are the blessings Jacob allotted to each of the sons and tribes.

D. 49:29–50:14: THE END FOR JACOB

Jacob is now very old and has nothing left to accomplish; it is time for him to die. But in death he does not want to remain in Egypt, the foreign place that is no home for him. It is home that calls to him, in particular the place where his family is buried. He makes Joseph promise to take him there; assured that his burial will be in the land God has given this family, Jacob can die. His sons are gathered around him, but only Joseph's grief is depicted. Overcome with tears once more, he throws himself upon his father torn with grief. Joseph is interestingly complex; at one and the same time the austere bureaucrat who parcels out food to the Egyptians in return for their land, seemingly without any feeling of remorse, and the man who bursts into tears repeatedly. One can equally well understand the lack of grief on the part of the brothers; shortchanged in their father's love throughout their lives, they have just received blessings that were very thin gruel indeed.

Joseph has his father embalmed in the Egyptian fashion. But what follows is a bit strange and off-putting. Joseph, the highly trusted administrator, seems not after all to be so secure in his position. Through intermediaries he asks Pharaoh for permission to travel to Canaan to bury his father. Permission is given, the mourning period for royalty is sanctioned and Joseph sets off, but he sets off surrounded by Egyptian military, and the narrator tells us that the young members of the family are kept behind. The soldiers and their equipment serve as protection in two ways. They protect the entourage from raids, and they protect Pharaoh from any defection of this most skilled technocrat or his equally skilled family. That the young members of the family are kept behind, apparently as hostages, makes us feel uneasy about the family's future. Clearly this trip to Canaan is not the Exodus (though it foreshadows Exod 10:9-11), and history has not ended for the family of Abraham.

D'. 50:15-26: THE END FOR JOSEPH

So our book comes to an end without any particular final climactic fanfare. It simply ebbs away, as the life of this now aging generation ebbs away. We note here that, despite years of living together, Joseph's brothers still fear him. He might, they think, take revenge now that his father has died. Once again they prostrate themselves before him. They proclaim that they are servants of their father's God and willing to serve him. Once again they ask forgiveness, and it is freely given.

Where has God been in all of this? Where has the savior been?—for, as I have said over and over, it is as savior that God is presented in this book. Joseph reiterates the theological stance that has helped him make sense of his life: whatever harm they intended, God used it for good (Gen 50:20).

Joseph lives out a full and ultimately happy life. He dies at the age of 110, the ideal lifespan in Egypt, and he is buried in a coffin, according to Egyptian custom. There is no funeral, however, nor any reprise of the grand journey to Canaan with burial there. Perhaps this is a hint of Israel's future troubles in Egypt when they will be reduced to the slavery from which God, always savior and always faithful to this people, shall free them in due course.

The book began with the story of creation, when God saved chaos from lifeless futility and made it very good. The story seems to end on a very different note, with so many things unresolved and unsettled. What do we as readers desire at the end of this book? More. We want to know whether the promises ever come true and whether God does save the people he has chosen. To whet the appetite for more life, more salvation, more meaning in the midst of apparent chaos—this has been our author's task, the purpose for which this book was given the shape it has today. Desire, longing, the vision of a world not yet achieved but just out of sight, of the very goodness that we once enjoyed but refused to cherish. This is what drives all of our religious longing, a desire whetted but unappeased until God finishes the history begun here. Amen.

Excursus

OUTSIDERS

The Use of Location, Movement, and Concentric Structure
to Highlight the Autonomy of Female Characters
(Genesis 38; 1 Samuel 25; 2 Samuel 11; 2 Samuel 13)

A. Introduction

The autonomy of women, their freedom to pursue their own goals as
they see fit without subservience to another character, is not an explicit
subject of concern in the narrative sections of the Hebrew Bible. The stories in which women function as characters are apparently about something else. Genesis 38 is about the origin of two Judahite clans. 2 Samuel
13 is about the reasons for Absalom's revolt against his father. Of course,
when these stories are read superficially as having a clear univocal
meaning, they seem to be about something other than the women who
appear in them. Yet it is just as true to say that, when women appear in
the narratives of the Hebrew Bible, those narratives are about them, how
they are to be in their world, and how they are free or unfree.

It is hard to imagine anyone arguing today for the view that these apparently historical texts simply describe in some unambiguously objective fashion what happened at some moment of past time. I would agree
that the concern of those who put these texts together was less to describe how it was, than to explain why it is. Etiology is all, but all is not
as it seems. Indeed, as we will see in the stories at hand, etiology is
sometimes a subterfuge, a way to insert profoundly subversive ideas
into a developing canon without it being noticed. We are made to look in
the wrong direction, so that while we think that we see meaning rolling
along toward us, another meaning and another way of explaining why
the world is the way it is, is slipped in behind us. As Phyllis Trible taught

us years ago, a text often used to explain and justify the etiology of the secondary role assigned to women might, in a more insightful reading, mean the exact opposite.[1] So too, texts that explain clan origins and loyalties might have other meanings hidden away in them.

Proceeding by a narrative strategy of indirection, the writers of the biblical books have provided us as readers with rules for judging the status of women, then and now. In this excursus, I will demonstrate one of the narrative rules, a particular motif, for the treatment of the freedom of women.

My thesis is simple enough. When women in the Hebrew Bible are outside they are free.[2] As they move inside, their freedom is lost or becomes increasingly restricted. Outside-ness may be either literal or metaphorical, i.e., the character may be outside of any physical structure and/or operating outside of the expectations attached to her position in the social structure of Israel. This movement towards or away from autonomy may be highlighted by the use of a concentric structure in which the woman's free act is at the center or, conversely, her lack of freedom is indicated by her disappearance from the center of the action.

The functioning of these rules will be shown here by an examination of four narratives in which women figure prominently: Genesis 38 (Tamar), 1 Samuel 25 (Abigail), 2 Samuel 11 (Bathsheba), and 2 Samuel 13 (Tamar).[3] In each case it will be shown that the narratives contain a sequence of movements on the part of the female characters that mir-

---

[1] Phyllis Trible, "Depatriarchalizing in Biblical Narrative," *Journal of the American Academy of Religion* 41 (1973) 30–48.

[2] Mieke Bal expresses the germ of this idea:

> The subdivision of locations into groups is a manner of gaining insight into the relations between elements. A contrast between **inside** and **outside** is often relevant, where inside may carry the suggestion of protection, and outside that of danger. These meanings are not indissolubly tied to these oppositions; it is equally possible that **inside** suggests close confinement, and **outside** freedom, or that we see a combination of these meanings, or a development from one to the other. (*Narratology: An Introduction to the Theory of Narrative*, trans. Christine van Boheemen [Toronto: University of Toronto Press, 1985] 44)

[3] Consideration of these four stories is a result of having read Gary Rendsburg's article "David and His Circle in Genesis xxxviii" (*Vetus Testamentum* 36 [1986] 438–46). In this article Rendsburg argues that the story is a ninth-century B.C.E. creation intended to entertain by poking fun at the Davidic royal family rather than to inform the reader about Judah and his family. My original interest in the story of Tamar in Genesis 38 led me to the Tamar of 2 Samuel and so backward to the tales of Bathsheba and Abigail. That the same structure is evident outside of this complex I will show by including a brief mention of the story of Sarai in Egypt in Genesis 12.

rors their movement toward or away from autonomy. In addition, all four narratives are concentrically structured in such a way as to place the free woman's act at the center or the unfree woman's being acted upon somewhere in the margin. The outlines of the scenic structure of the four passages in question have been provided; these form the substance of my argument. I invite you to read and respond to them but will not comment on the entire narrative in detail. I will simply advert to some of the principal features of the texts at hand that clarify this motif. Finally, a conclusion will summarize both the rules offered and the fruitfulness of their application.

B. Readings

1. GENESIS 38

The literature on Genesis 38 is vast, and I can do little even to summarize it. In the commentary above I have discussed two of the principal lines of exegesis that are found in both modern and historical critical thought and traditional interpretation. Some (e.g., Rashi, Speiser) would see Genesis 38 as completely divorced from its context in the Joseph story. Others (e.g., Alter, though the idea is already adumbrated in Rashi) see that the chapter has a function in its present context, particularly as furthering the character development of Judah. However, as we have seen in the earlier commentary, it is possible to read the story otherwise, not with Judah at its center but with Tamar (see the scenic structure outlined on p. 279).

The story falls into two well-balanced halves with their center in the free act of Tamar. Action begins with Judah's marriage to a nameless woman. Three sons are born, although he names only the first. The story ends with Tamar giving birth to twin sons to Judah, to whom she is not married. However, he apparently names (*wayyiqrāʾ*, 38:29-30) these two boys.

Judah's two eldest sons are recognized by God as evil and punished. The first marries Tamar, but dies leaving her a childless widow. The second marries her, in his unwilling levirate turn, but takes measures to assure that she not conceive. She remains firmly a member of Judah's household and firmly trapped in a marriage without marriage—bound to a dead husband, waiting for the maturity of the third son—even when she is eventually expelled back to the household of her father. Identified as Judah's daughter-in-law, she is condemned to widowhood in her father's home. Tamar is entirely bound up in relationships unsought and inescapable, in houses not her own, without will or future.

The story centers on Tamar's free act. Removing one persona, the widowed daughter in the father's home, as she doffs the garment that indicates that status, she puts on an ambiguous garment ("Is she available for use by men?") that reflects her ambiguous situation (A widow? A wife in waiting? A prostitute? A priestess? A sort of woman hitherto unseen?), goes outside of home and role, and seizes a future. Having acted freely, she freely withdraws into the only place her world provided for her, putting on her widow's garment and receding into her father's house. But justice demands restitution. Tamar has lost family, status, and future. These would be returned. Once again, she is brought outside, to the place where she is free, and identified as publicly sinful, as not having stayed inside her father's house and inside her widow's role. Here this outsider acknowledges what she has done, is recognized as righteous and given a new future, one in which she establishes a house for herself and raises up progeny for the future.

Tamar moved from the inside to the outside. Inside her role as wife, widow, and daughter she was futureless. Outside, with eyes open, with an appearance her world did not understand, but creating a future her world would have denied her, she bore fruit. No longer wife, nor widow, nor daughter, in fact no longer (after 38:25) even indoors in this narrative world, she is simply Tamar.

2. 1 SAMUEL 25:1-44

Unlike Genesis 38, the story of Abigail found in 1 Samuel 25 has excited relatively little interest among exegetes. Aside from the usual commentaries, Jon D. Levenson studied it in some detail in a fine article in *The Catholic Biblical Quarterly* in 1978.[4] The story provides information about the origin of David's growth in wealth and his connection to certain clans. But, again, the story may be read with Abigail, not David, at its center.

Nabal, acting the fool his name implies he would be, treats David with contempt. Abigail acts to save her household from David's wrath, and does so (in unwifely fashion) without even telling her husband of her departure. In the speech with which she soothes the angry David, she is so free that (1 Sam 25:31) she creates a possible future for herself

---

[4] "1 Sam 25 as Literature and History," *The Catholic Biblical Quarterly* 40 (1978) 11–28.

in which her current husband does not figure. Like the evil sons of Judah, husbands of Tamar, YHWH strikes Nabal dead. The story's scenic structure:

1. Narrator's report on the wider context (vv. 1-3)
   A. David sends to Nabal (vv. 4-8)
     B. Nabal's contempt (vv. 9-11)
       C. A report causes David's anger (vv. 12-13)
         D. A young man warns Abigail (vv. 14-17)
           X. Abigail acts (vv. 18-19)
         D'. Abigail soothes David (vv. 20-35)
       C'. A report causes Nabal's death (vv. 36-38)
     B'. David's joy (v. 39a)
   A'. David sends to Abigail (vv. 39b-42)
2. Narrator's report on the wider context (vv. 43-44)

Acting outside her role, barreling down a hillside, Abigail is centered on saving lives, and her righteous deed is rewarded.

In both of these cases, Tamar's and Abigail's, the free action of a woman who chooses to go outside of role and house is the center of the tale. In both cases, these free actions are deemed righteous and rewarded. But tragedy is found in the counterparts of these stories, where women are trapped inside and so disappear.

3. 2 SAMUEL 11:1–12:1

This most powerful of biblical stories has invited the most powerful of readings and retellings. These tellings range from the sublime to the banal. The former may be seen in Meir Sternberg, who makes it a centerpiece of his *The Poetics of Biblical Narrative*.[5] It appears repeatedly in popular culture where a deeply flawed retelling may be seen in Richard Gere's film "King David."

Telling where stories begin and end is notoriously difficult but is nonetheless an important part of the interpretative process. The temptation is to let typography rule and so see an end to this tale at the end of 2 Samuel 11. Read thus, the story ends with divine displeasure but without divine action. A more complete reading of the text will see that

---

[5] Meir Sternberg, *The Poetics of Biblical Narrative: Ideological Literature and the Drama of Reading* (Bloomington, IN: Indiana University Press, 1985) 190–222.

the tale ends at 12:1, where YHWH sends Nathan to David. The story's scenic structure:

A. Stage ambiguously set
    1. [narrator] David sends his servants (v. 1a)
    2. David stays in Jerusalem (v. 1b)
    3. David's action (vv. 2-4a)
B. Ambiguities clarified
    4. [narrator] Bathsheba is purifying herself (v. 4b)
    5. Bathsheba sends (vv. 4c-5)
    6. David sends (v. 6)
X. A deadly game called "Who Knows What?"
    7. David and Uriah meet (vv. 7-8a)
      8. Uriah's reaction (vv. 8b-9)
    9. Another ploy (vv. 10-12a)
    10. Uriah's reaction (v. 12b)
    11. Another ploy (vv. 12c-13a)
    12. Uriah's reaction (v. 13b)
    13. Another ploy (vv. 14-15)
    14. The ploy succeeds (vv. 16-21)
B'. Winner and losers
    15. David's reaction (vv. 22-25)
    16. Bathsheba's reaction (vv. 26-27a)
A'. Spectator heard from
    17. [narrator] The Lord sends his servant (11:27b–12:1a)

The text is extraordinarily complex, despite its brevity. On its surface it supplies background information about the revolt of Absalom and the eventual succession of Solomon. Yet it is the details of literary craft, the gaps in the story, the way repetition in used, that excite the reader's interest and participation. The repeated use of "send" makes David seem like the spider in the web, manipulating all to do his bidding. The careful use of names, appearing and disappearing, makes Bathsheba, for instance, at once both the daughter of a well-known house and a de-personified particle. The opacity of motivation on the part of the various characters solicits suggestions from readers curious to know why David is not at Rabbah, exactly what sort of bath Bathsheba is taking, whether or not her taking it on her roof is rather suspicious, how David can fail to know his immediate neighbors, what Uriah knows, and on and on.

Bathsheba first appears in the story bathing on her rooftop, probably undertaking an act of religious devotion. Despite her identification as a woman married to a supporter of David, she is sent for and she goes to the king. After 11:3, her name disappears from the text. Subsequently, David "took her" (unwillingly?), "lay with her"; "she" is the woman (11:4) or the wife of Uriah (11:26) or simply a feminine particle (11:26). The center of the narrative (11:7-21) is the long and deadly game of dialogue that pits Uriah and David against each other, as David tries to entice Uriah to go to his "house" (11:8 ff) and Uriah, instead, stays in David's house. What, or who, is in the house David does not mention. Interestingly, right in the middle of the dialogue (11:11), and so in the middle of the entire narrative, Uriah makes the identification explicit: in his house is his wife. To her, he will not go. So, in the middle of the story, Bathsheba has disappeared as a person with her own name and fears. She is so firmly inside that to speak of a house is to speak of her. Uriah tells us who is trapped in that house, but he will not go to her, nor can she leave. She acts, again without a name, inside her wifely role when she hears of her husband's death and mourns for him. She is still inside, and remains so, for she is brought to David's house and, still a nameless particle, becomes his wife.

Bathsheba is trapped inside a house, a marriage, a perhaps violent relationship, and finds no way out. She is brought from the outside to the inside, has violence done to her, and disappears as an actor, is never spoken to, is never again (in the present context) even a named person, but a nameless wife in a house from which she cannot escape.

4. 2 SAMUEL 13:1-22

The story's scenic structure:[6]

    A. Amnon in love with Tamar (vv. 1-2)
      B. Intervention of Jonadab (vv. 3-5)
        C. Tamar's arrival (vv. 6-9a)
          D. Amnon's servants ordered to leave (v. 9b)
            E. Amnon commands Tamar to lie with him; she refuses but to no avail (vv. 10-14a)

---

[6] J. P. Fokkelman, *Narrative Art and Poetry in the Books of Samuel: A Full Interpretation Based on Stylistic and Structural Analyses*, vol. 1: *King David (II Sam. 9–20 & I Kings 1–2)* (Assen/Amsterdam: Van Gorcum, 1981) 99–100. Cf. also G. P. Ridout, "The Rape of Tamar (2 Sam 13:1-22)," *Rhetorical Criticism: Essays in Honor of James Muilenburg*, ed. Jared J. Jackson and Martin Kessler, Pittsburgh Theological Monographs 1 (Pittsburgh: Pickwick Press, 1974) 75–84.

X. Amnon rapes Tamar, and love turns to hate
(vv. 14b-15a)

E'. Amnon commands Tamar to depart; she pleads
but to no avail (vv. 15b-16)

D'. Amnon's servants recalled (v. 17)

C'. Tamar's departure (vv. 18-19)

B'. Intervention of Absalom (vv. 20-21)

A'. Absalom hates Amnon (v. 22)

The story of the rape of Tamar by her half-brother Amnon sets up the rebellion of Absalom. David's ineffective response provides Absalom with the fuel for the anger that will eventually erupt in open revolt. From the beginning of the text in 2 Samuel 13 the reader's attention is directed toward Absalom, who, we are told, "had a beautiful sister named Tamar" (13:1). The story is dominated by language of family relationships, such terms occurring more than twenty times in the chapter. However, neither the terminology of relationship nor the movement of the characters is casual. Tamar is called, first to the house of her father, then sent to Amnon's house, and finally caused to come even further in, to his bedchamber. There, with the dialogue reminding the reader that they are brother and sister, Amnon rapes Tamar. After this act of violence, she is put away, no longer called sister, not named, simply the feminine pronoun.

This last is the clearest case of those considered here of a woman losing her freedom because she is trapped inside both a social role and a structure. There she loses her freedom and her self. Only when she is cast aside is she again a sister, again Tamar, but trapped in that violent moment in another brother's house.

C. Other Possibilities

Other texts suggest themselves as following the rule described here. In Genesis 12:10–13:1 Sarai, because she is a wife, must pretend to be a sister, and so is lost into the house of Pharaoh until rescued by God and brought back out to her husband. This story is carefully neatly centered on Genesis 12:14, "The woman was taken into Pharaoh's house." It is a structure with a difference however, since God acts to save her (see the earlier commentary on this passage). Hagar is free in the desert (Genesis 16) but a slave in the house of Abraham. Dinah chooses to visit the local women, is abducted, and is taken into the town and the house of Shechem (Genesis 34) where she awaits rescue. Over

and over for the women of the Hebrew Bible, to be outside is to be free
and to be inside is to be trapped.

D. Conclusion

My initial thesis was that a consistent motif could be discerned in
the narrative sections of the Hebrew Bible that would help us to evalu-
ate the status of women. That this pattern is consistent is now most
evident. When women are outside of role or structure they are free. To
move toward the outside is to move toward increasing freedom. The
converse is equally true. To be, or to move, inside is to lose freedom.
Sensitivity to the operation of this rule helps us to see that these stories
are not only about the etiology of events, relationships, or what have
you. These stories are about the women in them, and they tell us over
and over again that the God whose name is Freedom values freedom
and regards as righteous those who move toward it, even if they have
to go outside role and structure to achieve it. This latter is an idea no
less subversive now than then.

FOR FURTHER READING

It is not possible to compile anything like a full bibliography on methodology in biblical studies in general or on the book of Genesis in particular, so I append here merely some items that I have found useful in the preparation of this book and that might be useful to those desiring to study the book further. At the same time anyone familiar with the current discussions on methodology and Genesis will notice lacunae here. By no means do I agree with everything that appears in these works, nor would their authors agree with everything that appears in mine, but these are all voices worthy of being heard.

I have avoided using many abbreviations that would be unfamiliar to the non-specialists reading this work. However some are unavoidable, so a list of those used in this book appears at the end of the list of items for further reading.

Adar, Zvi. *The Book of Genesis: An Introduction to the Biblical World*. Jerusalem: Magnes Press, 1990.

Allen, Charlotte. "Is Nothing Sacred? Casting Out the Gods From Religious Studies." *Lingua Franca* (1996) 30–40.

Alter, Robert. *The Art of Biblical Narrative*. New York: Basic Books, 1981.

Alter, Robert. *Genesis: Translation and Commentary*. New York: Norton, 1996.

Andersen, Francis J. "On Reading Genesis 1–3." *Backgrounds for the Bible*. Ed. M. O'Connor and David Noel Freedman, 137–49. Winona Lake, Ind.: Eisenbrauns, 1987.

Anderson, Bernhard W. "From Analysis to Synthesis: The Interpretation of Genesis 1–11." *Journal of Biblical Literature* 97 (1978) 23–9.

Anderson, Gary A. *The Genesis of Perfection: Adam and Eve in Jewish and Christian Imagination*. Louisville: Westminster John Knox Press, 2001.

Andreasen, Niels-Erik. "Genesis 14 in Its Near Eastern Context." *Scripture in Context: Essays on the Comparative Method.* Ed. Carl D. Evans, et al., 59–77. Pittsburgh: Pickwick Press, 1980.

Aristotle. *Aristotle's Poetics.* Trans. S. H. Butcher. Boston: Hill and Wang, 1989.

Auerbach, Erich. *Mimesis.* Princeton: Princeton University Press, 1953.

Baker, D. W. "Diversity and Unity in the Literary Structure of Genesis." *Essays on the Patriarchal Narratives.* Ed. A. R. Millard and D. J. Wiseman, 197–222. Winona Lake, Ind.: Eisenbrauns, 1980.

Bal, Mieke. *Narratology: An Introduction to the Theory of Narrative.* Trans. Christine van Boheemen. Toronto: University of Toronto Press, 1985.

Banon, David. "Exégèse biblique et philosophique." *Études Théologiques et Religieuses* 66 (1991) 489–504.

Bar-Efrat, Shimon. "Some Observations on the Analysis of Structure in Biblical Narrative." *Beyond Form Criticism: Essays in Old Testament Literary Criticism.* Ed. Paul R. House, 186–204. Winona Lake, Ind.: Eisenbrauns, 1992.

Bar-Efrat, Shimon. *Narrative Art in the Bible.* Sheffield, England: Sheffield Academic Press, 1997.

Barr, James. *Holy Scripture: Canon, Authority, Criticism.* Philadelphia: Westminster, 1983.

Barr, James. *The Garden of Eden and the Hope of Immortality.* Minneapolis: Fortress, 1993.

Barré, L. Michael. "The Riddle of the Flood Chronology." *Journal for the Study of the Old Testament* 41 (1988) 3–20.

Barth, Karl. *Church Dogmatics.* Edinburgh: T. & T. Clark, 1957.

Berlin, Adele. *Poetics and Interpretation of Biblical Narrative.* Bible and Literature 9. Sheffield: Almond, 1983.

Berlin, Adele. "Characterization in Biblical Narrative: David's Wives." *Beyond Form Criticism: Essays in Old Testament Literary Criticism.* Ed. Paul R. House, 219–32. Winona Lake, Ind.: Eisenbrauns, 1992.

Berry, Wendell. *Remembering.* San Francisco: North Point Press, 1988.

Biddle, Mark E. "The Endangered Ancestress and the Blessing for the Nations." *Journal of Biblical Literature* 109 (1990) 599–611.

Bird, Phyllis A. "'Male and Female He Created Them': Gen. 1:27b in the Context of the Priestly Account of Creation." *Harvard Theological Review* 74 (1981) 129–59.

Bos, Johanna W. H. "Out of the Shadows: Genesis 38, Judges 4:17-22, Ruth 3." *Semeia* 42 (1988) 37–67.

Bos, Johanna W. H. "An Eyeopener at the Gate: George Coats and Genesis 38." *Lexington Theological Quarterly* 27 (1992) 119–23.

Breukelman, F. H. "The Story of the Sons of God Who Took the Daughters of Humans as Wives." *Voices from Amsterdam: A Modern Tradi-*

tion of Reading Biblical Narrative. Ed. Martin Kessler, 83–95. Atlanta: Scholars Press, 1994.

Brichto, Herbert Chanan. *Toward a Grammar of Biblical Poetics*. New York: Oxford University Press, 1992.

Brichto, Herbert Chanan. *The Names of God: Poetic Readings in Biblical Beginnings*. New York: Oxford University Press, 1998.

Brisman, Leslie. *The Voice of Jacob*. Bloomington, Ind.: Indiana University Press, 1990.

Brooks, Peter. *Reading for the Plot: Design and Intention in Narrative*. New York: Vintage, 1984.

Brown, Francis, S. R. Driver and Charles A. Briggs. *A Hebrew and English Lexicon of the Old Testament*. Oxford: Clarendon, 1972.

Brown, Schuyler. *Text and Psyche: Experiencing Scripture Today*. New York: Continuum, 1998.

Brueggemann, Walter. *Place as Gift, Promise and Challenge in Biblical Faith*. Philadelphia: Fortress, 1977.

Brueggemann, Walter. *Genesis*. Atlanta: John Knox, 1982.

Bruns, Gerald. *Inventions: Writing, Textuality, and Understanding in Literary History*. New Haven: Yale University Press, 1982.

Campbell, Antony F. and Mark A. O'Brien. *Sources of the Pentateuch*. Minneapolis: Fortress, 1993.

Cassuto, Umberto. *A Commentary on the Book of Genesis: Part I: From Adam to Noah. Part II: From Noah to Abraham*. Trans. Israel Abrahams. Jerusalem: Magnes, 1961, 1964.

Chatman, Seymour. *Story and Discourse: Narrative Structure in Fiction and Film*. Ithaca: Cornell University Press, 1978.

Clifford, Richard. "Exodus." *The New Jerome Biblical Commentary*. Ed. Raymond E. Brown, et al., 44–60. London: Chapman, 1990.

Clifford, Richard and John Collins, eds. *Creation in the Biblical Traditions*. Catholic Biblical Quarterly Monograph Series 24 (Washington: CBA, 1992).

Clines, David J. A. "What Does Eve Do to Help? And Other Irredeemably Androcentric Orientations in Genesis 1–3." *What Does Eve Do to Help? And Other Readerly Questions to the Old Testament*, 25–48. Journal for the Study of the Old Testament Supplement 94. Sheffield, England: JSOT Press, 1990.

Coats, George W. "Abraham's Sacrifice of Faith." *Interpretation* 27 (1973) 389–401.

Coats, George W. *Genesis: With an Introduction to Narrative Literature*. FOTL 1. Grand Rapids, Mich.: Eerdmans, 1983.

Coats, George W. "Joseph, son of Jacob." *ABD*.

Cotter, David W. *A Study of Job 4–5 in the Light of Contemporary Literary Theory*. Atlanta: Scholars Press, 1992.

Curtis, Edward M. "Genesis 38: Its Context(s) and Function." *Criswell Theological Journal* 5 (1991) 247–57.

Deurloo, Karel. "The Way of Abraham: Routes and Localities as Narrative Data in Gen 11:27–25:11." *Voices from Amsterdam: A Modern Tradition of Reading Biblical Narrative.* Ed. Martin Kessler, 95–112. Atlanta: Scholars Press, 1994.

Deurloo, Karel. "Because You Have Hearkened to My Voice (Genesis 22)." *Voices from Amsterdam: A Modern Tradition of Reading Biblical Narrative.* Ed. Martin Kessler, 113–30. Atlanta: Scholars Press, 1994.

Dorsey, David. *The Literary Structure of the Old Testament.* Grand Rapids, Mich.: Baker, 1999.

Doyle, Arthur Conan. "The Naval Treaty." *The Memoirs of Sherlock Holmes.* London: Penguin Books, 1950.

Driver, S. R. *The Book of Genesis.* London: Methuen and Co., 1904.

Emerton, J. A. "Judah and Tamar." *Vetus Testamentum* 29 (1979) 403–15.

Emerton, J. A. "The Source Analysis of Genesis xi 27–32." *Vetus Testamentum* 42 (1992) 37–46.

Emerton, J. A. "When Did Terah Die (Genesis 11:32)?" *Language, Theology, and the Bible.* Ed. S. Balentine and John Barton, 170–81. New York: Oxford University Press, 1994.

Firestone, Reuven. "Difficulties in Keeping a Beautiful Wife: The Legend of Abraham and Sarah in Jewish and Islamic Tradition." *Journal of Jewish Studies* 42 (1991) 196–214.

Fishbane, Michael. "Composition and Structure in the Jacob Cycle (Gen. 25:19–35:22)." *Journal of Jewish Studies* 26 (1975) 15–38.

Fishbane, Michael. *Text and Texture: Close Readings of Selected Biblical Texts.* New York: Schocken, 1979.

Fokkelman, Jan P. *Narrative Art in Genesis: Specimens of Stylistic and Structural Analysis.* Assen/Amsterdam: Van Gorcum, 1975.

Fokkelman, Jan P. *Narrative Art and Poetry in the Books of Samuel: A Full Interpretation Based on Stylistic and Structural Analyses,* vol. 1: *King David (II Sam. 9–20 & I Kings 1–2).* Assen/Amsterdam: Van Gorcum, 1981.

Fokkelman, Jan P. "Genesis 37 and 38 at the Interface of Structural Analysis and Hermeneutics." *Literary Structure and Rhetorical Strategies in the Hebrew Bible.* Ed. L. J. de Regt, et al., 152–87. Winona Lake, Ind.: Eisenbrauns, 1992.

Fokkelman, Jan P. *Reading Biblical Narrative: An Introductory Guide.* Louisville: Westminster John Knox, 1999.

Forster, E. M. *Aspects of the Novel.* New York: Harcourt, Brace & Company, 1927.

Fox, Everett. *In the Beginning: A New English Rendering of the Book of Genesis.* New York: Schocken, 1983.

Fox, Everett. *The Five Books of Moses.* New York: Schocken, 1995.

Freedman, David Noel, et al. (eds.). *The Anchor Bible Dictionary*. New York: Doubleday, 1992. Freeman, Gordon M. "Wives and Sister: A Contemporary Exegesis." *Conservative Judaism* 44 (1992) 50–5.

Fretheim, Terence E. "The Reclamation of Creation: Redemption and Law in Exodus." *Interpretation* 45 (1991) 354–66.

Friedman, Richard Elliott. *Commentary on the Torah*. San Francisco: HarperSanFrancisco, 2001.

Frye, Northrop. *Words with Power: Being a Second Study of the Bible and Literature*. New York: Harcourt, Brace, Jovanovich, 1990.

Fuchs, Esther. "The Literary Characterization of Mothers and Sexual Politics in the Hebrew Bible." *Feminist Perspectives on Biblical Scholarship*. Ed. Adela Y. Collins, 117–36. Chico, CA: Scholars Press, 1985.

Furman, Nelly. "His Story Versus Her Story: Male Genealogy and Female Strategy in the Jacob Cycle." *Feminist Perspectives on Biblical Scholarship*. Ed. Adela Y. Collins, 107–16. Chica, CA: Scholars Press, 1985.

Genette, Gérard. *Figures III*. Collection Poétique. Paris: Éditions du Seuil, 1972.

Goldin, Judah. "The Youngest Son or Where Does Genesis 38 Belong?" *Journal of Biblical Literature* 96 (1977) 27–44.

Goldingay, John. *Models for Interpretation of Scripture*. Grand Rapids, Mich.: Eerdmans, 1995.

Gordis, Daniel H. "Lies, Wives and Sisters: The Wife-Sister Motif Revisted." *Judaism* 34 (1985) 344–59.

Görg, Manfred. "Tohû wa bohû: ein Deutungsvorschlag." *Zeitschrift für die Alttestamentliche Wissenschaft* 92 (1980) 431–34.

Gross, Walter. "Zum Problem der Satzgrenzen im Hebräischen—Beobachtungen an Pendenskonstruktionen." *Biblische Notizen* 35 (1986) 50–72.

Gunn, David M. and Danna Nolan Fewell. *Narrative in the Hebrew Bible*. New York: Oxford University Press, 1993.

Hall, Robert G. "Circumcision." *ABD*.

Harrington, Daniel. "Hebrews." *The New Collegeville Bible Commentary*. Collegeville: The Liturgical Press, forthcoming.

Healey, Joseph P. "Faith (Old Testament)," *ABD* 2:744–49.

Hendel, Ronald S. *The Epic of the Patriarch: The Jacob Cycle and the Narrative Traditions of Canaan and Israel*. Harvard Semitic Monographs 42. Atlanta: Scholars Press, 1987.

Hoffmeier, James K. "The Wives' Tales of Genesis 12, 20 and 26 and the Covenants at Beer-Sheba." *Tyndale Bulletin* 43 (1992) 81–99.

Holladay William L. *A Concise Hebrew and Aramaic Lexicon of the Old Testament*. Grand Rapids, Mich.: Eerdmans, 1971.

Howard, David M. "Sodom and Gomorrah Revisited." *Journal of the Evangelical Theological Society* 27 (1984) 385–400.

Humphreys, W. Lee. *Joseph and His Family: A Literary Study.* Columbia, S.C.: University of South Caroline Press, 1988.

Humphreys, W. Lee. *The Character of God in the Book of Genesis.* Louisville: Westminster John Knox, 2001.

Hunter, Alastair G. "Father Abraham: A Structural and Theological Study of the Yahwist's Presentation of the Abraham Material." *Journal for the Study of the Old Testament* 35 (1986) 3–27.

International Commission for English in the Liturgy. "Ordination of a Priest." *Rites of the Catholic Church,* vol. 2. New York: Pueblo, 1980.

Jacob, Benno. *The First Book of the Bible: Genesis.* New York: KTAV, 1974.

James, Henry. *The Art of Fiction.* London: De Wolfe and Fiske, 1884.

Jeffers, Robinson. "The Purse-Seine." *The Collected Poetry of Robinson Jeffers,* vol. 2: *1928–1938.* Ed. Tim Hunt. Stanford: Stanford University Press, 1989.

Jenni, Ernst and Claus Westermann. *Theologisches Handwörterbuch zum Alten Testament.* Band I. Munich: Chr. Kaiser, 1984.

Jobling, David. *1 Samuel.* Berit Olam. Collegeville: The Liturgical Press, 1998.

Johnson, Luke Timothy. "So What's Catholic About It? The State of Catholic Biblical Scholarship." *Commonweal* 125, 1 (1998) 12–6.

Jongeling, Bastiaan. "Some Remarks on the Beginning of Genesis I, 2." *Folia Orientalia* 21 (1980) 27–32.

Josipovici, Gabriel. *The Book of God: A Response to the Bible.* New Haven: Yale University Press, 1988.

Joüon, Paul. *Grammaire de l'hébreu biblique.* Rome: Pontifical Biblical Institute, 1923.

Kamin, Sarah. "Rashbam's Conception of Creation in Light of the Intellectual Currents of His Time." *Scripta Hierosolymita* 31 (1986) 91–132.

Kilian, Rudolf. "Gen 1.2 und die Urgoetter von Hermopolis." *Vetus Testamentum* 16 (1966) 420–38.

Kselman, John H. "The Book of Genesis: A Decade of Scholarly Research." *Interpretation* 45 (1991) 380–92.

Kugel, James L. *In Potiphar's House.* San Francisco: HarperCollins, 1990; 2nd ed., Cambridge, Mass.: Harvard University Press, 1994.

Kugel, James L. *The Bible as It Was.* Cambridge, Mass.: Belknap, 1997.

Kugel, James L. *Traditions of the Bible.* Cambridge, Mass.: Harvard University Press, 1998.

Leibowitz, Nehama. *Studies in Bereshit.* 4th ed. Jerusalem: World Zionist Organization, 1981.

Lemche, Niels Peter. "The Chronology of the Flood." *Journal for the Study of the Old Testament* 18 (1980) 52–62.

Letellier, Robert Ignatius. *Day in Mamre, Night in Sodom: Abraham and Lot in Genesis 18 & 19.* New York: E. J. Brill, 1995.

Levenson, Jon D. "1 Sam 25 as Literature and History." *The Catholic Biblical Quarterly* 40 (1978) 11–28.

Leviant, Curt. "Parallel Lives: The Trials and Traumas of Isaac and Ishmael." *Bible Review* (April, 1999) 20–5, 47.

Lewis, Jack. *A Study of the Interpretation of Noah and the Flood in Jewish and Christian Literature.* Leiden: E. J. Brill, 1968.

Lockwood, Peter F. "Tamar's Place in the Joseph Cycle." *Lutheran Theological Journal* 26 (1992) 35–43.

Louth, Andrew. *Genesis 1-11.* Ancient Christian Commentary on Scripture: Old Testament I. Downers Grove, Ill.: InterVarsity, 2001.

Luster, Robert. "Wind and Water: Cosmogonic Symbolism in the Old Testament." *Zeitschrift für die Alttestamentliche Wissenschaft* 93 (1981) 1–10.

MacLeod, Alistair. *No Great Mischief.* New York: Norton, 1999.

Mann, Thomas. *Joseph and His Brothers.* Trans. H. T. Lowe-Porter. London: Vintage, 1999. Originally published as *Joseph Und Seine Brueder* in four volumes: 1. *Die Geschichten Jakobs* (S. Fischer, 1933); 2. *Der Junge Joseph* (S. Fischer, 1934); 3. *Joseph in Aegypten* (Bermann-Fischer, 1936); *Joseph, Der Ernahrer* (Bermann-Fischer, 1943).

Mann, Thomas W. *The Book of the Torah: The Narrative Integrity of the Pentateuch* (Atlanta: John Knox, 1988).

Mann, Thomas W. "All the Families of the Earth: The Theological Unity of Genesis." *Interpretation* 45 (1991) 341–53.

Mays, James Luther, et al. (eds.). *Old Testament Interpretation: Past, Present and the Future.* Nashville: Abingdon, 1995.

Menn, Esther. *Judah and Tamar in Ancient Jewish Exegesis: Studies in Literary Form and Hermeneutics.* Supplements to the Journal for the Study of Judaism 51. Leiden: E. J. Brill, 1997.

Meyers, Carol. *Discovering Eve: Ancient Israelite Women in Context.* New York: Oxford University Press, 1988.

Miles, Jack. *God: A Biography.* New York: A. A. Knopf, 1995.

Mitchell, Stephen. *Genesis: A New Translation of the Classic Biblical Stories.* San Francisco: HarperCollins, 1996.

Moloney, Francis J. *The Gospel of John.* Collegeville: The Liturgical Press, 1998.

Montale, Eugenio. *Satura 1962–1970.* Trans. William Arrowsmith. New York: W. W. Norton, 1998.

Morris, Paul, and Deborah Sawyer, eds. *A Walk in the Garden: Biblical, Iconographical and Literary Images of Eden.* Journal for the Study of the Old Testament Supplement 136. Sheffield: Sheffield Academic Press, 1992.

Moyers, Bill, ed. *Talking about Genesis: A Resource Guide.* New York: Doubleday, 1996.

Neusner, Jacob. *Confronting Creation: How Judaism Reads Genesis: An Anthology of Genesis Rabbah*. Columbia, S.C.: University of South Carolina Press, 1991.

Newsom, Carol. "Angels." *ABD*

Niditch, Susan. "The Wronged Woman Righted: An Analysis of Genesis 38." *Harvard Theological Review* 72 (Jan.–April 1979) 143–9.

Nikaido, S. "Hagar and Ishmael as Literary Figures: An Intertextual Study." *Vetus Testamentum* 51 (2001) 219–42.

Oates, Joyce Carol. *We Were the Mulvaneys*. London: Fourth Estate, 2001.

O'Brien, Edward J. *The Short Story Case Book*. New York: Farrar & Rinehart, 1935.

O'Callaghan, Martin. "The Structure and Meaning of Gen 38." *Proceedings of the Irish Biblical Association* 5 (1981) 72–88.

Orlinsky, Harry "The Plain Meaning of Ruach in Gen 1, 2." Jewish Quarterly Review 48 (Oct 1957) 174–82.

Orlinsky, Harry. "The Plain Meaning of Genesis 1:1-3." *Biblical Archeologist* 46 (1983) 207–9.

Petersen, David L. "A Thrice Told Tale: Genre, Theme and Motif." *Biblical Research* 18 (1973) 30–43.

Pontifical Biblical Commission. *The Interpretation of the Bible in the Church*. Rome: Pontifical Biblical Commission, 1994.

Price, Reynolds. *A Palpable God*. New York: Atheneum, 1978.

Price, Reynolds. *Things Themselves: Essays and Scenes*. New York: Atheneum, 1972.

Rad, Gerhard von. *Genesis*. Philadelphia: Westminster, 1972.

Rad, Gerhard von. *Das Opfer des Abraham*. Munich: C. Kaiser, 1971.

Rashi. *The Pentateuch and Rashi's Commentary: A Linear Translation into English*. Vol. 1: *Genesis*. Trans. Abraham ben Isaiah and Benjamin Sharfman. Brooklyn: S. S. & R. Publishing, 1949.

Rashkow, Ilona N. "Intertextuality, Transference and the Reader in/of Genesis 12 and 20." *Reading Between Texts: Intertextuality and the Hebrew Bible*. Ed. Danna Nolan Fewell, 57–73. Louisville: Westminster John Knox, 1992.

Reed, Walter. *Dialogues of the Word: The Bible as Literature According to Bakhtin*. New York: Oxford University Press, 1993.

Rendsburg, Gary A. "David and His Circle in Genesis xxxviii." *Vetus Testamentum* 36 (1986) 438–46.

Rendsburg, Gary A. *The Redaction of Genesis*. Winona Lake, Ind.: Eisenbrauns, 1986.

Reventlow, Henning Graf. *Opfere deinen Sohn: Eine Auslegung von Genesis 22*. Biblische Studien 23. Neukirchen: Neukirchener Verlag, 1968.

Ridout, G. P. "The Rape of Tamar (2 Sam 13:1-22)." *Rhetorical Criticism: Essays in Honor of James Muilenburg*. Pittsburgh Theological Monographs 1. Ed. Jared J. Jackson and Martin Kessler, 75–84. Pittsburgh: Pickwick Press, 1974.

Rilke, Rainer Maria. *Ahead of All Parting: The Selected Poetry and Prose of Rainer Maria Rilke.* Trans. Stephen Mitchell. New York: Modern Library, 1995.

Ronning, John. "The Naming of Isaac: The Role of the Wife/Sister Episodes in the Redaction of Genesis." *Westminster Theological Journal* 53 (1991) 1–27.

Rose, Martin. "Names of God." *ABD.*

Rosenberg, David (ed.). *Genesis: As It Is Written.* San Francisco: HarperCollins, 1996.

Ross, Ellen M. "Human Persons as Images of the Divine: A Reconsideration." *The Pleasure of Her Text.* Ed. Alice Bach, 97–116. Philadelphia: Trinity Press International, 1990.

Russo, Richard. *Empire Falls.* New York: A. A. Knopf, 2001.

Salm, Eva. *Juda und Tamar: Eine exegetische Studie zu Gen 38.* Forschung zur Bibel 76. Würzburg: Echter Verlag, 1996.

Santmire, H. Paul. "The Genesis Creation Narratives Revisited: Themes for a Global Age." *Interpretation* 45 (1991) 366–79.

Sarna, Nahum M. *Understanding Genesis: The Heritage of Biblical Israel.* New York: Schocken, 1966.

Sarna, Nahum M. *Genesis.* The JPS Torah Commentary. Philadelphia: Jewish Publication Society, 1989.

Savage, Mary. "Literary Criticism and Biblical Studies: A Rhetorical Analysis of the Joseph Narrative." *Scripture in Context: Essays on the Comparative Method.* Ed. Carl D. Evans, et al., 79–100. Pittsburgh: Pickwick Press, 1980.

Schlink, Bernhard. *The Reader.* New York: Pantheon Books, 1997.

Scullion, J. J. "Righteousness (Old Testament)," *ABD* 5:724–36.

Seth, Vikram. *A Suitable Boy.* San Francisco: HarperCollins, 1994.

Sherwood, Stephen K. *Had God Not Been on My Side: An Examination of the Narrative Technique of the Story of Jacob and Laban.* New York: Peter Lang, 1990.

Ska, Jean-Louis. "L'ironie de Tamar." *Zeitschrift für die Alttestamentliche Wissenschaft* 100 (1988) 261–3.

Ska, Jean-Louis. *Our Fathers Have Told Us: Introduction to the Analysis of Hebrew Narratives.* Subsidia Biblica 13. Rome: Pontifical Biblical Institute, 1990.

Ska, Jean-Louis. *Introduction à la lecture du Pentateuque: Clés pour l'interprétation des cinq premiers livres de la Bible.* Le livre et le rouleau 5. Brussels: Éditions Lessius, 2000.

Smith, J.M. Powis. "The Use of Divine Names as Superlatives." *American Journal of Semitic Languages* 45:3 (Apr. 1929) 212–3.

Speiser, E. A. *Genesis*. AB 1. New York: Doubleday, 1962.

Steiner, George. "The Uncommon Reader." *No Passion Spent*. Pp. 1–19. New Haven: Yale University Press, 1996.

Steiner, George. "Real Presences." *No Passion Spent*. Pp. 2–39. New Haven: Yale University Press, 1996.

Steiner, George. "A Preface to the Hebrew Bible." *No Passion Spent*. Pp. 40–87. New Haven: Yale University Press, 1996.

Steinmetz, Devora. *From Father to Son: Kinship, Conflict and Continuity in Genesis*. Louisville: Westminster John Knox, 1991.

Sternberg, Meir. *The Poetics of Biblical Narrative: Ideological Literature and the Drama of Reading*. Bloomington, Ind.: Indiana University Press, 1985.

Stewart, Columba. *Prayer and Community: The Benedictine Tradition*. Traditions of Christian Spirituality. Maryknoll: Orbis, 1998.

Streit, Judith. "The God of Abraham: A Study of Characterization." Final chapter of unpublished dissertation, University of Denver, 1996.

Thomas, D. Winton. "A Consideration of Some Unusual Ways of Expressing the Superlative in Hebrew." *Vetus Testamentum* 3 (1953) 209–24.

Trible, Phyllis. "Depatriarchalizing in Biblical Narrative." *Journal of the American Academy of Religion* 41 (1973) 30–48.

Trible, Phyllis. "A Love Story Gone Awry." *God and the Rhetoric of Sexuality*, 72–165. Overtures to Biblical Theology. Philadelphia: Fortress, 1978.

Tsumura, David Toshio. *The Earth and the Waters of Genesis 1 and 2: A Linguistic Investigation*. Journal for the Study of the Old Testament Supplement 83. Sheffield: Sheffield Press, 1989.

Turner, Laurence A. *Announcements of Plot in Genesis*. Journal for the Study of the Old Testament Supplement 96. Sheffield: Sheffield Press, 1990.

Van Seters, John. *Prologue to History*. Louisville: Westminster John Knox, 1992.

Van Wolde, Ellen. "Texts in Dialogue With Texts: Intertextuality in the Ruth and Tamar Narratives." *Biblical Interpretation* 5 (1997) 1–28.

Vatican II. Dogmatic Constitution on Divine Revelation (*Dei verbum*), *Vatican Council II: The Conciliar and Post Conciliar Documents*. Rev. ed. Ed. Austin Flannery, 750–65. Collegeville: The Liturgical Press, 1992.

Viviano, Pauline. "Genesis." *The Collegeville Bible Commentary*. Collegeville: The Liturgical Press, 1989.

Walsh, Jerome T. "Genesis 2:4b–3:24: A Synchronic Approach." *Journal of Biblical Literature* 96 (1977) 161–77.

Walsh, Jerome T. *I Kings*. Collegeville: The Liturgical Press, 1996.

Walsh, Jerome T. *Style and Structure in Biblical Hebrew Narrative*. Collegeville: The Liturgical Press, 2001.

Wenham, Gordon J. "The Coherence of the Flood Narrative." *Vetus Testamentum* 28 (1978) 336–48.

Westenholz, Joan Goodnick. "Tamar, QĔDĒŠĀ, QADIŠTU and Sacred Prostitution in Mesopotamia." *Harvard Theological Review* 82 (1989) 245–65.

Westermann, Claus. *Genesis 1-11: A Commentary. Genesis 12-36. Genesis 37-50.* Trans. John J. Scullion. Minneapolis: Augsburg, 1984, 1985, 1986.

Wilfong, Marsha M. "Genesis 22:1-18." *Interpretation* 45 (1991) 393–4.

Williamson, Peter. "Actualization: A New Emphasis in Catholic Scripture Study." *America* (May 20, 1995) 17–9.

Wright, G.R.H. "The Positioning of Genesis 38." *Zeitschrift für die Alttestamentliche Wissenschaft* 94 (1982) 523–9.

Zimler, Richard. *The Last Kabbalist of Lisbon*. Woodstock, N.Y.: Overlook, 1998.

Zornberg, Avivah Gottlieb. *Genesis: The Beginning of Desire*. Philadelphia: Jewish Publication Society, 1995.

ABBREVIATIONS

AB	Anchor Bible.
ABD	David Noel Freedman, et al., eds. *The Anchor Bible Dictionary*. New York: Doubleday, 1992.
AT	Author's translation.
BDB	Francis Brown, S. R. Driver and Charles A. Briggs. *A Hebrew and English Lexicon of the Old Testament*. Oxford: Clarendon, 1972.
FOTL	Forms of Old Testament Literature.
G-K	Kautzsch, E. Gesenius' Hebrew Grammar (Oxford: Clarendon Press, 1910)
HOLLADAY	Holladay William L. *A Concise Hebrew and Aramaic Lexicon of the Old Testament*. Grand Rapids: Eerdmans, 1971.
LXX	Septuagint.
MT	Masoretic Text.
NAB	The New American Bible.
NRSV	The New Revised Standard Version.
RSV	The Revised Standard Version.
Sam	The Samaritan Pentateuch.
TJ	Targum Jonathan.
VG	Vulgate

SCRIPTURE INDEX

SUBJECT INDEX

What follows is an idiosyncratic index of some of the themes that have emerged as especially important in this commentary.